the
Witch's
Guide
to
Life

Photo by Chris McKernan

About the Author

An active occultist for over fifteen years, author Kala Trobe believes that daily life may be lived in full metaphysical consciousness. She is ever in search of living magick, and has found it in many places, not least her native England. She is the author of several books, including *Invoke the Goddess, Invoke the Gods,* and *Magic of Qabalah.*

the Witch's Guide to Life

kala trobe

2003
Llewellyn Publications
St. Paul, Minnesota 55164-0383, U.S.A.

First Edition
Second Printing, 2003

Book design and editing by Joanna Willis
Cover design by Lisa Novak
Cover image © 2002 by Jonnie Miles, Getty Images
Illustration on page 168 by Kevin R. Brown, Llewellyn art department
Photos of Dion Fortune and Israel Regardie are courtesy of the HOGD private archives,
  P.O. Box 1757, Elfers, FL 34680

Library of Congress Cataloging-in-Publication Data
Trobe, Kala, 1969–
    The witch's guide to life / Kala Trobe.—1st ed.
      p.   cm.
    Includes bibliographical references and index.
    ISBN 0-7387-0200-5
      1. Witchcraft. 2. Magic. I. Title.

BF1566.T76 2003
133.4'3—dc21

2003040040

Llewellyn Worldwide does not participate in, endorse, or have any authority or responsibility concerning private business transactions between our authors and the public.

All mail addressed to the author is forwarded but the publisher cannot, unless specifically instructed by the author, give out an address or phone number.

Any Internet references contained in this work are current at publication time, but the publisher cannot guarantee that a specific location will continue to be maintained. Please refer to the publisher's website for links to authors' websites and other sources.

The remedies and recipes in this book are not meant to diagnose, treat, prescribe, or substitute for consultation with a licensed healthcare professional. Please use herbs within the guidelines given and heed the cautionary notes regarding potentially dangerous herbs or combinations of herbs. The publisher assumes no responsibility for injuries occurring as a result of herbal usages found in this book.

Llewellyn Publications
A Division of Llewellyn Worldwide, Ltd.
P.O. Box 64383, Dept. 0-7387-0200-5
St. Paul, MN 55164-0383, U.S.A.
www.llewellyn.com

 Printed in the United States of America on recycled paper

This book is dedicated to
Josie Rose Moore and her son
Samuel Anthony (Peanut),
and to my faery godson
Riley A. G. Elfinn Grothmoore,
with love

Contents

List of Spells and Meditations . . . . *xiii*

Acknowledgements . . . . *xv*

Introduction . . . . *xvii*

PART I—PHILOSOPHY AND ETHICS

1   What Makes a Witch? 3

     When Is a Witch Not a Witch?   7

     The Wiccan Rede, Verse and Proverb   9

     The Witch's Rune   21

     Does Being a Witch Make Life Easy?   22

     God, and Other Religions   26

2   The Witch and Morality 29

     The Eco-Witch (and the Neo-Pagan)   32

     What Can the Witch Do in Times of Global Crisis?   40

     How Can the Witch Respond to Personal Crisis?   46

3   The Witch and Love and Sex 49

     The Witch and Sex   53

     The Witch and Same-sex Sex   57

     The Witch and Marriage and Monogamy   59

4   Meaning and Magick 63

     Covens, Gurus, and Teachers   68

5   Karma Drama 73

 6   The Witch and Mental Health 79

    Mood Swings   79

    The Witch and Eating Disorders   82

    The Witch and Suicide   84

    Coping When the Wheel of Fortune Takes a Downward Dip   88

 7   The Witch and Drugs 91

    The Witch and Alcohol and Tobacco   94

 8   The Ages of the Witch 99

    The Witch and Death   102

PART II—FACTUAL WITCHCRAFT

 9   The Wheel of Death and Life 109

    Samhain (October 31st)   110

    Winter Solstice/Yule (December 21st)   111

    Imbolc (February 2nd)   111

    Spring Equinox/Oestara (March 21st)   112

    Beltane (May 1st)   113

    Summer Solstice/Litha (June 21st)   113

    Lammas/Lughnasadh (August 1st)   114

    Autumn Equinox/Mabon/Madron (September 21st)   115

    Folk Customs and Folk Magick by Paul Davenport   116

    The Esbats   127

10   Myth and Symbolism 137

    Gods and Goddesses   140

    Symbols Ancient and Modern   152

11   The Chakra System and Auras 165

    Chakras   165

    Auras   171

12   The Witch and Qabalah 177

    Use of the Sephiroth in Magick   189

13   The Witch and Divination 191

    The Witch and Tarot   191

    An Overview of the Tarot   192

    The Major Arcana   199

    The Minor Arcana   221

    Tarot Magick   244

    The Witch and Runes   245

14   A Brief History of Witchcraft 253

15   Who Influenced the Witching World? 267

    Moses de Leon   267

    Cornelius Agrippa   268

    John Dee   268

    Robert Fludd   271

    Jacob Boehme   272

    William Blake   273

    Eliphas Levi   274

    Helena Blavatsky   277

    Annie Besant   282

    Wynn Westcott   284

    Samuel Liddell MacGregor Mathers   287

    W. B. Yeats   288

    Moina Bergson Mathers   289

    Aleister Crowley   291

    Alice A. Bailey   297

    W. E. Butler   303

    Florence Farr   304

    Austin Osman Spare   305

    Dion Fortune   307

    Gerald Brousseau Gardner   315

    Maud Gonne   316

    Annie Horniman   317

    Israel Regardie   318

    Alex Sanders   320

    Doreen Valiente   321

    Gareth Knight   322

16   The Witch in the Arts and Media 323
     The Media Witch   329
     The Cyberwitch   332

            PART III—PRACTICAL WITCHCRAFT

17   A Witch's Working Tools 335
     Tools   335
     The Witch's Working Week   345
     General Correspondences   346

18   Magickal Techniques and Spell-casting 349
     Astral Magick   350
     Binding   351
     Candle Magick   353
     Casting the Circle   355
     Cone of Power   357
     Conjurations   358
     Creative Visualisation   360
     Enochia   363
     Evocation   365
     Familiars   366
     Fetches   368
     Ingenuity   368
     Invocation   370
     Music in Magick   371
     Poetry and Spellcraft   372
     Practical Magick, with Props   379
     Psychic Self-Protection   379
     Skrying   384
     Shamanism   384
     Sigilisation   386
     Sympathetic Magick   387
     Technology in Magick   388
     Thoughtforms and Telepathy   389
     Transference of Energies   391
     A Summary of Aspects of Spell-casting   391

19   Menstrual and Menopausal Magick 393
        Some Menstrual Spells   400

20   The Witch and Physical Health 407
        The Witch and Running by Dr. Radcliffe Morris   *410*

21   The Witch and Food 419
        The Witch's Cauldron: The Alchemy of Food by Syd Moore   *420*

22   The Witch and Wealth 437
        The Witch and Employment   439

Glossary 441
Bibliography and Resources 445
Index 451

Spells and Meditations

1. Neutralising an Aggressor 48
2. Mood Swings Spell. 80
3. General Chakra Meditation. 170
4. Visualising the Qabalah as a Whole 181
5. Justice Spell 244
6. Spell for Abundance 354
7. Visualisation for Recalling Life's Inner Mystery 361
8. Washing Up Spell. 365
9. Spell for Well-Being 369
10. Garment Spell 379
11. Simple Psychic Self-Protection Technique 383
12. Psychic Self-Protection II 383
13. Spell for Ridding Oneself of an Unwanted Thought, Memory,
      or Influence 386
14. E-mail Spell 388
15. Syd's Nan's Wart Spell. 391
16. To Define Your Psychic and Psychological Barriers 400
17. Exorcise Your Life of Unwanted Differences 401
18. To Bring an Idea(l) to Fruition 402
19. Spell for Menstrual Strength 403
20. Spell for Peace of Body and Mind During a Period or at Menopause. . . . 404
21. Money Tree Spell. 439

Acknowledgements

I AM VERY GRATEFUL TO my contributors: Paul Davenport, author of the unique and colourful section on folk customs and folk magick; Radcliffe Morris, whose knowledge and practise of physical fitness far outweighs my own; and Syd Moore, whose magickal recipes I've been lucky enough to enjoy on numerous occasions, and with whom I have enjoyed many a magickal Circle. Syd's help was also invaluable in the section "Magickal Techniques and Spell-casting."

Introduction

A GUIDE TO LIFE IS a tall order indeed, and this one lays claim to the title not because it is fully comprehensive—how could such a manuscript exist?—but because it spans intellectual and physical as well as magickal and philosophical aspects of a witch's life. Each seem to me to be of equal importance; a witch is not merely magickal, he or she is also a functional human being living in a community of others with, usually, widely differing beliefs. She has a body that needs maintaining, a mind that must be constantly questioning and learning, and everyday problems to consider on top of her magickal pursuits. I hope that at least some of these have been helpfully covered in this book.

Also included are sections on magickal systems that I feel are key to a witch's working knowledge. These include basics of colour magick, chakras, mythology and symbolism, the Qabalah of the Western Mystery Tradition, folklore and magick, and spell techniques. The roots of Wicca lie in Pagan beliefs native to the Western Hemisphere, which is why a section on British folklore as practised today has been included. Of course, Wicca and witchcraft are renowned for their eclecticism, and owe much to many diverse influences; I have endeavoured to include some of these too. A brief history of the Craft and biographies of some of its key players are also featured. As souls on the ascent employing—like the Tarot's Magician—every faculty to aid us, we should be aware of our intellectual as well as anthropological and spiritual roots.

This book is divided into three parts: "Philosophy and Ethics," "Factual Witchcraft," and "Practical Witchcraft." In the first part, we explore the ethics of modern-day witchcraft, as well as some of its roots and modern practises. The "Factual Witchcraft" section contains correspondences and systems used in magick, and biographies of some of the most significant and famous occultists of the Western world. The "Practical Witchcraft" section contains details on how such information may be put to use practically, both as spellcraft and in one's daily life.

Many of these themes are interlinked, and the reader is advised to use the word index at the back of the book for thorough references to each subject. For directions to specific spells, techniques, and visualisations, see the list of spells and meditations on page xiii.

Part I

PHILOSOPHY AND ETHICS

one

What Makes a Witch?

MAKING YOUR OWN MAGICK IS the essential tenet of being a witch. We do not sit around waiting for the world to offer us our dreams on a plate, knowing as we do that this will never happen. We are proactive, and seek to manifest our heart's desire, even when the odds seem stacked against it. We use the concentrated power of our Will, we Dare to be Different, we seek the Knowledge we need for autonomy, and about our beliefs we are Silent in the company of outsiders.

This does not make the witch a dysfunctional member of society. On the contrary, the witch is always ready to help others, he or she is conscientious as to the cause and effect of her powers, and the knowledge she gathers from every religion and every walk of life makes her about as well rounded as it is possible to be. Her mind is always open. She respects all cultures and the essential teachings of all other religions (though their practises may at times test her patience). She is acutely aware of the smallness of her place in the Universe, and in this world, she is grateful to the elements that bore her—and all of us—into being. Earth, air, fire, water, and spirit are never far from her thoughts. She is consequently ecologically aware. She loves nature; not as other people "love" chocolate or skiing, but with the real love of a daughter for her mother. She feels for the cosmos.

Though aware of her minuscule significance in the scheme of things, the witch is not afraid to make waves. She sees the making of her own magick as essential. This is partly because all action is a kind of magick, and if we make no moves, we may as well lay down and die, and partly because her expanded awareness makes her conscious both of what needs to be done, and how it might be possible. She knows that everything is linked by an invisible (to normal vision) electricity, and realises that she is a storehouse of this energy. She learns to accumulate and direct it in order to effect the changes she desires. This requires knowledge of yearly cycles and phases of the moon (see chapter 9, "The Wheel of Death and Life"), and the ability to strongly visualise and will a situation into being. It also means being semi-otically aware (see chapter 10, "Myth and Symbolism").

Witches do not have to go around in long black cloaks and pointy shoes (though it can be fun) to feel empowered. Being a witch is still not a popular life choice. People may want to burn you and chase you out of town. Normal clothing and demeanour is a handy way of throwing people off the scent. After all, if a rumour starts that there's a witch living down your street, and she turns out to be that woman in jeans and sneakers, you're hardly going to believe it, are you?

Even when stripped of dignity in the outside world, however, the witch knows she has power and grace within. Because she Knows, Wills, Dares, and is Silent, nothing can penetrate her inner sanctum of confidence. She can be as plain as a pikestaff and still know how to captivate lovers; she can be useless at math and still excel in intelligence. A quick spell and some applied will could turn her grades around and make her a straight-A student, as well as the most entrancing girl in town.

She also realises that there is more to magick than the mere fulfilment of petty ambitions. Films like *The Craft* emphasise the selfish possibilities of being a witch, and bear little resemblance to the type of person she wishes to be or become. A teenager using her psychic powers as a bludgeon is a scary thing indeed, and she does herself no favours either. Following the example of Nancy in *The Craft,* we stumble into the mire of unpleasant consequences (see chapter 5, "Karma Drama").

The best policy of all witches—white, grey, and black—is "To Know, to Dare, to Will, and to be Silent." Aleister Crowley's Thelemites are renowned for following the principle "Do What Thou Wilt shall Be the Whole of the Law." For them, magick comes first, morality second. Crowley is, of course, infamous for his lack of scruple both in the Circle and outside it. His "diabolical" behaviour provoked wide condemnation in late Victorian England (see chapter 15, "Who Influenced the Witching World?").

Wiccans and ethical occultists adhere to the creed "An' it Harm None, Do As Thou Wilt." Easier said than done. To truly follow this spiritually watertight method, all motives must be analysed and possible consequences assessed. Is your ceremony or spell really for the good of all concerned? Is it definitely not going to harm anyone in any way, however slight? If both of these questions can be answered with confidence, go ahead and cast your white spell. If not, don't forget that other rule of the "Craft of the Wise": the threefold return. All that we send out will return to us tripled (more or less); so cast good magick if you want to revel in good vibes, and send out hate if you wish to battle your way through this life feeling paranoid. There is no better way for a witch to destroy herself than to attempt to destroy another.

It is a popular belief that we reap what we sow, but some witches would not agree with the concept of threefold return, or with various other commonly accepted aspects of the Craft. Each of us is unique. Definitions vary and are often self-created, and aspects of belief vary with them. We are all individuals with perceptions of equal validity, and there are, in my eyes, no rules except the conscience of the practitioner. A witch, as I see it, is anyone who is aware of the Divine in the midst of daily life, who casts spells, and uses magick.

There is a difference between a Wiccan witch and a non-Wiccan witch. This book deals with the witch as an individual rather than as a product of specific schools of thought. Most of us are influenced by a host of philosophies, and every witch is unique and operates differently. However, a few basic guidelines on the differences between the main schools of witchy thought may be found in the following section, "When Is a Witch Not a Witch?", as many people like to belong to particular traditions or schools of thought.

So, the key points of modern witchcraft are inner strength, resulting in the confidence necessary to change one's circumstance, and spiritual and ethical awareness. Will power combined with effective ritual and moral conscience does not, however, differentiate the witch from any other positive religious person.

What, then, makes a witch a witch? There are several answers to this. One is that the witch does not merely ask for help, but she makes positive moves to bring the desired change to pass. This is a classically Pagan stance. As Hugh Lloyd Jones says of the ancient Greeks: "Faced with a difficulty, a Greek will first pray to a god; but he must then reinforce the god's action on the divine plane by applying on the human plane whatever action he is capable of making." Likewise, the witch.

Secondly, she admires and employs the aid of ancient deities from a huge array of pantheons. Many of these deities have remained dormant for long periods of time owing to the decline of certain empires, the growth of Christianity and other now orthodox religions, and the destruction of the cultures from which they arose. Modern magick has resuscitated many an arcane deity. She may take her pick of which to contact, supplicate, and work with.

Thirdly, at least in the case of Wiccans (Alexandrian, Gardnerian, and solitary practitioners), the emphasis is on the nature gods and the Goddess—both of which are usually held in equal reverence. If, however, there is discrimination, it will be towards the feminine, as the Goddess ultimately presides over the cycles of life and death. This reflects the fact that Wicca is predominantly a nature religion.

It must be remembered, however, that witchcraft, like any other spiritually effective path, is merely a means to an end. That end? Spiritual ascension. The witch realises that she is placed here, in this particular set of circumstances, for a reason. That reason is to grow and learn. The outer planes are manifestations of inner circumstance, and the goal is to see through the illusion and transcend it. Ultimately, we are aiming for reunion with the Creative Intelligence, the Ultimate Deity. This God is not thought to be cruel or punishing—we inflict suffering on ourselves rather than have it inflicted on us—but is loving, magickal, and perpetually sending us opportunities to grow closer to the Truth. All spiritual paths may be included in this. All apparently random events come under the same category.

The witch, with her awareness of symbolism, is well equipped to understand and rate her spiritual progress. Her stumbling block is being glamoured by lower psychism. Spells and magick are excellent tools when intelligently applied, but they can lead to terrible karmic tangles when meddlesome or ill thought-out. It is the first test of the witch to combat the lust for personal power and prestige. Many fail at this early stage. However, with constant application and interaction with earth and cosmic energies, she will accumulate power. If she uses this power for healing (when asked), blessing, helping (but not interfering), and, most importantly, for bringing light and love and positive energy down through the planes to earth, she is doing what she is meant to be doing on the path of witchcraft.

This leads us to another essential factor: the After-and-Beyond life. The witch's very nature dictates that she believes in life after physical death. The witch recognises the perpetual presence of other planes and the entities that inhabit them. She is adept at seeing behind the Veil of dense matter to the subtle etheric and causal levels, and she is acutely aware of the crossovers between levels. Certain sabbats are celebrations of the times when the worlds merge most obviously—Samhain is one example. She can interact with the so-called "dead" at will, but she will only do so when it is helpful to the spirits concerned (leading victims of accidents away from their bodies, for example, and ensuring their well-being before leaving them on the astral levels). She does not meddle with those who do not wish to be called, and she certainly does not expect other spirits to do her bidding any more than she would expect to be able to stop a person in the street and command him or her to be her slave. (Well, OK, some do, but this is not the type of witch it is desirable to become for numerous reasons. Plus, dominating another life-force requires a complete self-belief and consistent lack of conscience that few of us are, thankfully, able to possess.)

However, the witch is fluent in the languages of many levels. She learns, through years of experience and psychic encounters, that there is no end to the spirit (nor even to many aspects of individual consciousness), and that the flesh is not the material cul-de-sac it often seems to be. Her consciousness becomes a transdimensional crossroad; with her Hecate-self at its epicentre, she may follow the paths to the lands of both the astral (where we go between incarnations, and where more advanced spirits exist), and the higher causal (closest to Godhead). Yet her feet remain planted firmly on the earth. She knows that all levels are of equal importance.

The way that a witch operates can vary completely. Some get together in the classic coven of thirteen; others work alone. Some go through external training; for others this is impractical, and they teach themselves through experience and experiment, or even learn through a correspondence course or the many comprehensive books available today. Some like to feel the gods and Goddess around them by working skyclad, or naked; others go robed, or, for discretion's sake, dress as normal. There are all-female covens and all-male ones (though the latter are certainly rarer), and covens that meet only on the astral plane. The true witch is an individualist, and her *modus operandi* will reflect this. It is important to state here, at the beginning of the book, that *all witches are different.* Because Wicca and witchcraft are nondenominational, and because covens and individual witches have sprung up all over the world, rarely meeting together, if at all, there are as many opinions on the Craft as there are individual practitioners. Therefore I speak only from my personal standpoint. I take into account the huge body of work now available on the subject, but there are as many different practises as there are different witches on the globe—and believe me, there are quite a few now! However, all witches employ the sabbats to aid their work, and will remain aware of the seasonal and lunar tides from day to day (see chapter 9, "The Wheel of Death and Life").

This book aims to be helpful to the witch, whatever her personal specifications. It behooves us all to remember that the Craft is a progressive path, not an end in itself. There are higher levels to aspire towards; the point of our incarnations is to ascend. That means to seek the Creative, Benevolent Intelligence—in ourselves, in others, and in all manifestations.

When Is a Witch Not a Witch?

A witch is somebody who casts spells using the natural cycles as allegory and guide. He or she might also summon spirits, work ritual magick, and so forth. These spells can be of any nature at all.

A Wiccan, on the other hand, is a spiritual descendent of Gerald Gardner and/or Alex Sanders (see chapter 14, "A Brief History of Witchcraft") and operates under the tenet "An' it Harm None, Do As Thou Wilt." Although there are many schools of Wicca now—from Faery to Seax to Celtic (the word *eclectic* crops up time and time again in Wiccan self-description)—the general precept is that the Wiccan worships the Goddess and Horned God (usually with the Goddess in precedence). The Goddess and God are seen as manifest in all other gods and goddesses; the Divine is easily accessed and recognised in many forms. However, this aspect is shared with some other witches.

Essentially, all Wiccans are witches but not all witches are Wiccans. Within the category of witchcraft, there are more differentiations. This includes Traditional Witchcraft, which is animistic and polytheistic like many other types of magickal belief, but which admits no superior entity. The God and Goddess are seen as innate in nature rather than external, lofty forces (most Wiccans will see them as both), although spirits will often be called upon to help the witch meet her aim. These spirits are perceived as equal but different, as is all in the cosmos. There is no hierarchy in Traditional Witchcraft, while in Wicca, deities exist and are obviously our "superiors." (However, this is not in the grovelling, Judeo-Christian/Islamic sense. The deities are respected as evident in natural things—the trees and earth, for example, and stars and sky—and there is no aspect of fear or punishment in the sense of divinity.)

Wicca tends to be more ritualistic than Traditional Witchcraft, which is simple and often involves no paraphernalia at all. Traditional Witchcraft does not involve casting a Circle, for example, as all places are seen as sacred. The Traditional witch must therefore be naturally fully attuned to magickal thought processes at all times. A Wiccan or non-Traditional witch, on the other hand, can afford to "be mundane" (sometimes a necessity in this world), knowing as she does that a small ritual will restore her to her magickal persona and create a sphere in which the worlds intermingle.

Wicca is ethical, while Traditional Witchcraft is amoral. In Traditional Witchcraft, emphasis is placed on taking responsibility for one's actions, and on intent. The forces of the Universe are seen as neutral (like weather), rather than good or evil. Curses and hexes are used for self-preservation, whereas a Wiccan would never curse, believing in the law of threefold return and in the ethics of "An' it Harm None."

Like Wiccans, Traditional witches celebrate the seasonal sabbats and lunar esbats. However, no invocations to the Lords of the Watchtowers would precede a Traditional ritual; if protection were needed, spirits and elementals might be summoned to assist, but the mode would not be high magickal. Clothes would be kept on in most Traditional covens, rather than working in ritual robes or skyclad, as most Wiccans tend to do.

There are witches that belong to none of these categories, especially as magick and spell-casting have become so popular since the 1960s. Information has exited the broom cupboard and landed in the most public of forums. Thousands of books have become available, leading to this characteristic awareness of natural cycles, the widespread practise of magick, the emergence of new covens, and self-initiation. There are now as many types of witch as there are individuals practising the Craft.

In this book, the word *witch* is used in a Wiccan as well as non-Wiccan way. I believe that religious practises should be ethical, especially those that involve direct magick, but I do not perceive witchcraft as confined to the precepts laid out by Gerald Gardner and Alex Sanders. So I have used the word to define anybody, whether Wiccan or otherwise, who:

- Acts positively to enhance his or her life using magick

- Worships the old gods, in whatever form, even as simple energies inherent in nature

- Accepts responsibility for his or her own actions

- Follows the cycles of the seasons with magickal and practical awareness

- Works with lunar and stellar tides, and celebrates the full moon, however quietly

- Strives towards self-improvement, often involving "initiation" experiences

- Thinks of him- or herself as a witch

The Wiccan Rede, Verse and Proverb

To get an idea of what Wicca implies, the following are examples of specifically Wiccan ethics and proverbs. Some are based on ages-old principles of witchcraft; others are clearly new concepts. Much of the Gardnerian Book of Shadows, from which this is taken, is popularly recognised as falsely antiquated-sounding.

Bide the Wiccan Redes ye must, In Perfect Love and Perfect Trust;

"Perfect Love and Perfect Trust"—what are these qualities in this context?

When a Wiccan is initiated, he or she undergoes, in the true nature of all initiatory experiences, a symbolic death and resurrection process. In the case of first-degree and second-degree initiation, this is underlined by the use of cords to bind and a blindfold. In order to keep one's nerve during this compromising experience—bearing in mind that one is traditionally naked as a babe to boot—does indeed require "Perfect Trust" in the Goddess, and in fellow coverners.

So, the initiate is made as vulnerable as possible, but "Perfect Love" for the Mother-Goddess sustains her courage and pulls her through into successful rebirth. This symbolises the faith necessary to undergo each incarnation without becoming spiritually "warped" by its numerous difficulties. To remain a loving, giving person despite adversity is key to Wiccan faith, which admits no retaliation. "Perfect Love" means that love of self is not higher than that for the Mother, who represents compassion for all living creatures.

It is worth noting that there is scope for abuse of the "Perfect Love and Perfect Trust" clause. Wicca attracts some unsavory persons because of its ritual nudity, the Fivefold Kiss, and the Great Rite, and some of these go undetected by those they do not attempt to compromise. All religious paths are prone to attract the occasional megalomaniac, and Wicca and Paganism are no exceptions. What the clause does *not* mean is that "Perfect Trust" is to be invested in an individual human being, High Priest/Priestess or not. It refers to faith in the Divine, and definitely not the fallible human, however impressive and bona fide he or she may seem.

> *Live ye must and let to live, Fairly take and fairly give;*

This clause is simple enough to understand. It promotes exactly the ethics found in Christianity—to "Do unto others what you would have done unto yourself." However, being a nature religion, it also refers to the earth. Wiccans do not simply strip the land of its resources, but "fairly give" in return. This is done psychically, through thanks-giving celebrations, as well as physically. The "Perfect Love and Perfect Trust" has to cut two ways.

> *Form the Circle thrice about, To keep unwelcome spirits out;*

This of course refers to the casting of the Circle, or the invocation of the elements and Lords of the Watchtowers to protect the proceedings from unwanted influences. This procedure is one of the many arguments in favour of the concept's recent authorship; Traditional Witchcraft did not employ the Circle, as every space was seen as already sacred. Spirits might be convoked to protect the witch, but the Lords of the Watchtowers are a purely modern addition. Much of Wicca is based on mediaeval magickal and alchemical theory, the Circle not least. However, this by no means invalidates the technique, which is one of the most powerful psychological and psychic techniques of the Craft.

Bind fast the spell every time, Let the words be spoke in rhyme.

Binding a spell can be done in many ways: by the words "So mote it Be" and a mental full stop; or by burning, burying, or sending away on water an object used in the spell (such as paper on which unwanted traits or influences are listed, a doll, or any object symbolic of the task at hand). As the word suggests, a spell may also be "bound" with cord or thread quite literally. It does not matter which technique one uses (there are many others), the point is to believe and know that the spell is "done." Absolute confidence in one's abilities is the most powerful binding tool one could possibly have.

The words are "spoke in rhyme" because they facilitate a chant that is easy to remember, mellifluous, and magickally effective. Many of these verses were written by Doreen Valiente, others by Gerald Gardner himself. It is particularly powerful for a coven to author its own rituals and spells, of course, but many choose to stick to the prescribed Wiccan versions.

The main point about any magickal verse is its rhythm. It is this that works on the brain and body of the witch to create a mood suitable to the spell in hand. The chants are often danced to in circular motion, and the effect is autohypnotic. I do not mean that the participants become zombies—they most certainly do not—but the mood becomes more trancey, more magickal. The mundane world subsides, and excitement and intent become intermingled. If the words rhyme, one is unconsciously transported back to childhood, when cynicism had not spoiled optimistic belief, and when magickal realities were so much easier to access. There is much to be said for naïve verse for this reason.

Soft of eye and light of touch, Speak ye little, listen much;

The first line of this section seems to be for reasons of poetic ambience only. However, it may also suggest subtlety—and gentleness. To be "soft of eye" is to be kindly and nonjudgemental. "Light of touch" again suggests gentleness. The second clause, "Speak ye little," refers to the vow of silence taken by the initiate ("To Know, to Will, to Dare, and to be Silent"). This obviously befits the witch, who is likely to suffer through indiscretion. It is also a wise bit of advice in any scenario, especially a learning one, hence, "listen much."

> *Deosil go by waxing moon, Sing and dance the Witch's Rune;*
> *Widdershins go by waning moon, Chant ye then a baleful tune;*

Deosil, or clockwise, is the right direction for creative, positive, forward-forging magick, such as would be cast when the moon is waxing. Personally, I usually work deosil whatever the phase of the moon, but the reference to moving "widdershins," or anti-clockwise, occurs because at the waning of the moon, the tides are reversed and the flow is corrosive rather than augmentative (hence the tune being "baleful"). Therefore the time is right to perform magick relating to the past, and to the removal of unwanted obstacles. The witch might move widdershins to represent this "regression," but the action must always be counterbalanced by a clockwise movement later in the working.

"The Witch's Rune" referred to is the wonderfully effective verse written by Doreen Valiente and Gerald Gardner. It is usually chanted during a "ring dance," when coveners hold hands, face inwards, and rotate deosil, at first slowly, but gradually faster and faster until the Priestess deems that the relevant energy has been raised and bids them stop (and sometimes "drop" onto the floor!). It may be found in its entirety, with comments, in the next section.

> *When the Lady's moon is new, Kiss hand to her times two;*
> *When the moon rides at peak, Heart's desire then ye seek.*

These lines refer to the Goddess as Maiden, when her favour is best gained through gentle workings, and ideas are sown rather than reaped. The hand is kissed "times two" rather than the traditional three because she is still in a stage of incompletion. Also, two is a number of partnership—the first stage of initiating a project. In Tarot, the twos are cards of developing.

At the full moon, however, the time is right to take the plunge and put full energy into magickal projects, including requests for love, insight, and the conclusion of any healing work that may have been performed as the moon waxed. It is therefore the Mother who grants the "Heart's desire."

Heed the North wind's mighty gale, Lock the door & trim the sail;
When the wind comes from the South, Love will kiss them on the mouth;
When the wind blows from the West, departed souls have no rest;
When the wind blows from the East, Expect the new and set the feast.

This verse adds pseudo-folkloric proverb to the poetic melting pot. The references to the cardinal points are obviously relevant to witchcraft, as is the concept of interpreting the winds.

Nine woods in the cauldron go, Burn them quick, burn them slow;
Elder be the Lady's tree, Burn it not or curs'd ye'll be;
When the wind begins to turn, Soon the Beltane fires will burn;
When the wheel has turned to Yule, Light the log, the Horned One rules.

Nine is, of course, the number of the Goddess, being three times three, the triple aspect of the Triple-Aspected One. The Celts attributed the properties of trees to the lunar months, hence the beth–luis–nion tree alphabet. The woods are perhaps symbolic of the main seasonal/lunar cycles, though nine are mentioned rather than the full thirteen. They go into the cauldron of life, for, if literal, the woods would no doubt be *under* rather than inside the cauldron. The cauldron is another Goddess symbol, which stands on three legs. Aromatic fires may be burned, which also serve as incense. This is difficult, however, now that deforestation has rendered fine woods such as sandal and cedar both overpriced and rare. Personally I love the idea of such a fire, but would feel terribly guilty about it. Burning trees seems anathema to the witch's ecologically aware path, though of course anything that has fallen naturally is perfectly all right. Elder is sacred to the dark aspect of the Goddess, and thus must never be burned, at least by a Wiccan.

The references to the Wheel of Life are obvious. They are mentioned, presumably, to indicate the witch's constant awareness of the cycle, and the next stage in it. Foresight is as important to the witch as it was to the original Pagan who relied on successful seasonal cycles to bring him continued life.

Heed the flower, bush or tree, By the Lady blessed be
When the rippling waters flow, cast a stone—the truth you'll know;
When ye have & hold a need, Hearken not to others' greed;
With a fool no seasons spend, Or be counted as his friend.

Ecological awareness is again emphasised in the first two lines of this verse. Respect the Goddess and her botanical manifestations, and you gain her blessing. The next two lines, however, are vague in the extreme, and, along with those that follow, sound again like an attempt by Gardner(ians) to authenticate his verse with pithy folkloric sayings. There is potential for analysis here—the "waters," for example, may refer to lunar tides and their use in divination—but I do not aim to tackle it here. The final lines are common sense, and sound more like Blake than Gardner—keep good company, lest you be tainted by association! This could also refer to hanging out with nonwitches, and the potential unhelpful grounding that springs from being with those who do not believe. This is particularly relevant at sabbats, or "seasons"—the turning points of the year both seasonally and magickally.

> *Merry meet and merry part*

This has become the accepted witch's greeting and "goodbye"—rather a charming one at that. Witchy websites and chatrooms often abound with "MM!" and "MP!" when a person is logging off (see "The Cyberwitch" in chapter 16).

> *Bright the cheeks, warm the heart;*
> *Mind the threefold law ye should,*
> *Three times bad and three times good;*

Again, a reminder of the Wiccan rule of threefold return.

> *Whene'er misfortune is enow,*
> *Wear the star upon your brow;*

This refers to the "star" of perception and intuition at the third eye area, which can be used to counteract (or at least, to comprehend) adverse circumstances. It also implies the pentacle, symbol of all things witchy, worn in a ritual headdress. The witch undergoing misfortune is therefore bid to approach the Goddess for aid.

> *True in troth ever ye be,*
> *Lest thy love prove false to thee.*

Again, do unto others as you would have them do unto you.

'Tis by the sun that life be won,
And by the moon that change be done;

Symbolic of masculine energy, dominion, and power, the sun does indeed give life on the material planes. It is through "feminine," creative thought, however, that life becomes flexible; so lunar currents are employed to facilitate change. Considerations such as this affect both the day and the time of day a spell is cast; a Monday is best for workings concerning intuition or any psychic endeavour, for example, while a Sunday will work well for wealth, growth, and empire-building.

If ye would clear the path to will,
Make certain the mind be still;

Meditation is necessary before attempting magick. This is one of the many benefits of casting a Circle—it creates a sacred space not only externally, but within the practitioner's head also. Deep, relaxed breathing prior to embarking upon a magickal endeavour (or meditation) gives energy a flying head start. Certainly nothing is less helpful than a mind full of trivia; it is a dead certainty that an unstill mind will fail to create effective magick. This is one of the benefits of chants such as the Witch's Rune—though they may not exactly still the mind, they certainly sideline trivia and create a conducive set of brain waves through their rhythm. This sets the witch truly "flying."

What good be tools without Inner Light?
What good be magic without wisdom-sight?

Well, quite. The author goes to pains here to underline the truth-seeking nature of the Craft. The emphasis, as ever, is on Right Thought and Action, with motives properly scrutinised prior to offering them up to the deities for possible immortalisation.

Eight words the Wiccan Rede fulfill—
An' it harm none, do what ye will.

Spells and magick in Wicca are performed only when the results are guaranteed to be positive to all they touch. The "Do what ye will" part also underlines the unconventional nature of the Craft. In order to perform effectively, the Wiccan must "Dare" to be different, feeling safe in the knowledge that his or her unorthodox practises are indeed harming none.

> *For witches this be Law—*
> *Where ye enter in, from there withdraw.*

Could this be about living in full consciousness, rather than allowing encounters to be haphazard, as most people do? Perhaps. It could also refer to the casting of the Circle, and the importance of ritual at both ends. If a Circle is cast in Wicca, it must also be undone without being broken. Likewise must the Lords of the Watchtowers be thanked for their protection of the sacred space at its close. Ceremonial "withdrawal" is important both psychologically and through sheer politeness to the entities and energies concerned. It also means that loose energies are earthed rather than being left flailing about in an uncontrolled manner. It seems likely that here Gardner is talking about the necessity of conscious self-discipline to the Wiccan.

> *An' ye will secure the spell, Cast some silver in the well.*

By throwing silver into a symbol of the Goddess, we give back a little of what we continuously take from her. The lunar associations of silver coupled with the water of the well give strong psychic possibilities—focussing on them and willing the spell to come to pass "secures" it. Wishing wells have reflected this thought process for centuries, and it is second nature to many British to throw money into any well or pond they see and make a wish. In magick, the gesture is a significant full stop to a process, which may then be left to the subconscious (represented by the subterranean depths of the well).

> *Enhance thy trance*
> *With drug and dance.*

This shamanic advice is ages old. Spiritual seekers have long employed rhythm, dance, and various substances to achieve otherworldly states. Mescaline, marijuana, magic mushrooms, and a host of other intoxicants (not to forget good old alcohol) have been used for centuries across the globe by the magickally minded. This is one point that has been rejected by Americanised Wicca, now whiter than white and completely anti-intoxicant.

Personally, I think each to her own. Mantra and meditation can achieve similar states, but at a much slower rate, and the results are infinitely less dramatic. It depends on what the practitioner desires, and on her own body and her attitude to it. Drugs can scrabble the brain, there's no doubt about that. Perceptions may be less valid when drug-induced, though to the shaman they were more so. Gardner is here implying that the use of drugs does indeed enhance the trance that leads to psychic perception. Aldous Huxley, author of *Brave New World* and *The Doors of Perception* amongst many other fine books, was so convinced that drugs opened the doors to the astral and spiritual that he took LSD as he was dying. His mind was most certainly not scrabbled, as his numerous fine intellectual works attest. However, we all have different constitutions and varying levels of the self-discipline necessary to keep unleashed subconscious powers in check. It is certainly not normal or usual for witches, Wiccan or otherwise, to "enhance their trance" this way. Most people prefer a natural approach that, results attained, can be guaranteed bona fide. (See chapter 7, "The Witch and Drugs," for a more detailed discussion of this.)

Upon the Clock, Dependeth Not

Time is manmade, at least in the sense of hours and minutes and seconds. The seasons and lunar cycles, however, tell the true time: the stage of the Goddess and God, and our position in the cosmic cycle. When a Circle is cast indoors, clocks are turned to face the wall, and watches are forsaken by all who enter the sacred space, which is, of course, timeless.

Success pursueth the persistent.

This is simple common sense. Strive, and you are more likely to succeed.

Guilt flees when none pursueth.

This is an interestingly amoral sentiment, as presumably the clean-living, ethically astute Wiccan would incur no "guilt" anyway. Certainly the proverb reflects the idea of "Do What Thou Wilt," though there seems to be an implication of either actually doing wrong thereby, or of having such an opinion inflicted on one. If this "guilt" means the effect of personal conscience, where does that leave us ethically? Perhaps the idea is that the outside world could inflict a sense of guilt on the unorthodox religious practitioner, but that without this influence, it is possible to carry on pursuing one's own path, "An' it Harm None." However, it seems to me more likely that this proverb was injected by the concupiscent Gardner to excuse various indulgences, particularly sexual ones. It is certainly more the sort of sentiment one would expect from Aleister Crowley, who rebelled throughout his life against imposed social and religious mores.

Power shared is power lost.

It is true that talking about a spell or experience dissipates its energy in a similar way that "a problem shared is a problem halved." Obviously, this is less desirable in the case of magick! Despite the possible truth of this sentiment, many Wiccans would disagree with it and are keen to "share" their "power."

The first person to share magickal secrets on a large scale was Israel Regardie, when he published the rituals of the Golden Dawn. Certainly many initiates felt that their ceremonial power was lost thereby, and some members, such as Maiya Tranchell-Hayes, simply gave up the ghost and buried their robes in despair. There is much to be said for the power of discretion, both psychologically and for practical reasons. However, sharing it with the right people can enhance it hugely.

Seek thine enemy in secret.

This again seems a strange piece of advice to find attached to such a conscientious religious path. Hopefully most Wiccans and witches do not have enemies, and would not wish to "seek them in secret" if they did. Certainly the use of the subtle arts is suggested in lieu of confrontation, perhaps indicating the advisability of approaching a negative situation through magick in a carefully planned and controlled way. However, the implication of underhanded, scheming action is an unpleasant side effect of the way this Wiccan proverb is worded.

Thoughts are things: as a man thinkest, so he is.
If you think small, you become small.

This belief is fundamental to magick. It has also become much vaunted in popular psychology. Many magickal beliefs have filtered into the self-help arena, thanks to authors such as M. Scott Peck and Gill Edwards. Indeed, the idea of "living magically" through joyous thinking and positive action is now almost as widespread as the ancient belief that thinking and willing a thing will bring it to pass.

Remember the Passwords: Perfect Love and Perfect Trust, so trust the Universe and be at Home everywhere.

More very modern-sounding advice about faith in Universal benevolence. Sentiments such as this have strongly affected many recent schools of therapy.

If you imagine and fear 'I will get trapped', of course you will get trapped. Fear not, and you won't.

Same as "Thoughts are things . . ." above. Many of these proverbs seem to be unnecessary repetitions of one another. The use of the words "you" and "won't" jar badly when one has been lulled into arcane language at an earlier stage; there is no consistency in the style. "Thou" is certainly more affected, but at least it befits the vocabulary established earlier.

No one person can accomplish all.

This is plain common sense. It also indicates a group spirit in total contrast to the sentiment that "power shared is power lost." No one coven can "accomplish all" either, but it may stand a better chance than a single witch working alone (though not necessarily).

Danger is never overcome without danger.

Is the suggestion here that magick is required in order to effectively counteract danger, and that this magick is necessarily dangerous? Or simply that one should always take risks in a good cause? It is most likely the former, as many evocations to avert danger involve complete self- and external control in the magickian. This, however, refers to high and mediaeval magick rather than to Wicca, or certainly to modern Wicca. Gardner, however, was greatly influenced by mediaeval High Magick, so this is perhaps what is meant by the proverb.

The past is fixed, yet the future may be bent.

Some magickians would disagree that the past is fixed, but neither a witch nor a magickian nor any nonfatalistic person would argue with the second part of this clause. The word "bent" implies the subtle pressure of magick rather than the simple self-assertion most people would apply to their futures.

Where communication fails, confusion follows.

This is so obvious a statement that I am surprised it has been presented in "Wiccan lore" as a proverb. It may be applied to any situation in any walk of life. In witchcraft, it could imply anything from not arranging the coven-moot properly to messing up a group spell, obviously, but in fact, it is probably nothing more than evidence of an attempt to sound wise and pithy with very little actual material to work on.

Some things cannot be understood by mortal man. Many such must simply be accepted.

Here lies the difference between the Wiccan and the alchemist. Where the Wiccan accepts and worships, the alchemist strives to crack the code and master the energies concerned. However, one is left to wonder why the Wiccan, accepting his or her own ignorance, still seeks to change circumstances according to his or her own will. Perhaps the next proverb explains it all:

Rush in where angels fear to tread: the Gods are with you.

It seems that the conscientious observer of Wiccan ways is immune to nasty repercussions when attempting magick, despite the lack of understanding inevitable to "mortal man." The interesting thing about this saying is that the Pagan "Gods" are protecting the Wiccan from all that is dangerous to Judeo-Christian angels, apparently. Clearly this saying is based on another saying, but it has changed its meaning. Surely it is fools, and not Wiccans, who rush in? Ah, but this is different. Why? Because Wiccans have faith in the Goddess and the Old Ones, of course.

You are never less alone than when you think you are alone.

I love this idea. It has more truth in it—for me, anyway—than many of these other Wiccan sayings. One is most likely to reflect on solitude in an intense way when undergoing some kind of crisis. Indeed, it is at this time that one becomes a psychic beacon, and when beloveds from across the Veil, guardians, and gods can best see us.

Pray to the Moon when she is round
Luck with you shall then abound
What you seek for shall be found
In sea or sky or solid ground . . .

More of the same: ask the Goddess, and she will shower forth her bounty.

Clearly, these gems of Wiccan wisdom are of varied value. However, discernment is an essential tool in magick, and if such sayings help the aspiring witch to attain it, all the better.

The Witch's Rune

Eko, Eko, Azarak,
Eko, Eko, Zomelak,
Eko, Eko, Cernunnos,
Eko, Eko, Aradia!
Darksome night and shining moon,
East, then South, the West, then North,
Hearken to the Witch's Rune—
Here we come to call ye forth!
Earth and water, air and fire,
Wand and pentacle and sword,
Work ye unto our desire,
Hearken ye unto our word!
Cords and censer, scourge and knife,
Powers of the witch's blade—
Waken all ye into life,
Come ye as the charm is made!
Queen of heaven, queen of hell,
Horned hunter of the night—
Lend your power unto the spell,
And work our will by magick rite!
By all the power of land and sea,
By all the might of moon and sun,
As we do will, so mote it be;
Chant the spell, and be it done!

Eko, Eko, Azarak,
Eko, Eko, Zomelak,
Eko, Eko, Cernunnos,
Eko, Eko, Aradia!
Eko, Eko, Azarak . . .

I first heard the Witch's Rune performed during ritual when I was fifteen, and its effect is largely responsible for my interest and later participation in Wicca. Even today, when chanted with concentration, it sends shivers down my spine—the good ones you get when real magick is afoot. It doesn't matter that the invocations at the beginning are nonsensical, and drawn from mediaeval High Magick translated by MacGregor Mathers in the British Museum; nor does it matter that "Aradia," claimed by Leland, Gardner, and Sanders to be the Italian goddess of the witches, may never have existed at all. Who exactly "Zomelak" is, I doubt anyone would care to conjecture. But the Witch's Rune works. Why is this?

Rhythmically, it is highly compelling. Listening as a child, I could literally see the energy rising as it was chanted. The ending is open, and leaves room for as much repetition as is needed. Often, the High Priestess will raise the pitch of her voice at the end when there is sufficient energy in the group to guarantee successful magick, and her eerie, long, drawn-out shriek will bring the chant to conclusion.

The imagery in the Witch's Rune casts a spell of its own. "Darksome night" has a fairy-tale appeal; the "shining moon" may be imagined even if there are clouds (or a roof) overhead. The Quarters are reaffirmed (usually, they have been evoked prior to this stage), the tools are listed (most of them, anyway), and the practitioner commanded "Work ye unto our desire." The God and Goddess, the land herself, the sea, and finally the moon and sun are all called upon to add their power to the spell. The witch mentally adds the impetus of each as she circles, ever faster, through the billowing incense hand-in-hand with her fellow coveners, whose personal energy is also being raised. The power becomes tangible, almost visible. It's enough to turn any fifteen-year-old into a witch.

Does Being a Witch Make Life Easy?

Does being a witch make life easy? Apart from the obvious obstacle of harbouring beliefs that most people still consider superstitious at best, and delusional or even evil at worst, you mean? Well, I hate to admit it, but actually, there are more problems attached to being a witch than there are to not being one. The following are some key examples.

Responsibility

If one believes in magick, and that one has the power to perform it, obviously the question of cause, effect, and subsequent self-congratulation or blame must occur. Wiccan lore is strong on this—the law of threefold return symbolises the danger of sending out negative emotions or magick, either deliberately or by accident. Every adept witch is almost paranoiacally aware of the results of her actions, however small these may be. She looks right into the heart of any situation, and she accepts that her own interaction in it, especially if magickal, will have an effect for which she is culpable.

Self-blame

Then there is self-blame of another sort. When the chips are down, does it mean that you're a hopeless witch?

Whenever I have a problem these days—and believe me, I have plenty of them, just like the next person—nonwitches say, "Well, why don't you just cast a spell to sort it out?" This, of course, makes me feel worse, as it seems I am appearing to them as both powerless in the face of adversity, and hypocritical in that I cannot practise what I preach. Many other witches feel this too. Yet there is much more to spiritual existence than witchcraft, and that is the issue. Let me explain.

Witchcraft lends added impetus to doing everything in one's power to make a situation as positive as possible, but, as the saying goes, "In every life a little rain must fall." If life is a learning process—and it seems to me that each incarnation is a training module in a larger spiritual plan—then obstacles are not only necessary, they are inevitable. Some may be countered with magick, others may not. It takes years to become a truly effective witch, and even then there are things that are simply meant to be, no matter how annoying or painful they may seem at the time.

If a child knew how to change his circumstances using concentrated will, he would most likely use it to grab as much candy as possible, to avoid going to school, and to blast away anybody who annoyed him. The all-powerful infant would end up fat, ignorant, and despotic. Now, as adults, we have more conscience than this—or do we? Wiccans try to, as does any good human being, but all of us run the heavy risk of abusing our power, either deliberately or by accident. Alex Sanders has told of misusing his magickal ability to gain sex and money—pitfalls that are unfortunately natural to basic human instinct. There are enough people doing this on the material planes, without them doing it on the astral and spiritual ones too, so we have guardians. They only let us go so far. They also continually present us with new problems to overcome.

With each problem we successfully counteract, we become stronger and closer to our true spiritual selves. Yes, this often involves attempts at magick, but we as humans are not insurmountable, no matter what some witches might imply. Keeping a positive attitude and accepting each new problem as a challenge is the ideal standpoint. Keeping spiritual faith in an often harsh material world is one of the most difficult exercises in this life. Nobody, not even the witch, or the priest, or the Buddhist monk should punish him- or herself for occasionally losing sight of the Light. We all know of "dark nights of the soul" that often lead, eventually, to radiant new leases on life. Without the utter dejection of a temporary loss of faith, the epiphany would be paler. The contrast factor is a major spur in most people's incarnations.

The intelligent person is designed to question, and the magickal person is designed to be intense. This means that the witch, if she is more than just a sheep (and there are magickal sheep out there too, in coven-flocks of prescribed thought and action), must inevitably suffer both highs and lows (see the section "Mood Swings" in chapter 6). Many witches, Wiccans, and other spiritual/mystical types are psychologically, if not chemically, bipolar; it is often the lows that have led to the spiritual search. Again, this is the gem to be found in the head of the ugly toad of misfortune. Adversity breeds strength and is a necessary ingredient to epiphany.

Perceptions

Another factor that can make life more difficult is that witchcraft increases one's perceptions. The witch is sensitive psychically and psychologically—she trains herself to be. She is thus easily affected by atmospheres emanating from the living, the dead, the past, and often the future too. That's a great deal to handle in any situation. It requires discrimination ("Is it me, or is there really something going on here? If so, what?") and the ability to earth oneself when necessary. Astral armour is one of the first tools developed in magickal training—and necessarily so—but it takes years of self-scrutiny to rid it of psychic Achilles' heels, even just the minor ones.

Nobody is invulnerable. If one thinks he is, effective protection may take place for a while, but the degree of self-belief required on a permanent basis is nothing short of self-delusional. This is particularly applicable to working negative magick. (I mention this because those I have met who consider themselves the most invulnerable are all practitioners of "left-hand"—i.e., amoral or even immoral—magick.) The effective witch knows and acknowledges her weaknesses as well as her strengths. She is aware of her own neuroses. She has to be, otherwise they will destroy the magickal organism that is her mind, body, and soul working together to produce a positive, proactive, and spiritually aware incarnation.

Well-meant Judgements

If magick worked for the individual in the manner that most people imagine (creating an uninhibited path for the practitioner to the top of the social/financial ladder, and donning the witch with powers that impress and terrify in equal measure), human nature would abuse it. The chance for well-meant misjudgements would also be greater. For example, a witch might decide to save her best friend from dying of cancer, and do so at the flick of a wand. Yet perhaps that friend needed to pass over to progress to the next stage of development.

As it is, covens and individual witches can indeed perform healing at a patient's request, but healing will only take place if it is meant to. In the Wiccan's case, this is because of the proviso "An' it Harm None." If the patient will suffer more by staying here, will be harmed in any way, or if somebody else in the situation will suffer because of the magick, the person will be allowed to die, no matter how much healing energy is directed at him or her. In the case of the non-Wiccan witch who may not have added such a proviso to the working, all I can say is that there are powers out there far greater than the human, albeit a human empowered by magick. No, that isn't just an excuse to explain away ineffective magick. If I didn't believe it, through the power of my own experiences, I certainly wouldn't waste my time studying and writing a book on it. The same principle can be applied to orthodox science. We, as humans, can only do so much. There are larger things afoot in this cosmos than our individual lives.

Certainly, the witch does what he or she can in any given situation, gathering energy and fortitude from her magickal resources. She aims her will and fires—and there will always be an effect, it simply might not be the one she thinks she wants. Because she is spiritually aware, the witch knows that there are many invisible, almost imperceptible forces at work in the cosmos. At times, these will cause her great personal pain. She accepts that she can only do her best. She never lies down and dies; she strives. Because of this proactive attitude, she often succeeds in the end. Yet being a witch is no cop-out. Magick never was for the faint-hearted.

God, and Other Religions

Most people assume that witches do not believe in God, or that witches presume to usurp God. They might have Pagan deities that they worship, as did primitive man before he realised that the world was big and governed by many purposes, but these are mere demigods, or idols; or the witch worships the goat, as in the Goya depictions, right?

In reality, many witches believe in a Creative Intelligence that rules over the demigods, which are often worshipped as expressions of particular qualities. The god Pan, the capricious lord of the forest, is the nearest most witches wish to get to the goat.

Because she is eclectic, the witch respects all religions, though she may not agree with the expression of some of them. These days, the most popular orthodox religions with witches are Buddhism and Hinduism, as both are pantheistic (but with a supreme Cosmic Intelligence), and both contain creeds of mutual tolerance, reincarnation theory, and generous lashings of philosophy.

Witchcraft has become more than a nature religion or a crude quest for power; it has moved with the times and absorbed the principles and ideas of many other cultures and creeds. It embraces elements of many philosophies that span back thousands of years, a fact appropriate and natural to its initiates, many of whom participated in these ancient religions at the time they were practised.

As mentioned in the opening of this chapter, witches take their beliefs from whatever seems a genuine path to the Light. Admittedly there are some who adhere to the creeds of either Gerald Gardner or Alex Sanders with blinkered determination; there are always those who stick to the rules.

Then there are those who think we are plain crazy—atheists, for example. Witchcraft is often confused with simple superstition. Yes, there are crossovers, but these have more to do with understanding symbolism than with thinking one will die because her life-saving operation is taking place on the thirteenth day of the month and a single magpie was spotted en route to the hospital. Most witches are semiotically aware rather than superstitious.

Superstitions change so much from country to country that, in these days of global awareness, it is difficult to take them seriously. The Chinese and Japanese, for example, take issue with the number four. The word for it, *shi,* sounds very similar to the Cantonese, Mandarin, and Japanese word for "death." Many East Asian hospitals do not list a fourth floor, and a recent survey showed that Chinese and Japanese citizens are 7 percent more likely to die of a heart-related illness (such as a sudden heart attack) on the fourth day of the month than on any other day. Such is the power of superstition and psychological connection. However, in these climes, four is a number of stability, and suggests unshakable material foundations, as in "standing foursquare." We may be less likely to die on such a day.

It would be possible to argue from this standpoint, as did those involved with the Western Mystery Tradition, that belief systems from other cultures are not applicable to our own environment. In modern terms this would mean that feng shui, for example, is completely incompatible with the Western lifestyle and psychic atmosphere—a fact with which I would personally agree. However, I know some people who claim to have gained great benefit from practising feng shui in their British and American homes. I certainly use a great many Hindu and Buddhist techniques for which the same point may be argued (as did Dion Fortune, W. E. Butler, and others in response to the Eastern esotericism of the Theosophists).

I feel sure that few would agree that one is more likely to die on the fourth or thirteenth day of the month, but the point is, people do. Here in England, more car crashes occur on the thirteenth than on any other day. People are naturally out of sorts on this day (except for my mother, who has adopted it as her lucky number for some unknown reason!). It cannot be ignored that the belief system has a powerful effect. This is partly due to the impingement of the group mind, partly to the depletion of personal confidence when a thing is deemed inauspicious. It is clear, therefore, that *belief* is everything.

Any system may be applied with effect if the practitioner is completely convinced of it. I am not Christian, but I have seen Christians glowing with serenity and compassion, and having a powerfully positive effect on the lives of others. Nor am I Muslim, but I have seen the power of Islam all but possessing its disciples. A friend of mine who is agnostic witnessed her Transcendental Meditation teacher (a British-born Buddhist with Hindu tendencies) physically levitating, no strings attached. She acknowledged that her instructor knew how to accumulate psychic power, even if the path was not her own, or one to which my friend could fully relate.

Many will see witches as lunatics (we are, of course), as well as occultists of any discipline, and Neo-Pagans, and committed Christians, and Muslims, Buddhists, and all other religious groups. We all believe in unseen powers, and our "proof" is never enough. However, of two things we can be certain: belief and faith can move mountains, and, no matter how different our creeds and beliefs—and they are as different as it is possible to be—all are valid because they affect lives in real time and are paths to the Light.

two

The Witch and Morality

MORALITY IS, TO A DEGREE, subjective. Part of the nature of the witch is to refuse to allow others to inflict on her their own standards; she has always been, and always shall be, unorthodox. However, she is aware of cause and effect (the underlying principle of magick) and of the numerous layers of which the cosmos is composed. Thus, she cannot fail to notice that it is wiser and better, for a plethora of reasons, to adhere to the moral code "An' it Harm None, Do As Thou Wilt."

This Wiccan Rede is no new revelation. In Hesiod's *Great Works,* authored around 700 B.C.E., it is stated: "If a man sow evil, he shall reap evil in increase; if men do to him as he has done, it will be true justice." This simple psychological algebra is echoed by the Rede. Contrary to popular belief, the witch and magickian apply the principle of common sense to everything they do. This includes the avoidance of "sowing evil."

So, the witch lives according to her conscience, and is able to define between moods and rational decision. There is a great emphasis in magickal training on the dangers of the astral planes (Yesod in Qabalistic terms) where many a neophyte is glamoured. This includes a sudden, dazzling belief in particular personal powers (this is where magickal megalomaniacs are created), and being taken along pleasant-seeming sidetracks, their reality merely that of the imagination. The art of discrimination is one of the first the witch must learn.

When she is swept up with anger and black thoughts as we are from time to time, the witch has the wisdom to wait. Should she act in fury, she knows that her magick will be misguided by the "tygers of wrath," and will eventually unleash an entire pack of sharp-toothed, yellow-eyed beasts on their perpetrator. So she takes a few deep breaths, indulges in a salt bath by candlelight (with a sweet-smelling oil to soothe her senses), and waits until morning to reassess her assail. Perhaps it would be better to strengthen her own stance, rather than attempt to undermine that of her opponent? Maybe a little loving attention would transform her rival into a decent human being—after all, petulance and perversity are the products of misery. She might choose to cast a spell to pour metaphysical oil on the troubled waters of her rival's psyche, or she may simply ask the Goddess to bring mutual understanding and hope to the situation. The gods, ever gracious when prettily petitioned, are bound to bend a willing ear to one who does them faithful service and who is prepared to make an effort for the common good. The gods can see how the power-cravings of one person upset the communal balance. Most of them have been there, done that, and learned the lesson, as the Greek myths, for example, imaginatively attest.

One of the witch's first rules is not to do anything she is unhappy with. She understands that it is wrong both towards herself and towards humanity to be coerced into inappropriate action. She does not allow herself to be swept away by the group mind; she is immune to peer pressure. Such lessons can be dearly learned; we all put a foot wrong occasionally. When I was eighteen, for example, I allowed a self-proclaimed High Priest to talk me into all sorts of madness. I knew, fundamentally, that he was not sound, but I allowed my instincts to be overruled by apparent fact. He was very intelligent, well liked, and well respected. What did an eighteen-year-old girl have in comparison? Well, I'll tell you: discrimination. However, in this particular case she failed to exercise it, and paid the price with blood and tears. It was an initiation indeed, but barely the joyous process it could have been.

Protection against self-doubt is as essential a tool to the witch as self-belief. It is one thing to be full of confidence when surrounded by friends, or comfortably lodged in one's own surroundings, but this self-assuredness must be hermetically sealed against chance circumstance. It must stand untouched by alien environments, by aggressive interrogation, and by communal fire. Our sisters and brothers who were burned, drowned, hanged, racked, and crushed knew how to maintain their belief in any situation, the likes of which we shall hopefully never experience again. The Christian martyrs were similarly blessed with incredible spiritual and psychological strength. All who stick to their beliefs in adversity have learned the lesson known to every witch: that of psychic and spiritual self-protection. The soul that passes through life and through the gates of death with complete integrity is indeed immortal, whatever the creed that informed it.

Witches have long been popular symbols of complete immorality. We all know the confused images inflicted on the Craft by Christianity and Islam: the witch kissing the backside of the goat, the witch's orgies. Thank goodness so many white witches are out there—particularly in America, but in Britain and Germany too— who are improving public relations by demonstrating the absurdities of these claims. Yes, there's always some nutcase or group of nutcases who will satisfy their bizarre urges and give it some name (Satanism, maybe, or witchcraft), but it surely bears no resemblance to the Craft as it is commonly practised. Do we accuse all Christians of being witchfinder generals? Do we see all Roman Catholics as Inquisitors? Do we view every single Islamic person as personally responsible for the many atrocities (particularly perpetuated on women) committed in the name of Allah? Of course we don't. We try to act as luminaries in a dark world. We see the spiritual core in any creed, and respect it. When accused of idiocies such as goat worship, we calmly respond that the image derives from Pan, symbol of all demigods and of nature, and that yes, we do appreciate nature, but we sure as hell don't kiss any butts. (Crowley and his Thelemites did/might, but that's another story. Their aim was to counteract neuroses, which is another form of immorality—the crime against the self.)

The orgiastic image is again related to the Pan-Dionysus legacy, and bears more relation to shenanigans in ancient Greece than to those in any self-respecting coven I have known. Because the witch is intrinsically linked with nature, it is commonly assumed that she follows the laws of the beast of the field: mating as impulse dictates (though not even merely seasonally!), and, perish the thought, mating inappropriately with other species, and so on. This is a deeply unpleasant concept and one clearly bred in the sewers of the mediaeval imagination. Hieronymous Bosch's *Hell* scenarios sum up the common concept of the witch perfectly, as do Goya's haggish depictions.

Yes, the witch and magickian will employ sexual energy for rites. It is the strongest energy we possess; we would be idiots not to. It is the basis of life, of all creation. Artists, painters, and even scientists use it, sublimated—nine times out of ten—into inspiration. The witch takes her natural urges, without taint of fear or guilt, and channels the energy into her magick. It is the very breath of life to any spell. A sexual frisson can become an astral hurricane; enough to carry her plans to the desired location, enough to change things and rearrange the earth plane. This is why some covens encourage sexual interaction between members. (Personally, I feel this to be foolish, as it inevitably grounds the energy that would otherwise have "taken off" magickally.)

Working skyclad (naked) is a common image of the witch, and was once perceived as immoral. It does happen, yes. Working skyclad has partly to do with being psychically unveiled, partly with the symbol of being at one with nature, and partly with being an open announcement that we refuse to be ashamed of our physicality. Despite the magickal nature of being a witch, physicality is understood as being of equal importance—"Kether is in Malkuth, and Malkuth in Kether." Our physicality is important as a symbol of the particular energies that characterise us.

The witch refuses to kowtow to societal neuroses, which is another reason for her liberated attitude. If she wishes to work naked in order to feel the wind on her skin or to feel revealed before the Goddess, she will. If, however, she is not in the mood, or prefers to work cloaked, she will never be coerced into doing otherwise.

Morality is subjective, and the witch makes her own rules. The touchstone is her own informed conscience.

The Eco-Witch (and the Neo-Pagan)

I will sing of well-founded Earth, mother of all, eldest of all beings. She feeds all creatures that are in the world, and all that go upon goodly land, and all that are in the paths of the seas, and all that fly: all these are fed of her store. Through you, O queen, men are blessed in their children and blessed in their harvests, and to you it belongs to give means of life to mortal men and to take it away. Happy is the man whom you delight to honour!

—Homeric "Hymn to Earth, the Mother of All"

Ancient religions emphasise the connection between Earth and her children; Wicca does the same. The Wiccan and the Neo-Pagan seek to reunite human consciousness with nature, a principle considered as fact in many older cultures, but easily forgotten today. As Dion Fortune's Vivien Le Fay Morgan points out in *The Sea Priestess*:

. . . the gods are forces, and the forces are intelligent and purposive, being expressions of the nature of the One. And as It is, so is creation, for as the Chaldean Oracles say, "The wise man looketh upon the face of Nature and beholdeth therein the countenance of the Eternal." And human nature . . . is a part of nature, and you learn a lot about both Nature and the gods if you study it.

In the present era, many environments that are natural to us are in fact entirely unnatural; urbanisation has left very few places untouched. Once, the quest was to achieve civilisation in conjunction with, or despite, nature; nowadays, it is to reestablish contact with the Mother we are destroying. We are faced with a peculiar situation in which we may grow up surrounded by the natural or seminatural, yet be entirely closeted in our manmade environments. This, of course, still tallies with Dion Fortune's description of all as a psychic landscape (true of the city as much as of the forest), but establishing the Pagan rapport with nature is not always easy or possible. For example, I was raised in Northumberland (in the north of England) amidst fields and hills, but felt very little connection with them at the time, as I had no religious link; God seemed housed in church (though I could barely perceive divinity there either). The best to be hoped for were sunsets and moonlit nights in which the world seemed transformed, because at times of natural power, my pre-programmed antipathy to the great outdoors was nullified. The "outside" had always been presented to me as alien; "real life" and warmth were to be found inside, in a civilised environment. It was not until I left home and found my liberty and magick in the midst of nature that I came to truly appreciate it.

Conversely, many nowadays are raised in urban situations and have no opportunity to worship as our Pagan ancestors did; and not just worship, but connect. We have also created (as a species) a culture in which science and the rational are revered above the primal and intuitive, whereas, in fact, both should be taken in equal measure. The witch aims to reunite these forces. She works with the earth, and respects and nurtures her in return. Simply by relishing the tides of the moon, the sea, the greenness apparent in the few spaces left to us, and by being environmentally conscious, she gives something back.

This point is important for several reasons. One, we owe some sort of recompense to the physical organism and spiritual entity that produced us physically, and to which we are inherently attached. Secondly, it gives us great joy to appreciate our origins; it is an atavistic necessity. Thirdly, if we do not honour our Goddess, she will withdraw her bounty, just as Demeter, in grief for her snatched daughter, almost starved mankind in Greek myth.

The Homeric epigrams opine on this and on the apparent randomness of nature (a fact of duality, of which she is the intractable daughter): "Queen Earth, all bounteous giver of honey-hearted wealth, how kindly, it seems, you are to some, and how intractable and rough for those with whom you are angry" (Homer's Epigrams, sec. 7). However, the fact that she (Gaia, Themis, Rhea, call her what you will) is described as "angry" suggests something other than randomness. The cataclysms of the earth are viewed as punishments—for hubris (the sin committed most by mankind in our quest to quell natural forces and establish ourselves as somehow immune and superior to them), and for wanton destruction, an issue of great relevance in this era. We have taken and taken, as every witch knows, and since the dawn of the patriarchal religions, have given very little back in return as a species.

The witch endeavours to reestablish a sense of balance. She does not desire to mindlessly manipulate natural resources; she hopes to work with them without negative side effects. Capitalism, colonisation, and short-term thinking have led us very close to environmental disaster. Governments are always blithe about this because they think in terms of short spans of control. They certainly have no intention of preserving resources for generations not yet born, and other species barely get a look in. The witch is acutely aware of the natural balance of things, and of the karmic debts we have to less-fortunate cultures and other species.

Every witch and Wiccan is different, as previously discussed, so when I speak on current attitudes to these issues, I can do so confidently only for myself. I do not view natural disasters as punishments—the first word implies that they are merely cyclic—but I do think that they can act as warnings. However, the most obvious warnings and true punishments come from ourselves: oil slicks, factory explosions, air pollution—all that industry does to despoil our planet. These are almost always the affliction of the few on the many, but the effect is vast and damaging to the Mother and to us. Such factors and events need to be counteracted both physically and psychically. Wiccans, Neo-Pagans, and many witches aim continually to do this, our practical and magickal efforts aided by the Wheel of Life, or the eight-pronged cycle of sabbats.

Sabbats celebrate natural cycles; this is why they exist. They are an opportunity to say "Thank you," to work with natural conditions, and to revel in the change of the seasons. The progress and intrigues of the God of the Waxing Year, the Goddess, and the God of the Waning Year are of paramount importance to the practising Pagan and Wiccan. At Samhain, we mourn for the death of the Old God, but welcome the coming of a new cycle. We work with the apparently fickle Goddess, who slays her old lover in favour of a newer, younger version. She, too, mourns; she becomes oracular and translucent in her grief. Here, we find it easy to slip between the worlds; the dead are as clear to us as the living. Physical referents become less relevant.

At Yule, we harmonise with the bleak, unyielding earth. We celebrate her hibernation with festivals of fire, and nurture the hearth, enticing the gods to bring warmth to a Homeric mankind apparently devoid of celestial bounty. This is a Northern festival; in hot countries, the emphasis is similar, but involves the parching rather than the freezing of earth. There, it seems that an excess of warmth and light (in Qabalistic terms, excess of Chesed) is the problem; here, we suffer from an apparent withdrawal of bounty (a Geburic issue). Between the hemispheres we balance out, of course, but we are programmed as individuals, and as separate cultures, to experience life in terms of the immediate.

The spring equinox brings the upbeat vernal principle into play; the God of the Waning Year grows weak as the tides of fortune reverse. Now, nature is waxing, augmenting the strength of the God of the Waning Year's rival. The pulse of life grows high and strong; sap rises in plants and life-force rises in mankind. Here, we celebrate the beginning of the season of growth, which will climax at Beltane.

May 1st, or Beltane, falls opposite Samhain on the Wheel of Life. It is equal in power to this great sabbat, but its emphasis is entirely different. Where Samhain celebrates life beyond death, Beltane celebrates the nativity of new life. Qabalistically speaking, we could say that Samhain is Binah (the dark sea—saturnine and restrictive—but also the womb of life, at the top of the Pillar of Severity), while Beltane is Netzach (Orphic, perpetuating life through love and also lust [without which, animal husbandry and agriculture would not exist], at the bottom of the Pillar of Mildness). Both are powerfully uplifting: Samhain to intuitive and sometimes oracular/prophetic heights that often involve interaction with beings on the other side of the Veil; and Beltane to states of spiritual, emotional, and material aspiration. Both, of course, celebrate the Goddess in nature; at Samhain she is the Crone moving into her winter phase, and at Beltane she is the Maiden, flowers in her hair and her belly swelling with a ripening child (or her form could be slender and girlish, and enticing the attentions of the satyr-like God).

Between these are, of course, other sabbats: Imbolc (Candlemas) in February, Midsummer (the summer solstice), Lughnasadh in August, and the esbat of the full moon in every month. All of these involve us intimately with the cycles of our Mother, and ensure that the witch is fully attuned to her physical and spiritual origins. For as long as she is appreciated, the earth will, like any mother, continue to wish to bestow on us her bounty. However, we also need to help actively. (See chapter 9, "The Wheel of Death and Life," for further details.)

The witch is always environmentally aware. She recycles her bottles and as much of the rest of her refuse as possible, and does her bit for whatever issues she feels are of particular relevance at the time (saving a local wood from being turned into a parking lot, for example, or petitioning against the unnecessary fuel emissions from industry and on the roads).

Without nature to act as an analogy, we would find ourselves even more cut off from our communion with God (or the Creative Intelligence if "God" jars). Trees, for example, represent the whole of creation, as in Ets Chayyim, the Tree of Life. They also signify the mind of man striving, reaching up towards the Truth (and they bear a spookily acute likeness to the shape of neurons in the brain to boot). Water reminds us permanently of the fluidity of life—how easily it is spilled, how fast and forceful it may be, and how the great sea herself is influenced by the planets above (how could we not also be?). The planets symbolise a wealth of information, as every occultist is aware. The sun, which induced life on our planet, represents the earth-fructifying male principle in most cultures, and the health-giving life-force on the spiritual planes. The moon is our symbol of inner life, and is feminine to most perceptions. We are borne of the elements earth, air, fire, water, and spirit, and their living presence in our lives provides an analogy of our progress. It makes sense for us to preserve the environment for which we were designed, and many witches are prime movers in this cause. Most witches are green-fingered herb- and nature-lovers, after all.

Modern Wicca, as will be discussed in chapter 14, "A Brief History of Witchcraft," is very much an amalgam of traditions. It does not undermine it to be modern; indeed, in my opinion, its eclecticism is one of its greatest strengths. However, Wicca is profoundly influenced by Paganism, and this really is ancient. Now, the Wiccan and the modern Pagan often describe themselves as belonging to different schools of thought, but most of their core beliefs are identical. The Goddess is paramount, or at least of equal stature, in both schools, and they share an emphasis on the old gods, an acute awareness of natural cycles, and a respect and awe for Gaia, for example. The major difference is the practise of magick; witches do it, and many Pagans do not, reserving their energies for pure worship and celebration. However, the witch and Neo-Pagan work well together for the causes in which they are united, and they are most certainly siblings, spiritually speaking.

Wicca/witchcraft has swallowed Paganism whole, along with large chunks of Buddhism, Hinduism, diverse mythologies, the Jewish and Western Mystery Traditions, and many modern interpretations of these and lateral topics. The Craft includes aspects of Christianity through an understanding of the mysteries of Tiphareth (the mystical path of self-sacrifice) and through Gnosticism. It aims for intellectual as well as primal (physical, psychological, and emotional) satisfaction. It aims to influence as well as to partake. This interactive open-mindedness is the greatest strength of Wicca, and will, if the trend continues as described, become a force of great enlightenment. The practising of spellcraft, one of the defining chacteristics of witchcraft, is relevant in that it is important to know how to do it—to the witch, essential. It is then possible to choose not to. This gives a greater arena for discrimination and intelligent action, when necessary.

Most importantly, however, the Wiccan follows the Pagan in putting the Earth first. Through this, and in this, she sees her divinity. Second in her priorities, after God and the Goddess in nature, comes mankind as a whole, along with the other species. Then comes personal affiliations (friends, family, spouses, familiars), and finally her individual self. "An' it Harm None" is her first premise before action; "For the Good of All" is her second. After all, if a thing harms nobody, but is of no benefit either, it is barely worth wasting the energy on. Selfish gain always backfires, for nature is not designed to allow the rampant perpetuation of individual will. Looking at mankind as an evolving species, it might be tempting at times to assume that this is not the case. Nature is very much attuned to the survival and propagation of the strongest and most arrogant, but we are now beginning to witness nature being "Intractable and rough [with] those with whom [she is] angry." We are at the beginning of the backlash.

How does nature show her wrath at being so abused? It is not simply through volcanoes and earthquakes—these are themselves natural, and were occurring millions of years before man was even thought of. Neither do storms, which most witches thoroughly enjoy anyway, reflect the anger of the abused Mother. No, it is through small things that we at first perceive our environmental karma. Certain rare, delicate flowers that Persephone might have gathered in her skirts vanish from the earth, one by one. Herbs and medicines that might perhaps have been used to cure cancer or even AIDS are lost to us when acres of rainforest are destroyed (nature never produces a disease without an antidote, for everything in this plane has its equal and opposite reaction). We find our lives less filled with joy, for it is difficult to celebrate life when surrounded by concrete and sculpted chrome and glass. We find ourselves seeking ecstasy in Dionysiac activities (unfulfilling sex, drink, drugs) without the Dionysiac *primum mobile:* nature. Or, we become tied to straight jobs in straight lives in which there is little joy but material success. Abundance is sought materially and emotionally rather than through a physical connection with the Divine, and as sages of any culture will say, this creates further confusion.

There is no natural repose in the world we have created for ourselves through selfishness and greed. Instead of resting in the lap of our Mother, we are stung at every juncture by the results of our own propagation and actions as a species. Rather like Io relentlessly being pursued by the gadfly of Hera's envy, we flee from continent to continent (job to job, relationship to relationship, house to bigger house) in search of respite. By suppressing and attempting to control nature, by achieving a state of semicivilisation (there are many decent humans upon the Earth, but there are also many indecent ones, and few of us would even aspire to being as good as we possibly could be), by thinking only in terms of immediate gratification, we have created a bed of concrete and refuse. Now we must lie in it.

The idea that nature punishes us is actually more relevant to civilisations past than to us now. They were literally at the mercy of the weather gods. Indeed, we have striven and largely succeeded in shielding ourselves from the elements. However, recent events have given us cause for reassessment. For example, in normally mild-weathered Britain, where I live, floods and freakish seasonal fluctuations have shocked even the most environmentally blithe of persons. Will those in power learn and change their policies, as our houses are flooded, and as trains crash due to water-damaged railroad tracks? Probably not. These events are not punishments as such, they are natural consequences of unnatural actions and influences. We can, as witches and as green-minded citizens, merely attempt to reverse the trend by pointing a finger or a wand at the damage and willing not the Earth to be appeased, but the minds of men to absorb and act sensibly on the evidence.

I live on an island with a population of fifty-eight million people, and it is dramatically increasing by the day. I have visited New Zealand, which is bigger than Great Britain, and it has a population of three and a half million. It is clear that individuals from different countries will have differing views on the subject of global crisis. Were it not for individual governments preventing mass immigration, however, the world citizens who currently have so much space might find themselves thinking more carefully about the issue of space-sharing and procreation. (I am not suggesting that New Zealand is environmentally irresponsible—in fact, it is quite the reverse. I am simply using it as an example of a place with a different population density, and thus a different perception of available space in the world.) Even if overcrowding occurs only in a few countries, it will eventually affect many more, if not all. Because the things we as humans think we require to lead quality lives (things we are told are what we need) have powerful environmental side effects. Then, the more of us there are to create them, the greater the fall-out will be, and the lower the quality of life is available to all.

One of the (many) problems of being human is that we are cosmically small, and the Earth and universe seem huge in comparison. Not only are we prone to think only in terms of one incarnation's survival (and frequently, of less; a month or a year ahead is many people's outer limit), but we also feel overwhelmed by that which lies outside of us. I have heard Irish Catholics state that contraception should be banned in all cultures because "we need to fill all the spaces left on Earth." One particular "pro-life" activist actually cited the South American forests and African deserts as examples of the "plentiful space" left on Earth. I would like to see her trying to live there, especially with her numerous children to care for. It is inane and selfish to go on producing so avidly when resources are running so conspicuously low. Perhaps children born now will escape the effects of Gaia's depletion, but what of their children, and their children's children? Yes, the Earth is big compared to the individual—or to a single community or country even—but we are eating it up at an incredible rate.

The issue of contraception and procreation is not, I think, one that should be preached upon, except in the general sense of facing facts. However, *awareness* is essential to everyone bringing further beings into the world. Our position must be assessed first from a worldview, then from a spiritual overview (fundamentally, what kind of incarnation might one be able to offer the child/children in question?). Finally, it is for the individuals concerned to decide. Every human being is different, and circumstances vary wildly from person to person, be they Catholic, occultist, Hindu, atheist, or humanist. The point is to perform every act in full consciousness of its potential repercussions. When a pregnancy occurs accidentally, abortion might be the right choice for the woman at that time, but to use it as contraception (however semiconsciously) is a travesty against the life-force. Either way, it invokes terrible karma for all concerned. However, bringing a child into the world when the circumstances are wrong creates another karmic mess. For this reason, most witches are pro-choice.

Contraception, conversely, indicates responsibility towards potential beings, as well as towards society and the environment in general. We cannot deplete the Earth's resources whilst augmenting our demands on it; the equation will inevitably become imbalanced and future generations will find themselves devoid of choice in the issue. China is an example of this, and the results of overpopulation are inhumane beyond belief. They contravene all individual rights, and have created a generation of single, spoilt children, or "little emperors." Perish the thought that the rest of the world should ever come to this (or to that which China is attempting to avoid): an utter lack of resources, an inability to sustain life. History, of course, has seen numerous such scenarios in the days before contraception. Third World countries that cannot afford the luxury of choice, or that reject it on religious grounds, are perpetually suffering the repercussions of overabundance of life and underabundance of food, water, and the other reasonable props to any incarnation.

These examples may seem extreme to us Westerners, but even the most adamantine industrialists will now admit, when pressed, that perhaps we are not so very far from a global crisis. Plus, all of us are aware, thanks to the work of modern psychologists, of how essential it is not simply to provide a new being with just the physical essentials, but with positive emotional and mental sustenance too. We need to take the environment seriously on a minor as well as a major scale. All great movements begin in the home. The foundation of a single psyche can become magnified into an entire culture or movement, which in turn influences innumerable other lives. Every person alive on the planet will affect it in some way. We need to ensure that the trend changes from mindless abuse of resources to conscientious, spiritually aware giving and receiving. The witch and the Neo-Pagan carry this knowledge with them at all times, even when shopping at the corporate supermarket, travelling on the subway, or working in an office. There is no more effective way to influence others (subtly is best) than to be in the midst of them. An environment that is never experienced cannot be effectively changed. Contrary to the Biblical expression, "In the midst of Death, we are in Life." The witch, mistress of innovation and improvisation, knows this, and works with it as best she can.

There is a much more positive side to the concept of community than simply the gobbling up of the Earth, of course. Folk customs and festivals reflect the wealth of information, both practical and religious, built up by pockets of humanity over the centuries. This information is struggling to survive, and reflects with awe on our position in the cosmos, thanking the Great Mother for her bounty when it is received. These rituals are tribal. The British Isles contain many such living examples. As the year turns, we repeat the religious and magickal thought processes of our forebears through folk custom, music, and dance, often unconsciously. This point is key to witchcraft and Wicca. See Paul Davenport's section ("Folk Customs and Folk Magick" in chapter 9) for more on this.

What Can the Witch Do in Times of Global Crisis?

We have established that the witch aims to be in touch with the Earth both practically and spiritually. She makes the effort through her seasonal rites and her environmental awareness, and sometimes she is drawn like all of us into deep-rooted group awareness, such as the sabbatical scenarios described by Paul Davenport in chapter 9.

This is all very well when life is going according to plan, but what of war, flood, famine, or terrorist attack? Magick can seem very feeble indeed in the face of these acts of nature and of human nature. Often, evil is difficult, if not impossible to predict, leaving the witch and the visionary with a terrible feeling of guilt and futility in the wake of disaster. After all, what is the point of being psychic if the most apparently useful thing one can do is think of somebody just before they make an unexpected phone call, or have a vague feeling of unease just before a major catastrophe?

To take on personal responsibility for global events, even on a miniscule level, is tantamount to considering oneself a demigod. The forces surrounding our planet are way beyond human comprehension and certainly intervention. What we *can* do is act on a microcosmic scale to help those affected by the disasters that characterise life on this planet, and teach compassion and tolerance by always acting with it ourselves. This, of course, is not confined to the witch. There are compassionate people of all religions and walks of life. The witch, like these, tries to minimalise damage when it occurs. She is concerned with healing the planet and its inhabitants, not causing further destruction.

The pitfall of the magickally inclined is the absorption of the atmosphere in a crisis, rather than effecting its transformation. After the destruction of the World Trade Center and the deaths there and at the Pentagon, for example, many witches I know—including this one—felt or became physically ill. They empathised with the victims and took on huge quantities of strong emotion—fear, anger, despair— which were practically impossible to process. The only way to counter this was to make practical moves: donating to funds for the victims' families, sending messages of support to those affected, and directing as much healing energy as could be mustered, just like the rest of the world who wanted to help.

When disaster strikes, it fills humankind with a terrible fear of transience. The society that protects us from the uncivilised, and represents all to which we have become accustomed (even if it does compromise us in some ways), suddenly seems fragile, leaving us exposed to unknown influences. In the case of a national disaster, our savings, homes, and way of life also come under threat. The body is suddenly put into perspective as an intensely vulnerable vessel. Old age and slow disease seem like luxuries when lives in full flow are suddenly cut dead without a moment's warning. Timescales change, and grief moves from the microcosmic to the macrocosmic. This must be how life was before the age of medicine. For all of its faults to the homeopathic mind, we cannot doubt that orthodox medicine (often based on old herbal law) has prolonged many an incarnation, and that "modern" life, for all its pitfalls, has also preserved life within its manmade walls. However, we can prolong life and prolong it, but its sum total is still a blink in the eye of human history, and immortality is available only from within.

Because much of the world is so heavily populated, and death is cleared out of view, gathered into hospitals, hospices, and old-people's homes, we often get the impression that this life goes on forever. Everywhere we look there are young, robust, healthy bodies containing upbeat souls confident in their own longevity. Death, when it occasionally touches us, seems terrible, an outrage. A girl in high school who died of leukemia only a month or so after she was diagnosed with it shocked our youthful community to the core. A young woman in another community has battled and lost against breast cancer, and nobody can believe it—she was only thirty-two. We are not accustomed to looking the Grim Reaper in the eye.

In the centre of the ancient city of Prague, there stands a fine mediaeval clock. Every hour on the hour, a carving of the skeletal Grim Reaper begins to shake his bell. As he does so, statues appear in the two windows of the clock, processing in his direction; everybody cheers. They are priests, beggars, merchants, lords—all being called in by Death, regardless of their social standing. In mediaeval times, the End was always near, and lives were lived with this in mind. Now, however, unless one works with the dying, it is sanitised. A death in the family is a terrible tragedy, but life goes on. Life *does* go on, but the perspective gained by an encounter with death should not be forgotten, least of all by the witch.

The witch operates on both sides of the Veil, and she must always be aware of the fact that life continues there as well as here. Human bonds do not dissolve when the flesh dies (nor do animals' in many cases, for that matter). Spiritual progression continues in a more intense form, as it does not have the body left to interfere with it. After a while, the spirit might reincarnate, or it may move on; so witches believe. I'm sure none of us would claim that we are unquestionably right—therein lies the path to fanaticism—but we know what we have experienced, and that is all anybody can go by. The End is not the end. This feeling of hope, if not the actual specifics (which could jar on the grieving, and if so, should not be expressed as such), should be conveyed with certitude. Even simply on a psychological level, in times of crisis, the individual requires a strong shoulder. The witch can provide this, along with other practical action. She can also ease things along on the astral and spiritual planes by sending lines of light and strength to traumatised souls in transit.

The other things a witch can do are:

- Always act and speak with compassion towards all, regardless of their colour, creed, or affiliations. The witch avoids tarnishing everyone with the same brush; she knows all too well the effects of prejudice. That includes Christians! Being anti-Christian or anti-anybody simply reinforces mutual antipathy.

• Offer calm strength and support to the traumatised. An effective witch, like any other useful person, draws on her parallel experiences to gain empathy. She isn't self-obsessed (any comfort beginning with "Actually, I had a similar experience once, and it goes like this . . ." is no-go), and she isn't sickly sweet and patronising; she is simply a pillar of steady psychological support.

• Perform workings to add to the Universal fund of positive energy. Even a simple act such as lighting a candle and envisaging a person surrounded by healing light can work small wonders.

• Keep herself strong so that she can fight for what she believes in.

• Keep abreast of local and international politics so that she is well-informed and can act accordingly. Persistent petitions and peaceful protests have saved more than one plot of land from industrialisation, and have released more than one political prisoner.

Remember, our individual lives, and thus the world as we know it, are made up of small acts. There is no such thing as trivial action—each little event goes towards an overall cumulative total, and it is cumulative totals that create minorities and majorities. Most sane people want conscientious individual freedom to be the keynote of society, and it is towards this that the witch, in her own unique and valuable ways, continues to strive.

September 11th: An Example to the Spiritual Community

The beliefs of all free-thinking, spiritual individuals were severely challenged on September 11, 2001. I was in Northumberland writing this book at the time; I had just visited a beautiful ancient wood, and was feeling very much attuned to the spirits of Earth. I returned to my friend's cottage with, admittedly, few things on my mind except those delightful issues of my own sphere. Even if the day had turned from a beautiful autumnal one into one in which the wind blew up and the trees became quarrelsome and the atmosphere tilted into darkness, nothing could have prepared me for the shock I was to receive when I got back. My boyfriend rang and simply said "Turn on the TV." Like the rest of the world, I sat and watched helplessly, aware of being an onlooker at a critical point in human history—a watcher, merely. No spells or incantations could have stopped those towers from coming down, though it is true that the people inside them may have perceived the huge amounts of love and compassion that flowed to them from all around the globe during those terrible hours. Yet bricks are sometimes stronger than love, on a physical level anyway. So where does that leave our beliefs?

At times of crisis, practitioners of any spiritual discipline should try to bring hope and compassion where there is fear, harmony where there is discord, and love where there is hatred. Hopefully that's what we're doing already anyway. Faith is essential too; consistent belief in the Spiritual Source serves as the steadying, stabilising agent in human affairs during a time of global crisis and transformation.

There is practical action (discussed above) and then there is action on other planes. In his *Autobiography of a Yogi,* Paramahansa Yogananda described this life as "God's movie-screen" on which happy and sad films are projected—the inevitable effect of duality. It is our duty to avoid being sucked into the negativity, without burying our heads in the sand. There is a balance to be attained. As the Lucis Trust put it:

> The modern disciple, being a part of humanity, cannot escape the "drama of humanity." In this age there is no retreat for the disciple from the world's crisis. And clearly, the recent disaster highlights the crisis now confronting humanity.

What is this state of crisis, exactly? Spiritually, many would say that it is the beginning of the New Age of Aquarius. Physically, it is the product of overpopulation (there are more people alive on the planet today than have ever lived and died before—that should tell us something!), of global capitalism (when outlets of McDonald's are springing up in the most obscure of Third World towns, we definitely ought to worry), and of spiritual decrepitude in human beings; they run into one another. For a few to live comfortably, many suffer. Suicide bombers and -pilots are borne of a community that feels it has nothing to lose. It becomes self-righteously homicidal because it sees wealth here and hopeless poverty there. It sees injustice in the way material things are meted and doled out.

I am not naïve enough to suggest that it can ever be otherwise. Reading George Orwell's *Animal Farm* knocked that one out of me at an early age. Give most people an inch, and they will try to take a mile. It's true; it's human nature. Human nature is tribal and selfish without the universal spiritual influence. I say "universal" because the people responsible for the atrocities of September 11th were highly spiritual in their own way. They were prepared to die for what they see as justice and God. *Universal* spirituality respects all cultures and modes of being, respects all life forms, and is compassionate and sensible in its application.

Knowing this, we can use our spiritual imagination to ponder the choices available to humanity. Some say that humankind released evil into the world through immoral values and actions; others say that good and evil exist as naturally as light and darkness, independent of our species. To the occult mind, good and evil might create the dynamics necessary for spiritual progress. Admittedly, it is difficult to ever imagine it otherwise.

The Tibetan Master, one of Alice Bailey's spiritual guides (and coauthors), expresses the typical New Age view that, for humans, the Global Crisis will come through "wrong thinking, false values and the supreme evil of materialistic selfishness and the sense of isolated separativeness." Well, that makes perfect sense. What else could inspire it? This makes sense to all spiritual seekers, the witch included.

Involution comes from compassion, wisdom, and ethical action. It is time for us to choose between the temporary life of the body, and the eternal truth of spirit. We can combine the two, certainly, but only if we are primarily focussed on Higher Life. The microcosmic result of this is simple kindness; not altruism for show, or for gain, but for its own sake.

September 11th shook us all to the foundations. The falling towers shattered global, and especially American, complacency. All who are alert to esoteric imagery will appreciate the ages-old symbolism of what became a global spectacle. It put sorrow and fear into the hearts of those who believed themselves unassailable. It distressed the naturally compassionate to the core. Entire nations wept when they witnessed the sudden sacrifice of individual lives to ideals reminiscent of the Crusades. Nobody wants this kind of sorrow. No healthy human being could possibly wish to live in a world where such things occur. The same may be said of retaliation—more pointless civilian misery. So we have to learn from it. Learn to listen, to think for ourselves, and to step up the spiritual search. There is not a great deal of time left. Individuation is all very well, but now it's time to look outside our own narrow blinders and take a responsible attitude to what's being felt and experienced in other minds and cultures, often less privileged than our own. The "Age of Aquarius" so beloved of New Age/occult practitioners must not arrive covered in blood. It is the job of the witch to wash off preconceptions and political/sociological smears, and analyse them. Then she must decide how best to avoid future disasters. This takes communication and realism, and a genuine "Blessed Be" towards every human being who shares our planet.

How Can the Witch Respond to Personal Crisis?

The witch is human like everyone else. She is aware of magick and magickal realms, sure, but there are times for all of us when these seem like self-delusions, or simply irrelevant. There are times when we are in shock or depression or undergoing continuous difficulties, which makes a sense of magick almost impossible to access. There are times when our best efforts may simply seem useless in the face of other forces, or when a trusted friend turns, and our personal world crumbles. Sometimes something or someone we have invested our faith in fails. Sometimes life goes wrong.

The only thing we can count on when the chips are down is the Divine Spirit both within and without us. This finds its mundane expression as friendship and love. It really does make the worlds go round. Those in desperate circumstances, or on the brink of death, inevitably think of those they love in their final moments. A witch in crisis also turns to those she loves. Sometimes this is enough to get her through. They give support, both spiritual and practical. Sometimes she is left alone to deal with her problems, or she wears her supporters out with the depth of her demands. Because she is by nature a deep-thinking individual with a strong sense of justice, and is striving for the very best she can achieve in each incarnation, she suffers greatly when alone and in personal crisis. It wrecks all perspective. If supported, she will relate to her helpers enough to avoid total self-indulgence. If left to her own devices, she may simply plummet down into a vortex of despair (see the section "The Witch and Suicide" in chapter 6).

However, the witch knows her Tarot. She knows the images of Death, the Ten of Swords, and the Tower, and how each dire image promises light after the darkness. It might seem like rhetoric at the time, but in her heart of hearts, where hope always lingers however elusively, she knows that these images reflect a certain universal Truth.

The witch knows that there is no such thing as Death, no such thing as the End. Everything is a process of transformation. Sometimes this is pressuring and painful, and other times it brings sensations of delight and we are happy; but both processes are necessary for spiritual and mental progression.

So, when undergoing a personal crisis, the witch tries to maintain faith and perspective. Meditating (if she can manage it while distressed), taking soothing baths with comfrey oil and rose oil, lighting a candle to focus her mind—these are all simple techniques that can be used in times of stress.

After the initial impact of the crisis has faded, she begins to look for solutions to her predicament. If she is grieving, for example, she feels for ways to continue a rapport with whomever she has lost *without compromising their progress.* She knows, for example, that a spirit who has crossed the Veil will visit her at Samhain if such an act is necessary. She knows that bonds are eternal, and that interaction may be continued when she, too, crosses the Veil. If she is mediumistic, she may be capable of communication from this side, but she never harasses the dead, and certainly does not utilise equipment such as the Ouija board, which merely attracts chaotic energy and angry spirits. She is more inclined to work a ritual, preferably with others who knew the deceased, to act as a "rite of passage" for the person. This sends loving energy to the person in transition and helps ease the deceased into his or her new state of being. Like a funeral, this also serves to draw a line under her own bereavement. Like anybody else, she grieves, and then her life goes on. The loved one is never forgotten, but a temporary parting of ways is acknowledged. She gives thanks for pleasure received, anticipates reunion at an unspecified time, and then continues working towards her personal aims in her own incarnation.

Personal crises come in many shapes and forms, of course, and this witch has had her own fair share of them. Once the initial impact has eased off, it can be helpful to perform a ritual of closure on the past; perhaps by creating an object invested with the energies of the misfortune, and then ceremonially burning or burying it, or sending it away on a river (biodegradable substances are definitely preferable for this). A waning or dark moon creates the best psychic tides for such an operation. Then, at the new moon, she may perform a simple "new leaf" ritual, promising herself that she will rise from the ashes of disaster both purified and full of additional strength and wisdom. These are, of course, exactly the same processes undergone by any human being struggling to turn negative repercussions into positive. The difference is in the symbolism of ritual.

There are many detailed descriptions in print of rituals and visualisations for practically any requirement now. Ed Fitch's *Magical Rites from the Crystal Well* (Llewellyn, 1988) gives rite-of-passage rituals as well as seasonal celebrations, as does Janet and Stewart Farrar's *A Witch's Bible. Invoke the Goddess* (Llewellyn, 2000) and *Invoke the Gods* (Llewellyn, 2001) by yours truly offer detailed interactions with deities through creative visualisation for every situation from ending cycles of abuse, to turning over a new leaf, to letting go of partners who have moved on in whatever form. Scott Cunningham's books offer magickal ideas for working with the seasonal and planetary tides. Examples of positive magickal action may be found in chapter 18, "Magickal Techniques and Spell-casting."

Personal heroism may go unrecognised by others, but it builds up spiritual virtues, which create a stronger, more powerful spirit. Even if this goes nowhere on this plane (and, chances are, it *will* reap rewards), it affects conditions both internal and external on the next levels. We define ourselves by how we think, and when the body is stripped away (which is one thing each and every one of us can count on as a certainty), the build-up of our thoughts and actions across the aeons is all that is left. Even the atheist can envisage this as a certainty, only minus the continuity of any kind of consciousness. The path we have trodden becomes our legacy.

If you are feeling wronged by an individual, a simple remedy is to write him or her, and then burn or bury the epistle (unless, of course, sending it to the person is completely justified and will not cause you further aggravation). This is simple psychology, but wonderfully cathartic. In these modern days of e-mail, write the message as if you were going to send it (disconnect whilst doing this, lest the message send itself), and then save it in your "Drafts" folder. You can delete it when you've cooled down a little.

NEUTRALISING AN AGGRESSOR

If for some reason you are unable to innocuously shed your anger, it is time for a calming spell or visualisation. Props could include white, pale-green, or blue candles, and an oil, such as lavender or sage, for cleansing.

Visualise yourself glowing with as violent a red as you are angry. Imagine all of your resentments catching fire and smoking up into one big flame.

Take a doll that represents your aggressor. Take a long length of white ribbon, and wind it around the doll's torso and arms, saying:

> *With this ribbon*
> *I thee curb*

Pick the doll up in your left hand, and tell it to desist from its harmful actions. Place it on your altar, and bless it.

Then cut away the binds, and imagine yourself becoming free of the aggressor. As this occurs, your auric flames diminish and die. Collect up the ribbon, and burn it in your cauldron. Scrape up any ashes, and throw them into the wind. Next time you go out, throw the doll into a public refuse bin.

The intuitive witch will know what suits his or her needs and is likely to give her the catharsis and motivation she requires to change circumstances for the better. She may even be able to turn the situation around so that she enjoys it as a learning process, looking over her own shoulder at her reactions, and learning from them with affectionate humour.

The witch knows that, above all else, the most important thing is to strive.

three

The Witch and Love and Sex

LOVE HOLDS THE WORLD TOGETHER. It may sound sickly, but it isn't. Bearing in mind the amount of pain the average individual has to endure in each incarnation, no matter how privileged he or she may seem, love is the ultimate goal and really, the very least that each of us deserves. It is both personal and cosmic. We need to perceive ourselves as loved in both ways in order to operate properly.

Attaining love is the most common use of magick. Since time immemorial, women have sought supernatural aid in procuring and keeping their spouses, and men have striven to capture and enamour disinterested maidens by secret means. There is no energy as strong and capricious as sexual attraction, and when it is combined with love, it is almost insuperable.

The first move of the witch who wants to attain love, however, will not necessarily be the casting of a spell. Because every witch is self-assured, and because every witch understands her own intrinsic value, she may well be confident enough to go for what she wants without the aid of specific rites. The witch is a magickal creature, period. Her thoughts and beliefs, just like those of any human being, radiate from her and directly influence those in her sphere. She dares to be different.

Consequently, the witch is an accomplished suitor. She knows how to home in on the subject of her desire without freaking him or her out. Her sense of balance keeps her from growing obsessive, though intensity is both acceptable and helpful, as it aids her with the all-important visualisations. She knows how to focus her will to a specific purpose.

The first step, of course, is to get under the skin of the desired one. The world is full of pretty women and handsome men (of sorts, anyway); what the witch understands is how to stir the cauldron of the imagination. She zones in on the particular influences and affiliations of her potential partner, and gets to grips with the elements of which this human is compounded. She recognises the archetypes in the individual. For example, very intellectual people are, she knows, best approached from a cerebral angle. Give them a code to crack; let them know they have an admirer (for who ever minds that?), then give them clues. I've done it myself by e-mail. It's great fun, as long as the person knows that you'll stop if the tryst becomes tiresome. The person might be into symbolism or art instead, in which case the psyche may be penetrated simply by getting to grips with the symbols or works most significant to him or her. Analyse the person! Discover the triggers! But never be contrived. If his or her symbols and interests clash with your own, be sensible and take the cosmic clue. He or she is not for you.

And that's just the flirtations. What about the "big L," the soulmate scenario? This will occur very seldom in one's life—twice at most—and is the biggest magickal and chemical hit we will ever receive cosmically. It is a catalyst for all sorts of progress and, if handled with courage and faith, a blessing that can last a lifetime. Here we get as close to the "machinery of the Universe" as is possible except in birth and death.

Love calls to us on the most fundamental of levels (the physical urge to couple and procreate) as well as the most sublime (the enduring bond of spiritual union). If the Universe is created out of love, as many believe it to have been, then every interaction between lovers is a reenactment of the creative principle. It makes sense, considering the way in which all species are conceived. It is the sharing of the essences of two separate states that brings forth life; it is the gift of duality. Qabalah plays on this atavistic symbolism. Chokmah, the male thrusting force, is received by Binah, the feminine receptive and infinitely creative (yet paradoxically barren) state of being. (I say "barren" partly because she takes from the spiritual realms in order to deliver into the finite, material realms.) It works as an analogy of the physical scenario, but it is much more than simply that. There are always higher principles involved when the motive of a spell is love of any kind. They should never be undertaken lightly.

However, if you have met your heart's desire, and are totally convinced that he or she is your soul's other half, and the conviction has already lasted a number of years and seems immune to mood swings, I think a little magick may be excused as reasonable. By magick I mean setting your perfected will into motion. This may require a spell. It should always be general; to lure a particular person with magick is wildly unethical. If the person can respond to a general call, it is his or her choice and thus no problem ethically.

The best spell I have ever encountered of this nature is Jeni Couzyn's "Summoning for a Husband" (featured in Robin Skelton's *Spellcraft*). I discuss her work in the section "Poetry and Spellcraft" in chapter 18. In "Summoning for a Husband," Couzyn lists every aspect desired in her potential loved one, and compels him to come to her without compromising herself (or the subject of the spell) with individual details. Apart from the fact that it is riveting poetry, the spell is highly magickally evocative:

> *As your mind is a landscape, wide and changing*
> *is growing and dying, knows the seasons*
> *knows the flight of the bird and sleep of trees*
> **so let you come, so marry me.**
>
> *As your body is straight and brown and smooth as stone*
> *as your fingers are subtle as water*
> *as your eyes are quick and sharp, as your nerves are*
> *talking and listening*
>
> *as your life is a wide river on its course*
> *as I to you am bank and ocean and rain*
> *as your love to me is sky and womb and storm,*
> **so let you come, so marry me**

Jeni Couzyn goes on to describe, indeed evoke, the child who is "waiting in the forest"—the child they would have together if her desired husband comes to her (not that all of us would wish for such a thing, but Couzyn obviously had a baby on her agenda when she wrote this).

This spell is perfect because it summons precisely the type of person she would wish for. There's no chance of him being small-minded, as he cannot come to her unless his mind is "a landscape, wide and changing" due to the conditional "As." This technique is key to sympathetic magick. Not only must his mind be a "landscape," but a landscape as the poet/witch describes it. Likewise will she be immune from aged suitors, for he can only respond if his body is "straight and brown and smooth as stone." She wants a sensitive partner, so he is required to have "fingers . . . subtle as water," and "nerves . . . talking and listening."

Couzyn then goes on to depict herself as she would wish to be in the relationship—"bank and ocean and rain." She generates a powerful image that includes every relevant aspect of the sought partner and herself and the way they fit together—past, present, and future. She does so succinctly, and with that all-important compelling rhythm, which is key to the magickal wavelength.

A sense of cosmic love is the goal of every mystic and religiously inclined person; the witch is no exception. There are many books on Wicca and witchcraft available that concentrate on quick fixes—that is, spells. These are fine when taken in a wider context, but the witch *has* to be aware that she is one small person in a vast and complex universe. She has to know that true answers do not come from a sudden influx of Pentacles and Cups (money and affection), but from a joyous acceptance of being part of the organic and spiritual Whole. Because Wicca and witchcraft have been severely challenged by orthodox religions over the centuries, some of that sense of cosmic wholeness has been lost—it has become "them and us." This is fading now that the Witchcraft Acts have been repealed, and many new souls have been attracted to the subject on their spiritual search. However, it is my belief that we, as witches, need to take a long look at the mystical aspects of the Craft, and to realise that, at the core, the aim of all spiritual disciplines is the same— union with the Divine. There is not such a difference between the positive witch and the positive nun or yogi—all seek the spiritual elevation of the species. The techniques are different, yes. The mode of expression may be virtually antithetical. Yet beyond the ritual differences, beyond the mutual prejudice, we are all souls striving for happiness, both individual and collective. Love is everything, and to attain a sense of cosmic love is the ultimate aim of every person on the planet.

The witch, therefore, is not anti-, she is always pro-. When she encounters a religion with which she disagrees, she looks at its fundamental aims, and realises that it is not so very different from her own. She seeks the good in everything and everybody, though she is not stupid about it. Some creeds preach sectarianism, and clearly she would object to these. Yet she has an overview large enough to perceive the exception to every rule. She values other seekers, whatever their specific references. She attempts to communicate with those whose minds are closed, but never aggressively. She is interested and compassionate. She knows her own ground rules and is not swayed from them. She always remembers that "Love is the Law"—and it really is; not soppy love, but the force that keeps this cosmos hanging together. It comes from sources much higher than ourselves. The witch strives to understand, intuitively and intellectually. When she cannot understand— goodness knows, we all have our limits—she remains open-minded. This is all that any god could truly ask.

So, how do we access this cosmic Love on a day-to-day basis? After all, high ideals are all very well, but we have mundane life to cope with on top of the spiritual quest. It is never easy. If it is, we are not progressing.

The essential factor is to be aware of our position in the Universe as significant, developing beings moving towards higher states of consciousness. The ability to enjoy this process, its challenges, its serendipities, and its interactions with other growing spirits is the key to a happy incarnation. As occultists, we keep our sense of wonder and spiritual progress alive as we use our magick to draw us ever closer to Kether. It reminds us that all is relevant, that no effort is lost. We should cut ourselves some slack for those down days when clouds obscure the heavens, and use our pain to fuel esoteric efforts when we're feeling more capable. Living in magickal consciousness necessarily means moving in and out of Darkness and Light.

The Witch and Sex

> At the climax of the Mysteries of the Earth Mother all the lights went out, and the High Priest and the chief Priestess descended in darkness into the crypt and there consumed a union that was a sacrament just as much as eating the Body and drinking the Blood.
>
> —Dion Fortune, *The Goat-Foot God*

Sexual magnetism is essential in magick. It is the process of psychic circulation, of carrying energy from one polarity to the other. It is exchange, movement, and emotion. It is the only frequency other than death and birth that is able to encapsulate a thoughtform. Sex is magickal conception.

I am not talking physical sex, however, unless the body is sanctified as a vessel for divine currents (and not necessarily through ritual, but simply through the relevant, magickal mental state). Rather, this exchange takes place on the astro-etheric and spiritual levels, and may be performed without the Priest and Priestess even touching. Herein lies the rub; it is not the actions that count, but what they symbolise (as with anything in magick). The real sex happens on the astral plane.

We see, then, that sex is construed of as sacred in witchcraft. The energies of attraction that precede sex are of equal, if not greater, importance. Dion Fortune makes much of this in her novels, particularly *Moon Magic*, *The Winged Bull*, and *The Goat-Foot God*. In *Moon Magic*, Morgan Le Fay, the ultimate Priestess, quite deliberately provokes a sexual response in Dr. Rupert Malcolm in order to entice him out of his psychological hideaway and into a new mode of thinking. It works, and he comes to know magick, but Morgan is aware that she cannot "let him have it." To do so would break the spell. Their "Moon Magic" is reliant on the power of unacted desire. This is, indeed, the strongest bond of all. The witch knows this, and uses her knowledge well.

However, if the body may be used as it ought—as a key to higher dimensions—there can be no greater use of it. Sex in ritual in such a scenario is the archetypal creation process, and thus all-powerful.

Wicca and witchcraft are frequently referred to as "fertility religions." This applies well to the ancient Celtic principles on which many witches' festivals are based, but in the physical sense, it is pretty irrelevant in most covens today. Rather, the emphasis is usually on mental and spiritual fertility. Not in all, I'll grant you; some few have managed to acquire the necessary degree of the qualities described above by using sex as the motivational energy in a sanctified way. But at the other end of the spectrum, there are some covens that are little more than glorified wife-swapping groups, and there are people who claim to be witches for all the wrong reasons. The Fivefold Kiss doesn't help. Though there are doubtless many earnest individuals who perform this act in all innocence, the kissing of a male or female initiate on the breasts and just above the pubic hair by a Priest or Priestess seems to me—and if I get shot down in flames for this, I don't care—to be asking for trouble. What a wonderful fetish for the voyeur to witness or participate in such an act! Yes, the female body is utterly sacred and wonderful and is the door of life. Yes, the breasts are formed in beauty and yes, the womb is amazing, but the concentration on it in Wiccan ritual has always seemed to me innately dodgy. It all depends on who you are working with, of course.

Witches are not ashamed of sex or sexuality, and do not repress it. This is one of the fundamental differences between the Craft and most orthodox religions, in which physical functions are seen as negative. The witch sees in the male and female bodies an analogy of the God/Goddess functions—all is sacred. This much is good.

The obvious argument for an act such as the Fivefold Kiss is that it is honouring the body as a representative of the God and Goddess and all that is implied thereby. However, the author knows more than one other witch who has undergone lechery in the Circle, and whose integrity has been severely challenged and compromised by demands to "stop being neurotic/repressed" and allow the "energy" to flow. This can be extremely difficult to cope with. Let's face it, there are very few men in the world—even in the world of witches—who could avoid being aroused when faced with a beautiful naked woman blindfolded with her hands tied behind her back. Let's get real here! Sexuality is a necessary and wonderful gift, but it is *not* a free-for-all, "fertility religion" or not. It is a question of choice, never of compromise. So, if you're working with your own partner or close and trusted friends and you wish to get naked in order to be humble before the Goddess or to liberate your mind or whatever, and such details as the Fivefold Kiss seem apt and helpful to you, go for it. But I would warn all aspiring Wiccans that there *are* predatory people out there whose main attraction to the Craft is the nudity and physical contact aspect, however well they may cover this fact up (usually by being vociferously knowledgeable about spirituality, etc.).

During training and initiation, one is necessarily vulnerable. Ignorance and fear of upsetting Wiccan protocol through protest are major enemies to the neophyte. Don't forget, most of these rituals were written by a naturist with a concupiscent eye. They are pro-female in that they give worship to the great Goddess, but they are distinctly male in nature! Dianic covens, of course, are immune to this, though it seems a shame to lose all male interaction. (The male energy itself is available through women, just as feminine energy may be channelled through a man.) By far a better technique is to *write your own rituals* containing what you are happy with and is meaningful to you, and *work with friends, not strangers.*

Being comfortable with sex cuts both ways. As well as meaning that one is at home in the body, it also means that one is happy with the way the body is treated by others. Traditionally, according to Wicca, the "altar" is the female body, at which the men of the tribe worship "the circle within the circle." This is perfectly understandable as a principle, but it does not, to me, need to be reenacted in any way other than symbolic. Most Wiccans, when performing the "Great Rite" literally, do so in private with their life partners. However, some do not. It is always important to check such details out before getting into a ritual situation with anybody.

For example, when I was nineteen, I was in the middle of a (nonskyclad) ritual with a local coven who had accepted me for training. All was going well, it seemed to me, and high energy was in the room, ready to be utilised. Suddenly, the High Priest—a strapping man in his midforties—grabbed me and demanded that I perform the Great Rite with him. "Otherwise," he told me, "the energy of all the covens across England will crash tonight, because of your neuroses." Shaking and shocked, I refused. The working stumbled to an untimely end, with me cast very much as the baddie.

Had I been pressured into sex in the Circle, this would have constituted exactly the sort of "ritual abuse" the papers are always banging on about, usually completely wrongly. Witches and Wiccans have been fighting for years to improve their image and make it an accurate one of a caring, wholesome community, which it usually is. Many Wiccans, including High Priests and Priestesses, to whom I related this scenario, were horrified—but some confessed to undergoing similar encounters. So, let's not be naïve about this. In a religion that involves some physical intimacy, caution is the best policy.

Many covens employ a chalice and athame to symbolise the Great Rite, which is just as powerful, if not more so. The point is the energy raised, not its mode of expression. In bringing together the two principles of the life-force in ritual, the witch is experiencing the essence of creativity: true fertility. This may be used for any purpose through directed will; the Circle is a storehouse of psychic electricity. It may be transferred into another object, to an astral region, or used immediately. The remains are then earthed. However, should it be tainted by compromise or the discomfort of any member of the group, its quality and substance will be second-rate and it will most likely backfire. The karmic repercussions of compromising another's magickal and physical integrity are vast. There are few worse spiritual sins than using religion as an excuse for abuse.

That is the negative side. In the positive, Wiccan and non-Wiccan witches abide by pre-Christian ethics, and are thus body-friendly. The emphasis is on gender balance (either literally, or energy-wise), individual freedom and respect, and on the creation of magick through the most powerful means available. The energy of consensual sex is one of the most intense we can know. Many occult-orientated couples practise Tantra for precisely this reason. Beginning with "joint breathing"—a means of creating intimacy while at the same time slipping into a trancelike, concentrated state—the couple (whatever their sexual orientation) enjoy a carefully choreographed foreplay whilst focussing on their interaction and the goal in hand. Orgasm is rigorously withheld—usually by both partners or the male alone—while pleasure and ritual are given precedence. Sometimes this is used as a form of bonding, just as normal sex ought to be; at other times it is also employed to bring certain strong energies to magickal intent. This includes spiritual ascension through kundalini energy (which can also be used for other purposes), healing, and spell-casting. The couple does not earth their energy, they send it off to fulfil a specific purpose.

Austin Osman Spare developed the technique of "sigilisation," into which sexual energy—either of a couple or an individual—may be channelled. A monogram is formed using the first letter of the relevant words of intent, or utilising symbols that represent it. The important thing is to be aware of the meaning when the monogram is formed, but for it not to be obvious afterwards. This way, the unconscious knows, but the conscious doesn't. Once the monogram is formed—a symbol of all that the magickian wishes to bring to pass—the practitioner(s) focus(es) on it, and sexual energy is expended whilst staring at it. This has a "branding" effect on the mind. Afterwards, the practitioner allows the act to fade from his or her mind. Meanwhile, the subconscious works on it with all the gusto of one nearing the act of love. It is powerful, and it works. The energy raised through sexual stimulation is indeed magickal—both spiritually and in the most primitive sense—and it kick-starts (or swiftly brings to pass) the true will of the witch or magickian.

The desire to continue life (symbolised by union with another) and the urge to interact affectionately and/or sexually are very strong motivators in the human psyche. It is apparent that teens are frequently superpsychic—especially when repressed—as can be prepubescents. Stephen King hit upon this in his brilliantly perceptive, though rather melodramatic novel/film *Carrie*. Many ancient high magickal texts involve virgin youths and maidens—especially for such purposes as divination—because they are "pure" (i.e., have not dissipated their energy physically). They are still attuned to the spiritual creative force rather than merely the physical. So, teens who feel they are neurotic and oversensitive can comfort themselves with the fact that they are most likely at the height of their powers, if not their happiness. Most poltergeist activities revolve around those entering puberty. The results are powerful, but chaotic. The witch and magickian aim to direct this energy towards specific objectives. However, teen perceptions and dreams create levels of power difficult to reattain at a more advanced age when perspective has increased. Angst is actually a gift, difficult though it is to believe at the time. Teen witches are the best at generating energy, though their lack of discernment may be counterproductive (Silver RavenWolf's teen novels feature this; Bethany Salem and her crew only need to *think* before—hey presto!—a living incarnation of their joint ritual energy!). This is where a Wiccan/witch "community" comes in handy. If the elders can direct the intense but uninformed psychic abilities of the younger members of the coven, great results might indeed be attained.

The Witch and Same-sex Sex

The work of many Theosophists and occultists (notably Alice A. Bailey and Dion Fortune) repudiates same-gender sex as unbalanced. They claim that it is an act of vice rather than of spiritual progression, and magickally destructive—or void. However, it is worth remembering the straight-laced era in which they wrote, and that Dion Fortune was also opposed to masturbation, believing so strongly that it weakened the psychic constitution that she prescribes invoking the archangel Michael when the temptation is present! (see *The Problem of Purity*, written under her real name, Violet Firth [Rider & Co., London, 1928]). No doubt Alice Bailey would have thought similarly, if indeed the subject even crossed her mind—their backgrounds were poles apart from the liberated modern era. With magickians such as bisexual Crowley at the helm of gay liberation within magick, their reaction is unsurprising. Their morality was already Victorian; those brave enough to vaunt their homosexual inclinations merely served to increase outrage and disgust in pre-closed minds.

Some of this attitude continued in the early modern Craft. Gerald Gardner, for example, is known to have found gay men repellent, and to believe that they could never become witches. Clearly, this is a very personal attitude springing from one whose own preference was for bound, naked (and presumably heterosexual) women.

However, times have changed, and there are very few witches or magickians today who would doubt the validity of same-gender relationships, either in their own right or magickally. There are all-female covens that work with the Dianic current, and magickal lodges that include or even focus on homosexual sex magick. Gay male and female witches and Wiccans are becoming increasingly apparent "on the scene." Indeed, I have found the Wiccan/witch community highly refreshing on this score—bisexuality and homosexuality are generally considered normal. How could they not be, when the virtues of God and Goddess are recognised in all?

Reincarnation also plays a part in this philosophy. If we migrate from body to body en route to perfection, as witches believe, then quite obviously a mainly male soul will at times dwell in a female body, and vice versa. I know women who are definitely male spirits, and men who are female but for a detail or two. The body in which a soul finds itself is often irrelevant to the souls' interaction. If two people loved one another in a previous life, they will do so again whatever shape and form the physical vessel may take.

Social mores are totally irrelevant to the witch—after all, she is the victim of many of them. She values love above all ("Love under Will") and acts accordingly. If she wants to take a female lover, then she will; not as a fashion statement or to titillate her male witch friends (I have occasionally seen this happen, as in any walk of life), but because she is free and at ease with her body. She may also be (re)forging a spiritual link. Whatever the reason, it is her business, and it is not for others to approve or disapprove.

Likewise, the male witch or Wiccan; magick has involved male homosexuality for thousands of years, beginning perhaps (in recorded myth, on which much occult practice is based) with the incestuous and abusive relationship between the

Egyptian Horus and his uncle Seth. But magick involving male homosexuality has progressed and positively defined itself over the aeons.

In classical myth we find Artemis preferring the company of other athletic girls to that of men, and her twin brother Apollo is described in some accounts as effete and apparently bisexual—a trait, of course, perfectly normal to the Greeks. The Amazons have become a symbol for modern feminists, often aligned with the concept of lesbianism, or at least of female self-sufficiency. When initiates of Dionysus were "united with the god" in intoxicated mystical frenzy, who knows what sexual impulses were enacted? And the goat god Pan, along with other pastoral deities, may be associated with the idea of anal intercourse, a concept deepened through his later transformation into Baphomet (though our modern concept of sexual liberty ought not to be confused with symbols intended to represent debauchery in their original contexts).

Mythology aside, male homosexuality has been a key factor in magick (as female interaction will become)—vaunted by Crowley, but experimented with long before this. The modern witch sees the validity of all psychic currents and their potential in both ritual and everyday life.

Often, the meeting of souls in same-gendered bodies can prove more powerful than that of those who interact in a "socially acceptable" mode. This is partly a magickal challenge, and partly a factor of social evolution. When any spirit can love another, physically as well as spiritually (when mutually consensual), we know we're getting somewhere.

"The Witch and Sex" (above) and "The Witch and Marriage and Monogamy" (below) may be considered to be as relevant to same-gender relationships as to heterosexual.

The Witch and Marriage and Monogamy

Many witches and Wiccans are monogamous, some are not. The key point of both Wiccan and non-Wiccan witchcraft is honesty. The principles of both involve free growth of the individual, which may involve development through being in a couple, or may not. Most of us nowadays were brought up in families belonging to orthodox religions by parents who attempted to stay together for one reason or another; many of these failed.

Witches marry through "handfasting," a voluntary joining of energies not just on this plane, but on more permanent ones too. This is best performed in a sacred, ancient building (or one rendered effective through the Arts), or outside in a place of natural beauty and of significance to the couple in hand. In a wood, on a hill within the ruins of a castle, under an oak tree—the decision is down to the couple. The symbolism is not a cut-and-dried thing; a handfasting can be dissolved by the High Priestess who married the couple a year and a day afterwards should either party wish it. Cords can also be cut in other ritualistic ways, if necessary. In handfasting, the couple makes a spiritual commitment to one another. This bond lasts through future incarnations as well as the present one, linking those concerned spiritually as well as physically. Far better than being legally lumbered with an outgrown soulmate, or one who needs to move on!

In witchcraft and Wicca, handfasting is not necessarily monogamous. It is a statement of having bonded with a particular person, and sometimes it can take the tone of an orthodox religious wedding, implying that the couple is focussed entirely upon one another. It can also mean that the bond is indubitable, but that growth through other partners is still acceptable—the love will not die when so challenged. The founders of the American Neo-Pagan Church of All Worlds, for example, live in a community that includes their many hand-fasted partners. This is a more realistic approach to love than that of most religions in many respects, and it works for some people, though certainly it would create havoc for others. Accepting change and development in partners as nonthreatening is an attitude both tribal and avant-garde. Jealousy must necessarily be processed and dealt with. Children may be brought up by a mother and father, a community, and/or two mothers or two fathers. Admittedly this is rare—most Wiccans and witches bring their children up (if they have them) in ordinary heterosexual or two-partnered relationships, but difference is not frowned upon. The most important factors are spiritual growth and honesty.

Because of the witch's understanding of reincarnation, it is a fairly common experience to encounter friends, lovers, and hand-fasted partners from previous incarnations. It is a great thrill when recognition is mutual and memories are shared. This has happened to me a couple of times. It also gives leeway to creeps and manipulative people who might tell you that you did this, that, or the other in a previous life, but haven't remembered it yet. In the worst-case scenario, they might suggest that you owe them some kind of bond or debt. Never let anyone else tell you what you "were"—it is most likely incorrect or irrelevant. We recall our previous lives if and when we are supposed to. It is often far better to concentrate on the one in hand. If this happens to involve a friendly soul you recall from a previous incarnation, all the better.

The word *handfasting* conveys the fact that, during the witch's wedding, the bride and groom are attached at the wrist by a cord. This is loose, and may be untied at any time. It symbolises the bond—strong, but not inescapable. There is also a "length" to which the couple may go without breaking the bond.

Another characteristic of handfasting is the broomstick over which the couple jumps at the end of the ceremony. This symbolises brushing away past experience, and is relevant to the themes of homestead and magick also. The High Priestess often sweeps the Circle after the besom-leap to give the couple a "clear run" in the sacred space of their union.

The handfasting is frequently backed up by a legal wedding too.

four

Meaning and Magick

My words fly up, my thoughts remain below;
Words without thoughts never to heaven go.

—William Shakespeare, *Hamlet*

RITUAL IS NOTHING WITHOUT INPUT; spells fall flat without belief. The key to magick is the knowledge that everything on the earth plane is symbolic of what lies behind; solids represent rather than define. The witch is aware that all she sees is not a material cul-de-sac, but the physical expression of something greater. With this knowledge, she is capable of moving mountains.

Just as in the Qabalah, where Malkuth is the final expression of creation, all that we experience and witness on the earth plane is the final result of a particular mixture of energies and influences. The witch is adept at identifying and extracting the original ingredients and working with them. The astrological witch can observe a person and, on analysing his or her birth chart, recognise the pertinence of particular planetary attributes to his or her predicament, whatever that might be. The spiritualistic witch might see the preincarnational factors that either help or hinder the individual he or she is studying. The Wiccan/Neo-Pagan witch might recognise a divorce from the natural state, inducing neurosis or self-doubt. Many witches will do all three, and more. The witch is as adept as a forensic scientist at distilling the compound into a set of identifiable, workable elements. This is where our correspondence tables come in handy.

Self-belief is more essential to magick than any tool or ritual. It grows with time, of course; few of us are arrogant enough to assume, from our very first working, that all we intend will come to pass. Trial and error, and effect and side effect will lead to an eventual understanding that magickal action influences its subjects on a plethora of levels. Usually, we attempt to affect the outer or emotional planes—spells to bring specifically conducive circumstances, for example, or the ever-popular love spell. However, often the results may be subtle, and until we learn to recognise the signs, they may appear to be circumstantial. Yes, the element of chance is active in any given situation. We are, after all, pretty small creatures in the scheme of things. It is unrealistic and arrogant to expect to command heaven and earth for our own petty ends. However, we can work within the peripheries of what is possible, and, preferably, of what "Harms None." The latter point limits us, of course, but for our own good as well as that of others. A heavy debt of karma is unhelpful to any developing soul; and that, when all is said and done, is what we all are.

Remembering our origins is helpful both to spellcraft and to our sense of self-belief. When we recall that we are spirits in a material world, we inevitably reflect on our place in humanity, on Earth, and in the cosmos. We are all aware of the dire effects of petty tyranny; it is the bane of history. The aim of the witch is to cling to her sense of identity as a spiritual being—complete with responsibilities to her fellow entities—and with power. The disempowering of the individual is the key to the witch-hunts. The latter occurred because it seemed atrocious to the authorities—religious and proprietal—that an individual might have a direct link with God, or the Cosmic Intelligence. They wanted us to go through the middleman, and bring tithes both emotional and physical. The other major cause, of course, was simple fear (see chapter 14, "A Brief History of Witchcraft").

The witch recognises the present as the point of power, though the past can come in handy too. She knows how to create reserves of energy, maybe by visualising an emotionally charged glyph (a pentagram perhaps, or an ankh) at a significant time for later use in magick. This gives a gateway to that moment, trapped in time. She manipulates energies and applies them to the spell in hand. She is able to move her consciousness about so that physical reality provides no obstacle to her intent. She does this through a concentration of will power. Without self-belief, this would be impossible.

This self-belief should then be tempered by intelligent compassion, as Amber K points out in *True Magick:*

> A sense of drama and a strong ego can be useful tools for the magickian; flamboyance and egotism, however, are not required. Far, far more important are reverence, courage, and love: these are the qualities of the greatest of

magickians, and their names were not Cagliostro and Crowley. Their names were Lao-Tzu, and Buddha, and Jesus, and a host of feminine names now forgotten.

So we have the "flamboyance" of ritual and self-identity, discerning perception, and perspective. What else is required for effective magickal work?

Also it serveth nothing to speak without devotion, without attention, and without intelligence; nor yet to pronounce it with the mouth alone, without a true intent; nor yet to read it as do the ignorant and the impious . . .

The above, by Abra-Melin the Mage, is a distinctly Judaic attitude that involves a type of humility alien to the latter-day witch, but the principles remain of relevance. The element of devotion is as important today as it ever was—devotion to the Craft, which takes much effort to get off the ground, and equally, devotion to the "Great Work," which is of significance to every occultist. There is no point in us sailing through this incarnation in cracked eggshell boats, invoking the winds that will carry us to the destination of our choice, regardless of other ships on the waters. Devotion to a greater plan is as essential to us as to the world in general. If we lose our power, which the selfish witch inevitably does, we will be consumed by the crosscurrents of our own making. Devotion assures that we maintain the essential perspective on our lives and abilities. Giving thanks is rewarding in itself. We have much to be grateful for, and the gods, whichever we chose, will appreciate our attentions. A thankful heart does much to enhance any situation.

The relevance of attention cannot be overstated. A love spell cast at the dark of the moon on a Tuesday is blighted from the start. A little attention to detail, and a productive spell might be produced on a Friday when the moon is waxing. The further the witch delves into her correspondences, the easier it is for her to identify the right time to perform her magick.

Nor will she perform a ritual in a half-hearted, perfunctory manner. She will only work when the spirit is in her, thus filling her words and actions with a carefully directed energy that cannot fail to take effect. Intelligence coupled with raw power is her aim.

"The ignorant and impious" are not to be made privy to the magickian's words or intent: Abra-Melin underlines the clause "To be Silent." It is not that secrecy is a boon in its own right; rather, that to speak to an unbeliever can create all sorts of side effects, from making us sound insane, to offending the listener (who will inevitably have his or her own cosmology to contend with), to creating the dreaded situation of disbelief.

Self-belief is the grail that we must guard against all odds. It is the sweet wine of the soul, the gateway. We have all witnessed in the day-to-day world the way in which self-belief affects functions such as speech. Those who lack it might stutter, or find themselves unable to articulate properly under pressure. It is not that they are physically disabled; rather, the blockage is psychological. Normally, I am a fluent speaker. If I am excessively tired or nervous, however, I might find myself stammering. I would never attempt to perform magick in such a state, or when depressed. Lack of self-confidence severely undermines magick. Balanced self-belief (rather than megalomania), however, can perform small miracles. Every single person is perfectly capable of applying his or her will to any situation. We witness it all the time in those who succeed against the odds: paraplegics who excel at the Paralympics, or blind people who walk the streets with as much confidence as those with sight. These people have made the decision to disbelieve their apparent inabilities. The occultist disbelieves that life is merely a set of irrevocable circumstances. She knows that the sky is not the limit.

> Unless the whole heart and soul and faith go with the ceremony, there can be no reliable result produced.

Here, Abraham the Jew is describing how to pray and evoke. The system he describes involves calling up demons and angels, so "reliable" refers not just to the issue of self-belief, but to that of balance. We must believe in the forces of light and darkness in equal measure—otherwise we tip the scales of our consciousness and sanity.

For example, there are people in the New Age movement who focus entirely on the light. There's nothing wrong with that, until it becomes a reality block. We are living in a world in which darkness and light exist in equal measure, and to cut off from the real world by only acknowledging one aspect is no more effective than floating in a water tank all one's life. We may receive stunning insights and gallons of spiritual bliss, but it is a cul-de-sac. Believing in love and light and denying all else is as damaging as its opposite. When combined with the real world, it creates a sickly cocoon of sanctimony that only serves to put other people off the Path.

Some people in the Western world have attempted to live off light, or prana, to be more precise. They have been encouraged by some New Age "gurus" into total denial of their physical needs—most relevantly, food. Their belief in the light alone has been so strong that they have given themselves over to it entirely. At least three people are known to have died following this path.

There is no doubt in my mind that it is possible for certain saints and gurus to live off spiritual sustenance alone. Hinduism and Catholicism have produced many immaculate souls who have defied all scientific statistics and become living miracles. However, for most of us, this is impossible, especially in a well-informed, educated society into which self-disbelief has been allowed to enter. Programming goes so deep that reading a few books and performing a few meditations cannot possibly prepare most organic systems to live off celestial manna alone. We are designed to interact with the symbol of celestial manna—that is, real, solid food. On the astral planes we will indeed exist on cosmic electricity. On this plane, however, we relate to it in its solid, molecular form. The few exceptions to this rule are highly evolved beings who certainly do not need to read a book to discover how it is done. The people who tried it and failed must be celebrated for their faith, but their belief was sadly misguided. We must pay heed to balance.

As to those who focus only on darkness, they may be active—powerful even—as magickians, but the duration of their abilities is necessarily short. Qabalah, which originally entered Wicca and witchcraft via Alex Sanders, teaches us to balance the forces.

In the higher realms, we can accept that light and goodness reign supreme. All religions teach this, and millions of us feel it. Without belief, and self-belief in Right Action and Right Living, we are lost in chaos. However, overemphasis on this plane leads to gullibility, vulnerability, and overconstraint. Those magickians who believe that immorality will lead to power are equally constrained, and their worldview is equally warped. Self-belief in both camps works for a while, but then inevitably backfires.

Equally impotent is the spell or ritual delivered whilst wondering what we'll eat tonight, or why that house alarm is going off, or what's happening in the latest episode of *Buffy*. It is difficult in Malkuth to focus on spiritual reality, but that is part of our quest here. Self-belief implies both faith in one's abilities, and faith in higher forces—of both extremes. Without the grounded reality of the physical planes where all is dualistic, and the knowledge that we are part of this bipolar cosmic entity using darkness to push us towards the light, the witch is lost in space.

Thus, belief is much more than in the self. It is in the many potent energies of the Universe, and the continual quest towards spiritual enlightenment, with emphasis on the "Light," or Godhead.

Covens, Gurus, and Teachers

What is a witch without a coven? A witch.

It makes no odds whether one is flanked by twelve robed women and men, or has been officially pronounced of this or that grade; if you know you are, and you act your knowledge, you are.

Many witches prefer to be solitary, and there is much wisdom in this choice. As in all social groups, petty issues can arise that completely distract from the original point of the exercise—and there is nothing worse than a pack of bickering witches. "Bitchcraft" is neither fun nor helpful, and the solitary practitioner avoids its pitfalls.

However, if one can find a like mind or two—preferably chosen from amongst friends—the results can be triply spectacular. A single mind can work modest wonders, but two or more can create entire universes of possibility.

Joining a coven blindfolded (usually literally) is rarely a sensible thing to do. Just because somebody says he or she is a witch or a well-meaning Pagan does not mean that he or she is to be trusted. Even within Pagan and Wiccan networks, unpleasant persons may lurk. After all, the organisers do not have time to vet every person who claims affiliation with the group, and there are often strong feelings against the censorship so many of us suffer on the "outside." At the end of the day, a male witch is still a man, and ought to be treated with the same caution you would treat any man you do not know from Adam, especially when the coven involves ritual nudity. Personally, I would not be caught dead in such a scenario. Call me a prude if you like, but the nature of the beast should never be overlooked. Yes, Wicca is a type of fertility religion, but that does not mean that the women are up for grabs! I have met enough dodgy men disguised as witches to know what I am talking about here. Whether you are male or female, remember: never get yourself into a compromising situation. Physically, this means never practise with strangers or without a trusted friend at hand, and magickally, always vet your coven first. Working magick with the wrong people can defile your integrity. It doesn't look too attractive astrally either.

The best covens are those that spring up spontaneously out of a group of like-minded friends. They do not recruit—no true occultist ever does. There are certain cases in which a person or group might advertise, as sometimes it can be difficult to get linked up with empathetic thinkers, but this is never for direct initiation.

Pagan moots are a good place to start if you require company; meet in a public place initially. However, as a witch friend of mine pointed out, many of these take place in pubs (in Britain, anyway), which is a real obstacle for those who have issues concerning alcohol. There is a big drinking culture surrounding British Paganism, which is great fun for most, but a danger to others. We could do with learning from our American cousins on this one, although we are inhibited by restrictions on where it is comfortable and practical to meet and discuss what we need to without provoking too much attention. Real ale and Paganism/Wicca do not necessarily go hand in hand, however. If you are mooting for the first time in a pub or bar, it is wise to limit your drinking, as occasionally there may be unsavoury persons there "probing" astrally. Alcohol can compromise you and open you out to unwanted influences.

In ritual, sipping from a chalice of wine is wonderful indeed, but it compromises the involvement of those to whom alcohol has been a particular vice in the past. Some covens now circulate a chalice of spring water or grape juice for those who do not wish to taste or smell alcohol. This is another example of the importance of knowing with whom you are working—compromise can come in many forms. Every one of us has our limits, and in a coven to which one is new, these may not be known or respected.

A coven is any group that performs Goddess-aware magick in relation to the seasons and lunar phases. It usually comprises a High Priestess, a High Priest, and other members to whom particular roles are ascribed. However, one man and one woman are perfectly capable of covencraft, such as Morgan Le Fay and Dr. Rupert Malcolm in Dion Fortune's *Moon Magic*. Two or more women are equally able, as is demonstrated in Dianic Wicca. A solitary practitioner often finds him- or herself in astral company during ritual. There are a thousand ways for a coven to exist—the trick is, to choose the one that is right for you.

Gurus in the West are a legacy of the sixties, a hangover from our attempted "mergence" with the East. Many of them reflect this in their demeanour—they will have long hair, hippie garb, a laid-back attitude, and are usually either as thin as sticks, or pot-bellied like the Chinese god of luck, except the luck they bring us is not always good.

How do you spot a fake guru? He will probably make a beeline for you, and say something intended to be profound, such as, "Haven't I seen you somewhere before? Oh, sorry, it was in another incarnation." He will not even be embarrassed by his own cheesiness, and appear to totally believe every cliché he utters. He may also act aloof, sitting with a clique of apostles (usually hippie or "alternative") and emanating coolness and wisdom (he thinks). He is usually an older man, at least in his forties. He will be able to quote from the Bhagavad-Gita, the

Rig Veda, Timothy Leary, the Bible (in order to point out its contradictions), and any number of Zen philosophers. He is often multilingual. He will profess liberty, especially sexual. If you disagree, you are neurotic. If you argue, you are conditioned by society. Still, you will feel that the fault is yours, because he carries the weight of clique approval with him.

The Western guru can be an entertaining buffoon, or he can become a real menace. He will start to addle your brain if you let him, telling you which star or planet you came from, why you incarnated here and now (usually, to pay some karmic debt—to him!), and what you ought to do about it (sleep with him immediately!).

He will couch his unreasonable demands in the most astonishing reasonings. He can see further than you can, you see, so you have to trust him; it is essential to the "Perfect Love and Perfect Trust" he hopes will flourish between you. He will know exactly how to pull your strings; if you have a childhood trauma, never tell him, or he will reenact it at every opportunity. If you have an adult issue that is your Achilles' heel, you may be sure he will find it out and use it to his optimum advantage. As far as manipulation goes, the guru is king.

The guru also abounds in creation myths. "In the Beginning . . . ," he will tell you, as if he was actually there. It will be something far-out: Atlantis, space-gods, him, maybe, enacting Adam Kadmon. I am not saying, incidentally, that bizarre-sounding theories are necessarily incorrect (what could be more bizarre than our mortal condition?), but simply that they should not be taken as definitive Truths—not from the mouth of a wannabe swami, anyway.

The witch should avoid the guru at all costs. He is interested in Wicca because he thinks it means sex; beneath his tales of mortifying the flesh (for the sake of universal peace, or whatever), there lurks a rampant carnality. He might teach you a thing or two, but whether it is anything you want to know is another matter. Essentially, he loathes the idea of free, independent women (and is often jealous of other men to boot). He hates the thought that these young lovelies might evade the traps he lays for them to slip into. Do not even try to outwit this character. Ignore him, and if you're lucky, he will go away. If not, warn him, and get your friends to warn him. If all else fails, alert the police.

There are one or two good gurus around, but the best ones are mostly discarnate. The lure of power is usually too much for mortal man to bear; a taste of worship, and he becomes enslaved by it. I have seen this happen to several people who have set themselves up as founts of wisdom.

It is possible to learn from spiritual teachers, of course, without falling into the trap. The touchstone is this: Is the person trying to encroach on my personal space?

This means both physically and psychologically. If he seems in the tiniest bit creepy, bin him. It really isn't worth it.

When it comes to learning, books are best. My own favourite gurus, in whose integrity I totally trust, are Paramahansa Yogananda and Sri Yukteswar of the Self-Realization Fellowship. Wisdom may be safely gleaned from a thousand others by simply reading the tracts that are inevitably available from metaphysical bookshops.

The worst enemy of the witch is her quest for knowledge. It is also her best friend, the thing that drives her out of the norm. The solution is discrimination. This cannot be overemphasised. When we enter the world of magick, we risk glamour. It is the pitfall of all who tread the magickal and mystic paths. This means that we need to be alert on all levels—physical, mental, and astral. We need to keep a foot in both worlds, interact with those whose opinions differ from our own, find solace in those who empathise, focus on higher purpose, challenge our own motives at every juncture, and watch out for the prana-suckers who are inevitably drawn to those with fresh psychic energy.

Because Wicca and Paganism have spread so widely over recent decades, there are also many good teachers out there to help the aspiring witch along the path. However, as these teachers are necessarily going to take the novice along a deeply psychological route, it is essential to find one you trust and with whom you have a rapport. There is no ground rule for this except intuition; trust yourself. Never hand your soul over on a plate to anybody, no matter how impressive he or she may seem. The best teachers are often the least obvious ones. They are married or hand-fasted or happily celibate, they live quietly (possibly with their families and/or animals), and they have a vibe that you know is right. If no such person is apparent, take advantage of the wealth of excellent books now available on the subject. Many magickians and witches have produced works of outstanding value. Read Eliphas Levi, Israel Regardie, Dion Fortune, Gareth Knight, Dolores Ashcroft-Nowicki, Janet and Stewart Farrar, and anything else that appeals; follow your intuition. Books often come to those who need them. Try sending out a request on the astral plane to be led to what you need. It makes popping into bookshops a whole lot more interesting!

five

Karma Drama

THE WORD *KARMA* CAME TO us from Hindu and Buddhist belief, from the Sanskrit verb *kri,* meaning "to do." Its implications may be roughly translated as the spiritual and physical repercussions of intelligent action. This in turn creates another type of karma: one's unwitting deliverance into a new set of circumstances, a new life whose referents are informed by the past. The idea is to be offered the opportunity to reform, to learn a particular skill on the spiritual path.

The Bhagavad-Gita discusses the issue of karma in great depth, beginning with Arjuna's dilemma: Should he do as Lord Krishna tells him and kill his kinsmen on the battlefield, or should he save them from his sword? For lofty souls, the choice between good and bad is rarely easy. Krishna tells Arjuna: "Arise . . . ! Win the glory, conquer thine enemies, and enjoy thy kingdom. Through the fate of their Karma I have doomed them to die: be though merely the tool of my work." Krishna is testing Arjuna's faith (and that of his kinsmen): Will he fall for the illusion of death, or realise that the soul cannot be killed?

The concept of reincarnation, which goes hand in hand with that of karma, is often said (by such as Paramahansa Yogananda) to have been accepted by the early Christian church, but declared a heresy in 553 C.E. Certainly, Gnostics embraced the belief, which is innate also in Judaism (though less often taught these days). Christianity, of course, is a branch of Judaism. The idea that we perpetually reincarnate until we reach God certainly makes more sense than having one brief, random chance at it and then going either to heaven or to hell. Nowadays, most witches are conscious of the fact of reincarnation, and strive to elevate themselves against *maya,* or delusion; that is, the sense that consciousness and our present lives are finite. Like the yogi, the witch strives to understand and work with her karma, and to elevate herself, through selfless action, above "the Wheel of Life and Death."

The influence of Hindu and Buddhist philosophy on the Western Esoteric Path has been considerable since the Theosophists began their work in the Victorian era. Helena Blavatsky (see chapter 15, "Who Influenced the Witching World?") was a key figure in the impressing of Eastern philosophies onto the Western spiritual template. Indian gurus such as Krishnamurti became acceptable, bringing with them an innate belief in concepts such as karma. By the time the 1960s struck, Hindu and Buddhist beliefs were ready to blossom in the West. They merged with other schools of thought, such as modern Wicca, and became easily integrated into a spiritual overview. Nowadays, it is very rare to find a witch who is not enormously influenced by these ancient Eastern schools of thought, and who does not take concepts such as those of karma and reincarnation entirely for granted.

Karma is the result of action. It is the spiritual equivalent of the scientific principle that "every action has an equal and opposite reaction." Thus, it is not so much a process of judgement, as is often imagined, but the necessary answer to an equation of events. It is the energy-balancing result of a conjunction of circumstances. However, that moral lessons are innate in karma is beyond question.

Most witches recognise three types of karmic influence. One is the result of past lives. This influences our temperament, magickal inclinations, and life aim. Usually, if past-life issues are particularly prevalent or powerful, it is because they need to be resolved. These issues may be broached via meditation, regression, and analysis. They are particularly difficult to work with because of their apparent obscurity. Anybody with a sense of self-parody will know what I mean here. It is preferable to work on these issues quietly and privately.

The usual function of past-life contacts coming through to this one is emotional and practical debt. If we owe, the potential recipient may well appear in this incarnation and offer us the opportunity to do something worthwhile for him or her. If we are owed, he or she might do us a particular favour. There is usually a sting in the tail for the giver, of course, as the entire point is that of self-sacrifice, selfless action, and spiritual development. Often those in need of help are actually doing a significant favour to those able to offer it. Karma is one of the necessary dynamics in a dualistic world!

The Babe that weeps the Rod beneath
Writes Revenge in realms of death.

In his "Proverbs of Hell," William Blake echoes the popular Christian idea of judgement after death, when "The meek shall inherit the earth" and the cruel be punished for their misdeeds. However, Blake was in fact less simplistic than this, and implies also that the effects of evil are death-bringing in the sense that they destroy the spirit. The person who beats a child, the man who beats his wife, and the harridan who makes others suffer beneath whiplash words, are all in the process of spiritual suicide. Those who are cruel are always unhappy; the natural state is one of intelligence and compassion. They are lost in maya (delusion), and their negative actions will, as Blake points out, "Write Revenge in realms of Death." There is no possible extrication from this scientific fact—the equation must always balance out. We live between two Pillars—that of Severity, and that of Mildness. If we err more to one side than the other, we will inevitably be called upon to rebalance our positions. Duality exists, it seems, in order to teach us to be skilful jugglers of light and darkness.

The second major karmic influence is that of actions in this life. The idea of "threefold return" is popular in the Craft. Basically, if we put out good, we receive it. If we pollute the environment with selfish deeds or cruel words, we will suffer an inevitable backlash, probably much greater than our original transgression. Again, this concept has an almost algebraic sense to it. If we emanate darkness, we will attract dark forces to us. The witch endeavours, therefore, to think before she acts and speaks not just of the immediate repercussions, but of the subsequent effects also. Sometimes karma is second-, third-, or fourth-hand; the results can be of an action on others we may not even have been aware of. Everybody is connected to a strong network of developing spirits, both on this plane and on others. If we hurt a person, that pain travels along the subtle cords that attach that person to his or her group, and all are affected. A similar phenomenon occurs on the material plane, where chains of negative events may be so easily perpetuated by unwise actions and words. So, the witch knows when to hold her tongue, when to stop herself working magick (when she is angry and blinded by subjectivity), and how to divine the possible results of any of her actions.

A truth that's told with bad intent
Beats all the Lies you can invent:

Blake's words sum up another important aspect of karma—that of motive. It is not simply a question of adhering to what is popularly construed as "right" or "wrong," it is a question of the intelligent interpretation of any situation. We have all witnessed the manner in which Christianity and Islam, for example, were built on fundamental, compassionate truths, and then became tools for the torture and destruction of any who were not of their school. "Goodness," when carried to an extreme and made rigid and punishing, becomes a type of fascism. We see this reflected in the Qabalah where Chesed, sephirah of mercy, is necessarily balanced out by Geburah, the Destroyer (of all the excess mercy "allowed" by Chesed). Without Geburah tempering it, Chesed becomes bigotry and hypocrisy.

The point here is to be as ethical as possible without becoming a morality fascist and cancelling out any good inherent in a good deed. Sanctimony is a terrible danger to any with religious/occult inclinations; it can be easy to be swept up on a cloud of "oversight," but we must watch out for raining on anyone else's karmic parade. If we do, we become involved with that person or group of people, and repercussions may ensue. There is nobody in this world better than anyone else. We are all simply at different stages of evolution, and are obviously fallible, or we would not be here at all. Therefore it is always best to gently advise rather than to interfere or instruct, for our own sakes as well as those with whom we are involved. The witch is adept at discriminating between what is necessary and productive, and what is truth- or lesson-concealing.

Along with ethical action exists the knowledge that all that happens does so for a reason. There is no such thing as chance or coincidence. We attract circumstances from a higher level in order to respond to them in a certain way. Every witch knows that her life is an outer analogue of her inner condition, and reflects it symbolically. With this in mind, everything—even adversity—becomes both precious and fascinating.

Recently I was standing by the roadside waiting to cross. My body was on autopilot; my mind was on aspects of the occult, and which book would give me the best input for a project I was considering. My mind was reaching out for inspiration. I looked to my left, and the car approaching me bore the numberplate "777 LAW." I don't know whether the driver was an occultist and aware of the significance of this combination (I imagined he or she may have been, though the person might simply have been a rich police person), but it certainly told me which book to dip into when I got home!

Another example of this living symbolism came when I had just moved to the seashore. It being winter, I rarely bothered to go down to the waterfront to listen to the waves or watch the light on the water, even though I love both and they always have a magickal effect on my mood. I was also socialising a great deal—too much, to be frank. Instead of writing or meditating in the evenings, I was going to the pub and having fun. Well, there's a time and a place for everything. However, I was beginning to feel peevish. My spiritual sources seemed distant. Then, one day I realised that my proximity to the sea, which I was not bothering to visit or give thanks to, represented my proximity to the creative source—so near, and requiring so little effort on my part to be accessed. I began to visit the water's edge every morning and psychically recharging there. The slight effort it took to carry myself physically to the sea's edge each morning soon reflected itself in my dreams. I began to leave my body again at night, flying over the water's edge, liberated. Spiritual inspiration flooded back into me. I had, with this small symbolic effort, reversed my tides. Life is living metaphysics!

The third major source of karmic repercussion for a witch is the result of her own magick. This is one of the most spectacular to behold, of course, especially as many early spells misfire, usually to act as lessons. A typical example is the love spell—one of the major allures to the teenage witch, and to which I was no exception.

The first major spell I ever cast was on a boy named Meredith. I was fifteen and he was sixteen. I wanted him to ask me out, essentially, and I was too shy to approach him directly. It was a simple candle-magick spell and involved burning our names together in a red candle on an altar on which were arranged things that reminded me of him in all ways. I strongly visualised us together in various situations. That done, I waited. Suddenly, I saw him everywhere. We were at separate schools, and we had not run into each other much prior to my working (hence, partly, my doing it). Now we were bumping into each other at every juncture—usually when I was alone, and he was with his friends. It simply tortured me.

Then, one Saturday when I was working at my pocket-money job at a local café, and wearing a horrific white overall for hygiene's sake, in waltzed Meredith with a large group of his mates on their way to watch the football game. I had to serve him red-faced, knowing that I looked horrible and that it was probably my own fault because I had forgotten to add the clauses that not only should we be together, but alone, when I was ready for it, and in conducive circumstances. Serving him and his fellow footie fans lunch whilst dressed in lab-coat apparel was not exactly what I'd had in mind! I learned my lesson, decided Meredith was a lost cause, and made up my mind to move into more constructive modes of magick.

We might forget our spells, but they never allow us to forget them. Six months later, by which time I was besotted by somebody else (but resisted the urge to use magick), I ran into Meredith on the bus. This time he was alone, and I was looking about as good as a sixteen-year-old punky goth girl can manage. Our eyes met and lo! I got my spell's desired result: he asked me out. But guess what? I didn't want to go by then. I thanked him very nicely and explained that I was seeing somebody else. The emotions that had driven me to find Meredith attractive in the first place had been exterminated by the results of my own spells. I now associated him with the most mundane of circumstances—Saturday jobs, footie matches, greasy-spoon cafés. Lesson learned!

The point is: never cast a spell on a whim. The motive may feel overpowering at the time, but a spell cast in a flippant or temporary frame of mind boils down to unnecessary meddling.

Every spell we cast leaves its trails in our auric and causal bodies. The more spells we cast, the more auric and karmic baggage we must carry around with us. The wise witch, and those following the Wiccan Redes, restricts her spellcraft to that which is essential, helpful to others, healing, and compassionate. She may also work for her own benefit not as "selfish gain," but simply to provide conducive circumstances for her to materialise her aim. She begins every spell with the adage "An it Harm None . . ."

six

The Witch and Mental Health

Mood Swings

ALL WITCHES HAVE MOOD SWINGS. They are essential to a fully functioning sorceress.

For a start, we need intensity in order to focus our power. Secondly, if we look closely, we notice that our moods are directly related to the Great Priestess herself—Lady Moon.

A typical female witch will feel attuned to the moon both psychologically, and physically through her menstrual cycle. At the dark of the moon she may be tetchy and intense, perhaps depressed, and with a temptation towards spite. As the moon begins to wax, she will start to feel optimistic again, bringing inspiration and increased clarity of intent to her work. The climax of the full moon could bring about an epiphany. The waning of the moon will turn the mind inward again to thoughts of preparing for the future and to more mundane concerns. We need both the creativity of the waxing moon and the pragmatism of the waning moon in order to lead balanced lives.

Of course, it would be good if we could be happy all of the time, but feeling depressed and disgruntled often acts as a prompt to greater things. We may consider ourselves at the mercy of our hormones and the phase of the moon—and undoubtedly, there are times when we are—but these usually (perhaps always) occur in accordance with our subconscious. If there is a repressed urge for change, it will manifest as a "mysterious" feeling of disgruntlement. We should listen to our irrational side as well as to common sense. As witches, we understand the value of both currents.

Depression is a difficult one, as it often closes the imagination and intuition, making everything seem flat and one-dimensional. It could bring the feelings that our spiritual and magickal beliefs are phoney, or the guilt that we are not living up to our own ideals. If the cosmos is a magickal place to be, then why are we feeling this way? Were we just kidding ourselves when we thought we felt attuned to the Universe? No! Yet unfortunately, it is impossible to go around this world on a permanent magickal high. For a start, we would alienate everyone who lacks or has never tried to have vision. We would irritate them beyond description, and lose our humanity.

Though unnecessary pain is certainly to be avoided, there is a degree on this plane to which we need to *suffer to learn*. It's in the witch's creed, and with good reason. It is a basic tenet of any viable religious belief; it is the only explanation for our predicament. I am not saying that suffering ought to be brought into one's life deliberately; absolutely not. There is plenty of it in the world as it is, and all of us will naturally encounter obstacles from time to time, and misfortune. It is a question of appreciating the positives hidden inside the apparent negatives—"At the heart of the dark, sterile Goddess is the bright, fertile Goddess." Depression keeps us from getting too airy-fairy; after all, we exist on this plane not merely so that we can peer into other, preferable ones. We need to spend plenty of time here too, and if we have high standards, as most witches do, this realm will sometimes seem very bleak indeed.

Do not punish yourself for your mood swings and inevitable lows—allow them to teach you. Study their relation to the moon, and to your menstrual cycle (if you are female), one of the most powerful springboards possessed by the witch (see chapter 19, "Menstrual and Menopausal Magick"). You will gradually notice the patterns, and then, when something is irregular. Learn to listen to your own darkness. It can be eloquent when our conscious mind is paralysed with fear or conventional issues. Also, note the astrological details. You will soon find that a full moon in Pisces brings far more chaos than a full moon in Aries, when problems might start to clear.

MOOD SWINGS SPELL

If the instability of your emotions is making you seasick, you might like to try this simple technique. Take a lump of rose quartz and soak it in cold water at the bottom of your bath for as long as is practical. Envisage the warming, healing properties of the rock vibrating out into the water, affecting every molecule and atom.

Tie a handful of camomile petals in a piece of cheesecloth and place it under the hot tap (you may use any herb or flower you find soothing).

Remove the rose quartz, but remain aware of the influence it has had on the water. It has charged the water effectively.

Light ten rose-coloured candles and place them around the bath. Begin to allow the hot water to seep through the cheesecloth, carrying with it the powers of the herbs and flowers in the sack. Add ten drops of rose oil, or any other rose-scented bath accompaniment.

Take a small handful of salt and hold it up in the direction of the east, saying, "Cleanse and balance me, by the power of Air." Feel the sylphs on your skin as you do so, already getting to work on your polluted aura.

Now hold it to the south, saying, "Cleanse and balance me, by the power of Fire." See the salt blaze with purity as you do so. Now, to the west, say, "Cleanse and balance me, by the power of Water." You will soon feel the effects of this one.

Finally, to the north, say, "Power of Earth, keep my mind, body, and spirit in sacred equilibrium."

Now throw the salt into the bath, and get in yourself. Feel the relaxation and rebalance seeping into you with every inch of your body you submerge.

When you are fully relaxed, imagine yourself as three layers. The bottom and heaviest one is your dense, physical body. The second, which is lighter and higher than this, does not touch the bottom of the bath, and ends higher up than your physical body. The third repeats the pattern, beginning at a higher point and floating quite a way above your physical head. How dramatic the differences are will depend entirely on your state of being at the time.

With your inner eye, assess the state of each layer. Are any of your bodies grubby, cracked, or overemphasised? Take the time to mentally bring them back into shape. You can do this by using rays of light from your mind to "laser" them into better condition. Visualise them in perfect condition until they are. If they revert, put them back again. This may take some mental effort, but with any luck, the soporific warmth and scented steam of the bath will serve to give your mind free range of your bodies and make the operation relatively effortless.

When your bodies seem of equal emphasis to you, and all are clean and bright, imagine a bolt of rose-coloured light descending from the ceiling and landing in you. This is the final ray required to have you physically, mentally, and spiritually balanced again.

You may find that a return to your workaday life has you frayed again before too long. If so, repeat this exercise as often as possible. If performed once a day, it should definitely keep those mood swings that are not conducive to our progress at bay. (Some, as already discussed, are ultimately productive. You will probably know the difference!)

The Witch and Eating Disorders

I felt it essential to include a section on eating disorders because they affect the lives of so many witches and nonwitches alike. One of the first spells I was ever asked to cast was by a bulimic friend who wanted to lose twelve pounds at the flick of a wand. She was desperate. Needless to say, the spell was not performed. There are magickal techniques that can be used to help one out of this hellish mindset, and even to tone the body into a more suitable shape, but like any form of exercise or discipline, it takes the affected person to work for it.

Eating disorders are a form of obsessive perfectionism. It is ironic that one of the motivations behind anorexia is to look model-like and thus, theoretically attractive, when anorexics look vile and skeletal, not to mention the loss of hair, the skin problems, and so forth that accompany the disorder.

Anorexia and bulimia are running at epidemic proportions in Britain and America. I know of one girl's high school in which eighty out of ninety-three of the fifteen- to sixteen-year-old year group were anorexic. No less than five of them, including another good friend of mine, ended up in the hospital on a drip—and that was only the beginning of a ten-year struggle for her. If the neurosis is allowed to get a grip, it very quickly spirals into insurmountable self-hatred, especially when accompanied by competition—usually between girls. It is hysterical, deeply damaging behaviour.

Fashion and peer-group pressure, however, are but two of the many complex reasons that eating disorders occur. It is commonly recognised that many people feel this is the only control they have over their own lives, so they eat or don't eat in order to experience this control. In other cases it is a sign of severe depression to reject what sustains us in this life. Often this is a genuine will to die, and at other times it is a cry for help, like any other suicide attempt.

Eating disorders make the victim feel isolated and trapped in a body that won't cooperate with his or her will. Anorexia and bulimia are forms of self-torture and self-punishment that indicate a dysfunctional view of one's right to exist in the world. One cause is simple sensitivity—the fear of being called or thought of as "fat." Yet "fat" in itself is not a sin, nor is it found universally unattractive. Rather, the fear is of being seen to be greedy, or dependent on factors over which one has no control. Refusing to eat, or eating to excess and then disgorging, are attempts at seizing this control.

There are no permanent standards in the world regarding physique—of the female, at any rate. The well-rounded women we would now call plump was the height of desirability only a century ago, and the sticklike creature would have been seen as disgusting (and still is by many people). In those days, thinness was related to poverty (as it still is in India and Africa, for example, where chubbiness is also seen as attractive because it is pro-life); now, of course, it is related to city-slicking sleekness. The most glamorous women in *Sex and the City* and *Ally McBeal,* for example, are often—though admittedly not always—slender in the extreme; certainly, their lead women are. Thinness is expensive now—you have to be able to afford to eat really well to stay so slim, and avoid the cheap junk foods with their sugars and starches and so forth—theoretically, anyway.

The fact is, some people are naturally slim, while others are naturally larger. Which is more attractive will depend entirely on the onlooker. It is certain that a healthy, confident, engaging person will prove infinitely more desirable than the depressed person who will drink only mineral water or who rushes off to the toilet after every meal.

The stupid thing about bulimia is that it actually doesn't work. It's completely illogical. Have you ever seen a thin bulimic? I haven't. The fat from the food consumed is absorbed almost instantly, while the proteins, fibres, and vitamins are expelled by the vomiting process; not very bright. Meanwhile, the body is strained, and permanent damage can be caused to teeth, intestines, and the entire constitution. Anorexia is no sensible alternative either. Even very tightly controlled eating is dangerous as it is on the brink of an eating disorder. The best thing is variety. Eat when you feel like it, and not when you don't. Allow yourself sweet and savoury snacks once in a while or you will begin to crave them.

The witch, ideally, will remember that there is so much more to life than the body that she will not spend too much time thinking about hers. She will spend some time thinking about it, of course, for general maintenance and enjoyment of her image (why the heck not?—we only have this body once, we may as well enjoy it), but most of her focus will be on other planes. Imagine the owner of a fine car who was so worried about the contents of the gas, and which sort to use, that she stood there fretting over the stationary tank of the vehicle and never let it leave the garage! That is what eating disorders do to the brain—they are so time-consuming that they severely halt progress. Obsession with food is about as trivial as we can get.

However, it does not seem trivial at the time. It seems like your life's crux, and the ultimate cure-all once the "ideal weight" has been achieved. The same obsessive compulsion applies to overeating; it is less common, but it is a similar neurosis. This time, however, one simply lets go of all control and self-respect and blobs out mentally and physically.

We all have neuroses and phobias. They are a natural part of the human make-up, and can often be positive in the long run if intelligently scrutinised. There is a reason for everything. However, those neuroses that dice with death, ultrasignificant though they are, can only threaten our incarnational integrity. They are a challenge, and must be met as such. Nobody can be blamed for wishing for self-improvement, but self-immolation on the fire of physical fashion, which comprises so many modern eating disorders, is far from clever. Radiance comes from within. Beauty, too, is spiritual—there is nothing more beautiful than a truly happy, generous person, no matter what his or her physique. This is the kind of beauty we are aiming for—along with the charming confidence of being at home in one's own body.

We are given our specific bodies because they facilitate what we need—they are the tool we have no choice but to work with. Very few people, if any, are entirely satisfied with theirs, as this type of narcissism thankfully goes against the human grain. We always crave what is better, and sometimes, what is unobtainable. Yet we need our physical vessels in order to learn and grow spiritually. Learning to be at peace with your body takes time, but when achieved, reflects the Hermetic motto, "As Above, So Below."

We are spirits in the midst of matter, and to be at one with the body, with its inevitable imperfections, can only bring us closer to Spiritual Truth. Remember, the real key to happiness lies within your self. "He who Seeks, will Find."

The Witch and Suicide

What is a section on suicide doing in a guide to life? Doesn't that contradict the proactive, megapositive stance of the sorceress highlighted in the first chapter? Well, I don't think so. As far as I can tell, witches and occultists suffer as much as ordinary mortals, if not more so, because our standards are so high and our perceptions are enhanced by magick.

A witch can suffer terrible repercussions for her follies, as we know from the law of the threefold return (whether it is believed specifically, or simply as general karma). Even if she doesn't believe in this, she can fall from great heights. She flies high on the currents of nature, magick, and cross-dimensional interaction, and then finds her broomstick called back to earth by mundane considerations. The perversity of the material plane (in some of its aspects) may be recognised, but it is not necessarily easy to overcome. The contrast factor can be harsh. Not only this, she also suffers from all the other dilemmas of the human condition. It is unrealistic to think that even the most naturally buoyant of witches can avoid the occasional dark night of the soul. This is inevitable—and deeply productive—to any thinking individual.

Suicide does not have the same connotations to a witch or magickian as it does, say, an atheist. Witches are accustomed to interacting with spirits, and we know that the inner self never dies, no matter what the outer shell undergoes. Experience of the astral plane teaches us that astrally and spiritually one appears as one is on those levels, not the way one looks in daily life. So, a very pretty witch who thinks evil thoughts will seem as revolting as her motives on the astral—at least, to anybody good. A shamanistic person might appear as an animal with human characteristics; a very petite person might be twenty feet tall over there. As you think, so you are.

Because of this, the witch/magickian is keen to think positively. If she walks around feeling weak, she will look it on the astral plane. If she is depressed—which any suicidal person is obviously likely to be—she may appear slouched and covered in black gunk, or an equivalent substance. She is even less likely to want to appear on the astral like that, than in the street on which she lives. After all, both realities are equally real. This is one of the reasons for the great emphasis on ritual cleanliness in witchcraft and magick. One would not wish to appear in a Circle covered in grime, astral or otherwise.

So, no matter how low a witch is feeling, she knows that were she to dispatch herself to the next level in this state of mind, she would find her astral integrity severely compromised. The gunk from this life is best washed off on *this* plane.

That's just one of the selfish reasons to avoid inducing an untimely end. The Wiccan would be reluctant to do so anyway because the proviso "An' it Harm None" could barely apply to such an act, no matter how unwanted or hopeless a person might be feeling at such a time. Suicide creates terrible trauma for the ones who love you most, and the spiritual person knows that he or she is likely to have to witness some of this from beyond the grave. Spirits may be sent back (or just naturally gravitate) to abide with those they love and/or have made to suffer, and suffer in equal measure, or more. The idea of one's beloved family and friends going through hell over you, and you unable to fully interact with them and comfort them, is not a tempting thought.

Then there's the question of incarnational objectives. The witch believes that she is here for a reason—she has certain tasks to fulfil. That one of these might be suicide is very difficult to believe. Although I am of the school that it takes great courage rather than cowardice to dispatch oneself to the Other Side, suicide *cannot* be a positive end to an incarnation; suicide is defeat. Should the witch pick herself up off the floor and struggle on, the Wheel of Fortune will turn again. She will find great relief, and deeper inner strength, when the depression or trauma has passed. She will have moved up a psychic grade or two. She will be a survivor, and her courage and power will be greater for it.

Most witches believe in reincarnation. This adds another angle to the suicide issue. If each life is for a purpose—which it has to be, in such a scheme—then not only is the suicided witch failing in this life's objectives, but she is precipitating compromise in the next one. The lesson will still have to be learned, but with all of the physical learning processes repeated. It is a rare person indeed to whom such a thought appeals.

Some witches, similarly to Buddhists and Hindus, consider karma from the last life to affect the present one. I agree to a point, but am reluctant to think that anybody is ever being "punished," or that any misfortune is deserved. Compassion is one of the most important lessons anybody can learn, witch or otherwise. However, what is certain, in my opinion, is that an act such as suicide would negatively affect one's circumstances in the next life. If incarnations are progressions, then a regression (or some would suggest, a transgression) of this sort must have a price attached—not as a punishment, but as a simple equation. The last life did not equal success. The quest may simply become more ambitious to counteract the negative repercussions caused by the act of suicide (the same goes for cruelty and other negative acts). However, achieving x, y, and z in the next life will create the next stepping stone.

Then there is the issue of euthanasia—the compassionate killing of those in great pain, or suffering from a terminal illness. This topic is being hotly debated in Britain at the moment, as such patients who require this "dignified death" are having to travel to Switzerland to attain it. The process is illegal here, and a murder charge is inflicted on those who help. For the witch, such a choice would require many angles to be taken into account, not least karmic, and how the process of suffering may (or may not) be "refining" the soul. Buddhists and Hindus believe such afflictions to be a blessing—burning off bad karma and purifying one in preparation for the next life. However, there are many situations in which such a concept would clearly be inappropriate. Certainly it is very difficult to watch a loved one suffer, with no hope of recovery, especially when he or she has asked to be released. If the patient wishes to live out all of his or her days, fine, but some would rather not.

A good witch strives to be nonjudgemental, whilst maintaining perspective and those all-important skills of discrimination. This is one of the characteristics that separates the Craft from more conventional religions. Witches do not proselytise, nor do they cast any stones, having had so many pitched against themselves in times past. (Still, today, in some Eastern countries, anyone suspected of sorcery or witchcraft may be dramatically "punished" in the street.)

Being pro-life does not mean recoiling from the problems inevitably thrown at us, as humans, on this plane. Depression should be treated with empathy, and attempts to counteract it with magick are a natural recourse if the witch concerned is willing. Orthodox help should also be sought in some cases; the impulse to commit suicide and constant depression (or manic highs and lows) usually have a chemical origin that can be treated on that level. There is nothing shameful about taking medication when it is needed (quite unlike the popping of happy pills, or the addiction to valium undergone by so many women in the '60s and '70s). Therapy is another path that might be of help, although it is vital to get the right psychotherapist with the right techniques for your "issues." You don't want to be made to beat up a pillow pretending it's your father, or make yourself feel complicated by reiterating your past if what you really need is to focus positively on the future. Most witches are already pretty good at sorting out their own pasts through self-analysis and ritual.

Depending on the issues in hand, it is possible to construct psychospiritually helpful rituals that enact the healing process either symbolically or literally; an underworld quest is an obvious example. Every initiation is a death and rebirth, after all, and such extreme emotions may be harnessed and used to create a dramatic epiphany. These are best based on mythology, or "theotherapy"—the healing of archetypal wounds in the individual. There is no issue that does not have its parallel in the universal unconscious, and a tale or a symbol may be chosen by the individual or her helpers that best befits the scenario.

A potentially helpful archetypal dynamic for myth reenactment is the despair of Persephone when she found herself imprisoned in the Underworld, married to Hades, and the despair of her mother Demeter on losing her. (See *Invoke the Goddess* [Llewellyn, 2000] for full details and suggested visualisations.) The witch may do this for herself (though, if her get-up-and-go has got up and gone, this may be difficult), or with helpful friends and coverners. If the witch is alone, she may use guided visualisations, of which there are many now available either on tape or in books. If she has the energy, she may attempt to invoke a godform, though it is unlikely that a witch suffering from depression will be able to summon the inspiration required for this. Another alternative is the use of astral doorways (such as the Hindu tattva colour symbols); this is good as it may be done whilst lying down and drifting (see chapter 18, "Magickal Techniques and Spell-casting"). Whatever the course of action, the important thing is to strive.

We may never fully understand what goes on in the minds of even those who are closest to us. Suicide is a deeply personal decision that, if chosen, must be accepted as self-euthanasia. Sometimes, the fault is with the physical mind, rather than outer circumstances or inner turmoil. These terribly sad situations can result in release when the body comes to an end, either naturally or otherwise. The individual made the decision to move onto the next level, and that is that person's right. The witch strives to be pro-life, self-supportive, and helpful to others in any given situation, but her spiritual overview informs her at all times, and she will not mourn unnecessarily, either for her own life, or for those of others. She knows that life never truly ends.

Coping When the Wheel of Fortune Takes a Downward Dip

The witch knows that life works in cycles—all of it. Sometimes we are at the top of the Wheel of Fortune, and at other times we are at the bottom of it up to our eyes in bad karma. The trick is to remember that the Wheel will turn again, elevating us out of misfortune as it does so. This is indeed "the Starlit Mire"; when life is bleak, it becomes particularly evident that earth, or Malkuth, is a launching pad rather than a resting place. Thus, there is good to be gleaned from the bad patches, not to mention the opportunity to try some magick to get us back to where we'd rather be. Yes, the Wheel will turn again, but if we know how to speed the motor along a little, it seems foolish not to do so.

Through challenge, we learn. As Shakespeare put it in *As You Like It,* "Sweet are the uses of adversity,/Which like the toad, ugly and venomous,/Wears yet a precious jewel in his head." Without experience of conflict, we would be smug and spineless. Often, trouble is a gift, offering the "precious jewel" of victory over circumstance. Self-respect and the admiration of others come only when obstacles have been overcome and one's mettle proved. The most tempestuous lives are often the most constructive.

However, it is important to recognise when adversity is a challenge from the fates and when it is self-inflicted and pointless. Some people, even some witches I have known, have been so emotionally overindulgent that their lives have been permanently strained; every little issue is a crisis, and the day-to-day an exhausting melodrama. The key is to maintain perspective and self-control; then the real incarnational issues can make themselves known.

Once the true issues have been extricated from the dross of attention-seeking and mental laziness, it is possible to tackle them one by one. When we are at the bottom of the Wheel of Fortune, we often realise, "This serves me right for _____," or "This is my karma for being [proud/unkind/inconsiderate/selfish]." As long as we are being honest rather than self-punishing, this is positive. Unresolved guilt surfaces as we seek a justification for our plight. This inner scrutiny is one of the bonuses of misfortune.

Karma is the result of past thoughts and actions. I discuss it in chapter 5, "Karma Drama." It can be a friend, despite often seeming otherwise. Karma is spiritual (and physical) logic. If we act stupidly, we reap the consequences. If we act stupidly for the right reasons, we reap the consequences but remain spiritually intact. We know that spiritual rules are not completely applicable on this plane—nothing could be more blatant. So we have to tread the line between rectitude and what is physically sensible. We do not wish to catapult ourselves into chaos by standing up for what we believe at every juncture, necessarily. Some of our karma is programmed into our genes, and there are those amongst us who will do exactly this—suffer in order to enlighten others and themselves. Yet martyrdom is not the path of all. We each have our roles to play.

When we find ourselves in adversity, we must look at what brought us to this point, assess it, and make positive moves to extricate ourselves from it, always bearing in mind the higher purpose that informs our incarnations, obvious or not (usually not at such times). Witches, Wiccans, and other magickally minded people have several options. Firstly, there is the very human response of seeking the advice of others on the same path. This does *not* mean asking others to "cast a spell to help." It is a downfall of many who believe in magick to ask for such aid—it isn't the answer. I myself and other authors and witches I know receive such requests frequently— sometimes for trivial purposes ("I lost my luggage at JFK. Can you get it back?"), sometimes for very serious problems ("My husband has just been diagnosed with Parkinson's. Can you cast a spell to cure him?"). A better approach is to ground one-self (often difficult, but nearly always possible), assess one's role in the scheme, and then look for support if necessary, always being aware that you should be giving as much as receiving. Quick-fix spells are like Band-Aids on gangrene: no point. There is more to life and death than we can sensibly influence—at least sometimes.

Secondly, the witch looks at her own fund of experience—which must be con-siderable, otherwise she would not be a witch—and assesses what she can do to improve her own state of mind, thus enabling herself to be helpful to others involved in the situation. This may involve spells and rituals for strength and endurance rather than instant solutions.

Thirdly, she appeals to higher entities. I write much about this in *Invoke the Goddess* and *Invoke the Gods*—there are godforms and wavelengths out there that can aid us in any situation.

Finally, she bears in mind at all times that *things will change.* Having done all that she possibly can in any given situation, she can rely on the hand of Time to turn the Wheel of Fortune. This is not to say that improvement is inevitable—sometimes it is not within a life span—but usually it occurs, and the learning process proves priceless.

Fortune is fickle, as priests, poets, and prophets have always pointed out, but to endure, to strive, and to learn—these things are eternal. Faith and fortitude will pay high dividends to witch and nonwitch alike. One thing we can rely on above all others is that circumstances on this plane will always change. If we can guide that change with intelligent magick, all the better.

seven

The Witch and Drugs

THERE ARE FEW SUBJECTS AS likely to cause an argument between pro- and anti-camps in the Craft as that of drugs. Crowley flaunted his own experimentations with mind- and magick-altering substances in his magickal journals and his novel *The Diary of a Drug Fiend,* and Carlos Casteneda took peyote and mescaline with Don Juan in order to access alternate realities. Many other seekers have spurned drugs as negative or delusional. Certainly those following the holistic lifestyles that often go hand-in-hand with modern Wicca, Paganism, and Goddess-worship would be reluctant to taint their systems with drugs. Many witches and psychics believe even hashish to cause auric damage.

Barbara Ann Brennan's book *Hands of Light* (Bantam Books, 1987), for example, contains descriptions and an illustration of "etheric mucus" caused by cocaine usage. She also describes the aura of a man "who has taken many LSD trips and drunk a lot of alcohol" as "dirty greenish-brown. The dirty green spot, which was slowly moving downward and was not released, correlated to his mixed, undifferentiated, withheld feelings of anger, envy and pain." This, states Brennan, could have been cleared were it not for the mucus blocking the man's energy field.

What Barbara Ann Brennan is identifying here is a man who is suppressing his feelings with drug and alcohol usage. His aura is smeared by his own frustrations as much as by the drugs. Obviously the use of any substance or mental attitude to cause selective amnesia is damaging.

Drugs have been used by medicine men in a spiritual context for centuries. Any brief study of shamanism will tell us this. They have also been used more recently to elicit responses to difficult situations. When the Zulus famously defeated the

Victorian British Army, for example, they had been provided with snuff by their medicine men. This snuff contained a particular type of hashish that causes paranoia and fast physical response to danger. The Zulu warriors thought that even the birds in the skies had been commanded by the British to turn against them, and responded accordingly. The result was a devastating defeat for the British, despite the guns that should easily have fended off near-naked men with spears. There were other factors, of course, but essentially, the medicine men were wise enough in the ways of drugs, music, and ritual to counteract the attack of an army sophisticated in all types of physical weaponry. They manipulated their men into a single, concentrated force of defence.

Following on from this, the other major issues we as witches have with drugs are: Will they impose behavior on their subject, or do they bring out what is already innate? Are visions and perceptions received whilst "tripping" real or not? I cannot comment on LSD or acid as I have always avoided taking them (for precisely the reason that I needed to know that my natural visions were "real"), but several of my friends have had their consciousness expanded by these experiences in a noticeable and positive way. I am not recommending them per se, but I am saying that sometimes one must go with what is right, rather than sticking to "the rules." Only the individual can decide whether such an experience will be of value or not. Running the risk of paranoia, terrifying hallucinations, and temporary psychosis, very few magickally minded people would go into such an experience flippantly. Grown-up witches, however, ought to be able to decide for themselves.

In the novel *The Sea Priestess,* which is renowned in occult circles for its esoteric insight, Dion Fortune's hero Wilfred Maxwell is only able to communicate with the moon (initially anyway) through the exhaustion, hunger, and "dope" he undergoes after an asthma attack. As he puts it himself: "It seemed to me a marvellous thing that I should lie there, practically helpless in mind, body and estate, and yet trace my lineage to the stars." In this condition, he is able to abandon his straitjacket of social mores, and allow his spirit free range of the astral and spiritual realms. He goes on to conclude: "I dare say I owe a great deal to the Dangerous Drugs Act."

Now, Dion Fortune was far from an advocate of drugs per se. Indeed, both the group she founded, the Society of the Inner Light, and its daughter, Servants of the Light, spurn drug usage—the latter to the point that it denies access to any who have experimented in such areas. Still, she recognised the shamanic quality of liberation from the body that sometimes—but certainly not always—may be facilitated by drugs.

With street drugs (as opposed to pure ones such as peyote straight from the cactus), another major problem exists for all users—that of their composition. Because of their illegality, no trade standards are applied, and drugs such as Ecstasy can be cut up with all sorts of pernicious substances. Each pill is a matter of trust—there is no way of knowing where it comes from or what its effects are going to be. Some contain ketamine, a horse tranquilizer, and others are spiked with harder-core drugs. This is a far cry from the seratonin-enhancing MDMA supposed to constitute Ecstasy!

The concept of Ecstasy is a fascinating one. It smacks of *Brave New World,* in which Aldous Huxley's characters lose themselves in "soma"—an idea based on the mythologies of many cultures. In Hinduism, *amrita* is the intoxicating drink of the gods, which confers eternal youth, happiness, and beauty. In Greek mythology, *ambrosia* does the trick. The idea of perfect happiness in pill form should not be brushed off without consideration. Is it a gift of the gods to mankind?

Once again, I believe that it is up to the individual to decide. Spiritual seekers should not be told to do this and not to do that; life is a process of learning, and each of us has a conscience and discrimination to guide us. The only true judge is oneself. An Ecstasy pill taken in a nightclub with strangers will be very different from one taken at home with a close friend or friends. One taken in a field or forest during a ritual, again, will be different. Chances are, the latter will far from enhance the magick, as it accesses an entirely different wavelength from the one the witch normally uses, which is more concentrated and determined. Attempting a ritual with a space cadet would be trying indeed, and affect everyone else's energy to boot. Most likely, it would ground proceedings completely.

What Ecstasy does, of course, is stimulate one's sensation of happiness; it causes the impulse to reach out lovingly to others (though this emotional and physical tactility is rarely sexual). It induces a sense of cosmic well-being and connection with the Universe that is very similar to the magickal high, but lacking in normal referents. These referents are essential in magickal proceedings. The difference is partly its duration—one pill can cause a constant high and energy-rush for up to eight hours solid. The discrimination is not compromised, and the high is not "irreplaceable." (Some think of it as "borrowing happiness from the future." This may be a karmic issue, but I do not personally believe it to be the case, although with excessive usage, essential seratonin in the brain may at times be used up, or even blocked.) It must be remembered that magickal highs may be compromised by the use of such stimulants. A ritual might begin to seem little in comparison— the subtle frissons that herald magick may seem like nothing once the sky-high sensations of Ecstasy have become "normal," or at least been tried. However, many cultures are known to have used drugs that create the best sensations possible in ritual. Experimentation truly is the personal choice of the informed adult.

One pitfall of Ecstasy (and cocaine, hashish, acid, etc.) is paranoia. Unless one is already extremely happy naturally and in "ideal circumstances," the risk of psychological discomfort is always present. Of course, many of us undergo that on a day-to-day basis (working with an obviously embittered colleague, for example), but, under the effect of drugs, or having used them, the sensation becomes magnified. The guarantee, therefore, is not so much of a taste of bliss, but of an enhanced state of consciousness.

There are arguments for and against the use of drugs in the search for enlightenment. Some seekers are destroyed by them; others find them helpful. Personally, I avoided them for years, and still would not touch several with a ten-foot barge pole. It seems obvious to me that drug abuse when young (by abuse, I mean continual usage for no reason other than pleasure) causes emotional and psychic dysfunction. It also instils the bad habit of escapism rather than the confrontation of issues, and is likely to lead to association with highly unspiritual types—and that's legal issues aside.

However, we as adults have hopefully developed a sense of responsibility to ourselves and those around us, and must decide for ourselves what is good for us and what isn't. To deny another person this choice is to deny that person of his or her free will.

The Witch and Alcohol and Tobacco

Any doctor will tell you that alcohol and tobacco are far more harmful than most of the illegal substances mentioned above. However, they are also a social habit as much as a personal one, especially in countries such as the U.K. where bad weather often drives us indoors, usually into pubs or bars. Many Pagan moots take place at pubs for they are neutral territories. "Cakes and Ale" is a popular addition to any coven meeting, and provides a relaxing, social arena after the celebrations and magick. And we all know of the pleasures and pitfalls of tobacco (if not personally, then at least through the testimony of others), often going hand-in-hand with alcohol. Between them, alcohol and tobacco kill four hundred people per week in Britain alone, which is far more than any other cause. So, what should our attitude be towards these two commonly enjoyable, but ultimately pernicious substances?

It is my opinion that we should each decide for ourselves. Throughout my own incarnation I have had a completely ambivalent relationship with tobacco—having started smoking at the age of seventeen, I thoroughly enjoyed it to the age of twenty-three, and then gave it up for a year. I have been on and off with it ever since—at the moment, off. Hopefully I will stay that way, but I say that only for the sake of my lungs and future in this body. To be frank, if I could smoke with impunity, I would spend most of my evenings in a fug.

As for drink, again, it is the individual's choice. Unless one is consuming danger-ous amounts regularly (by which I mean any amount that affects the faculties to the point of uncharacteristic behaviour or [partial-]amnesia [definitely time to stop!]), it really does have to be an issue of free will. This is the key point: as witches, we believe that we "cross the Veil" when we are meant to, and though this does not curtail personal responsibility (the body is also a temple, of course), it does mean that some of the normal rules of science do not seem relevant. The implication of spiritual belief in any culture is that one is not scared of shedding the body, but the danger of this is, of course, irresponsibility. Knowing death to be a simple transition, the witch is not paranoid about her physicality. That said, she has plenty she wishes to achieve in each incarnation (why go through yet another childhood, when you could just continue in the here and now?), and this instils common sense. Rather than becoming rampaging Hedonists, we know when to party, and when to stop. Waking up every morning with tight lungs and a stonking headache is not con-ducive to a productive life.

So, if you are a witch struggling with a tobacco habit, here are some handy points to remember. (This is only relevant if you want to stop. If you're happy smoking, and it fits into your incarnation comfortably, fair enough. Every effective occultist knows not to proselytise on any subject.)

- You are damaging your lungs, which represent your capacity to interact with the Universe in its purest form.

- You are affecting your relationship with the element of air. Tobacco stimu-lates the creative centres, but not without a price. You are going for the fast-burn equivalent of a lifetime's productivity, the latter of which may be cut short as a result.

- To be a Crone is wonderful, but not before your time. Smoking ages the skin, and often curtails the present incarnation.

- Lavender oil is a huge help when quitting smoking. It smells much better than stale tobacco after being burned or evaporated too.

- "An' it Harm None, Do As Thou Wilt"—it is every tobacco-toking witch's responsibility to avoid smoking over children or nonsmokers, or at least ask the latter whether they mind. Otherwise, we are breaking the Wiccan Rede or, if one is not Wiccan, simply being selfish.

- Breathing exercises are also an excellent tobacco substitute. Instead of a cigarette, visualise white light (or smoky light, if you prefer!) flowing into your lungs from the Universe. Breathe in the same way you would when smoking—enact the process if it helps, but without the cigarette. Much of the relaxation and euphoria gained from smoking comes from the deep breaths we take when inhaling.

- If you know all this and still wish to smoke, so mote it be. It is not up to the witch (or anybody else) to impose rules, judgements, or standards. We all get to where we're meant to be going in the end.

As for alcohol, it is widely recognised that independent women with disposable incomes are becoming the new alcoholics, most notably in the U.K. It's "Bridget Jones syndrome"—a bit of room for indulgence in one's own home, often accompanied by a tinge of guilt, but not that much. This includes many witches, who work hard, and wish also to play hard. Fair enough; however, alcohol is rarely of benefit to magick (though it sometimes is), and can often have a grounding effect. Psychically, it slows perception in most people. It is also worth remembering that the female body lacks the quantity of enzyme required to break down man-sized dosages of alcohol. Thus, though we may be happy to "drink our men under the table" (this witch has done so on more than one occasion), there may be a long-term debt to pay. Like tobacco, alcohol in excess ages, and causes damage to a vital organ.

Again, however, karmic circumstances and personal constitutions vary wildly from individual to individual. Each witch—indeed, each human being—should decide for herself what is right and what is wrong for her. Many people who disapprove of alcohol are actually terrified of losing control, which is the attitude of a nonadept. The initiate at least should be trusted to know what is right and what is wrong for him or her.

The liver was thought of in Elizabethan times as the seat of the emotions, and there is much in the idea that alcohol stupefies the emotional centre, whilst also damaging it. Many unmagickal alcoholics "drink to forget," even if their activities seem to be entirely social. When life lacks depth, the same scenario can befall the witch. I recall when I split up with a beloved boyfriend, undergoing the perpetual urge to go to the pub in the evening—ostensibly to socialise, but in reality, to drink myself to sleep. Without a few whiskey shots to help me along (and the accompanying cigarettes, of course), I found myself besieged by grief. However, all I really managed to do was drag the process out, instead of confronting it at the time. Because I suppressed my natural reactions so effectively at the beginning, it took me four years to get over that relationship!

The characters in Dion Fortune's novels, who are based on members of the Golden Dawn and other prominent occultists, survive on diets almost solely of caffeine (usually strong, sweet tea "you could stand your spoon up in"), cigarettes, brandy, and fry-ups that would send the calorie-counter into orbit. We know for a fact that most of these magickians drank and smoked in real life, some even venturing into experiments with narcotics. They were highly proficient—far more so than many a teetotal New Ager—and that is why we know of them today. So let's be realistic about this, and accept that alcohol and tobacco are not the devil's own. This attitude is indeed highly Christian, and far more prevalent in the more recently Christianised United States than it is in the U.K. Alcohol and tobacco, like all of the ingredients available to us in Malkuth, exist for sensible use by the definition of the individual.

Even the cautious witch will most likely agree that an occasional blowout is fine; dionysiac, one might say. There is a vast mythology behind wine, ale, and some liquors (such as the mystical green elixirs absinthe and chartreuse) that renders them sacred. Even the mystical frenzy, once in a while, has its place in a witch's incarnation—just not every night!

Aleister Crowley is one example of a magickian who pushed his body to the limits with drink and drugs, and there are many others. What one has to learn on a magickal path is to be nonjudgemental; nobody can doubt the enormous contribution Crowley has made to modern occult knowledge, and he did this by breaking every rule (see chapter 15, "Who Influenced the Witching World?"). We ought each to know what is personally productive for us, and what is not. When we feel uncomfortable, when constructive pleasure becomes a compulsion, or when we know we are attempting to suppress our feelings, it is time to stop.

Some ideas to lower alcohol intake, should you wish to, are:

- Start the evening with a green tea. The sensation of detoxing rather than retoxing can be equally enjoyable!

- Socialise in coffee shops rather than bars. Again, a caffeine-high can be just as good.

- Go to bed early and get up early.

- Remember that excessive alcohol consumed regularly causes infertility, premature aging, and liver damage. In Britain alone it kills one hundred people per week.

- Treat alcohol ritualistically—as a celebration, for example. This means not consuming it at every available opportunity, but on special occasions (if you wish to at all), and with the respect you would treat any other magickal substance. We do not drench our temple in sacred water, we sprinkle it. We do not burn so much incense that we choke on it. We don't dance so fast that we fall flat on our faces. There is much in the adage (boring cliché though it may sound), "Moderation in all things."

eight

The Ages of the Witch

THE PERCEPTIONS OF THE WITCH operate outside ordinary aesthetic standards. A witch has "it" at every stage—as Maiden, Mother, and Crone. An aged witch is at the top of the hierarchy, and is a living representative of Hecate, Greek goddess of witches, the celestial High Priestess.

Just as we find that every stage of the moon represents an integral part of a month's activities (sowing ideas at the new moon, bringing them into fruition at the full moon, harvesting them when the moon is waning), so do we respect every stage of human development for its intrinsic value. More to the point, we know how to celebrate it. In the "Seasons of the Witch" we equate the female form with the cycles of nature and the powers of the Universe.

Not wishing to exclude our masculine counterparts, the ages of man also play a role in our symbology. The youthful consort is essential to the propagation of life, traditionally represented by the God of the Waxing Year. During this time he is ever at the side of the Goddess, receiving her favours and enjoying his position as Lord of Spring and Summer. However, come Samhain (see chapter 9), the seasonal tides turn, and with the death of the old year comes the death of the Old God. The Goddess no longer casts glances of love and longing on her youthful beau, but instead turns a pale, cold cheek on his appeals for attention. He is literally slain by her indifference, his blood seeping into the earth and refertilising it. The seeds of spring and summer lie dormant, while in strides the God of the Waning Year confidently takes the Goddess's hand in his own. He, older and darker, is now her partner of choice.

Because of their close affiliation with the cycles of nature, Wiccans celebrate new life and old in equal measure. Belief in the cycle of rebirth means that an infant may be greeted as more than just a screaming baby of a certain genetic heritage; he or she is also a spirit brought into this particular set of circumstances for a reason. The parents, as guardians of this developing individual, will do their best to create an environment of both support and freedom to develop.

Menstruation is something to be celebrated in the Craft. Not in a cringe-worthy sense (some people tend to be quite over the top about these things), but as a quiet acknowledgement of a girl's progressing maturity. Another point of note to the witch is that with puberty comes a massive increase in psychic power. Dreams will become intense and symbolic (sometimes actually astral), intuition takes a quantum leap, and the intensity we all know so well in teenagers gives a significant boost to one's powers of creative visualisation.

Periods also attune themselves to the phases of the moon, adding a new dimension to the fledgling witch's awareness of nature's cycles. Now, her own body gives a visible analogy to the concept of seasonal tides. She is clearly a part of nature and its mysteries.

Sex is also seen as a natural function (as discussed above), but the young neophyte should be schooled in what is curiosity, what is choice, and what is unwise. Because Wicca is famed for being a "fertility religion," it is sometimes assumed that the men involved are free to scatter their seed where the spirit guides them. Not so! As in any decent religion, the fundamental rule of mutual consent applies—and that means that both parties must also be of an age to make a sensible, well-informed decision. Whether that age coincides with civic law or not is a matter for anyone—witch or nonwitch—to decide. The witch, assured of her autonomy, may choose to celebrate the life-force with a partner, or she may make the choice to wait. She never allows herself to be guilt-tripped into sex (see "Covens, Gurus, and Teachers" in chapter 4). If there is the slightest hint of her being forced, she screams blue murder.

The rite of passage into adulthood is the gateway to greater spiritual integration. It is therefore a key stage of initiation, if not the single most important one between birth and death.

The Great Rite, or the conjoining of male and female cosmic energies, is something that happens on a level much greater than the transient enjoyment of two bodies. The witch recognises the symbolic significance of sex as well as its procreative and pleasurable potential. It is illustrative of the God and Goddess creating everything that exists. Similarly, just as in Jewish lore, couples unite at midnight on a Friday in a reenactment of the Shekhinah reuniting with her male counterpart (the Shekhinah represents the exiled, female side of God, and also represents the Children of Israel). In other words, creation is brought back to its Sacred Source. In the witch's Circle, this process is symbolised by the gradual descent of the male athame (witch's dagger) into the wine-filled chalice. Likewise does the energy of God filter down from beyond Kether, the highest sphere of the Tree of Life, into Malkuth, the "bride" who waits on earth. The adolescent witch is a potential magickal bride or bridegroom.

Aging is approached with a positive attitude, as death is not the taboo in witchcraft that it is in some other religions. To a witch, there is no such thing as death; there is only transition. Therefore, signs of age are those of wisdom and experience rather than mortality. The Death card in the Tarot depicts the Grim Reaper riding over a scorched field straight into a baby and a kneeling bishop (Death pays no heed to age or status) while the sun begins to rise over the horizon. Likewise are we mown down by the inevitable, only to be "ploughed" back into the cosmic field, and to eventually "rise again" as the sun does every morning. Ergo, "crow's feet"—not a problem (theoretically, at least!).

The witch evinces the same attitude towards death as the Egyptians did; it is a period of temporary darkness, like the descent of Ra or Osiris beneath the horizon. Because it is a natural part of the cycle that we should return again, attraction does not have a sell-by date in witchcraft. Thus, the aged witch is as beautiful as the Maiden; she is simply closer to the other end of the Source.

Duality plays an important role in the beliefs of the witch. However, unlike the Christian attitude, there is no "better" quality between darkness and light, night and day, female and male, and so on. Nor is there the materialist's preference for young over old, or new over "outmoded." There is "right" and "wrong," of course, but these are very much for the individual to decide on. The basic ethic of Wicca— "An' it Harm None, Do As Thou Wilt"—says it all. If it injures nobody, an action is not wrong, regardless of the opinions of others.

The ancient Greeks held a similar stance. The dark and light sides of the human psyche were considered part of the whole, rather than as separates struggling for domination, and one of which required total banishment. The *daimon* of Greek lore—the spirit—was neither good nor evil, unlike the *demon* of Christianity.

Instead of a psyche over which angels and demons battle for control, the witch evinces a balanced psychology, in which all aspects of her being are accepted. Those that she does not find conducive to her growth, she takes positive action to eliminate. Those that are helpful to her—however unconventional these might be—she keeps. Thus, every stage of physical life—youth, adulthood, and maturity—and the varied circumstances that accompany them, become opportunities for further affiliation with the Creative Spirit.

The Witch and Death

Death, as it is commonly defined, is not a witch's or magickian's estimation of mortality. Instead it is a most wonderful portal that leads to spiritual judgement (that is, individual karmic adjustment)—reunion with friends across the Veil, 24/7 access to many interesting spheres, and the chance to take a refreshing break on the astral, essentially, between incarnations. If the magickian, witch, yogi, or other spiritual person is particularly advanced, that person will find him- or herself in the causal rather than astral plane. This is closer to Godhead, the eventual goal of the mystically minded seeker of any creed.

So much for death, an opportunity to get closer to the Creative Source. Death is neither sought nor feared by the witch—Kali comes when our time is up, and deconstructs the body with her weapons of inevitable physical demise. She is time, and even the adept is unable to fight that indefinitely on the physical level. If we walk into her arms willingly, and surrender to the darkness with the spiritual faith that is the test of every incarnation, the process is a great deal less painful.

> The majority of persons who are buried are still alive, while a number of others who are not buried are in reality dead. Incurable madness, for example, would be with them an incomplete but real death, leaving the earthly form under the purely instinctive control of the sidereal body. When the human soul suffers a greater strain than it can bear, it would thus become separated from the body, leaving the animal soul, or sidereal body, in its place . . . Dead persons of this kind are said to be identified by the complete extinction of the moral and affectionate sense; they are neither bad nor good; they are dead.

The above quote is Eliphas Levi on the magickian's attitude towards death from his book *Transcendental Magic: Its Doctrine and Ritual* (Rider, 1923). As it indicates, there are other types of death within the range of occult perception. Death-in-life is the common condition of most human beings. Life is spirit, and life without spirit is zombism. The living dead have taken over the world since the destruction of the great mystery religions and the establishment of materialism and rationale over religion. Don't get me wrong: I'm perfectly keen on rationale and a degree of materialism—both are essential tools to an effective incarnation—but only when balanced by spiritual energies. If a person is focussed solely on the material, he or she will at least stifle, and possibly eliminate the spirit (at least temporarily), and be nothing but a walking automaton; not a pretty sight to the psychic eye.

Luckily for us all, there is currently a resurge of old souls coming back and helping to reconstruct a more effective path to Godhead—to Kether and beyond, to put it in Qabalistic terms. There are more people alive on the planet today than have ever lived or died before, so it figures, then, that many of these will be Old Ones. The regeneration of interest in ancient mystical techniques, the ability to receive and exchange information with high speed and accuracy, and the ability to assimilate it on many levels not available in centuries past makes this era one of the most powerful ever known. Humans are right to fear death, for it truly is the end of them; but the spirit is immortal, and is ascending with every day that passes.

The spirit also exits the body for reasons other than death. On a positive note, there is astral projection. During this process, the projector is completely mentally lucid—possibly more awake than in daily life—and the spirit is able to roam the astral planes (or visit specific locations) whilst relaying information back to the brain. Consequently, the faculties of free choice and decision remain intact, while the participant is more often than not entirely aware that he or she is "out of the body." Often, it is possible to see the body in its state of inertia—it appears as a separate entity.

Similar sensations can occur when one is ungrounded. This is usually not as positive or conscious—one simply feels that one is floating over the body, which may seem numb or slow as a result. I have had this happen in shopping malls on numerous occasions when the piped music, neon lights, advertisements, and air conditioning have affected me. This is no doubt a deliberate ploy on the part of consumer giants—it is shocking how much hypnotism and subconscious programming goes into the retail industry. We walk around in a trance, and get home to find we've bought all manner of unnecessary items that seemed like "bargains" at the time! We have, in fact, been zombies throughout the excursion—the living, buying dead.

Trauma can create a similar dissociation of mind from body and spirit, however subtle it may seem on the outside. Overaffiliation with the Other Side, ironically, can have the same effect, when the "silver cord" connecting spirit and body is constantly stretched to its limit. Drugs and other addictions are likely to render body and soul asunder, particularly heroin. Every day in London and Oxford I see these walking bodies who have dissolved their spirit and every trace of their humanity in heroin. They have lost touch with their souls, and are what a witch would most certainly define as the living dead. That is not to say that the soul could not be induced back, however, with treatment both physical and magickal, but it becomes more difficult with every hit.

Some illnesses also cause this death-in-life condition. Various forms of psychosis and other mental afflictions such as Alzheimer's can send the spirit into complete dissociation with the body. In such cases, the spirit is usually resting and refreshing itself elsewhere, while the brain and body keep going on autopilot.

Dion Fortune, who worked as a psychoanalyst (as did Israel Regardie), makes much of these forms of spiritual plight in her book of esoteric short stories, *The Secrets of Doctor Taverner*. These are based on her real experiences under the aegis of Dr. Moriarty, her mentor. "Mona Cailey," for example, in "The Soul That Would Not Be Born," suffers from what we would nowadays define as a type of autism. She neither speaks nor employs any cognitive skills—she is dead in life. "Dr. Taverner" and his trusty accomplice manage to induce her into birth (i.e., to bring the soul into realisation of the body). They disentangle the karmic events (from an Italian Renaissance life, as it happens) that had led to the reprisals Mona was due to receive, and from which she was procrastinating. It is a common belief amongst the magickally minded that physical events have a spiritual origin and a purpose.

Not all forms of physical demise are of vast occult significance—if a person is not an occultist, why should he or she die an occultist's death? Still, "Once an initiate, always an initiate." Magickal people, even if for some reason they have undergone an unmagickal incarnation, will find their amnesia cured as they enter the death designed for them. It is, of course, rebirth into more vivid realms.

Many of the most powerful deities are directly connected with death, dissolution, and/or the Underworld: Siva and Kali, Hades and Persephone, Inanna and Tammuz, Osiris and Nephthys, to name but a few. Initiations of all sorts involve death and rebirth scenarios, and in occult work this is often carried through with deliberate symbolism, such as blindfolding the initiate and binding his or her limbs. Again, death is seen as part of the ourobouros snake of continuity and self-sustenance (the ourobouros swallows its own tail).

On a practical level, it is now possible to have a Pagan or Wiccan funeral in the Christianised West. This is an important act of dignity for those who have lived with "alternative" beliefs and who do not wish to be buried or cremated with the trappings of another religion. (Ecologically sound coffins are, importantly, also available now.) This process is likely to be a celebration of the deceased's last incarnation, and a process of bridge-building, or simply of sending energy to the "Other Side." Loved ones are sometimes recontacted at Samhain, if such a communication is appropriate. More often they are remembered with candles and simple offerings, and they come willingly if, again, interaction is called for. As I mention in chapter 2, the witch does not harass the dead.

Ritual is immensely important to the deceased and bereaved in witchcraft, as with any other religion. There are some beautiful "passing over" ceremonies in publication—see Janet and Stewart Farrar's *A Witch's Bible* for one example—and of course, it is always possible (and often preferable) to construct one's own. The successful sending of love and light to a being on the Other Side is an immensely uplifting experience for all concerned.

This understanding of death and the "Darkside" as powerfully positive is a key stage in spiritual development and insight. Without fluency in immortality, the witch is simply involved in power-play. With it, she is a Kether-seeking missile.

Part II

FACTUAL WITCHCRAFT

nine

The Wheel of Death and Life

WICCA IS BASED ON THE legend of the Goddess, the God of the Waxing Year, or Oak King, and the God of the Waning Year, or Holly King. During this time, the Goddess shows her many aspects: as dark, barren Crone in winter, as Maiden in spring, Mother in summer, and Wise Woman in autumn into winter. She is also approached through the lunar cycles, which similarly wax and wane over each month.

The God of the Waxing Year represents all that is forward-forging and pro-life. He "courts" the Earth Goddess in spring in her aspect as Maiden; in Beltane they are bought together. By Lammas, August 1st, his work is done, and the seed is to be harvested. He has given his life to the earth, and now he dies. John Barleycorn is cut down. His flesh and blood (bread and beer, if taken literally) feeds the community after his sacrifice. He descends into the Underworld, just like many other solar gods—the Egyptian Osiris and Assyrian Tammuz being but two examples. Later, he will be resurrected, just as the sun will rise again at dawn and the fields and trees will again be green in summer. While the Oak King is dispatched to the earth, his brother and rival, the Holly King, takes over. He rules until the longest night has passed—so, until December 22nd—and then the God of the Waning Year steps in again.

This cycle has been repeated time and time again in mythology and religion, nature being the most obvious analogy for our predicament as humans. Christianity adopted it in the symbolism of Christ crucified, dormant, returned to earth, and ascended. Even if they are not Wiccan, all witches, magickians, and occultists will recognise this theme—in microcosmic form at least—in their day-to-day lives.

Samhain (October 31st)

The pronunciation of Samhain [*SO-veen* or *SEW-en*] depends on who is talking. Many witches pronounce the word as it is written, which is always a pitfall of adopting languages unfamiliar to the modern tongue! Samhain is employed by the witch to access and process issues from the past. Its major themes are divination, purification, death, and potential rebirth, and the carrying of the life-impulse through the dark winter months ahead. It is the old Celtic New Year.

Samhain is the most powerful sabbat of the year, in conjunction with Beltane, its "opposite." Of course, it is the celebration most traditionally associated with witch-craft. The dead do indeed walk on this night, and we witches do our best to interact with those who are willing and helpful. Old friends come back to say hello (I light a candle for each as an invitation or welcome), and are usually related to this incarnation, but sometimes are from others long passed. Time knows no bounds on this night. Often, food, drink, and other creature comforts are left out to welcome these visitors from the Other Side, a tradition known as the "Dumb Supper." It is possible to attune with one's previous and future incarnations at this time too. The witchy catch phrase for this sabbat is "The Veil between the Worlds is at its thinnest."

In the days before year-round central heating and deep-freezers, this was the time when cattle would be slaughtered, ready to be salted and stored for use in the winter. The harvest, of course, would have been gathered up by now, and the fields would look barren without their crops and herds. The world had died, it seemed. The final leaves were falling from the trees, and the cold and dark were becoming more intense.

Samhain represents the gateway between the old year—now fully harvested—and the new, when all must begin again. The Goddess is "pregnant," but it will be a while before she shows signs of birth. She mourns for the God of the Old (Waning) Year, who is represented by the animals who have been "sacrificed" to keep mankind fed throughout the winter months. She is also worshipped at this stage as the Crone, usually represented by the Greek goddess Hecate. The fertile earth mother is gestating a child of hope, while the barren dark goddess has progressed to wise and ancient archetype. They can exist simultaneously, of course, because there is futurity in the fallow field, and we have faith that abundance will eventually follow. Both processes are necessary to ensure a healthy crop. Symbolically, the witch accepts the processes of dissolution as equally essential to those of growth. In Qabalah, this is represented by the Pillars of Severity and Mildness, and in the balance between the sephirah of mercy (Chesed), and that of restriction and destruction (Geburah).

Magick at Samhain often revolves around "letting go"—of obsolete emotional ties, such as those to people who have passed through the Veil, or of those from whom we have necessarily separated on *this* plane. It follows, then, that the Samhain tides are ideal for ridding oneself of old habits—rather in the tradition of the "New Year's resolution." It is also a superb time for divination. Mediumship is easy; telepathic conversations flow when the time is right, and the witch is perceptive. Tarot readings are intense and, if properly performed, extremely accurate.

There is always a mischievous feel to Samhain, which is represented nowadays by trick-or-treaters knocking at the door. Elementals will be playing up, and if one is not prepared for the new year to come, old efforts may be forfeited. So it is always best to take stock of one's life prior to Samhain, harvest one's resources, and face the longer, darker nights ahead with confidence. Otherwise, even the witch may indeed be spooked.

There are many suggestions for Samhain group rituals available in other books on Wicca, though, ideally, these will be written by the people performing them, using the seasonal motifs mentioned above.

Winter Solstice/Yule (December 21st)

Yule symbolises the death of the Holly King, who is vanquished by the Oak King. He will be reborn, of course, when the Wheel of Life turns again and the days begin to wane once more, but now, at Yule, the sun is reborn. There are bleak months ahead (at least, in the British Isles) until spring really announces the reign of the Oak King, but the tides have begun to turn. The longest night is over.

This is the sabbat of the rebirth of the sun. The Holly King, Lord of the Waning Year, is slain by his brother, the God of the Waxing Year, and his fruitful presence in our lives is reborn. The perpetuity of life through the dark winter months is represented by evergreens—holly, pine, and mistletoe being obvious favourites to the Pagan and non-Pagan alike. Themes to consider at this time include fire in darkness, represented by the Yule log (which may be used to wish upon, rather like a birthday cake when its candles are extinguished), and the Goddess in her harsh aspect—she is the "leprous-white lady" of snow at this time.

Imbolc (February 2nd)

This sabbat welcomes the oncoming light borne of the winter darkness. It is also the time for "spring cleaning" and quickening fertility. Imbolc is the "feast of lights," as its Christianised name "Candlemass" reflects. The darkness of winter is subsiding—life is germinal but increasingly in evidence. Imbolc represents the last day of winter, and the beginning of spring. The Goddess is no longer Maiden (as she is pregnant with life), yet not quite Mother. The Roman festival of Lupercalia also took place in February, when the priests of Pan would run through the streets striking people—particularly newly wedded women—to bring them fertility. The festival heralds spring.

Spring Equinox/Oestara (March 21st)

Next we have the minor sabbat of the vernal equinox, when spring reaches its apex. The words *Easter* and *oestrogen* (*estrogen*) were derived from the Anglo-Saxon "Ostara," goddess of fertility. Night and day stand in perfect balance, with the powers of light on the ascent. Naturally, the actual date of this equilibrium shifts from year to year, but March 21st or 23rd (some say 25th) are the times it is habitually celebrated. The God of the Waxing Year confirms his Yuletide victory over his twin, the Lord of the Waning Year. The Goddess in her Maiden aspect is wooed by the young sun god's embraces and conceives a child. The child will be born nine months from now at the next winter solstice.

It is posited that the customs surrounding the celebration of the spring came from the south, though megalithic sites suggest that early inhabitants of the British Isles celebrated it too. However, in the Mediterranean it was certainly more popular, and was celebrated as New Year's Day. Inhabitants of southern climes claimed Aries as the first sign of the zodiac. The vernal influences all around explain this connection with new beginnings, and life made manifest.

Christianity adopted this obvious natural tide of rebirth by celebrating the resurrection and Ascension of Christ at this time; the solar hero returns from the Underworld. The egg symbolism of this time indicates new cycles and new beginnings, as does the hare, a symbol of fertility.

This resounds with the theme of the Goddess dressing herself in green and returning also from the Underworld. Persephone is restored to earth after sharing Hades' gloom, and Demeter, her mother, celebrates with her. In Christianity, the three-day absence prior to Easter suggests a Goddess-origin to the symbolism.

Needless to say, the tides of this sabbat are employed to initiate new projects, symbolise a "new leaf" (habits may be broken, as at many sabbats), and to give thanks for sustenance and faith restored.

Beltane (May 1st)

The tides of this sabbat are harnessed by the witch for energy, new ideas, and empowered sexuality. Like Samhain, its opposite on the Wheel of Life, Beltane is full of mischief-making influences, both elemental and through those just beyond our vision behind the Veil. This is the night when the Gates to Faery swing open, and mankind is able to cross over. It is full of all the pulsing energy of the natural world yearning towards its fulfilment in summer, and full of the vigour of the wild hunt. Beltane is primarily a fire and fertility festival. The lighting of Beltane fires, usually atop hills, served the purpose of purifying and fructifying—cattle, crops, and communities.

There are many traditions for Beltane eve and morn involving beautification for potential coupling. One such tradition that has survived to this day is the maiden washing her face in May Day dew. The Maypole is another—the phallic symbol around which young people frolic, celebrating life and the return of the easy summer season. In days gone by, the winter months were spent encased in vests greased with lard to keep the cold out. Bathing was not believed to be of benefit to the health then, but in May it was deemed warm enough to peel off the winter vestments, have a bath, and don lighter apparel. The filthy old rags were normally burned, and everyone emerged looking relatively clean and wholesome. This was the time to find your partner, as the tradition of "June brides" attests.

Witches celebrate the marriage of the God and Goddess, who has finally been "caught" by her lusty partner (in some respects this happens at the spring equinox, but by Beltane, her fecundity is indubitable). This leads us to the subsequent role of the Goddess as Mother. Because of the emphasis on fertility, the Great Rite is key to Beltane celebrations. Literal coupling is apt, but the symbolic form in ritual—the joining of athame with wine-filled chalice—is equally effective.

In covens workings, a candle is often lit to represent the fire of old energies, and a bonfire is lit to represent the new energies. The High Priestess "extinguishes" the old tides when she snuffs out the candle flame. Altars are decorated with blossoms and young leaves, oak and hawthorn (symbols of the God and Goddess in their bright aspects, respectively) being particularly appropriate at this time.

Summer Solstice/Litha (June 21st)

This minor sabbat is employed by witches to relate the mystical to the physical, for spiritual enlightenment and for working on new levels. The longest day of the year is clearly a solar festival, with all its associations. Despite this, it is also the time at which the Holly King comes into his own again; the year will decline from this point onwards.

The Goddess at Litha is still in a maternal role—the harvest is yet to arrive. Many people stay up all night at the summer solstice to welcome the dawn. In England, celebrations are orientated around Stonehenge, though these have become more of a clash between travellers and the police than anything of real spiritual significance. Rave culture hits its peak, which is not necessarily a bad thing, but sometimes it is an encroachment on the quieter beliefs of other members of society. As with anything of this nature, it all depends on how it is done.

The essential message at this time is to "gather ye flowers while ye may"; we know that the year will decline in the wake of the summer solstice. (This is especially the case in England, where I once spent a freezing summer solstice on Ilkley Moor in Yorkshire [see the Tiphareth section in *Magic of Qabalah*].) It is certainly a time of celebration of warmth.

Lammas/Lughnasadh (August 1st)

This sabbat is employed by the witch to celebrate the harvest of past efforts, and to reflect on industry and the theme of replenishment. It is "loaf-mass," and it celebrates the beginning of the harvest. In days of yore, bread was baked from the first of the harvest and laid on the altars of local churches as offerings.

The theme of sacrifice emerges here because the Corn King must, of course, be cut down when the crop is reaped. This sacrifice is willing, as echoed in the Wiccan ritual: "He has embraced the Great Mother, and died of his love; so has it been, year by year, since time began." Nowadays, when harvesting is down to farmers in machines, Lammas seems to fall rather early—crops are not usually harvested until September. However, the sabbat marks, again, the changing of the tides—this time from waxing to waning.

It involves the concept of sacrifice in that "John Barleycorn must die." In days of yore, this was represented by a large wickerwork figure (to represent the vegetation spirit), which was then burned, as depicted in the popular film *The Wicker Man*.

Paul Davenport speaks of the mediaeval mummer's play tradition below in "Folk Customs and Folk Magick." As in many mythologies, the young king is sacrificed, then cured and resurrected. He is the sun, in his many guises. The doctor, "quite calmly and horribly mad," bends over the dead god, plies his magickal cure, and the Prince arises hale and hearty to the cheers of the crowd. This clearly symbolises the death and resurrection of nature, as is visible to us.

It was upon a Lammas Night
When corn rigs are bonny,
Beneath the Moon's unclouded light,
I held awhile to Annie . . .
The time went by with careless heed
Between the late and early,
With small persuasion she agreed
To see me through the barley
Corn rigs and barley rigs,
Corn rigs are bonny!
I'll not forget that happy night
Among the rigs with Annie

Lammastide was also a time of marriage (though many marriages would be performed earlier in spring and summer) and of Craft. Mediaeval guilds displayed and advertised their wares with much gusto on this holy day, sometimes even with play and dance. Industry and creativity were underlined. A highlight of the festivities might be the "Catherine wheel," now a popular firework. In the days described, a wagon wheel was placed atop a hill, smeared with tar, set alight, and ceremoniously rolled down the hill. Similar events still occur in Britain to this day, usually with absolutely no overt spiritual significance whatever. They are literally gatherings of wild, uninhibited males expressing their masculinity after many pints of ale. Academics may see this ritual as the remnants of a Pagan rite symbolising the end of summer, the flaming disk representing the sun god in his decline, but the participants are unlikely to have any idea as to its import. This was true, fundamental, and essentially brutal Paganism.

Autumn Equinox / Mabon / Madron (September 21st)

This sabbat is employed by witches to give thanks for temperance, stoicism, balance, and altering tides of fortune. It is the time of the second harvest after Lammas; physically, of fruit and root vegetables after the Lammas corn, and spiritually, of longer-term projects than those that came to fruition around Lammas.

The Mabon festival (a name springing from Welsh origins, and adopted by the Craft), is also known as Harvest Home, or the Harvest Festival. Naturally this is still celebrated as a holy festival of thanksgiving by the Christian church. It is one point at which the magick of nature can be ignored by no one!

In the following section, we look at aspects of the sabbats and Pagan worship as they survive in living folklore today.

Folk Customs and Folk Magick
by Paul Davenport

When Pope Gregory sent the first Christian missionaries to Britain, he instructed them to build their churches where the people already worshipped, and to structure the worship of Christ to the familiar practices of the Pagan population. In giving those orders, Gregory became an important preserver of the Pagan heritage of the British Isles. Throughout the ensuing years, the common people have continued much as they did before the coming of Augustine, missionary-in-chief of Gregory's regime. We can still feel the resonance of our ancestors when we witness or participate in seasonal celebrations. Antiquity is not actually an issue here. It is not how long something has been going on in a community, but the existence of that activity on other planes that lends authenticity and credibility to its appearance.

I want to take you to five places as examples of what I mean. I will describe them as they appear on the mundane level, and as the participants see them. Then I want to examine them as they manifest on a higher plane, and to discuss the symbolism that causes them to resonate in the greater unconscious. Finally, I want to examine a modern festival and its importance for understanding the interaction of these celebrations and events with contemporary life.

The Long Company

Reluctant to leave the warmth of the bar crowded with singers and brave the biting January wind, we huddle in the press of bodies while the chorus swells:

We are not of the ragged sort
But some of royal trim
We'll sweep away the old year
And let the New Year in!

We have come to this place high on the Pennine foothills to the west of the Yorkshire town of Halifax. The event in which we are participating occurs annually, each evening in the first week of January.

The smell of night floods through the now-open door and we are propelled into the dark. The wind bites with frost in its breath. The lanterns held by the cloud-breathing crowd flicker and sway. Voices fade and an anticipatory silence descends.

Out in the darkness there comes a faint sound, which reminds the listener of flames in an autumnal fire. The sound is there, yet there is no fire, no light in the darkness beyond the watchers who cluster together for warmth against the chill wind. The sound is growing and there is a dull roaring now, which draws closer; yet no conflagration, no accompanying glow. The watching eye searches for the source of the sound, and there, beneath the shadowed trees, there is a movement. They move slowly—each figure stands taller than a man. Their profiles are indistinct and appear to shift and blur, avoiding sharp focus. They glisten as if wet or covered with scales, and their gait has a slow relentlessness, which tells of a long journey. Two are armed with swords and shields, while another carries a cooking pan. The others carry long staves, which are bound with indistinguishable items.

The press of the watchers' bodies shifts and they enter the circle of lanterns. Each acknowledges the watchers and takes his place in a line that shifts and blurs with the touch of the wind. The figures are dressed in a mass of strips of shiny material that flutters and creates the unclear profile. Their faces do not exist to the onlookers, for a tall headdress with strands of material, which completely hide the face, tops each head. The headdress extends the height of each celebrant who, already tall, seems to be around seven feet in height. Each has a different colour scheme representative of his place and part in the celebration.

The first to step forward is Beelzebub, rustling in red and black and waving a pan in his hand. It is he who begins the incantation calling for room to play. He threatens the watchers, who steadfastly maintain their circle enclosing the figures. Each figure is introduced in turn by Beelzebub, who "calls them in." His words are formulaic and have a strangely repetitive air to them. Each answers as he steps forward with the formal announcement, "In comes I . . ."

We are introduced to "Old King Christmas," "Saint George," "The Prince of Paradine," and "Common Jack." One remains in the shadows, unannounced. Each regales the audience with a description of his status, deeds, and fame. There is a disagreement, and Saint George and the Prince face each other for combat.

What follows is the heart of this ceremony. The combatants clash with a ferocity that, even though announced, is startling in its sudden violence. The noise of shields clashing and swords striking is in stark contrast to the tense atmosphere earlier.

Saint George knocks the Prince to the ground and turns to the audience, but the wounded Prince recovers and strikes George down from behind. It is as if a dam has broken and the world's tensions are contained in the brief and bloody moment. Saint George falls dead. Common Jack prances around the circle scream-ing: "Send for a doctor!" There is no comedy, only a stillness and unease. The last, unannounced figure moves slowly into the light. The most bizarre of these figures, his body appears to be completely made up of silver tubes. He announces simply, "I am a doctor." "How came you a doctor?" questions Common Jack. "By my trav-els," comes the quiet reply.

In the exchange that follows, we learn that this is no ordinary doctor, but a crea-ture skilled in the most insane behaviour and practices. His credentials do nothing to create confidence. He appears quite calmly and horribly mad. The doctor bends over the dead man who lies still as if on a catafalque, and he pauses. After a number of incantations, he produces a potion, which he pours into the open mouth of the corpse. The dead man rises and a cheer goes through the crowd of watchers.

The figures reform their line, and then begin slowly to circle within the space before the watchers are forced to part and the figures once more depart into the outer darkness. For a short time, no one moves. Then the watchers jostle back toward the welcoming warmth of the bar and its fire.

This is the mummer's play; in this instance, the Hero Combat version. There are many other types. The Long Company's version has been constructed so as to open the minds and the eyes of the watchers to other levels of consciousness. The cre-ators and participants have made deliberate attempts to produce a mystical experi-ence by making references to old texts and a much older form than the sometimes pantomimic renditions dating from the nineteenth century. The text is not old, but the symbolism speaks of an ancient past.

If we examine the whole performance, we can detect some of these elements. Ritual combat is an ancient practice and is at the root of the bloody gladiatorial contests of ancient Rome. These battles were actually religious rites and were asso-ciated with funerary rites. The gladiator was not simply a trained thug, but rather an intermediary between the soul of the deceased and the Goddess in her aspect of Persephone. The whole presentation of the Halifax Long Company play has this sense of darkness and foreboding. It is funereal and dignified. Here the actors are dressed to create a sense of ambiguity. The strips of plastic rustle and flicker. As one watches them they recall armour, scales, and wetness, and their blurred profile gives the sense of "otherness."

We can pursue this line of thought by referring to the mention of an annual combat in which the Cymric deity Gwynn ap Nudd is condemned to battle with Gwythyr map Greidawl every May morn for the hand of Creidlawd, daughter of Llyr. Thus George claims as his feats not only the slaughter of the dragon, but also the winning of the hand of the king of Egypt's daughter. This in turn leads us to the epic battle described in the first section of the Mabinogion, in which Arawn, king of Annwfn, the Celtic Otherworld, must annually battle at the ford with an adversary named Havgan, who can never be defeated. Fortunately he is able to persuade the reluctant Pwyll, prince of Dyfed, to exchange places with him, and by shape-shift-ing, the two exchange likenesses. Now this story related to our mumming play is very important since Arawn has on him a geas or taboo that forces him to grant his opponent's wish. Each year Arawn wins his combat and wounds Havgan, who promptly demands to be put out of his misery by death. Immediately Arawn grants this wish and kills the wounded warrior, and the latter returns to full life and vigour. The cycle continues. Havgan in the old Welsh language means "double" or "twin." It seems that Arawn must fight himself. Pwyll, who at this point merely looks like Arawn, does not have the geas upon him that creates this unbroken circle. When his enemy begs for the mercy stroke, Pwyll is able to refuse and thus break the cycle.

The circle is broken and the warrior must live forever wounded without hope of healing. Here is the cause of the anguish of the Fisher King in the Grail legend who is the king of the Underworld. We may draw further inference that this is so from the names of the Prince of Paradine, originally "Paradise" (that other world of the dead), and from Saint George, who is a christianised hero figure whose dragon-slaying fame makes his resonance one with Siegfried and Heracles. We further note George's death by treachery in this rendition, the proper way for heroes to die.

What the Long Company has tried to do is to create a rite using traditional material that is readable by all who see it. The play is ancient, and the characters have names from the nineteenth-century view of such things. Despite this, the real meanings of the ritual drama lie beyond and behind these outward trappings. There is a depth and a reverence here that all can relate to. There are transformations of time and place that occur. Magickal symbols of sword and staff reveal the inner workings of the play, whilst the threatening presence of Beelzebub himself is revealed by closer inspection to be the Horned One, Lord of Animals. His simple domestic cooking pan reminds us at once of Cernunnos of the great Gundestrup cauldron. This also reaffirms for us the sanctity of all food and drink, which must proceed from the natural world if we are to be sustained.

Rites of Spring

As the wheel of the year turns, the sun lifts in the sky and the leaves return. Like Gawain, we are heartened and uplifted by the return of green. In the ancient island of Britain there are stirrings, too, in human hearts as the Morris Dancers practice their ageless rounds. One of the oldest manifestations of these spring rites is in the tiny north Oxfordshire village of Kirtlington, where once the rite involved sacrifice and a ritual feast. Nowadays the scene reflects this to a marked degree on the mundane level, whilst on higher planes the ether positively sparkles with Earth magick transmuting through all of the elements like the great kundalini serpent before returning into the Earth herself. This is the only Morris festival in Britain to actually include overt worship of our Mother. The fair is on the village green and the lights are on in the pubs that echo to the sound of ancient songs. The English revels are still as Washington Irving described. Beer, that mystical drink that proceeds from the earth-born waters and the blood of the Corn King (known here as "John Barleycorn"), lubricates the throats of the lusty singers:

> *There were three men came from the West,*
> *Their fortunes for to try,*
> *They shouted up, and they shouted down*
> *John Barleycorn should die*
>
> *They have ploughed, they've sowed, they have harrowed him in*
> *Put clods upon his head*
> *Then these three men made a solemn vow*
> *John Barleycorn was dead.*

The song goes on and the silent street, with its stone cottages that stood when King Charles I was beheaded, watch with dispassionate windows behind which drawn curtains await the dawn. The singers chant on as John Barleycorn is butchered anew and then thrown into a well to rot.

> *They took him out of that same place*
> *And flung him into a pail,*
> *They pour him out of a nutbrown jug*
> *And call him home brewed ale*
>
> *Now the hunter he can't hunt the fox*
> *Or so loudly blow his horn*
> *And the tinker he can't mend kettles and pots*
> *Without John Barleycorn*

The night wears on, and eventually silence falls. The village awaits the cry of the one creature who knows when daylight and dark change. The farmyard cockerel, as the rooster is called hereabouts, signals the dawn, which stands, as Shakespeare put it, "On tiptoe, twixt mountain and sky." From the distance comes the sound of bells.

The Kirtlington Morris are a large group, and all are men. They dress in white as befits the role of these celebrants of spring, and their top hats are bound with ribbons of pink and blue with a fine rosette on the side. Their chests are crossed with wide sashes, or baldrics similarly coloured and decorated. They dance to melodies that were old when Nelson died at Trafalgar. Their dances circle and cross somewhat in the manner of a contra dance, but performed here as if by combatants, opposite against opposite. They stamp and swagger, and swing stave and scarves. They have the snap and drive of flamenco and the aggressive ease of capueira. Their dances thrill the watcher with a sense of otherness, a feeling of being in a cleft between worlds.

All through the day on Saturday, the Morris men traverse the neighbourhood. Once, they fought with staves at the crossroads with other teams, but now the journey is less violent. The final performance of the day is at the great house of Woodstock. The main ritual part of the festival occurs on the third day.

The performers begin with a religious service in the local church; Pope Gregory would have awarded Brownie points in this parish! The procession begins to wind its way through the village. Morris teams from all over the country have come to share this moment. Some have been here all through the three days; others arrive for the final day.

The procession begins in the church and winds out along the street and across the village green. The squire of the Morris accompanies two diminutive figures, the Lord and Lady of the Lamb. This ceremonial is well documented in the past, and is of some antiquity. Here, the lamb is now a small soft toy carried by the young girl, an equivalent of the May Queen. Once, the lamb was a living creature, borne with its legs bound across the shoulders of a shepherd. The lamb was killed later and its head, complete with wool, was baked in a pie over which the villagers competed. The Sacred Head and the Sacrificial Lamb were, of course, old before Christianity came to these islands.

When the procession arrives at its destination, there is a spectacle that is unique in Britain. The Lady stands in the centre of a circle of nine other girls. They dance a ceremonial dance that depicts the shifting seasons and the rhythmic tides of the moon. The tune, called "The Silver Berry," is used only for this dance and is found only in this locality for this dance. The girls salute their Virgin Lady, and the Lord of the Lamb enters the space to lead her back to her place of honour. This is possibly the only female ceremonial dance to occur in such a context. The occurrence of such a dance is again a matter of antiquity.

The dance has recently taken place under a blazing noonday sun. Despite the bright light and the setting of a schoolyard, this is another moment of mystery and age that one can feel beneath the puerile surface. Throughout all of the day the white shirts and dresses cast a deep and dark shadow that, like a penumbra, haloes the moment of striking stick and flames darkly from the white handkerchiefs.

The Kirtlington Lamb Ale is a ceremonial meal—an Agape, as the early church called these ceremonies of love and feasting. The searcher will recognise here many aspects of the Grand Sabbat. Initiates may raise their eyebrows at how this ceremonial, thinly veiled with Christian trappings, can occur in broad daylight in an English village.

To Kill a King

The evening sun, dipping over the hill, silhouettes the ruined castle above the town. The shadow falls over the small slate-roofed cottages and the slumbering church. Deeper darkness lies in the great hollow below the castle where a massive cavern gapes and clear water streams out in a brook to water the town and the stretching valley. High above the valley is Mam Tor, a great carven hill that whispers sleepily to itself like a snoring giant. Such is the setting in which the sacred king is to be slain.

Since early morning he has ridden with his consort—a woman who rides, berobed, beside him; she on a white horse, and he on a black. The beasts sweat under the constant press of a crowd that seems bigger than the population of this tiny Peak District village. Police marshal the throng, their caps and helmets bearing the ubiquitous green spray of oak leaves. Music can be heard in the distance, and the band—instruments carving shards from the sunlight—play the ancient melody. The procession moves from place to place, and at each the king must sup. The dancers, who once carried swathes of greenery, though now that has gone, follow king and consort.

It is in the churchyard that the full impact of this sombre occasion is felt. On the street below the dancers pass—young girls who age, becoming mature women, then older still; wrinkled faces and shaking legs replace the sun-warmed cheeks and the rounded limbs. The procession, moving in space, moves time. The king is concealed beneath a great cage that covers his body, its weight binding him to the horse on which he rides. This cage or garland is covered in flowers and greenery celebrating life and love.

The moment arrives when he is beheaded—and the head is placed on the stone that names the war-dead of this sleepy place. The headless body rides on into the churchyard and fades into the shadows of the church tower and the ancient mouldering tombstones. In the deep shadows there is a movement, and an object, dark and amorphous, moves up the darkening tower. Suddenly, there is a blaze of colour high above the crowded heads as the great cage of blossoms is touched by the sunlight: "The king is dead, long live the king!" There is little more than this, yet somewhere in the corner of one's eye can be seen pale figures. The ceremony of the Castleton Garland is a rite of continuity. It is joyful, and yet there is a sense of sadness too. The dead are about and their loved ones greet them. There is a passage of time that touches the past and draws it and the present into the same place.

In that dark churchyard there is a real sense of the circle of life unbroken and unchanging, the living and dead sharing their identity. For are not the living merely the dead who have not yet passed over? Are not the dead but those yet to be reborn? Thus the king dies each year and is elevated to Godhead, whilst the commoners marvel at the Becoming. The woman who accompanies him is the personification of the Goddess. A man previously played this potent role. This is common in English custom, and recalls the foolish King Pentheus in ancient Greece who would not acknowledge his feminine side and was torn to pieces for this hubris.

The whole of this ceremonial reveals a symbolism that recalls the Major Arcana of the Tarot. The initiate can observe levels of meaning beyond the mundane within the black and white horses, the sacrificed king, and the woman who is Death. Each level unfolds from place to place as the procession travels through the town beneath the blasted tower on the hill above. This is the quietest, yet most moving of the rites that have measured the year, bringing us to the dying sun at autumn.

Carts and Reindeer

The ceremonials that mark the fourth quarter of the year are fewer in these islands, but the seeker should not miss the formidable rush carts of the Pennine towns of Yorkshire and Lancashire. These great spectacles mark the equinox with processions of hundreds of people who throng around the great carts. They are drawn by scores of men whose iron-shod feet strike sparks from the roads over which they drag their ponderous loads. The most famous are those at Saddleworth and Sowerby Bridge.

Viewing these structures, we might recall the procession of Jaganath in India, or the cart of Nerthus described by Tacitus in his *Germania*. Originally, the rushes were strewn on the floors of the churches to provide a warm covering for the cold flag-stone floors and, one supposes, to make rush lights for commemorative or votive purposes.

The carts themselves are structures on which rest pyramids of rushes. These are carefully constructed in a quiet ceremonial in which selected members of the community go out onto the high moors to collect the rushes and bear them home. On the day of the carts, the men assemble and each pair takes ahold of the "stang," a wooden bar that is attached to long ropes. The weights moved are huge, and a set of "brakemen" follow the cart to prevent it running over the men in front.

It is the noise that touches the nerve that tells us of the strange and unworldly. Listening to the sound of the cart approaching is an eerie experience. In the silence is a sound like an approaching train. The men appear heaving and sweating, feet moving in a rhythmic stamp. The feet of the brakemen move at exactly twice the speed of the front team. Mounted high on the heaped rushes is a woman, often a young girl. It is a dangerous and precarious vantage point, and a great honour to ride the cart.

It is difficult to equate the carts with the quiet and restrained English, who have so carefully guarded these hidden ceremonials. Yet even these pale into insignificance when compared with the six creatures that prowl through the small Staffordshire town of Abbots Bromley in early September.

In the mist of autumn, early in the day, a strangely clad group makes their way to the church of St. Nicholas. In the darkness of the sleeping church they take down the six wooden heads that hang on the walls of the nave. Each head is adorned with reindeer antlers, despite the fact that such animals have been extinct in Britain since prehistoric times. The antlers themselves have been dated to around one thousand years old. The village green is coming to life with people young and old. They gather to witness the spectacle as a mock hunt is performed, with dancers bearing a set of horns and crossing and recrossing as if the great reindeer bucks were rutting. The hunter fires a bow whose captive arrow makes a rhythmic snapping sound. A triangle is struck and a man dressed as a woman rattles a collecting box. None of this carries the slightest air of mystery, and yet it stands as one of the most ancient seasonal festivities in the British Isles.

Of all customs, this is the easiest to read. Only a slight shift is necessary to feel the resonance of this rite. The atmosphere is alive with crowding entities, and one feels strangely vulnerable and alone in this friendliest of English towns. There is a sense, perhaps because it occurs on a working day, that this ceremonial is private and for the initiated only. There is a warmth here that does not embrace, a sense of community that the outsider may witness but not fully join.

Late in the evening, the dance begins for the last time, and then moves out of the village centre with its half-timbered pubs. Then the astonishing juxtaposition of ancient and modern leaps forth. The ancient dance in a suburban lot. The streets are modern and the dance is not.

The procession moves, and suddenly the watcher is in an open field, animal men prancing beneath the trees. Without warning, the street returns. There is a sense of standing still and places moving, which is drawn inwards by the dance that twines its serpentine path within the mind as within the street. Finally, back in the village heart the dance unfolds for the last time. It is then that one sees figures that eluded the memory, and the dying light touches the deepest recesses of the heart. Hair stands on necks, and we are for a moment in the cramped cave-dark of our ancestors. We have returned to the heart, and our footprints are those of our ancients.

Of these seasonal rounds, the most mysterious is the most modern, and the least so is ancient. The English are adept at this sleight of mind, cleverly understating the ponderously important whilst attaching great significance to the trivial. Even Shakespeare places some of his best jokes in the weightiest of tragedies. Understanding is available, however.

Founts of Wisdom

Every August, the seaside town of Whitby in Yorkshire is host to a week of music and dance. This week provides the acolyte with opportunities to learn something of the range of magickal activity that abounds in this ancient land.

The streets throng, as in every seaside town in summer, with families burdened with the accroutrements of a summer holiday. Yet in this week there are also figures who carry black cases containing musical instruments. The music can be heard at all hours from pubs and bars, floating above the seagulls' incessant cries. The players are far from religious in their actions, though if we examine their dedication to playing and learning, we discover a mantralike approach to musicking. Watching their faces, we might recall the words of Thomas Mace in 1679 who observed that "Musick [is a] divine magical spell against all diabolical operations in the souls of men." Thus we can stand in the shadows of the bar and watch spells and memories being created before our eyes. The magickal aspects of this activity lie in the uses to which it is put. This is not a concert for the listener; the musick is not sophisticated in that way. The complexity lies in the act of a group who are all aware of the others inside their heads. Watch and learn; there is only one tune because there is only one musickian, and he/she is many.

Beyond, in the street, there is the sound of screaming. There is no one in distress; the sound comes from the throats of ragged figures that leap and gyrate to the sound of another musick. Their faces are black and their hands heft large staves, which they swing against one another with Bacchanalian abandon. Often, men are attired as women, and women as men. The dance is full of stamps and hops and the dancers appear less like men than animals. Such is the ancient and wild Morris against which Puritans railed in earlier times. Witches have burned in earlier times for just this act. They dance back to back, they turn widdershins, they affront the sensibilities of those pious souls who can see what they do. Yet these dances have survived the persecutions whilst the Puritans are gone. If the searcher asks these figures from whence they come—where the dance originated—she will discover fellow travellers on the Path. They are not all such, but a significant number are seekers after the ancient truths.

Finally, an extraordinary aspect of this week-long gathering should be noted. The uninitiated can attend workshops and tutorials that allow the nonmusickian to learn to play, the singer to learn ancient songs, and the would-be dancer to learn the dances of their ancestors. The heart of the festival is available to all, and allows each to listen and learn. Having learned, the individual can carry forth this new knowledge into his or her everyday life—some to bond family together, others to meet new friends, and some to extend their work in the Craft.

The festival is not an occult affair, and one has to look hard to see the fellow seekers. Its significance lies in just this—the apparent ignorance or lack of concern for the hidden depths, which seems to be all around. Yet scratch the surface, start up a conversation with a stranger, and a strange transformation occurs. The average watcher can suddenly and often alarmingly turn out to be an adept. For the seeker after ancient knowledge and the hidden rituals of our ancestors, this is the place to start. Forget the dead stones of Avebury and Stonehenge, which are as the empty beer barrels stacked in the yard of the Plough Inn on Whitby's harbour side. The ancient mysteries live on in the hearts and minds of these island people. Seek here my friend; when the pupil is ready, the teacher will arrive.

Paul Davenport is a folklorist who, not content merely to research his subject, also has a habit of bringing old practices back to life. His researches in the 1970s led to the revival of the Kirtlington Lamb Ale Morris festival and his later work on the lost dance traditions of East Yorkshire resulted in a similar resurrection in the 1990s. Paul edits English Dance & Song, *the quarterly magazine of the English Folk Dance & Song Society, and has published a number of books of tunes and traditional songs. When he was a student, he was drawn to folk dance and song in the late 1960s through his interest in occult matters. Paul's viewpoint reflects that group of folklorists who see the Pagan past as lying at the root of many of our folkloric practices, even if those practices might only be a few years old.*

The Esbats

The minor sabbats, or esbats, revolve around the moon. They are celebrated at the full of the moon, but other stages are also taken into consideration for magickal and thanksgiving purposes throughout the month.

The new moon is a time of beginnings, as one might expect. Any new projects are initiated at this time, along with resolutions to improve oneself, spells and plans concerning love, and health issues—anything, indeed, that one would wish to "wax." The best time to cast new moon spells is during daylight hours.

The crescent moon is a time for movement and increase. Thus the witch focusses on strength, business, and any change she wishes to effect (though of course all stages of the moon are times of change). The times of optimum magick energy when working with a crescent moon are from midmorning to the hour after sundown.

The moon's first quarter is a time for crafting the initial impulsive energy. More detailed plans are made regarding any project in hand, and a stronger, bigger energy is sought to push the witch's intent into fruition. The gods of luck might also be supplicated at this point—Ganesha, for example—usually between midday and midnight. The moon's strongest time of influence is shifting as she waxes.

The gibbous moon indicates that energies and projects have nearly reached the climax of their cycle. All that is needed is continued faith to see them materialise. A final boost of energy may be given to anything begun at the new moon, or the gibbous tides may be employed to give an extra push to anything the witch wishes to bring to pass within the near future.

At the full moon we give thanks to the Lady who has guarded and guided us over the month. Each full moon brings new correspondences both seasonal and astrological (see below). It is a time of declaration of intent, communication, decision, and of course, all things magickal and psychic. It is also a good time for divination and attuning oneself spiritually.

At the time of the disseminating or waning moon, energies run counterclockwise and it is therefore a time of wearing down or out. Thus, it is a perfect time for the removal of anything unwanted in one's life. These workings are best performed at night.

This influence is carried into the moon's last quarter, when the ability to remove unwanted influences hits its peak. Again, these workings are best performed at night.

The balsamic or dark moon is renowned for its potent, potentially negative or destructive energy. This is the time traditionally used for black magick, particularly against enemies or to cause strife (not that any good witch would even dream of such a thing). It can similarly be employed to *stop* strife—obviously a more karmically wholesome version. Spells are best performed between three in the morning and three in the afternoon.

The twelve minor sabbats, or esbats, are those of the twelve or thirteen full moons in the year. In Dianic Wicca, the esbats are more important than the major sabbats, as they celebrate the lunar rather than seasonal cycles. A Dianic coven might meet to celebrate the new moon (Maiden), the full moon (Mother), and the waning (Crone). The dark moon brings the transition from Crone, through Death, to Maiden reborn. Most other covens meet only at the full moon and major sabbats.

However, there are as many interpretations of Wicca and the modern Craft as there are witches, and we all have our special affiliations and techniques. The important thing is awareness of the cosmic tides, the flow of the seasons, and the magickal potential of each day of the year, whether it is officially a sabbat, an esbat, or just a run-of-the-mill Monday.

The sabbats and esbats represent power points at which we plug ourselves in psychically. They arise when the currents are particularly strong. The current is always there, but it is especially easy to access on these special dates.

The esbats are the occasions at which the famous Charge of the Goddess is made. The High Priestess "draws down the moon"; that is, she fills herself with ancient lunar energy with the words below, or words like them. The Charge itself is doubtlessly of recent origin, but the point is that it works.

Listen to the words of the Great Mother, who of old was also called Artemis, Astarte, Athena, Diana, Melusine, Aphrodite, Cerridwen, Dana, Arianrhod, Isis, Brid, and many other names:

Whenever you have need of anything, and better it be when the Moon is full, then shall ye assemble in some secret place and adore the spirit of Me Who am Queen of all Witches. There shall ye assemble, ye who are fain to learn all sorcery, yet have not won its deepest secrets; to these I will teach things that are yet unknown.

And ye shall be free from slavery, and as a sign that ye be really free, ye shall be naked in your rites; and ye shall dance, sing, feast, make music and love, all in My praise. For Mine is the ecstasy of the spirit and Mine is also joy on earth. For My Law is Love unto all beings. For Mine is the secret door that opens upon the land of youth, and Mine is the cup of the wine of Life, and the cauldron of Cerridwen that is the holy grail of immortality. I am the gracious Goddess, who gives the gift of joy unto all hearts.

Upon Earth, I give the knowledge of the spirit eternal; and beyond death I give peace and freedom and reunion with those that have gone before. Nor do I demand aught of sacrifice, for behold, I am the Mother of all things and My Love is poured out upon the earth.

Hear ye the words of the Star Goddess, she in the dust of Whose Feet are the Hosts of Heaven, and whose body encircles the Universe:

I Who am the beauty of the green Earth and the white Moon among the stars and the Mysteries of the waters, and the desire of all hearts, call unto thy soul. Arise and come with Me. For I am the soul of nature who gives life unto the Universe. From Me all things proceed, and Unto Me all things must return; and before my face, beloved of Gods and of men, let thine innermost divine self be enfolded in the rapture of the Infinite.

Let My worship be within the heart that rejoices, for behold, all acts of Love and pleasure are My rituals. And therefore let there be beauty and strength, power and compassion, honour and humility, mirth and reverence within you.

And thou who thinkest to seek for Me, know thy seeking and yearning shall avail thee not, unless thou knowest the Mystery: for if that which thou seekest, thou findest not within, then thou shalt never find it without. For behold, I have been with thee from the beginning, and I am that which is attained at the end of desire.

Though the Charge is a constant for any full moon esbat, each of the celebrations has a very different implication, depending on when it falls in the year. The full moon before a major sabbat brings the energy of that particular current to a climax. Major sabbats are often celebrated on the full moon preceding them.

However, the full moons themselves have implications, depending on their correlation to the zodiac. This both intensifies the qualities (and vices) of the sun sign of that period, and calls into play the zodiacal correspondences of the sign in which the moon is actually full—the opposite to the sun sign. For example, a full moon in August—a Leo full moon—operates in Aquarius. Though many witches would thus call a full moon in August an Aquarian Moon, I have always related it (by title) to the month in which it actually falls. Bearing seasonal, sun, and moon influences in mind, the full minor sabbats, or esbats, may be summed up as follows.

Full Moon in the Sun Sign of Aries

This esbat brings strong links with the Cosmic Masters, or with more evolved souls whose care is directed towards earth and the evolution of humanity. Falling around the time of the spring equinox, it is of course a time of hope and of burgeoning potential. Another cosmic theme is that of resurrection—the living presence of transcended masters amongst us. This obviously fits in with the vernal season—regeneration and life springing from what once seemed dead. Likewise, new life and opportunities are presented to the developing soul. It is a time to concentrate on goodwill towards our fellow beings on the planet (of all races and species), and to plan creatively.

Libra—the sign of balance—is the constellation through which the moon is actually passing at this time. This is reflected in the spring equinox, and it makes dawn and dusk times particularly powerful (at those times, light and darkness exist in equal measure). Energy is becoming externalised at this point of year, and with the Aries fire at hand, a huge boost is given to aspirational energy. This can be tempered by the strong sense of justice emanating from Libra, so that goals are worthy rather than hot-headed decisions. So, carefully planned projects are best planted now. The full moon will enhance prospects for creative and spiritual endeavours particularly. Aries is the seed, Libra provides the nurture (being ruled by Venus), and the moon waters it. If the seed-project is full of inspiration and pure of motive, it is bound to flourish.

Full Moon in the Sun Sign of Taurus

This is a time of inner illumination. Life practises should be scrutinised, the third eye opened, and the cosmic plan perceived. Encompassing the Beltane current, this powerful esbat represents promise. We have the ability to transcend mundane consciousness and aspire towards perfection. With nature as an example, we strive towards the perfect purity of a flower, opening up our petals of perception to the higher purposes of the Cosmic Intelligence. Petty concerns and base instincts will be highlighted, in order that we may overcome them.

Scorpio is the constellation in which the moon is full at this time, which emphasises the mysteries of nature and new life now burgeoning all around. With the influence of the full moon, the atmosphere is at its most magickal. The energies of its opposite (the full moon in sun sign Scorpio, and moon sign Taurus) become accessible, and these include the potent currents of Samhain. Thus, in the presence of flourishing life and huge uprushes of energy both physical and cosmic, we are also aware of the natural cycle that will lead to death in winter.

Until that time, we may dance the dance of life. The emphasis is on joy, fertility, and abundance. This is a good time to give thanks and aim for the stars. The moon, as ever, deepens this influence on the psychic planes. All that we do at this time will be magnified, just as our magick is magnified on the astral plane.

Full Moon in the Sun Sign of Gemini

One of the main issues for those born under the sign of Gemini is conflict between the celestial and the terrestrial aspects of one's identity. When the moon is full in Gemini, these issues are spread to all of humanity. Thus, the opportunity is given to discriminate between the lower self and the higher in a continuation of the last sabbatical theme. This is a time to combat maya (delusion) and to recognise the many levels of being that exist simultaneously to the realm of solids, which is most obvious to us.

Encompassing the energies of the summer solstice on the waxing side, the Gemini esbat again echoes the theme of balance. We are striving, waxing towards identification of the true self and the ensuing spiritual elevation. The waning side of the year represents the removal of that which has become obsolete. Both sides are necessary, and are helpful to us when kept in balance. We cannot operate on this level without our bodies and mind, and there is no point in existing at all without the spirit. At this time of year we receive the opportunity to bring the "twins within" into a harmony that can transform our incarnations.

Sagittarius is the sign through which the moon is travelling at this point. This brings into play the lofty ideals at which the Archer shoots. Combined with the mercurial qualities of Gemini, this makes the full moon an excellent time for projects involving or concerning communication, particularly of spiritual aims and ideas. With Jupiter's expansive qualities available through Sagittarius, the embracing of ideals and philanthropic action become easier.

Full Moon in the Sun Sign of Cancer

This esbat brings opportunities to advance through humanitarian thought and action. The pitfall is an overenhanced sense of personal identity; the key is recognising that one is part of a much larger consciousness. Summer is at its height, but the days are already growing shorter. Our thoughts begin to turn towards Lammas and preparation for the months to follow. The Cancerian full moon is a festival of light both inner and outer. The light shines on us all, uniting us as one. It is an ideal time to perform philanthropic action and to teach.

The other influence is Capricorn, through which the moon is passing at this time. The key note with Capricorn is striving towards higher and higher mountain peaks, labouring in the cause of spiritual ascent. Ambition is highlighted, however, the moon brings her influence into play, so that ambitions of an intuitive, spiritual, and magickal nature are especially propitious at this time. Hard work will pay off in these departments. Saturn rules both Capricorn and boundaries and restrictions, so this esbat is good for encouraging lunar tides to wash away outmoded codes of practise, unwanted habits, and so on.

Full Moon in the Sun Sign of Leo

As one would expect from an esbat relating to the sign of Leo, the theme here is rulership. Organisation is good, but the inflicting of one's will on others is not. Again, the theme of balance is present. This makes sense as we spend our entire incarnations trying to find a balance between personality, mind, body, and spirit; that is one of the reasons we come here in the first place. So each esbat contains a particular energy pertaining to the theme of balance.

Self-expression is key here; individuality is important. At the Leo full moon we may celebrate our unique nature, and that of others—the wonder of being "apart" from the Cancerian crowd. However, we must ensure that our personalities do not become overbearing. They are, after all, simply one aspect of the many qualities that make up an incarnate being. Special talents related to the body are a gift, but they do not go with us onto the next plane (usually, anyway). The spirit, however, does, so we should temper the ego with its eternal influence and lofty perspective. The same goes for the celebration of the personalities of others.

At Lammas we celebrate the sun (metaphorically, the personality/mind), but prepare for the summer's demise. Likewise should we reap the harvests of our individuality in the awareness that it is temporary.

The Aquarian influence is brought to bear on this esbat and its Leonine traits. Humanitarian pursuits are underlined, which find their echo in the generosity and philanthropy associated with Leo. With the Aquarian ability to operate happily outside of social mores (as opposed to the approval-seeking Leo), this esbat represents a time suitable for sticking one's neck out in aid of a good cause. In Tarot terms, it is ideal for themes we would associate with the Hanged Man.

Full Moon in the Sun Sign of Virgo

This esbat encompasses the autumn equinox, and thus brings atavistic themes of shelter-seeking and the danger of materialism. As the God of the Waning Year takes over and the leaves begin to drop from the trees, we consider the theme of death and rebirth. This is a potent theme for both this esbat and that of Libra, which concentrates the powers of Samhain when the Old God really is slain.

This is a good time for the seeker to strive against emotional attachments that are unhelpful, to strive against vanity, superstition, and prejudice. It is a time for nurturing the soul and of going inward again. The Pisces influence brings enhanced psychism and perception—very suitable for this season of natural withdrawal, our analogy for spiritual reabsorption into the Underworld. With Piscean fluidity added to the Virgo equation, it becomes easier to be flexible and to go with the magickal flow.

Full Moon in the Sun Sign of Libra

The themes of Libra are justice and balance, so of course these energies will be heightened during its full moon. We are aware that the seasonal tides are changing, and that we must say goodbye to the abundance of summer and embrace the darkness ahead. Likewise, with the approach of Samhain, we are increasingly aware of the theme of duality; in this case, of the visible world and that which can only be perceived by using the third eye.

What we seek at the time of this esbat is the "centre point" within; the part of ourselves that is still and balanced despite any flux of circumstance. This is what Hindus and Buddhists strive consciously towards, and what meditation and self-discipline can teach us in the West. The fearless self-honesty of the sign of Aries contributes a very positive quality to this search. With the lunar influence active on Aries, it becomes easier than usual to assess one's spiritual progress at this point, to ditch negative attitudes, and to strive towards a purer, more aspirational way of being.

Full Moon in the Sun Sign of Scorpio

Again, the theme of this esbat is illusion—this time, along with the opportunity to fight it. The headstrong energies of the Scorpion become available to humanity, and the poison of its sting may be used to paralyse and destroy maya (deception).

This esbat encompasses the witch's new year, Samhain, the most darkly intense of all the sabbats, so it brings the power of the warrior spirit. We move into winter ready to fight, to fend off the darkness and depression of the long winter months, and the voices of deception that tell us that the summer has gone for good and we may as well curl up and die (obviously this is more relevant to those of us living in cold or temperate climates!). We are offered the opportunity to arise victorious from the battle, just as the God of the Waning Year does at Samhain.

Taurus also affects this esbat, for it is in that constellation that the moon is full at this time. We may harness the energy of this steadfast beast to help us through the long winter months ahead. We can use the scorpion to goad the bull out of ruts we may have become stuck in—and to inject a little magick into our workaday lives.

The combination of Scorpio, Taurus, the moon, and Samhain is incredibly potent. The sensuous nature of Taurus means that intuitions can become solidified or made manifest at this time. The secretive, self-protective nature of Scorpio shields the mysteries revealed by Samhain, making it a good time to perform anonymous magick. Invisibility shields, and so on, will work especially well. The danger is the compulsive, obsessive Scorpio nature being overly influenced by the moon, leading to confusion and delusional behaviour. Magick must be given a reality-check at this time, for glamours are particularly strong.

Full Moon in the Sun Sign of Sagittarius

Embracing the energies of Yule, this full moon evokes themes of sociability, creature comforts, revelry, and other jovialities we also associate with the sign of the Archer. These are all positive attributes, especially in the heart of winter, but the trick is to see beyond the fulfilment of immediate desires to the longer-term and loftier goals for which we are actually placed here.

Thus, the energies become available to the witch and spiritual aspirant to expand perspective and to aim for the most celestial of ideals. The inquisitive, restless nature of Gemini redoubles this influence, particularly in lunar modes such as psychic and spiritual perception. It is possible to be spiritually experimental during this esbat, casting off old habits and seeking to develop in the year to come. Old cycles are celebrated and closed in the final stroke of the spiritual scythe of Samhain.

Full Moon in the Sun Sign of Capricorn

A full moon in the tenth sign of the zodiac concentrates the steady, hard-working qualities of Capricorn and turns them toward humanity in the mode of sacrificial service. In the Western world, inner light must make up for the lack of outer, elevating the spirits of others through humanitarian thought and action.

Cancer is the sign through which the moon is actually passing at this time; the Capricorn influence may be used to steady and discipline a normally moody psyche, or for any other purpose that requires restriction for positive ends. The tenacity of the Cancerian influence contributes to this, and allows one to look at the influence of family and friends in one's development. Capricorn helps the Crustacean leave her shell and bravely face the waters and shore ahead. This is a time for shedding unnecessary defence and trusting in the Universe.

Full Moon in the Sun Sign of Aquarius

In this most New Age of signs, the danger is again of materialism and distraction from spiritual elevation. Still, it becomes possible to drink "the water of life," the spiritual revitaliser carried by the Water Bearer. Imbibing this brings true sobriety; petty concerns seem like drunken distractions, as, indeed, they are.

At the time of this esbat we are given the opportunity to flow with the spiritual and cosmic tides. The Leo influence brings determination and creative intent to the process.

Full Moon in the Sun Sign of Pisces

The emphasis at this time is on teaching and discipleship. As this full moon reaches towards the energies of the spring equinox, the theme of rebirth is also emphasised. We find ourselves emerging from the cosmic tides of Aquarius as full-fledged fish. Now we look upwards for further direction.

This esbat brings us full circle to the Aries esbat, and the influence of higher consciousnesses on our own. With Virgo under the influence of the moon, we can make this a very specific, precise process, rather than a vague Piscean endeavour. It becomes possible to be intellectual as well as intuitive about our spiritual search. We are able to assess our progress over the year, and anything that our Virgo conscience tells us we have missed, we may retry in the year to come.

It is helpful to keep a magickal/spiritual journal throughout the year. Often influences occur that we are unable to interpret at the time, but with the luxury of hindsight, it becomes possible to witness the celestial flow in action on our lives and our reaction to them. Sometimes we may be helplessly influenced (full moons especially have this effect), and at other times we are able to sensibly employ the energies available to us. Either way, it is fascinating to observe one's progress over the years, and as they go by, to deliberately elicit the desired results from each stage of the year. It is a ladder waiting to be scaled.

ten

Myth and Symbolism

As Jung indicated, and as anthropologists such as Joseph Campbell have amply demonstrated, myth is integral to an understanding of the human species. Not only do the ancient stories of practically all cultures boast recognisable archetypes, but they are also mutually compatible. It has been the cause of much speculation that there are characters in Hindu mythology almost identical in nature to those in ancient Greek mythology, for example, and that vast geographical and chronological gulfs have been so easily bridged by parallel mythologies. Some attribute this to human nature, others to the collective unconscious, others still (such as Madame Blavatsky) to the ability of all visionaries to tap into the Akashic Records, astral home of all spiritual information and, indeed, of the "blueprint" of all thoughts and creations.

The importance of a working knowledge of mythology to the witch cannot be overstated. Significantly, most witches are naturally drawn to it from an early age— Egyptian, Greek, and Celtic mythology being especially popular. The symbolism inherent in the tales, the wisdom that emanates from them (particularly evident in Hindu mythology), and the archetypes apparent in the characters provide a priceless insight into mankind, magick, and the gods themselves. There is endless fun to be had with an ever-growing table of correspondences, another vital magickal device.

The scope of comparative mythology is too vast to be broached here, unfortunately, but the interested reader is advised to build up a repertoire of diverse mythologies, and to study the links between them. The *Larousse Encyclopaedia of Mythology* is an excellent place to start, with its summary of the beliefs of many cultures and civilisations, and its introduction by Robert Graves (whose books on Greek mythology are perfect to get the mind whirring). There are many useful sources available, and some of them are listed in the bibliography at the back of this book. It is good to absorb the thoughts of others to pick up ideas for lateral thinking, but nothing beats reading the original myths and then interpreting and connecting them oneself. They will soon take on a personal hue, and a magick that is both ancient and intimately connected with the modern world of the witch.

The witch is always semiotically aware; she has to be. She knows that the Universe is always whispering clues in her ear, for a start; life is a series of symbols waiting to be understood. At particular times of the year, she is especially attuned to sign and symbol (around the major sabbats, for example). She also knows when to stop. Nothing could be more irritating than a person who sees every little thing as representative of a mind-blowing cosmic truth. There is also normality, Malkuth in the Universe, and the cogs that turn the wheel of the Universe. Each cog is significant, but does not require an in-depth examination. The witch's intuition and sense of irony helps her sustain a balanced perspective.

Symbology is, of course, a huge topic, and one prone to subjectivity. A witch will have a wide understanding of universal symbolism, but, like any good Tarot reader, she will also endow certain symbols with her own interpretation and experiences. If she is into Chinese astrology, for example, and a man she is concerned with was born under the sign of the rat (perhaps he has particular feral traits that compound the attribution), she may begin to be aware of rats on television or on the rail track on the way to work as symbolising him. She will then watch the behaviour she encounters with interest; it could be telling her something. It's a simplistic example, but typical of the idea that one is being "signposted" along life's route. Hermes, the magickian and guardian of travellers in ancient Greece, used to direct the lost even when he himself was invisible. The witch, of course, pays special heed to the whispers on the breeze, and, it might be said, goes out of her way to rustle up some wind to deliver them. Her senses are always open, like her mind.

The witch uses symbols as portents, much as did the old Pythias, the priestesses of Apollo (the flight of birds was particularly telling in ancient Greece), or the Druids with their divination by animal entrails. She knows by these when best to weave her magick, and when definitely not to. She interprets her own dreams with discrimination, knowing that at least half (and probably much more) will be junk— mental flotsam and jetsam—and the rest of possible significance.

Some common symbols and their interpretations follow the section on god-forms below. These act as an example; it would require an entire book to cover this subject properly (see bibliography for suggestions). See also chapter 17, "A Witch's Working Tools," for descriptions of the symbolism of specific items used in ritual.

Wiccans see the Divine forces represented in two main forms: the Horned God and the Goddess. However, within these symbols, many others are contained. The Goddess herself has at least three main aspects: Maiden, Mother, and Crone. She is essentially all goddesses, especially those manifest in nature.

All deities have sprung from mankind's longing to connect with the Divine. We have the ancient fertility goddesses with their wide hips and sagging, milk-filled breasts representing the procreative process in nature and in woman as an individual. We have cruel gods whose appeasement was seen as essential to a species struggling against the unpredictable forces of weather. Then, as the vicissitudes of nature became less pressing, there developed sophisticated gods and goddesses, deities of music, cultivation, and of intellectual pursuit.

It may seem absurd to think that somebody living in the British 'burbs or the American Midwest could access an Assyrian or Egyptian godform and have a valid experience. I have toiled over this idea in two of my other books, *Invoke the Goddess* and *Invoke the Gods.* I say "toiled" because there are indeed times when such a connection seems near impossible, but it is in fact no less likely than connecting with one of the more orthodox godforms. It all depends on one's personal spiritual history. However, if a personal rapport exists and the deity (a living astral/spiritual entity) is approached with the appropriate history and symbolism in mind, the results of a simple meditation or ritual can be startling. For example, I find Isis easier to relate to than her Christian equivalent(s), and have extremely powerful experiences with Her—and I do see it as Her—as a result.

Sometimes it takes effort, and sometimes it happens spontaneously. However, a bit of work beforehand and a little ritual or visualisation go a long way in magick. Despite the illusion of separation, these godforms, invested with the spiritual energy of the many who have worshipped them over the aeons, are alive and accessible. Even the cynic will usually admit that the gods and goddesses of yore represent powerful psychological forces. Much magick begins with a psychological response.

I go into much greater detail about the gods and goddesses in the books mentioned above, but no witch's guide would be complete without at least a cursory glance at some of the demigods we are still able to interact with. At the very least, knowledge of mythology is an essential tool to the occultist and witch. It teaches psychic and psychological patterns, and at the most, when the student is ready and the gods are willing, a personal encounter of great significance can occur. Let us look now at some of these ancient godforms and their potential functions in a magickal context.

Gods and Goddesses

Amaterasu

Amaterasu is a sun goddess of Japanese Shinto, and is still worshipped today. Her brother Susano-o is an undisciplined storm god, while Amaterasu is refined. Susano-o excels in crude and inappropriate behaviour, often reminiscent of the Hindu god Siva when caught in one of his frenzies of destruction. Amaterasu represents all that is fitting to any given situation.

For a long time Amaterasu put up with her brother's domineering behaviour, but eventually she tired of his wanton destruction and shut herself away in a sky rock-cave. Just as when Demeter withdrew her bounty from the earth, mortals and even other gods suffered from the lack of Amaterasu's life-giving presence.

Uzume, a shaman goddess, came up with a brilliant trick to restore Amaterasu's light to earth. She placed a mirror outside the sky rock-cave. Then she stood atop a washtub and started a striptease, complete with raucous comments and general humour. The gods and goddesses came to witness it, presumably by fire and candle-light, and began to laugh. They laughed and laughed until Amaterasu in her lonely cave heard them and decided to take a peek at what was entertaining them so much.

A peek was all it took. As soon as Amaterasu moved the rock at her cave entrance, her rays flooded out and caught the mirror. The modest goddess witnessed for the first time her own splendour. Enchanted by herself, she returned to earth.

Amaterasu is a goddess of order and enlightenment. She may be approached for freeing oneself of depression and low self-worth, and to counteract the habit of "hiding your light under a bushel." She is especially good for this because, being a deity of moral rectitude, she will not lead those who give her honour into pointless egoism. She has experienced quite enough of this from Susano-o.

Anubis

Anubis is the Egyptian guide of the dead, as represented by his jackal's head. He leads the lost back home, and knows the secrets of the pyramids—of life after death. He is also, therefore, psychopomp—a guide between worlds. Anubis is particularly associated with the transitions between states or Underworld "chambers." Once the Judgement process is complete, Anubis accompanies the deceased in the Barque of Ra—often with Isis, Thoth, and Khephri—to join the righteous soul with "those who are among the stars which never rest." He is also associated with embalming, funerary prayers, incantations, and the mummification of the "Osiris" (corpse). Indeed, all that is preserving may be attributed to Anubis. He is sometimes depicted holding serpents in his hand, which represent his immunity to their venom, and his ability to turn the sting of death into the preservative of life. He also presides over lustral and purification rites.

Anubis is one of those who presides over the all-important weighing of the heart in the Hall of the Assessors, the judgement day faced by all Egyptians. His particular role was to balance the beam of the scales to ensure an accurate reading. This process determines a soul's future between a quick termination in the waiting jaws of the monster Ammut, or an eternity amongst the stars.

Anubis might be supplicated or invoked for purposes of vigilance, overview, and properties as a guard dog. This role may be both material and spiritual. Rites of passage are also Anubis's domain.

Apollo

Apollo is a sophisticated sun god, the intellectual and civilising luminary of the Greek pantheon. Arts, music, prophecy, medicine, beauty, and youth are amongst his domains. As celestial archer, he shoots his arrows from afar—the disease-cauterising, ignorance-dispelling, and sometimes punishing lasers of his sublime overview.

Twin of Artemis (see below), Apollo displays the same skill, grace, and fierce pride as his lunar sister. Apollo and his sister represent the principles of artful strength. The rudimentary vigour sought in primitive sun gods is replaced in Apollo by the refined, carefully honed strength of the intelligent athlete. This was particularly relevant to the male youth, often represented at its Grecian ideal by the archaic *kouros* statue. Youth and vigour are here brought to perfection. We witness some of the skills represented by Artemis and Apollo every four years at the international sports event named after the mountain on which they dwelled.

Apollo is a god of high moral codes and religious discipline. He presides over initiations (particularly from boyhood into adulthood), lustral rites, and expiations. The healthful rays of his divine person are called upon to cleanse his subjects. Healing is therefore one of his roles, usually by removing the spiritual or psychological cause of the ailment (such as the effect of hubris or the breaking of a taboo).

His faculty of music performs another purifying function by taming the beast with enchanting finesse. In one paean of Pindar, his golden lyre creates a "spell" so effective that it lulls even Ares, the ever-aggressive god of war. Here, Apollo's music symbolises moderation. Apollo epitomises codes of law.

The purposes for which Apollo might be approached, therefore, are cleansing and civilising. Musicianship and sporting skills—particularly those requiring precision work from afar—are also Apollo's concern. Naturally these activities can be seen as an analogy for other situations. We do not have to be *too* literal in our interpretation of such things, though an idea of the nature of the god and his precise function will prevent unwanted consequences.

Artemis

Artemis is the huntress of the Greek pantheon. She chooses to run free with her pack of dogs rather than involve herself in the roles typical of womanhood. She remains in an adolescent state: chaste and headstrong and ever-active in pursuit of her own pleasure. She is therefore a suitable deity for women who wish to remain independent or who prefer the company of other women to that of men. With her traits being both lunar and active, she allows intuitive response and psychism with feet placed firmly on the ground. Thus she is also an appropriate goddess for aspiring witches and Wiccans, particularly teens.

Brahma

Brahma is the four-headed god who, along with Vishnu and Siva, forms the Hindu Trinity. Brahma represents the formative, Vishnu the sustaining, and Siva the destructive aspects of Brahman, the Absolute God. His name meant, originally, "sacred utterance," as the world is believed to have been created through sound. This is why mantras are of such great importance in the Hindu religion; like the Trinity itself, they have the power to create, sustain, and destroy.

In the Upanishads, written around 800 B.C.E., Brahma is *Atman;* that is, both the individual soul and the cosmic self. His power is all-pervasive. He is eternal, like man's spirit, and everything is Brahma, everything sacred. This is pretty much what Brahman signifies today, while Brahma is a major cult deity with a specific personality—a member of the Hindu family pantheon. As Brahma represents the Vedas, so his wife Sarasvati represents their wisdom and practical application. They combine to produce Ultimate Sagacity.

In Hinduism, we find ourselves perpetually surrounded by and cradled in the sacred. This contrasts with the "good" and "bad" dualities of, for example, Christianity. It also makes for a decidedly liberating outlook on life, for nothing is finite and life itself an illusion, thus ridding us of the need to worry. Emotions are transient, and to be under their sway is to be in the grip of maya, or illusion.

Brahma is said to have issued from the golden cosmic egg. This naturally renders him entirely self-created (or self-laid), and allies him with a whole body of mythology concerning such sources of origin. In Hinduism, the most pertinent comparison is with the purple Akashic egg, the symbol of all knowledge past, present, and future. Obviously the golden egg predates this, as all knowledge springs from Brahman. However, both represent pockets of inestimable futurity, and potent capsules of potential. From the golden egg springs creation in its entirety, just like the later Orphic egg of Greek mythology. Other sources locate Brahma's origin as a lotus growing in the navel of Vishnu.

The *Shakti* (female counterpart) of Brahma is Vac (meaning "speech"), later known as Sarasvati. The latter is worshipped for the creative intelligence innate in the holy sound "Om." All humankind originated from the pair, most notably the wisest and strongest of leaders, who are purported to be direct descendants.

Brahma is depicted with four heads, which represent the quarters of the globe. He also peers into each of the four Yugas, or eras, aware of the secrets of each and observing the conduct of his creations throughout. Brahma's four faces are said to have arisen when Vac was dancing around him, and he wished not to miss a single move. It reminds us that Brahma can look in every direction and every dimension simultaneously. There is no level of reality that cannot be observed by him, and states of linear time—past, present, and future—provide no obstacle to his searing insight.

Brahma wears a robe of brilliant white indicative of his celestial purity. He rides on either a peacock or a swan, both birds of resplendence and royalty—literally in the case of the former, spiritually in the case of the swan.

Brahma is clearly one of the most spiritual of the deities, and as such may be meditated upon for spiritual clarity, perspective, and insight.

Brigit

In the sixth century, this goddess of the Irish Celts became famously Christianised—she is now known as Saint Brigit. Her father was a Druid, but he was converted by Saint Patrick. So keen was Brigit to be a bride of Christ rather than of a man that she made her eyeballs pop out to put off her suitors!—certainly a novel technique. Then she set up a convent in County Kildare, and worked in her community of women (Saint Brigit is the patron saint of women).

Brigit was once Dana, mother of the god Ecne, meaning "bardic knowledge." She presides over learning, cultivation, and culture. She represents a process of refinement, rather like Amaterasu. She is also connected with fire (her name means "bright") and illumination, as the eye-removing trick showed. Outer darkness brought inner light to the young seeker. Essentially, she dedicated herself to the Divine, and eschewed the temporary pleasures of this realm. Fires are kept lit in her honour to symbolise spiritual tenacity and healing in a dark world.

Brigit represents flexibility (she survived the shift from Goddess-worship to Christianity in Ireland), and thus self-preservation. She may be appealed to for help in times of threat, especially by women. Inspiration and understanding are also amongst the qualities Brigit can bestow.

Ganesh (Ganesha)

The elephant-headed Hindu god of luck is to be found in many Indian surgeries, and presiding over the doorways of businesses. Ganesh protects portals, removes obstacles, and enhances business. He is an ideal deity to appeal to for luck in a new venture, and for the ability to succeed against the odds. Incense or an offering of flowers always go down well with Hindu deities. Mantric meditation is also a suitable means of connecting with this pot-bellied god.

Hera

Wives whose husbands have a wandering eye can appeal to Hera for aid in keeping him in check. The Grecian deity has certainly had enough practise with her own husband, the thunderous Zeus, king of the gods. However, Hera can be highly malicious towards the innocent women who attract this attention, so it is well to tailor your meditation or visualisation to a more politically correct perspective. Concentrating on remaining strong during times of great provocation is another possible attitude, though Hera is certainly no martyr. She knows, despite her husband's straying, that no one else will replace her as the queen of heaven. She is far too feisty, innovative, and competent to ever be replaced.

Isis

Isis is a supreme goddess of witches, as she presides over the arts magickal. Isis originally gained her power by tricking her uncle Ra, the sun god, into telling her his magickal name. Once she had it, she was able to dominate him. Her name means "throne," and she ruled the hearts of the Egyptian populace for many centuries. She became the moon goddess, and her husband Osiris became the new god of the sun. Their son Horus also performed a solar role as "Horus of the Dawn Horizon."

Isis presided over agriculture, marriage, women's issues, and sorcery. She opens the inner eye, restores the lost soul to life, and specialises in the subtle arts. She presides over the tides of the ocean and its unplumbed depths, which are symbolic of the subconscious. Therefore she also presides over other lunar-influenced systems, such as the menstrual cycle. Isis can give help in dreams, and is best approached at night by moonlight.

Khephri

From the most divine of goddesses we shift our attention to the humble dung beetle! Yet both are of importance in Egyptian mythology. Khephri is the scarab ubiquitous in Egyptian sacred painting and talismanic jewellery. The beetle was believed to be—like Thoth—self-created, as it emerged from dung with no apparent parentage. This may seem an unpleasant and polluting origin to the hygiene-conscious modern mind, but in a hot land wholly dependent on agriculture, the good compost of dung would not be scorned, and the effect of heat would have an overall purifying effect. The emergence of life from waste matter is integral to organic existence, and it indicates positive forces at work. The beetle was lucky, and its apotheosis, Khephri, was a powerfully positive and protective force.

The scarab is son of the sun, Atum, Ra, or Osiris. Khephri often represented the rising sun (thanks to the imaginative analogy mentioned by both Pliny and Plutarch in their writings on Egyptian custom and belief) between the way the scarab beetle rolls a ball of dung before it and the idea of the sun being "pushed" into and along the sky.

Khephri's name means "he who comes into existence," owing to the belief that all scarab beetles were male and the insect's subsequent appearance of self-renewal. The verb *khepher* also means "to believe." This reflects the idea that the beetle, apparently borne of its own matter, could replicate itself through self-belief, an important point in a magickal context.

Khephri is a powerfully positive force because he is born daily, and is thus in a state of almost perpetual purity. His regenerative powers represent those of the hopes of humanity—both for rebirth in the afterlife and for "new leaves" in the present. His essential message is alchemical; dross can be transformed into the gold of potential. The second implication is that it is never too late to begin anew. All that is required is self-belief and will power.

The scarab beetle was one of the most popular icons of Egypt. It was used in the household to bring luck and prosperity, about the person for protection, and in the sarcophagus to ensure a blessed afterlife. The symbol and its god may therefore be approached for regeneration, new beginnings, transformation, health, and protection.

Laksmi

The Hindu goddess of wealth and status can confer much more than just worldly goods. She provides what is necessary for an incarnation's progress: a sense of well-being independent of physical referents. She is associated with light and luck. She brings beauty, supreme carnal pleasure, and righteousness, or "right living" (despite the carnal pleasure, which is much more than just sexual!). She carries with her a flagon of *amrita,* which confers bliss and immortality on those who drink it. It is the life-stuff of the gods (i.e., supreme spiritual insight).

Laksmi is therefore an ideal goddess to approach or include in a working for the provision of what is needed on this plane as a means to progress both materially and spiritually.

The Norns

The Scandinavian and Germanic peoples paid homage to the three Mistresses of Fate, who are practically identical to the Grecian Fates (or Morae). This perhaps betrays a classical influence on their mythology; the three sisters may have been more in number originally. They meted and doled out the destiny of individuals according to their merit, an idea reminiscent of the concept of karma. Even the gods were at the mercy of the celestial spinner, weaver, and cutter.

The Sisters lived by the Yggdrasill tree of Norse mythology. They protected its roots and watered it daily. They kept the Tree of Life alive by bringing new souls into the world, and by creating light and darkness in the lives of mortals. Duality is key to Western and Northern mythologies and religions.

The Norns are the spinners of time. Wyrd, the eldest, represented the past. Verdandi, the middle sister, symbolised the state of being in the present, and Skuld, the youngest and most mischievous, had power over the future. They were approached for advice by the gods themselves, for when evil entered Asgard, the realm of the Divine, even the gods became mortal. They gave Odin information about the fate of his people—his major concern—but refused to speak on his individual destiny.

The Norns or Fates can be meditated on for purposes of divination, but also for accepting the trials and quirks of our individual lives with good humour. Each new obstacle is a challenge; the Norns send conflict in order to encourage their subjects to fight and prove themselves.

Osiris

Osiris was the vegetation/solar god of ancient Egypt. Like Isis, his function was civilising; on attaining the Egyptian throne, one of his first acts was to abolish cannibalism. His story follows the pattern typical of sun gods: he is cut down in his prime by his jealous brother, and in this case set adrift on the Nile. Only the faithfulness of his wife Isis saves him from his demise; she seeks him relentlessly, and eventually reconstitutes him. She cannot quite restore him to his former glory, but she manages to conceive a son by the shattered and deposed deity. This son, Horus, resolves to avenge his father's murder, and fights against his uncle Seth. Isis's magickal ministrations protect the young Horus and perpetuate the honour of her husband. The battle between light and darkness continues, but Osiris is in some part avenged.

Osiris became god of the Underworld. The corpse and soul of the newly dead in ancient Egypt were known as the "Osiris." However, as vegetation god, he represented irrepressible life. No matter what Seth did to thwart him, Osiris remained in evidence. He therefore symbolises justice, transmutation, and life after death (whether this death be literal or not).

Prometheus

It was Prometheus who brought fire to man in Greek myth at the expense of his own liver. As a punishment for his compassionate action, Zeus had him tied to a rock and tortured every night as a vulture picked out the newly grown organ. Like Odin who hanged from the Yggdrasill tree of Norse myth for nine days and nights in order to rejuvenate himself and to bring runes to mankind, Prometheus represents transcendence of immediate circumstances in order to create a worthwhile change. He represents great courage, insight, and compassion. Therefore he is a suitable godform to meditate upon when planning some sort of unconventional or philanthropic action. Prometheus went where his spirit led him, and mankind has benefitted ever since.

Some myths have it that Prometheus was later rescued by Heracles, and inevitably, there is release from all cycles. The point is that Prometheus, despite his great pain, took comfort in the fact that he had irrevocably improved the condition of sorry mortals. He is indeed a cosmic martyr, but an effective one. He may be contemplated prior to drastic action for the good of all, or simply in the cause of one's own progress.

Rhiannon

Rhiannon was an early Celtic fertility goddess. Her name means "great queen," though it may also derive from *Rhian,* meaning "maiden." She was accompanied everywhere by three magical birds. Their voices could "awaken the dead, and lull the living to sleep" for seven years. Like Apollo's lyre (Apollo's sacred number is also seven) that worked its will on unruly gods and mortals, the birds of Rhiannon could be used to enchant; they caused Bran and his company to lose track of time in the Mabinogion, for example.

Rhiannon is associated with the horse goddess Epona, and rides a white mare that could run faster than any other (that is, the moon). She is also associated with white rabbits, another lunar symbol.

Pwyll, lord of Dyfed, caught sight of this scintillating goddess near the gate of the Underworld. He sent his fastest horsemen after her, but her horse was swifter than any other and she easily outstripped them. For three days they pursued her. On the third, Pwyll called to Rhiannon, declaring his love for her. She challenged Pwyll to meet and marry her in a year and a day, that well-known time span used to determine worthy initiates. Pwyll proved true, and won her hand.

Things did not go too well for Rhiannon after that. She gave birth, but the child was stolen from her maids. In fear of reprimand, the careless women smeared Rhiannon's face and bed with dog blood and bones (urgh!) so that she would be blamed for his murder. Their cunning scheme worked and Rhiannon was forced to do penance for a crime she never committed. She sat day and night at the gate of Pwyll's stronghold at Narbeth, told strangers what she was believed to have done, and then offered to carry them on her back into his hall. This continued until the son was found and returned to his parents. He was accordingly named Pryderi, meaning "worry" or "anxiety."

Rhiannon is a goddess whose attributes include the lunar domain (therefore magick and spellcraft), speed, frankness, and endurance. She is wrongly accused but eventually her innocence is proved, so hers might be an appropriate mythos to work with in situations of injustice. She remains steadfast in adversity and carries with her the powerful insight and auspices of the Great Goddess.

Thoth

Like Rhiannon and Isis, Thoth represents the moon. In respect to its colour, he is symbolised by the ibis bird. He is also depicted as a dog-headed baboon, often with a crescent or full moon on his forehead. Sometimes, like Siva and Horus, he is depicted with the moon as his left eye and the sun as his right, which reflects cosmic balance. As a god of wisdom and knowledge, this befits him.

Like Brahma and Sarasvati of the Hindu pantheon, Thoth created the universe through the faculty of sound. This gives us an important clue regarding a dimension of Egyptian magick that is not recorded: the relevance of the rhythm and pitch of the incantations, prayers, and spells that accompanied the amply illustrated Egyptian sacred ritual. It has long been recognised in the science of magick, of which Thoth is a patron, that sound has the power to create and destroy on all levels—physical, etheric, and spiritual. That the ancient Egyptians were aware of this there can be no doubt; and though their religious ceremony was spectacularly visual and involved an immense amount of creative visualisation, we may deduce with confidence that it was also very carefully structured on an aural level, like a Hindu ritual.

Thoth, like Brahma, is associated with the primordial cosmic egg, which underlines this creative faculty. Both gods split one shell (or reality level) to reveal the creative potential of the hidden reality within. This in turn develops its own shell (the flesh of maya, or illusion), and thus the cosmic egg forever retreats within, waiting for a god to extract it and again reveal the new realities of inner consciousness. In the same way, the self-begotten Thoth and Brahma seek to release the innate spiritual consciousness of mankind.

Although Thoth has been extensively linked with the Greek Hermes, in several ways his functions are more akin to those of Apollo. He is intimately associated with the art of prophecy, and like Apollo's Pythias, the priests of Thoth would sit in caves and underground temples delivering answers to the divination-hungry populace. Thoth is variously referred to as the "tongue" of Ra and Ptah, which emphasises his role as divine channel. Sometimes his priests would wear ape masks to reflect Thoth's chimerical connection with the baboon; at other times, an actual ape would provide, through its erratic barking, the answers sought by the supplicant. The servitor of Thoth would then interpret the message.

A natural progression from the spoken sound is the written word. Thoth the scribe is said to have invented hieroglyphs, known as "the words of the gods" and the encapsulation of the essence of Maat, or sacred truth. In other religions it is believed that the word has the power to manifest its import on the physical (and always on the etheric and spiritual) planes. Likewise, the faculty of sound and meaning are a sacred commodity to the ancient Egyptian. To misuse the word would be sacrilege, and a dangerous one at that. We may safely guess that the sacerdotal caste kept its hieroglyphs and incantations well concealed from the bulk of the populace.

Egyptian priests claimed metaphorical use of Thoth's library; one can only imagine the wonders that a primordial magickian's grimoires might contain. Tarot cards, thought in occult lore to have come to Europe from India via Egypt, are often referred to as the "Lost Book of Thoth." The Major Arcana represent stages of initiation, while the four suits of the Minor Arcana signify processes of development, and of control over the elements that constitute the human condition. Thoth presides over all of these stages, from the apparent mundanity of the suit of Pentacles to the most elevated initiation symbolised by the World card. Every footstep, however dull-seeming, is of significance in one's overall progress, and the neophyte and initiate alike will recognise this.

All metaphysical knowledge stems from the source of the divine magickian's wisdom, and the Akashic records are another name for the Library of Thoth. Many European magickal tracts, particularly from mediaeval and Elizabethan times, are attributed to "Hermes Tristmegistus," the "thrice-great Hermes" who devolved from the legend of Thoth via ancient Greece and its association with Hermes. The cap of invisibility worn by his Greek counterpart recalls Thoth, and both might be connected with sleep and illusion, but there seems little else to convincingly connect the great Egyptian master of magick with the Olympian messenger, trickster, and god of thieves.

Thoth is said to have helped Isis perform the resurrection of Osiris by lending his "true" voice to her spells, and to have caused Osiris to become victorious over Seth in the House of Ra. This is a civilising quality, as Seth represents (amongst other things) the cannibalistic urge, while Osiris signifies agriculture, or the growing of crops, and alleviating the necessity to consume human flesh.

As infallible scribe, Thoth was able to record and proclaim the Truth at the celestial tribunal between Seth and Osiris and Horus. He is continually invoked to aid the destruction of foes and situations of enmity.

Isis was tutored in magick by Ra and Thoth, the latter of whom shielded the infant Horus from pestilence and the negative energies of his cruel uncle Seth. Thoth provided antidotes to those diseases that beset Horus, and frequently displayed the traits of a divine apothecary. His lunar associations were reflected through the science of plant and herb use, and the all-important timing of ritual workings. He rescued the eyes of both Ra and Horus, the latter having lost one during a battle with Seth who had shape-shifted into the form of a black pig.

It is Thoth as scribe who records, and thus renders eternal, the verdict passed in the Hall of Assessors. He transfers the cosmic into the tenable, and thus irrevocable. The power of the word, both spoken and written, cannot be overestimated in Egyptian magick (see the section on Brahma above for more on this).

Assessing some of his many qualities, we can see that Thoth would be a suitable godform to invoke for all types of magick, especially written, or any involving sacred alphabets, sigils, and monograms. Chants and aural wavelengths are also his domain. Antidotes to magickal attack may also be sought from the celestial magickian.

Wodan (Wotan, Odin)

Wodan was the warrior god and mythical king of the Angles and Saxons when they invaded Great Britain. He was originally a savage sky god, the lord of the wild hunt who thundered overhead at night leading his troops of frenzied warriors. He therefore became associated with heroic death and the Afterlife. He also evinced a healing capacity.

The Scandinavian version of Wodan, Odin, has a less savage aspect. He reigned over the nine worlds of Yggdrasill, and was also called Allfather, as he ruled over men and gods alike. He was said to speak in intricate, beguiling rhyme, and did not even need to fight his enemies—one look at Odin and they were paralysed. Warriors appealed to Wotan/Odin for success in battle. He was skilled in magickal arts, and brought rune stones to man through self-sacrifice. He hanged on the Yggdrasill tree for nine days and nights "wounded by [his] own spear" and absorbed some of the secrets of the Norns. This was partly in order to regain his own life-source and stop himself from aging. Whilst hanging there, he spotted the runes, reached out for them, and was instantly revitalised by their magickal effect.

From infancy, Odin craved knowledge. His maternal uncle, Mimir, was a water demon whose fountain of wisdom lay close to the roots of Yggdrasill. He allowed Odin to drink from his fountain in exchange for an eye. Odin gladly forfeited part of his terrestrial sense-perception for insight into the Eternal.

Two ravens sat upon Odin's shoulders: Hugin (thought) and Munin (memory). He also possessed an enchanted spear, Gugnir, that could never be broken, and a ring of fertility known as Draupnir. He was main partner to Frigga, earth mother. Though Odin is associated with the After-and-Between life, he represents fruitfulness and fertility in a manner reminiscent of Osiris.

Odin was god of law—social and divine. Amongst his retinue were those famous biker-chick role models, the Valkyries—blonde, buxom goddesses of beer, war, and death. They rode into battle and determined who should die, and were visible only to those chosen. Odin ruled Asgard, the bountiful Valhalla to which warriors slain in battle were dispatched. His wisdom and magick found their union in poetry, over which he presided. He attained the "hydromel" (the mead of inspiration) by stealing it from the giants who had come to own it.

In many ways, Odin is akin to the Egyptian Thoth, with his connection with magickal alphabets, incantations, and wisdom. He resembles the Greek Hermes (or Egyptian Isis) in his capacity for cunning in order to attain what he wants. Like Hermes, he is handsome and wears a wide-brimmed hat. In some dialects, Odin means "wind," and like Hermes he could become the wind—powerful, invisible, and able to fit into any space. However, his martial connections are not echoed in any of the obvious parallel deities. Odin/Woden is quite unique in his ability to bestow ferocity on his subjects in battle, as well as the gifts of philosophy, magick, and poetry. He is a benevolent god who might be appealed to in virtually any situation. Intelligence and versatility are two obvious examples, particularly when these are operating in the face of opposition. A magickal connection with Odin, either personal or in ritual, is a link to the ancient wisdom of a passionate, violent race who nonetheless had the ability to contemplate the sublime, as Odin's finer points represent.

Symbols Ancient and Modern

As I said earlier, the witch is always semiotically aware. She looks for "whispers from the universe" to guide her, employing her intuition to tell when a spade is a symbol of digging deep into the subconscious, or when it is simply a spade. Much of what we see, dream, and experience is without profound significance, at least most of the time. Discrimination is required to select and interpret a "sign."

The following list is a selection of symbols relevant to dream, divination, and skrying, with examples of how they *might* be interpreted. All are based on universal archetypes as explored by Carl Jung and Joseph Campbell, but it is often relevant to add a personal flourish to one's understanding of the clues. After all, it is what they mean to the recipient that is of utmost importance. The symbol itself, however, often has an important history. A dream or experience should be interpreted by beginning with the symbol's original meaning. A combination of research, intuition, and common sense is the surest way to successfully interpret the import of a symbol.

Aisle (in church)—Route between the worlds. Naked in aisle (a common dream for adolescent church choir members such as myself!) means exposure, both to the Divine and to society. Fear of criticism. Self-scrutiny.

Alcohol—Celebration, initiation. The actual beverage is of importance—wine, for example, might represent life-force, while spirits may mean something more pernicious. See "The Witch and Alcohol and Tobacco" in chapter 7.

Alien—The alien has truly invaded our collective conscious and unconscious. Ever since Roswell, we have been pondering extraterrestrial life in a very specific form: either small and green, or small and silver with big slanting eyes. The perception of many gods has been replaced in the West by one god and aliens. The latter are often more intelligent than we, and often have malicious intentions. However, when they appear to the witch in well-aspected visions or dreams, they represent guidance of a distinctly positive nature.

Many occultists have intimate relationships with "extraterrestrials." Aleister Crowley, for example, took dictation from Aiwass, an entity who heralded the aeon of Maat and Horus (the Aquarian Age). The Theosophists founded their society on interactions between their mediums (originally Madame Blavatsky; see her section in chapter 15, "Who Influenced the Witching World?") and astral/causal entities, the Ascended Masters. These, however, were believed to have incarnated on this level at various junctures, and thus are not extraterrestrials strictly speaking, though they exist at present outside our immediate sphere. This is what the vilified populist alien actually represents: interaction with beings from different or higher levels than our own. It is therefore a symbol, at the very least, of progress and change of the individual spirit in conjunction with unfamiliar, usually positive forces.

Alligator/crocodile—Aggression, assertiveness, unseen forces that may pose a threat. Fear of facing the subconscious; fear of the past.

Angel—The symbolism of the angel is vast and is comprehensively covered in other publications, having reached a peak of popularity over the last decade. A more pallatable guide than the alien, an angelic visitation is now accepted as possible by many Jews, Muslims, Christians, and members of nonorthodox religions. Stories are recounted in magazines, such as the American publication *FATE,* of angelic intervention in times of need. The angel is normally an entity with a bright aura, or simply a helpful individual appearing against the odds (and vanishing afterwards), rather than a winged hermaphrodite in a nightie. Angelic experiences go hand-in-hand with the popular near-death experience, also now very much part of our culture.

In an age of orthodox religion versus "scientific proof," the angel has become the mystic medium of the masses. The angel may be found in the city preventing muggings, in suburban homes comforting the bereaved, and at almost any other time and place of significant stress. The angel, if not also the doctrines that first presented him to Western consciousness in the traditional form, has moved with the times. This is, of course, because the angel, the intermediary between the mortal and the eternal, existed long before the written word, and before our capacity to compartmentalise.

Ant—Ants always appear in lines or organised swarms. They represent group industry, self-sacrifice, and hard work. The Roman Army is an example of humans in ant-mode. On an alchemical level, ants represent fire in earth. They are renowned for their group intelligence and ability to bite and cluster. To humans they are often perceived as a pestilence, and thus may also symbolise group minds that are efficiently and determinedly taking over others. They might therefore represent organised oppression if they appear (in dream or vision) in negative aspect, or utilitarian efficiency if neutral or positive. They also represent the incremental effects of a new philosophy or mode of being.

Apple—Apples are the symbols of Avalon, and are intimately connected with Arthurian and Druidic lore. The Druids used to purify their systems prior to ritual by drinking apple juice and eating only apples for several days in advance. Certainly this all-fructose diet gave them clear, compelling visions.

The major saga of the ancient Greeks involved an apple—the golden one that was to be awarded to the goddess of Paris's choice. Athene, Aphrodite, and Hera all competed for the prize, the question being, who was the fairest? Paris, of course, selected the goddess of the greatest physical beauty, Aphrodite, and from this decision sprang the disastrous Trojan Wars.

The obvious Christian influence on the apple as a symbol is that of the Tree of Knowledge in Eden. Genesis demonises the sacred fruit, making it the cause of the downfall of mankind from Paradise to the dualistic earth plane. As a consequence, apples also get bad press in fairytales. The fatal apple obviously proffered by an ugly old witch became, for example, the cause of the temporary death of Snow White. Thus, we find the apple commonly perceived as a symbol of temptation.

One of my personal connotations for apples is bobbing for them at Samhain. It recalls our sisters who were ducked, but with an element of fun now involved, as in the Day of the Dead celebrations. Remembrance does not have to be solemn to be meaningful.

So, apples seem to represent fundamental purity that is then diverted by the "evil" side of our natures—according to major mythological sources, anyway. In many depictions, the Judaic Tree of Life (Ets Chayyim) is represented as an apple tree, and the sephiroth are spherical fruits hanging from every branch. The apple— sweet, versatile, and easy to ferment—appears as a gift of the gods of green lands, but has become a portent of ambivalence and possible downfall. Its mode of operation is instinctual—Paris and Eve both opted as their instinct dictated. They represent the first stages of human development: existence on an almost entirely biological level. The apple is also a simple fruit—half of heaven and half of earth—and represents a basic duality with which we must live on this level.

Attic—The attic usually symbolises the mind; the loftier parts that are accessed every so often and then forgotten. This is due to having to descend back into the material world for practical reasons rather than deliberately abandoning one's aspirations. This is, of course, the opposite of the basement: the subconscious in which things are abandoned, often because the subject dares not face them.

Ball or balloon—As in the Tarot symbolism of the Fool chasing his bubble, balls and balloons symbolise dreams and aspirations.

Barefoot—Religious types have gone discalced for centuries, possibly reflecting an original intention of contact with the Mother Goddess, the earth. Lack of footwear also represents humility and poverty. Witches often work barefoot, and sometimes entirely naked. Clothes and shoes, symptoms of civilisation, can place a psychological barrier between us and the Divine, as in the Eden myth in which Adam and Eve become modest and cover themselves up before God. This is the first sign of the rift between the Creator and the created.

Footwear represents the outside world and its pollution. In Thailand, all shoes are left outside the house for this reason, as in Hindu temples. This helps keep a private and sacred space free from negative external influences. Magickal work is almost always best performed shoeless, weather permitting.

Basement—The basement represents the subconscious; *see* Attic.

Bath—The bath is connected with lustral rites—purification that is spiritual as well as physical. It represents passing from one state to another—a person may be transmuted via water (especially with salt added) from ordinary citizen to magickian. A magickal bath may become a baptism, a rebirth. A clean tub is one of the best places to shed one persona and adopt another, the latter being more relaxed and spiritually awake. Its import in a dream or vision may be that ritual cleansing is required, but it depends on the context.

Beach—The beach is where the land meets the sea; that is, the conscious meets the subconscious, the mundane meets the spiritual. All interpretations can be safely based on these fundamental points!

Bear—The bear was sacred to Artemis in Greek mythology, and is connected to a wealth of correspondences in American Indian folklore. Its essential meanings are strength, cunning, and protection of one's kin and family.

Bee—It would be difficult to dislike this furry, stripy, and endearing insect. As bees sting only when in dire distress and die as a result, they symbolise constructive nonaggression. They create magnificent combs dripping with nature's bounty: wax that lightens our nights, and honey to sweeten our bread. They also represent complete attunement to nature. Their actions help us bridge the gap between the inedible/untenable in the natural world (in this case, pollen) and what is delicious and nourishing to us. Thus bees represent a positive, transformative synthesis. Honey is now being recommended to hay-fever sufferers as immunisation against pollen allergy; again, the bee is intermediary between man and nature!

Because bees work so efficiently and positively together, they represent harmony. Some societies have been founded on the idea of bees: the drones all working together to sustain the queen who will in turn sustain the species. Like ants, they represent efficient group work, but the bee tends to be less martial in implication.

Bird—Every bird has a different connotation; there are too many to list here. Some are mythological connections; for example, the ibis pertains to Thoth and the moon, and thus represents "left-side" issues (femininity, intuition, psychic arts, wisdom, spiritual growth). Another white bird, the dove, has entirely different connotations thanks mainly to the widely known Biblical peace associations. However, one thing that may be said of all flighted birds in visions and dreams is that they represent potential; goals and projects that could raise one from a current position and give a helpful overview, leading possibly to new fields of endeavour. They often represent ideas.

Black birds have darker links (we have all heard of the raven of doom), and because they seem like feathered darkness, they may symbolise the descent (or ascent) of powerful, possibly negative forces. Odin (or Woden), the gigantic Teutonic/Scandinavian magickian, warrior, and bard, had two black ravens as his familiars. However, they represented thought and memory, and were positive in aspect. Isis and Nephthys transformed themselves into kites when looking for Osiris, thus bringing connotations of mourning to this flighted friend. Crows and ravens, however, are generally seen as signs of dark forces, though the ravens at the Tower of London protect it from crumbling by guarding *against* encroaching forces of destruction.

Other birds such as ostriches and flamingos can represent petty malice and the power of pettiness. Another bird famed for lateral connotations is the peacock. Hera of Olympus was partial to this regal bird, as was the Hindu Krishna (*see* Peacocks).

There are many possible interpretations for any symbol; to be sure, the best thing is to research the mythology of the individual species and then attempt a creative interpretation of the vision, dream, or intuition. We are always sent clues at the right time, and analysis might be just the thing to clarify an underlying intuition.

Blindness—This is often a symbol of great insight; many seers are depicted in mythology as blind. Blindness also symbolises the rejection of outside influences (usually to the dismay of those with whom one is intimate), and the rejection of sensible advice to follow the inner calling.

Boat journey—This is a wonderful symbol much employed in mythology, usually to represent the transition from life to death. The boatman Charon of Greek myth who ferried the dead across the Styx to Hades is an obvious example.

Transition is guaranteed when this symbol crops up—under what circumstances depends entirely on the finer details of the vision. Water is symbolic of emotional and psychic conditions, and the boat itself of one's ability to rise above them and allow the will to prevail.

Box—*see* Chest

Bridge—Like the journey across water, the bridge represents transition. However, one is in a position of greater control when on a bridge than when directly on the water. Progress in the scenario is likely to be driven by intellect and reason. Reconciliation and communication are clearly indicated by the symbolism of the bridge.

Butterfly—The butterfly is often regarded as a symbol of the soul, though it is rather too flimsy a representative for my own liking. Butterflies, to me, symbolise rather the transience of youth and beauty, and the shocking frailty of the material condition. However, the analysis depends on the species. There is a world of difference between a cabbage white (a harmless, unmarked insect) and a peacock butterfly. This is largely due to the markings; the semiotics of a vivid, eye-shaped pattern are very powerful, a fact that is echoed by the bright, eye-shaped symbols of many cultures, including Tibetan and ancient Greek. Eyes such as these are used as warnings. The butterfly, with its gentle frailty, employs one of the most alarming psychological modes of self-defence. They therefore represent the power of life-force in the physically weak—hence, perhaps, their associations with the souls of the dead.

In Tarot symbolism, the Fool is sometimes depicted chasing a butterfly rather than a bubble. Of course, the subject of the Fool's fancy represents the virtually untenable, the principle of aspiration. The butterfly/bubble symbolises life as a work of art in which adventures must be had and ideas chased despite the possible pitfalls. Here, the butterfly represents the idea of truth to one's instincts as fleeting, flimsy, and brightly coloured as its own wings.

There is a famous Buddhist saying that the flapping of the wings of a butterfly in one continent can cause a tempest in another. The idea is, of course, that all things are interlinked, and that even apparently minuscule actions can have enormous repercussions. Thus we find butterflies also interlinked with the theme of karma.

A vision, dream, or perception involving a butterfly usually indicates the presence of a subtle but strong spiritual and/or psychological force in one's life. The process of change is clearly indicated—from what is in chrysalis form to its full potential. This is a delicate process that may involve fear as well as joy.

Cat—The cat is a symbol of intuition and guile. Long connected with magick and particularly witchcraft, this favourite of all familiars is respected for its sixth sense and ability to perceive spirits.

In Egyptian mythology, the fiery goddess Sekhmet is a fierce lioness. Here, the savage cunning of the feline species is emphasised. The same traits were recognised in diminutive form in mediaeval moggies. Because of their uncanny slanting glances, their habit of staring intensely into space, and the fact that they were often companions to solitary persons (particularly old ladies), they became associated in orthodox religions with evil, Satanism, and thus, of course, with the witch. True to say, witches have long enjoyed a rapport with this most superb of creatures, but very rarely in anything like the sense of latter-day common perception. Cats were hurled onto pyres in America or drowned in England along with their owners.

Many old buildings reveal cat skeletons trapped between walls. In some cases this may be an unfortunate accident, but as stuffed cats have also been discovered there, it seems more likely that they were used to fend off rodents. Possibly, the sly, territorial spirit of the cat was intended to scare off interlopers, both physical and incorporeal. They are certainly employed by many witches as psychic alarm consoles as well as beloved companions.

A large cat such as a panther or leopard is a popular choice as a totem. In shamanism, this form may be used to prowl the astral in a heightened state of sensitivity. Cats are excellent, subtle, psychic detectives when they are not too busy lying on their backs being adored.

Cemetery—This is where life meets death, and is a positive place for the spiritual and the ascetic. Devotees of Siva and Kali meditate and chant mantras in cemeteries in order to confront death and their fear of it, which is illusory. I used to dream all the time in my teens of graves in our family garden, of houses backing onto cemeteries, and many other versions of dreams symbolising our close, friendly proximity to death. Cemeteries also represent change within one's life—of location, job, and so forth. As with all of these symbols, much more can be interpreted from the specific details of the vision, perception, or dream.

Chest, trove, box—These things symbolise hidden documents, potential wealth, or potential disaster (as in Pandora unleashing the miseries (and hope) on the world). Secrets. Also, the female reproductive organs.

Crocodile—*see* Alligator

Dance—Integration, joy, harmony.

Dolphin—This graceful sea mammal has become a favourite symbol of the New Age. It represents the ability to harmoniously combine the conscious and subconscious—that is, the powers of successful mediumship. I do not mean this in the Gypsy Rosa Lee sense, though psychism is also indicated. Dolphins are cerebral creatures (an association redoubled by their being sacred to Apollo, god of intellect and civilised accomplishment), so the emphasis is on reason and intuition in perfect balance. Dolphins are always a good omen when they appear healthy, especially leaping.

Egg—Of course, an entire thesis could be written on the symbolic significance of the egg alone in world culture and mythology. It appears in many creation myths, unsurprisingly, and on the Hindu astral plane as Akasha, which contains all that has ever been and all that ever could be. The egg signifies fertility, potential, and new beginnings.

Fire—We all know that fire is purifying, literally burning away the outer shell and setting the spirit free. The Greek goddess Demeter attempted to confer immortality on the son of Queen Meteneira by placing the infant in a fire, but the queen, on discovering her at this, panicked and grabbed her baby from the blaze.

Demeter, as a corn goddess, has a natural rapport with the element that is used to transform grain into bread. Fire is transformative; it acts as synthesis between earth and man, and between mankind and immortality. Another representation of this is the phoenix. Symbolic of the human spirit rising from adversity or physical death, the golden firebird is a distillation of all our striving—the spiritual gold that cannot be destroyed, but which is only made stronger through pain. Of course, what seems to us to be pain—the agony of fire—is here revealed as illusion, a concept found also throughout Hinduism and Buddhism.

Another obvious connotation of fire is its light-giving properties. This makes it central to all world religions, in which the flame is used to represent the eternal spirit, and God in this world. In synagogues, a candle is kept ever-burning to symbolise this very principle.

In witchcraft, fire relates to the south, the wand (or sword, depending on one's school of thought), and to active, transformative principles. Many sabbats are fire festivals (Beltane being an obvious example), when fires were lit by the Celts on hilltops and at the centre of the community (one to represent the old season, the other the new). Cattle were driven between them for cleansing and to increase the milk yield. It is likely that the fire also served to symbolically cleanse the cattle.

The Vikings sent their warrior dead out on ships for glorious fire-and-water funerals; in India, bodies smoulder on the banks of the Ganges, similarly transported from one realm to the next. In Parsee fire temples, similar rites are performed. Using fire is not simply a convenient way of preventing the spread of disease and economising on burial space, it is an act of transformation. Through fire, the spirit returns to air and the body to earth.

Dreams of fire often represent crisis, just as the burning Tower in Tarot indicates shock, horror, and sudden release. It is often of disastrous implication in the short term. Emotional overdrive is always indicated by images of fire. It is the element that jolts us into sudden change. In its condensed form, it is the lightning bolt striking apparently at random with devastating consequences.

Fish—At home only in the water, the fish represents spirituality that is not necessarily in its element in one's everyday life. It was adopted by Christians as a symbol of purity, compassion, and the ability to share. It denotes psychic and mystical experience. In shape-shifting myth, the fish nearly always appears, as it is the perfect symbol of fluidity and swiftness.

Flying—A symbolic act intimately connected with the witch, flying usually denotes the ability or will to rise above a problem, or actual astral travel. Spiritual aspirants often leave their bodies in sleep (or meditation if especially deep), a sensation often most easily expressed as flight. Levitation and flying dreams and visions usually occur at particularly potent times in one's incarnation, and denote strong spiritual influences pending, guidance, and big incarnational changes for the better.

Furnace—The hearth, the home. Household gods—that is, values and aspirations instilled in childhood. Creature comforts, essential foundations. Our individual ability to understand and process the outside world.

Horse—The horse symbolises the Goddess, especially if it is white; if it is black, then it symbolises Death. Either way, it indicates poise, balance, and powerful progress. Nowadays the horse often relates to previous incarnations. Also, old allegiances, faithful companion spirits, forging forward with discipline.

Key—Knowledge, understanding. Initiation.

Lamp—Divine light in a dark material world.

Left/left side—Creativity, the Goddess, emotions, the unconventional side of our natures. The left has been demonised in the past, particularly by the Puritan and Victorian Christians, and is associated with uncleanliness and devilry in Islam. It is now being recognised as intimately connected with processes of assimilation and creative ability.

Lightning—Power flowing between the worlds; dramatic emotions; high energy being or about to be earthed—therefore, magickal opportunity if one acts swiftly.

Lion—This regal beast represents the sun, health, intellect, pride, and strength. All, in other words, that is beneficial to our well-being. Lions are paternal and represent social endorsement, wealth, and popularity.

Nudity—Again, a symbol associated with the witch. The lack of clothes represents oneness with nature, lack of social inhibition, and the shedding of neuroses; also, ease with one's body and sexuality. Stewart Farrar, who performed most of his magickal work skyclad, calls skin "the livery of the Goddess."

Owl—Wisdom and age, sometimes conventional, as in Athena's familiar; sometimes unorthodox, such as Lilith's owl form. Either way, the owl represents insight and magickal ability and the strong influence of one's past and the arcane. Perhaps it is most aptly demonstrated in modern literature by the appearance of hundreds of owls on Harry Potter's lawn in the English suburbs, which heralded his spiritual and genetic connection to Hogwarts School of Wizardry!

Peacock—To many, the peacock represents pride. The big-tailed bird with the ugly feet and screech—its finery seems to be all show. However, in Hinduism the peacock is both regal and spiritual. Krishna has peacocks as his special consorts; when he plays his celestial flute, they gather. Their beauty is seen as a tribute to the god.

In Greek myth, peacocks are sacred to Hera. The eyes in their tails seem to mirror the many eyes she must keep on her husband Zeus and his extramarital affairs.

Peacock feathers are seen by many people as unlucky. Some will not travel in the same vehicle as a peacock feather as they represent the evil eye. Very few people are immune to their uncanniness. Perhaps the primal imagery of an eye set on a stalk is too overbearing.

Right/right side—The right represents the intellect and orthodox. It is widely accepted as the side of virtue and of reason.

River—The river is a symbol of connection with the Divine, of spiritual flow, and creativity. "You can never stand in the same river twice." Rivers symbolise change and thereby mortality (*see* Boat journey).

Rose—Purity, virginity, and innocence, particularly if white. Pink: modesty, budding sexuality. Red: love, passion. In all cases, the Venusian influence.

Sea—The most powerful symbol of the subconscious. Again, it depends on the condition of the sea to determine its exact meaning, but it may safely be connected with spirituality and the emotions.

Sewer—Naturally, the sewer is associated with pollutants and evil influences. Usually it represents a need to reassess and cleanse, and often to detoxify. Dreams or visions involving sewers indicate unpleasant influences lurking beneath the surface.

Ship—The ship represents one's ability to "sail on the seas of life," and also enterprise, adventure, and potential gain.

Snake—The ourobouros snake (which swallows its own tail) symbolises eternity. Regular snakes represent healing, guidance, and wisdom. Of course, a vision involving an aggressive snake would signify hidden enemies, slyness, and cunning. Generally though, the serpent is a symbol of fire, regeneration, and male sexuality.

Spider—The spider indicates tireless industry, and the "if at first, you don't succeed . . ." philosophy. They also signify money, luck, and good auspices in travel.

Star—"Every man and every woman is a star," wrote Aiwass via Crowley, referring to the spiritual and magickal luminosity of the individual soul against its backdrop of cosmic blackness. We are patches of coherence in a chaotic universe, or potentially so. The star has long represented guidance from higher sources, and hope in an often bleak-seeming universe. Of course, the individual constellations have their own wealth of significance attached. The solitary star, however, symbolises guiding light during times of adversity.

Swan—Transcendence of mundane concerns. Supreme spirituality. In Hinduism, having reached the perfected state of Samadhi, or release from all earthly ties.

Tidal wave—Another frequent feature of my teenage dreams! The tidal wave represents unstoppable emotion, overwhelming circumstance, and the vastness of the spiritual quest in relation to individual circumstances. It is not necessarily a bad sign, but it certainly denotes inner striving, and the need to remain strong in adverse circumstances.

Tree—Many mythologies feature a Tree of Life, such as Yggdrasill in Norse myth and the Tree of Good and Evil in Biblical myth. They connect the sky with the earth, and symbolise knowledge both terrestrial and divine. Trees in general represent the sacred earth; the species of tree also carries great significance. The Druids and Celts used trees to represent the passage of time, and created a magickal alphabet around their attributes:

Beth (birch)—December 23 to January 20
Luis (rowan)—January 21 to February 17
Nion (ash)—February 18 to March 17
Fearn (alder)—March 18 to April 14
Saille (willow)—April 15 to May 12
Uath (hawthorn)—May 13 to June 9
Duir (oak)—June 10 to July 7
Tinne (holly)—July 8 to August 4
Coll (hazel)—August 5 to September 1
Muin (vine)—September 2 to September 29
Gort (ivy)—September 30 to October 27
Ngetal (reed)—October 28 to November 24
Ruis (elder)—November 25 to December 22

Triangle—Trinities are ubiquitous in religion and mythology. From the Egyptian Isis, Osiris, and Horus and the Hindu Brahma, Siva, and Vishnu to the Christian Father, Son, and Holy Ghost or God, Mary, and Jesus. The triangle reflects this, as well as the triple aspects of the Goddess—Maiden, Mother, and Crone. It also symbolises meditation. With its point upright, it is fire, air, and aspiration. With its point downwards it is earth and water and the channeling of the Divine into material form.

Trove—*see* Chest

Whale—True spiritual ideals surfacing. Large, worthwhile projects. Awe for and potential interaction with the forces beyond the visible. Mediumship and guidance.

Wine—The blood of life, menstrual and internal; our ability to interact with the outside world. Mystical experience, and, in its extreme, delirium. Communion. Friendship, celebration, reward.

eleven

The Chakra System and Auras

Chakras

CHAKRAS ARE THE PSYCHOSPIRITUAL ENERGY centres of the body. The seven major ones run from the tailbone area up the spine to the crown of the skull. They were once unique to Buddhist and Hindu belief and practise, but the system is now widely recognised in "New Age" and magickal practise.

As with all beliefs and practises, there are those who believe the system to be fundamentally flawed. Some adepts believe the chakra system to be outmoded, with little to offer but self-delusion and the possible rupturing of the energy centres with concentrated mental energy. My great-aunt Alice A. Bailey also believed the practise to be too "ancient" to be of use. However, I have used the system successfully for years, and am aware of a great many others who have also benefited from it. As far as I am concerned, it offers an excellent means of visualising and attuning with specific physical, mental, and spiritual functions. At the end of the day, the choice is your own. If you try it and it feels "wrong" to you, desist. If, however, you feel an elevation of energy or increased perception, use it! These systems are tools to help us climb the ladder of consciousness. Sometimes, we will learn by trial and error, and other times, our efforts will result in success.

The Hindu-Buddhist system of chakras was introduced into Western esoteric practise by the Theosophists. C. W. Leadbeater, a key Theosophist at the time of Annie Besant and Krishnamurti's involvement, wrote a book on the system (published by the Theosophical Publishing House). It came into print as early as 1927. The teachings of Helena Blavatsky had paved the way for the introduction of this Eastern meditative system into Western practise. Today, it is so widely employed that "chakra rainbow meditation candles" and so forth are ubiquitous in New Age shops.

The chakras are, essentially, power points in the body. There are thousands of them, each one existing on the etheric, astral, and causal levels. There are seven major chakras, which run from the crown of the head to the tailbone area. To each is assigned a colour and various properties on the physical, emotional (astral), and spiritual (causal) levels. In their original form, these colours vary from those popularly employed today: a spectrum, fading from brilliant white at the crown through purple, blue, green, yellow, and orange to red at the base chakra. It is certainly easier to visualise the colours thus, and I personally like the correspondence with the rainbow, "the bridge between the Worlds."

There are many basic books available on auras and chakras; the unversed reader is advised to seek one out for an invaluable mental map of the psychic bodies. For a more advanced read, Dr. Jonn Mumford's *Chakra and Kundalini Workbook* (Llewellyn, 1995), and Barbara Ann Brennan's *Hands of Light* (Bantam Books, 1987) are recommended. There are also several befuddled texts available on the subject, but it is rare for a book to have absolutely nothing to offer. The problem is exacerbated by the conflict between traditional Hindu-Buddhist symbology and modern interpretations of the chakras. For the sake of clarity I have adhered to the Westernised version here, with its spectrum colours that makes them simple and effective to visualise. However, the arcane symbols and colours are invested with a great deal of energy, and may be of more relevance to some readers. It is good to experiment in both schools of thought to find what is best for you. Trial and error is not such a bad method, so long as one's discrimination is constantly exercised.

The word *chakra* means "wheel" or "discus," and indicates the shape of the energy points known by that name. These discs of coloured light are spiritual and emotional energy centres both to the physical and etheric bodies, and their condition tells much about their owner. They are in some respects the digestive system of the soul, the part of the constitution that takes sustenance from the cosmos and makes it usable to the individual.

As each chakra relates to a separate part of the body and psychospiritual function, its speed, depth of colour, and condition is indicative of physical, emotional, and spiritual health alike. For example, a cardiac complaint will be visible in the heart chakra as a rift or murky colouring at the centre. Manifestations are as various as their subjects, but, as with the visualisations themselves, certain symbols are universal. A broken heart might manifest as savaged auric fibre or bruised or bloody colouring, while unwillingness to love for fear of rejection may be apparent as an armoured area in the chest, or a small tight box.

We see here the root of psychosomatic illness; emotional problems stored in the aura "overlap" with and infect the relevant part of the physical body. The emotional grievance of a broken heart subsequently disrupts the physical health of the body, and can actually bring about a cardiac condition. For those of a sensitive constitution, it is all too easy to literally die of a broken heart (and not just for love; all sorts of disappointments may be responsible). Clearly the maintenance of a healthy astral body, chakras included, is of paramount importance to all-round well-being.

Chakras are also the generators of the aura, the glowing body-sheath of equally telling energy (see below). By maintaining and conditioning the chakras, we influence every aspect of our manifestation and its well-being.

The Seven Major Chakras

There are seven major chakras in the human body (in descending order): the crown, third-eye, throat, heart, solar plexus, intestinal, and root. Each relates to a particular gland: the pineal, pituitary, thyroid and parathyroid, thymus, pancreas, adrenal, and reproductive, respectively (see Figure 1). Each also performs specialised functions, as follows:

Crown (Sahasrara/Pineal)—The crown chakra is located at the centre of the top of the skull. It is a major inlet for *prana,* the universal life-energy. This is the chakra most relevant to spiritual matters, and its Sanskrit title translates as "thousand-petalled," the lotus of perfection in meditative symbolism. It is an indication of the soul's essential purity that its colour is an effulgent white.

Third Eye (Ajna/Pineal/Pituitary)—Located between and slightly above the eyebrows in the bindi position, this is the centre of inner vision, intuition, and innovative ability. Through this chakra we access Akashic information, the contents of the cosmic library, and organised universal subconscious. Its colour is purple.

Throat (Vishuddha/Thyroid)—Connected with communication, spiritual guidance, and the ability to listen (and hear), this is an important "people-skills" chakra. It is sky-blue and located in the middle back of the throat.

Heart (Anahata/Thymus)—This is the green zone in the centre of the sternum. Its position allies it to pulmonary as well as cardiac functions. It is strongly associated with the faculty of hope, and is the emotional centre regarding love-ties, particularly those of an innocent or aspirational nature.

Figure 1—The chakra system

From the heart chakra extend astral/etheric cords that connect the individual karmically and emotionally to relevant people and places over many time-spans. It is consequently possible to use these cords to trace, for example, a soul-bonded partner from a former incarnation, or to employ them as telepathic communication cables.

The properties of this chakra are so extensive (covering literally the entire body) that it becomes clear why the proper functioning of the psychophysical organism requires affection and love, and why the pursuit of it consumes so much of our time on earth.

Solar Plexus (Manipura/Pancreas/Liver)—Seated a few inches below the heart chakra in the soft tissue at the bottom of the rib cage is the yellow solar plexus chakra. This zone is intimately connected with feelings and emotions, and is often the real cause of gastroenteric discomfort in times of nervousness and stress, and of "gut reactions."

Like the heart chakra, the solar plexus is also a centre for telepathic and empathetic communication. The cords that extend from it are representative of one's interaction with other entities; their thickness depends on how frequent the contact has been, and the level of its impact.

Unfortunately, these ties bind us just as tightly to people we hate as to people we love—sometimes more so. There is no better way to build up a lasting psychic rapport with someone than to feel strongly about them, either positively or negatively. Conversely, the best way to avoid being bound up with another is to block them from your mind, thus rendering them irrelevant from the start. There is more to the advice "turn the other cheek" (i.e., fail to react) than straightforward pacifism. Ignorance really is the best form of defense.

Those lines connecting us with people and places of little personal significance are, of course, the thinnest and most difficult to trace.

This centre is also connected with morality issues, worldly ambition, and vice, particularly of the cheap-thrill nature.

Intestinal (Swadhisthana/Adrenal)—This orange spinning disc is connected with our faculty of interpretation, as well as with digestive and endocrinal functions. Body fluids are controlled from this zone, as are charisma and vitality levels. It therefore affects our ability and desire to interact with others. The intestinal chakra lies halfway down the stomach between the belly button and genitals.

Base/Root (Muladhara/Testes or Ovaries)—The red base chakra relates to sexuality, and instinctive feelings such as fear in life-threatening situations. If we have a purely sexual relationship with somebody, that person will be connected to us primarily through this chakra. (Though purely sexual relationships are in fact very rare, being more of a function of incomplexity than our constitutions will normally allow.)

The intestinal and base chakras share the function of sustaining our physical response to sex, though all of the chakras have an influence in one way or another on our proper response to psychosexual stimuli. The immune system and basic survival modes are also controlled by the root energy centre.

Some teachers have warned that concentrating on the chakras burns one out psychically. As mentioned above, I do not personally agree with this, but if you have the slightest doubt about it (your intuition should tell you), do not proceed. The last thing we need is a lot of psychically self-immolated witches!

For those of us who are confident that we will not "rupture" our bodies with our visualisations, there are many meditations one can follow or improvise to connect with the chakras. The point? For me, psychic lucidity, aura-cleansing, and "checking up" on how one is doing in different respects. A psychic overview of the major chakras will tell a great deal about the condition of their owner, as mentioned above.

GENERAL CHAKRA MEDITATION

Sitting comfortably—cross-legged or in lotus posture if you can manage it, and spine straight—inhale and exhale as deeply as is comfortable for as long as you need to get relaxed and psychically attuned.

Start at the base chakra, and visualise a wheel of delicate red light. If anything seems amiss in it, mend it. Ensure that the colour is bright and regular throughout, and proceed.

Next, we have the orange intestinal chakra. Again, check for the clarity and regularity of colour, and if anything seems wrong or unusual, change it.

Continue with this technique through the yellow of the solar plexus, the emerald green of the heart chakra, up through the blue of the throat, the purple of the third eye, and finally into the brilliant white of the crown chakra.

Once you have finished, stand up, stretch, and place your left foot in front of your right, and your left hand under your right at the solar plexus to seal your aura.

Now, assess what you encountered at each major chakra. It might help to write this down. If it was the first time you attempted to cleanse your chakras, you may have discovered many irregularities. Even so, it is worth writing your impressions for future reference. Recurrent impressions may indicate more permanent issues such as physical problems or unresolved emotional issues. If, for example, every time you reach your solar plexus and heart chakras you discover that they are leaking or otherwise compromised, you can begin to look at possible causes—either relating to physical issues, such as diet and the health of your heart, or to emotional issues concerning past relationships and the damage they may still be doing you. As with magick, always look at the symbolism of what you see. It is amazing what your subconscious can tell you when you are willing to see the signs.

Regular cleaning of the chakras keeps the aura well oiled. They are essentially the engine that generates the body-sheaths of which the physical is the centre. Ritual salt baths with this kind of meditation included are of immense value to the practising witch.

Auras

The aura is the electromagnetic and etheric body-sheath visible to psychics. It manifests in many ways; moods are reflected there, as well as spiritual (causal) and physical aspects. Physical, emotional, and spiritual health and history are all indicated by the aura.

It is not always easy to discriminate between the three. For example, I have witnessed extremely black auras a couple of times, but in both cases they belonged to fundamentally sound people who were simply in terrible moods. Conversely, I have seen a person addicted to fundamentally bad behaviour (sexual and mental abuse of others) display a shiny golden aura. This is because the person concerned knew how to use magick for his own personal ends, including how to present himself to others who were psychically proficient. He had many friends who were witches and mediums who had no idea of what he was capable (and enacted every day) because he knew how to dissimulate. So, the aura is not always to be trusted on the surface.

Other things that can be reflected in the aura include past incarnations and past emotional traumas. Sometimes people can become "possessed" by their previous personalities. In extreme cases, these previous personalities perpetuate themselves in the auric field, living off particular connections with the past. For example, I had a friend who was (still is, actually) a prodigious classics student and university teacher. He once told me that he thought in Latin and Attic Greek, and had done so since he encountered the languages at boarding school. He was not a spiritual person, but he had a clear recollection of one other life in Rome. Despite his disbelief in reincarnation theories, he admitted that, on going to Italy years ago, he had known exactly how to get to what had once been his home. He had been a Roman senator. This man's previous personality existed in his aura so clearly that I often saw it slip across his face and obsess him completely—hence, no doubt, the thinking in Latin. Though blessed with a kindly personality in this incarnation (no doubt in order to make amends for past atrocities), when the senator took over, he became despotic. Clearly he had come into this incarnation (in which he suffered horribly from health problems) to make amends for the many terrible acts of this powerful incarnation.

However, he was a frail soul with a very strong mental body. I am sorry to say that, despite my efforts to help him detach from this previous malicious (though outwardly liberal) personality, it was too strongly attached to him aurically to be severed. He was so preoccupied with the past, and so in denial of the present, that he allowed his previous personality to return continually, wooing it with the language and references most familiar and dear to it. Bad karma caused by extreme behaviour in the past had lumbered him with problems almost impossible to conquer. (Not that I ever told him this, of course. As far as he was concerned, I believed him to have been as respectable in that incarnation as he is in this.) He could have overcome his problems with extreme effort and remorse, but he allowed himself the luxury of arrogance, and his previous personality thrived off it.

This is a rare case, however. Usually auras are rather more straightforward, but often they offer us clues in symbolic rather than empirical language. Strange shapes might be visible in the aura, and colour codes offer a wealth of interpretation. Allowing one's intuition to flow is essential whilst aura-reading; there are no set rules as to what means what, although there are guidelines. Here are some of them:

Auric Colour

Red—Forceful personality; possessive, emotional, proud, materialistic, creative, a good leader. Also, strong sexuality. Physically, often relates to pain. Red pain is healable, though it will get worse before it gets better.

Orange—Basic instincts, faculty of absorption and interaction.

Yellow—*Bright:* Spiritual health, physical health, optimism, wealth.
   Dull: Tired-out, conventional ideas. Need for rejuvenation.

Green—*Emerald:* Love, fertility, creativity, abundance.
   Murky: Illness, overabundance (as of cancerous cells), effects of hedonism.

Blue—*Bright:* Power of mind; psychic power.
   Dark: Old spiritual habits, established patterns.

Indigo—Astral activity of a positive (probably lunar) nature; intuition, spiritual health.

Purple—Religious inclinations, love of ritual, deep thinking, spiritualistic, "heaviness" of personality.

Pink—Joy, love, excitement, frivolity.

Spectrum—Health on all levels, gentleness, and nurturing. Pregnant women often have rainbow auras.

Auric Shape

Angular—Often indicates a being from another sphere. One aura I encountered looked like a molecular structure with the person in the middle—rather similar to a space suit (which, indeed, it was).

Animal—Could be the totem of the person concerned, or a lifestyle and attitude he or she is unconsciously projecting. Shamanic personalities will shape-shift aurically almost as they speak.

Atoms dissipating out of it—Lack of self-discipline, determination to let others know how one is feeling.

Boxed—Oppression. Fear. Habit.

Ever-changing—Those who experience very strong but changeable emotions will appear as auric chameleons. Those with a particularly strong ability to visualise will also project images of their thoughts into their aura. This is the first step of telepathy. For example, if they are thinking about being thrown into a lake during a thunderstorm, auric streaks and flashes might ensue. It does not mean that the subject is undergoing stress or danger, but simply that she is recollecting it.

Flaming—Magickally active, astute, experiencing a significant time incarnationally.

Open—As one would expect—receptive, inwardly confident.

Radiant—This indicates either a very pure, happy person, or an occult adept. As I mentioned earlier, it is possible to change the appearance of the aura so that even those with "second sight" might be fooled sometimes. These saintly auras, however, are usually genuine. The Christian halo is the descendant of the radiant aura.

Spikey—Anger. Defensiveness.

Swirling—Stirred-up emotions, powerful inner activity.

Auric Texture

Auric textures also vary. We all know the phrase "He was slimy," or "He's really smooth!" Neither make sense literally, except when we look at the aura.

Dry—When the life-force is running low, or the person is overly intellectual, the aura becomes parched and brittle. It indicates a soul mummified by the brain with little hope of progressing in this incarnation. This is often due to some early emotional disappointment or severe strain. Miss Havisham in Dickens's *Great Expectations* is an example of somebody who would have a dehydrated aura.

Fine, radiant—Pleasant people will usually have rays of light emanating from them—some gentle, some on full blaze. The texture is therefore fine and horizontal to the upright body.

Mealy, buttery—Those who are fundamentally generous of nature will have buttery auras. These are the maternal or paternal spirits amongst us, full of goodwill and love. They are the providers of spiritual, emotional, and often material sustenance.

Slimy—Some auras really *are* slimy; they are covered in astral gunk, and self-loathing is a major cause. Those who make the flesh crawl are usually mean-spirited individuals obsessed either by money, power, or sex, and the fundamental reason is excessive lack of self-confidence. Aurically, these people look like bog monsters.

There are many other variants on the aura; each one is unique. The easiest way to interpret them is to allow your mind to come up with natural connections. As with all skrying, letting thoughts flow and listening to intuitions will work wonders.

Not everybody *sees* auras as such—sometimes perceptions come more as a general feeling. Whether we see it or not, however, the aura is an electromagnetic fact, and one that is capable of telling us much about the soul at its centre.

Trees, plants, and all living creatures also have auras. So do places, countries, and planets. Objects owned by a person for a long time will absorb and emanate the aura of their owner. Tarot cards, diaries, and clothes are particular examples. Jewellery and watches are also well known for eliciting affirmative results in psychometric experiments. This is because they often have sentimental value, and are held in the mind and close to the body for long periods of time. They can thus become incorporated into the aura. The fewer possessions the individual has, the more likely this is to occur. There is certainly more value in one cherished object than in a thousand untouched diamonds in a jewellry case—psychically speaking, at least!

Cleansing the Aura

An excellent place to clean the aura is in a candlelit bath. The combination of water and fire stimulates growth and helps remove stale energies and old issues. A handful of charged salt in the water works wonders too. Envisage the water glowing white and dissolving any negative "black" substances attached to the aura.

A sachet of sage and thyme tied under the hot tap so that the water runs through it is also of great benefit to the aura.

Salt is a good addition to any bath. When held towards the east and imbued with cleansing energy (through conscious request and visualisation), it will be of great benefit to mind and aura alike. Hospitals often recommend salt baths after operations, as the salt both purifies and is a natural antiseptic. More unorthodox belief recognises that it also helps "dissolve" the memory of physical trauma, is reminiscent of the womb (so one is reminded of preincarnational issues), and that it disinfects the astral body. Salt that has been blessed or concentrated on is a strong enemy to anything inimical to its subject. It grounds (being an element of earth), cleanses, protects, and easily conducts.

Splashing the body with salt water has a similar effect (hence its use at church entrances, and at baptisms and exorcisms). A few drops of charged water will clear the aura if thorough cleansing is visualised in conjunction with the actions.

Visualisation is the key, as with much magick. This needs, however, to be backed up with inner conviction. What is imagined, is—in ritual circumstances, at least. To thoroughly cleanse the aura, or to perform any act of will effectively, cast a Circle first. Whatever is "imagined" in the Circle becomes certain on the astral planes. This "solid" energy can then be accessed from the material levels, and brought to pass.

Habits are often aura-defiling. Smoking when one wishes to give up, drinking to excess once too often, or dwelling on the past are all pollutants. The worst, however, are negative emotions such as jealousy and malice. These psychological habits and impulses cause the aura to look revolting—so the prettiest of girls will appear very ugly indeed to psychic vision. Oscar Wilde's *The Picture of Dorian Gray* describes a similar scenario, in which the main character is aesthetically divine, but, as his ever-deteriorating portrait depicts, spiritually and morally corrupt. He is soon so ugly that he cannot bear to look upon his own portrait, his spiritual and auric reflection. So it is with those who fool themselves that their bad behaviour will have no effect. Because auras and the spirit are invisible to most, it is often assumed that they do not exist—how wrong! The shock received by those who make no moral and spiritual effort, and who do what they know to be harmful to themselves and to others, is enormous upon death, when physical circumstances disappear. At that time, the true self emerges from within the walls of flesh, and there is no disguising it. The aura is the short-term prognosis.

The aura, which overlaps with the body, has a huge effect on the physical vehicle too. This is how spiritual and emotional issues affect the body, a fact recognised by all metaphysicists (see chapter 17, "A Witch's Working Tools"). It is best cleaned through the elements. Air, fire, water, and earth (salt) all have very positive effects. Their synthesis comes in bright sunlight in a natural surround, with a stream or other body of water. This apparently mundane (if delightful) combination is both spiritually and aurically refreshing, so long as one is open to its influences.

The most important thing to remember about the aura is that "As we think, so we Are."

twelve

The Witch and Qabalah

QABALAH WAS INTRODUCED INTO MODERN witchcraft by Alex Sanders. For examples of how each sephirah might be used in magick, see the very end of this section.

The form used in the Craft comes from the High Magick of the Western Mystery Tradition, but its roots are mediaeval and Judaic. I tend to spell this genre *Qabalah,* and the purely Jewish version *Kabbalah.* In both cases, it is a system of integration—inner with outer, above with below. The Qabalistic glyph contains all that has ever been created, both positive and negative. The witch's Qabalah is hypereclectic, and many of its key references come from general occultism rather than Jewish lore. Crowley gives a summary of these in his classic reference book, 777. Dion Fortune and Israel Regardie also produced invaluable works on the subject, partly based on the ideas of Samuel MacGregor Mathers and Eliphas Levi (see chapter 15, "Who Influenced the Witching World?").

The symbol of the Tree of Life (see Figure 2) is an astral "map." It describes ten main states of being, the sephiroth, and twenty-two states of becoming, the paths. The whole of Creation is represented, including the "negative" or "Qlipothic" side, and the premanifest. To each sephirah is ascribed a specific relationship between Creator and Created, along with its archetypal deity aspect (for example, merciful fathergod for Chesed, or mother of binding and synthesis in Binah), an archangel, and a fleet of heavenly bodies (a choir of angels). There are various ways to approach these entities, usually involving telesmatic imagery-building and ritual evocations.

Each sephirah on the Tree of Life represents a stage in existence between the Creative Intelligence and the intelligent creature. The unthinking too, and all else, have their place in the system. Even other religions are encompassed in the Qabalah

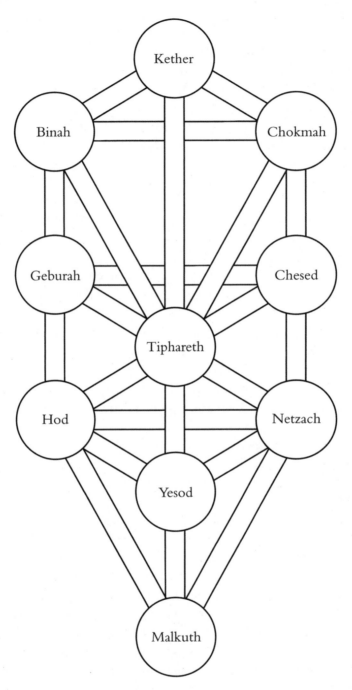

Figure 2—Tree of Life

of the Western Mystery Tradition; for example, to Tiphareth, the solar sphere, are ascribed both Jesus as Christ, and Krishna.

The Tree of Life is based around three pillars, on which the sephiroth are placed. The right pillar, comprising Binah, Geburah, and Hod, represents form, severity (because form is restrictive), and the *ida* currents of Hinduism. It is construed of as feminine, though in fact it is balanced.

The left pillar, comprising Chokmah, Chesed, and Netzach, symbolises force, mercy, and the *pingala* currents of Hinduism. It is construed of as masculine.

The middle pillar is the Pillar of Mildness, or Equilibrium. Its four visible sephiroth—Kether, Tiphareth, Yesod, and Malkuth—represent a balance between the polarities of female/male, form/force, and severity/mercy. Both male and female traits are represented, and each sephirah contains an element of the other nine. Power descends from Ain, Ain Soph, and Ain Soph Aur (the boundlessness beyond Kether) into Kether (the "Crown of Creation"). Then it spills into Chokmah, then Binah, and so on down the Tree in what is known as the "Lightning Flash." It finishes in Malkuth, whose physical expression is the earth plane. Here, it is "received," just as originally the Word of God was received by Metatron, Angel of the Presence. He then passed it on to Moses, who passed it on to man by word of mouth, or so the traditional story goes.

The witch's Qabalah, or the Qabalah of the Western Mystery Tradition, is an ever-developing network of consciousness with new references continually added as Creation itself progresses. It is a tool of great value both for meditation and for classification. Just as everything is visibly attached in the glyph, everything is psychically adjoined. The Qabalah is an incredibly helpful tool of classification.

There are four "layers" in Qabalistic cosmology, each representing a different aspect of reality. All of the sephiroth exist simultaneously on all of these levels.

The one in which we physically abide is that of Assiah, the world of physicality and action. Here, symbols are perceived in material form; the spiritual luminary Yesod, for example, is the moon, while Malkuth relates to Earth. The occult symbol of Assiah is the bull and its Tarot suit is, of course, Pentacles. It relates in the system I use to the four Tarot cards of the Page.

Yetzirah, the next step up, represents the formative stage in creation. Its sephiroth are those that form the "inner body" of the Qabalah: Yesod, Hod, Netzach, Tiphareth, Geburah, and Chesed. The orders of angels, deities, and godforms belong to this level. Its symbol is cerebral man, and its Tarot suit is the intellectual Swords. In the system I use, the four Knights belong here.

The creative, receptive level is known as Briah, and to it are ascribed the archangels. The sephiroth encompassed in this level are Binah and Chokmah. Its symbol is the eagle, its Tarot suit is Cups, and the four Queens correspond to it.

Finally, the layer of Atziluth represents the highest conceivable proximity to God. As far as the Tree goes, it is composed of Kether (some ascribe Kether and Chokmah). Its attributes are the archetypal world, or world of emanations, the lion symbol, and the suit of Wands. The God-names manifest through this level, and its Tarot attribution in the system I prefer is the four Kings.

These four worlds represent the "thought" of God coming into being, descending through the planes from the very refined and conceptual to the solid and physical. Of course it is in the world of Assiah, of physical fact and action, that we abide, but the whole nature of Qabalah is aspiring towards Kether in Atziluth, or ultimate Godhead. A key point to this aspiration is that the latter may be found at the heart of the apparently mundane. Malkuth is not only as important as Kether, but it also reflects and contains it. Likewise are all other sephiroth interlinked, composed to a greater or a lesser degree of one another.

Each sephirah exists on all four of these levels, hence the four different colours (popularly referred to as "the flashing colours") ascribed to each. These symbolise the impulse of creation from its archetypal expression in Atziluth (at which point it is very pure thought), through Briah (where the concept is created), into Yetzirah (where the concept grows and becomes evident), and finally through to Assiah (where it manifests in its fully tangible state). Each deity force is attributed to one of the four different "worlds" of the Tree.

Between the sephiroth are the paths. These are processes, or states of becoming; the sephiroth themselves are states of being. There are twenty-two of these processes, each ascribed (within the Western Mystery Tradition) with a particular Tarot card, a planetary attribution, a Hebrew letter, and a title. We will look into the Tarot in the next chapter. It is essential to the witch, Qabalistically inclined or not, to have a good working knowledge of the seventy-eight cards and their meanings.

The Qabalah may be visualised as a whole as ten symmetrically positioned coloured spheres, or sephiroth, each glowing with its own particular properties. All of the sephiroth exist on all of these four levels. They are arranged into three columns, the middle of which is the longest and lowest. The columns to the left and right each consist of three regularly placed spheres. As you approach each sephirah in meditation, you will feel yourself being drawn into and assimilated by the position and colour of that sphere, which will quickly lead you to its inner properties.

The following visualisation is featured in the introduction of my own book on the subject, *Magic of Qabalah* (Llewellyn, 2001). I have included it here as many people have told me they find it useful. For more detailed visualisations concerning the sephiroth and paths, please see the aforementioned book.

VISUALISING THE QABALAH AS A WHOLE

To help establish a "map" for your meditations, envisage yourself surrounded by a tentlike sphere of four colours—as if you were inside a giant juggling ball or beach ball—its segments yellow, green, dark red, and blue, respectively.

See yourself standing at the centre of this construction. Their colours unite at the top and bottom of the sphere, at the points above your head and beneath your feet.

Facing you is the yellow sector, representing air. To your right is the red of fire. Behind you is the cool blue of water. To your left, the verdure of green earth.

Really try to invest your sphere with the elements—be aware of the fresh, redolent earth; the sighing, lapping ocean; the crackling brilliance of fire; the relief and freedom of air.

With the wind comes the spirit world; all the beings who abide with us, yet are rarely perceived by us, nor us by them. Some of these are elementals, others are restless spirits caught up in their personal woes, long obsolete in the worlds from which they came, but still as fresh as yesterday's dreams to them. Still others are intelligent entities on missions between planes. Some, of course, are good, some neutral, and others malign. Obviously, any occult work increases one's sensitivity to the astral/spirit realms, and psychic self-protection is a good anti-spook device. Entities known as Qlipoth abide in the sephiroth; they are the product of imbalance in the spheres. Certain areas have become populated with Qlipoth, whose sustenance is this pernicious (because imbalanced) energy. These prana-draining mosquitoes of the spirit realms can be kept at bay using the simple techniques described above.

Inside this tent of four colours exists all material things, and everything that you connect with your life as an individual personality—especially those that are obvious. The tent, as you have no doubt gathered, is symbolic of the first station of the Qabalah: Malkuth, the Kingdom.

So, to begin your mental map of the Tree, focus on the properties of the earth kingdom of Malkuth:

1. See your abode (you do not have to own it), your possessions, your work.

2. Think of all the practical skills you possess, and those you would like to develop.

3. Consider those companions with whom you have the most dynamic and enjoyable conversations.

4. Feel your animal presence in this realm. The stamping of feet usually facilitates this.

5. Prepare to explore, knowing that you are strong on this most fundamental of levels.

When these thoughts are established and you feel ready for anything, you are ready to progress—or regress—to Yesod.

This purple-silver orb hangs directly above you, like a strange moon whose tides you know on a semiconscious level, but whose laws elude you. It reminds you of half-remembered dreams that slip away under scrutiny; you know you will have to induce a semiconscious state to tune in to the reality of Yesod.

1. Lie down flat on your back on your bed, arms to your sides and your eyes shut, and focus on the inside of the middle of your forehead at the top of the bridge of the nose. Allow whatever thoughts and images you have to float through your mind and drift away.

2. Now, think back through your life to those events and personalities that have affected you. Try to maintain an objectivity whilst doing this; view them as you might someone else's televised biography. Try to observe any patterns or astral networks you may perceive cropping up.

3. See your soul in silver ascending the line that connects Malkuth to Yesod. As you ascend, feel the increased lightness of being—a shedding of burdens, a mental holiday. Here, all is less personal and more essential. It is by inner nature that all is defined on this plane.

The beautiful and the strange process before you on this level, and many seem familiar, like the forgotten paintings of childhood. Others give you the feeling of dreamy déjà-vu; did you dream them only yesterday?

Don't fall asleep! There are further tasks to perform.

Now you must fly to the strong, orange sphere of Hod, which hangs above you to your left.

1. Still lying on your back, concentrate on travelling up and to your left.

    Even on thinking this, the subtle forms of Yesod disperse and seem unreal again; in Hod you know there lies a defining strength that emphasises rather than romanticises the inner nature of things.

2. Take time to perceive the qualities of Hod, a very different genre to those of Yesod.

    This is the realm of mental energy, the seat of empirical learning, patience, and effort. The geniuses and thaumaturgists of our realm are strongly affiliated with Hod.

3. Note how, even on so brief a visit, you feel a similar respect to that which you might if, visiting the British Library, you suddenly discovered that all the Nobel Prize winners were gathered within. The atmosphere is distinctly intellectual, but do not be intimidated by your own shortcomings in that respect (or overly proud of your own achievements!). Any entity worth its protoplasm knows that intellect is a component often latent in the human condition, and that emotional intelligence is its equally worthy counterpart. Many to whom Hod is a natural abode have lessons to learn in the more emotional and often practical spheres.

    Here, ideas manifest in the abstract, and civilisation progresses to the ticking of the mental clock.

4. Feel yourself assimilating these qualities along with the deep burnt-orange of their vibration.

As Charles Seymour, a member of Dion Fortune's Society of the Inner Light, says in his magickal diaries *Dancers to the Gods* (edited by Alan Richardson), "Every day the Magician should ask him or herself—is my brow wet with mental sweat?" For it is the vice of the magickian to spend time creating fancies rather than on progression, and it is to defining Hod that we can refer when this temptation is particularly strong.

After the effort you feel in the atmosphere of Hod, you will be pleased to take a break in the verdant greenery of Netzach. There is a strong relationship between this sphere and our own Malkuth—it is faery country. Those who are attuned to nature will be very at home here, and the urban Pagan will find in it a refuge cheaper and more accessible than a trip to the countryside.

1. Reach Netzach by travelling right in a straight line. If you prefer, you can also touch down on purple Yesod, slightly below and to the centre of your line, before ascending to brilliant green Netzach. You may undergo some discomfort, like the change in pressure when diving underwater, but do not be alarmed. Remember your strong protective armour.

2. Relaxed and still supine, explore the sephirah.

   In the earthy, elevated natural world of ultragreen Netzach, refreshment pours forth from the ground and is innate in the vital elements that celebrate themselves here. To a true Taurean this is home; its ingredients are both nurturing and natural, it is steady yet creative.

3. Consider the most sublime aspects of your love life, past, present, and future. Allow the ensuing feelings of pleasure to infiltrate your heart and soul.

   This beautiful faery realm is the starting place of many a true romance; its qualities are rapturous, enchanting. Opposite a sun of white-hot radiance, aureoled by rainbow hues, the violet moon of Yesod hangs in the sky. Energy is everywhere; you can feel the force of every object you encounter pushing out, externalising.

   Perspective here is not what we are accustomed to. Angles follow strange rules of elfin geometry and many objects seem out of kilter and likely to slip through dimensions at any moment. A large seven-pointed star hangs in the blue-purple sky, along with other celestial bodies of deep buttery-yellow and startling silver. Here is the perfect place to recline beneath a tree, like Omar Khayyam, and write or dream about the lifting of veils, the dissolving of maya, the emotional truths inherent in the religious urge.

4. Abide here for as long as you feel inclined; there is plenty to explore and many paths of fancy to be skipped along. This trip to Netzach should leave you feeling sprightly and inspired.

Now for Tiphareth. Remember the sun of Netzach? It hangs above you, to your right, and you are going to surf the cosmic ley lines that attach it to your present station.

1. Imagine the line linking the green orb with the yellow; feel yourself positioned at its base, and then, by the power of your will, feel yourself impelled along it, slanting upwards towards Tiphareth.

2. You enter through the outer atmosphere and feel a change in your constitution as you do so. This is a mystical realm of elevated love, of soul mates, and infinitesimal beauty. It smells of strange, heavy, entrancing perfume; one likely to make you lose your head at any moment. Remembering Malkuth, however, you resolve not to do so.

3. This is the Leonine sphere and it emanates strength, solar power, and love. Healing is performed here and sent down through the planes. If you have any requests of this nature, now is the time to divulge them. There are many golden beings of light ready to receive every twitch of your thought processes. If you can focus your thoughts and visualise the desired end, so much the better.

4. Bask in the life-giving properties of Tiphareth, and feel the excitement they engender. This is also a good place to visit when faced with a difficult choice or decision, particularly between two possible paths. You may, if naturally psychic, find yourself involved in high-level communications of an emotional nature (as opposed to those more academic concepts of Hod) with a particular guardian. Try to maintain equilibrium during this procedure, and especially afterwards. Pride is one of the pitfalls of this level, and self-respecting humility a boon.

As you find yourself heading for the red sphere of Martian Geburah, you may feel arrogance rising in your blood, for you have seen and experienced much on this short preliminary journey. Do feel strong, but try not to approach Geburah in a bombastic manner, or you will have the stuffing knocked out of you. Geburah is, on a microcosmic level, the harsh part of ourselves necessary for self-protection. Here we can shed what has become obsolete in our lives, rid ourselves of unwanted influences, and fill ourselves with warrior strength.

1. Travel up and to the left.

2. Note that everything here is red; the tone is either positively sanguine or sacrificially bloody, depending on your personal state of being.

3. The forceful atmosphere of Geburah is a philosophy in itself. Denoting war, it embodies possibly the oldest impulses of man: to protect and acquire.

Consider these properties and their ambivalence. Uplifting and courageous, the spirit of Geburah has frequently degenerated into wanton cruelty and destruction. Still, for those with a gentle nature, possibly self-sacrificing and too emotionally generous, Geburah provides a healthy antidote to self-dissipation.

Theoretically, Geburah is one of the seats of justice, especially when counterbalanced by Chesed, and it should be possible to have wrongs righted courtesy of this sphere if the powers deem that they are indeed wrongs. It is not a particularly pleasant stop, but its might is impressive. Walls, forts, and military constructs define it; stone, metal, and spilt blood are its main components. This is, of course, the sphere in which wars are fought and lost, or won.

Before it all gets to be too much, let us counterbalance the experience with a visit to the calm blue sphere of Chesed, also known as Gedulah.

1. Travel up and to the right.

    This blue-violet sphere is also known as the Mercy Seat or the Temple of Love. It is the abode of gurus and masters, and the atmosphere is at once challenging and reverend. You may well hear an inner narrative whilst visiting Chesed; chances are, it will instruct you. As obedience is one of the virtues of this station, it is well to follow the dictate you feel is authentic.

2. This is a place of dedication to a path or discipline—an astral hermitage. Here you may consider your life's greater purpose and the steps necessary to secure its coming to pass. This will involve effort, for the rewards of the gods are not easily earned. However, one's shortcomings should be given a sympathetic "viva" in Chesed.

3. Meditate on the following theme:

    The nature of gurus is various, but it is fair to say that the number of true gurus incarnate in Malkuth today is minimal. There are many false prophets and unsavoury self-proclaimed spiritual leaders who are more likely to lead us into the abyss than to the bright lights of Kether. It is foolish to trust such figures on the outer planes, but on the inner planes one's intuition may be employed. There is too much room for confusion on the material level, where countless forces prevent us from making accurate judgements. With the help of one's guides in the sphere of Chesed, disinterested help may be sought. The guru devoid of personal motive is so rare, especially in the West, as to be unicornlike in its elusiveness. Still, it is good to know that such beings exist, somewhere.

Chesed is quite a solemn place, with an atmosphere akin to a court of justice. It will be a relief, especially to feminine spirits, to prepare to ascend further still—this time into the bitter, receptive sea that is Binah. It is the most menstrual of female planets—at once pregnant, menopausal, and steeped in mystery.

Placed at the top of the left-side column, black Binah feels as if it might at any moment absorb all of the other sephiroth into itself and fold creation up like Sylvia Plath reabsorbing her children in "Ariel." Indeed, one of the paths to Binah is "Plathological," borne of deep neurosis and masochistic pain. However, in a balanced state Binah is healthy understanding, compassion, and the ability to empathise.

1. Try to free your mind of analytical thoughts; centre on "blind" feeling.

2. Allow thoughtforms to rise in your mind as you intuitively explore this dark sephirah.

    Binah has a very special relationship with female mysteries and Goddess-related issues, and emanates primal femininity in its most potent aspects. Binah flows with the tides, and women often access it through lunar Yesod, though this path is not commonly, or deliberately, used. There is a telling silence in the atmosphere of Binah; a tacit sense of knowing. Much is thought here in the caves of intuitive and atavistic wisdom, and little spoken.

    The light of Kether bathes the top of this sphere, which revolves and sends reflections scudding across its dark, miasmic surface. The heat of Geburah filters up from beneath, but there is no reflection of its brilliant red. This is absorbed into the dark seas of Binah's strange anti-matter.

3. Abide here for as long as you feel comfortable. Note your reactions: Do you feel at home, claustrophobic, restricted? Do not interpret these reactions yet; simply feel them. You can write down your experiences and interpretations when you return.

Opposite this disturbing yet restful sphere—rather like a graveyard just prior to mass resurrection (Stanley Spencer's paintings, though bright, evoke this atmosphere admirably)—hangs the grey sphere of Chokmah.

1. Journey straight across to your right.

2. Meditate on the following:

   Chokmah, the top sephirah of the Pillar of Mercy, is solemn as a cathedral and yet joyous, for the goal of the ascent is imminent. The Creative Intelligence permeates this sphere like hallucinogenic incense, and faith in oneself and the benevolent nature of the sublime infiltrates the still soul. The traditional imagery, as with all of the Tree, is deeply Biblical. Needless to say, the system is peopled with Rabbinic men, bearded and with robes, for the imagery is archetypal and borne of thousands of years of Judaism. However, the mind conversant in many cultures should not find this an obstacle; alternately, it may translate to your own inner tongue and imagery as quickly as a spiritual linguaphone. Take what comes to you; as time goes on the impressions will change and deepen.

Remember that Chokmah is the place where one identifies one's own Jehovah/Yahweh/Buddha/Vishnu/Isis, and prepares for personal dissolution in its most positive form. Such tasks are not lightly undertaken, and there is a nervy feeling in the air, for this is the vestry that leads to the temple of God. There is also a sense of great accomplishment within this sphere.

The living light of Kether is growing ever more attractive to you, the astral pilgrim. Standing in the grey stone vestry that is Chokmah, you yearn towards the light that has informed you during the entire journey.

Your mind flicks over the nine stages you have so far accomplished: The rise from earthly Malkuth to dreamy Yesod. The left turn to determined, orange Hod, and the right turn to emerald Netzach, the Ireland (or, mythologically, Tir Nan Og) of the Tree. You recall the solar resplendence and beauty of central Tiphareth, then the left-hand turn to bellicose Geburah. Remember how pleasant it was to zig from there to Chesed, the violet-blue home of guides and gurus, then zag to dark Binah, place of female mysteries.

1. Now, here you are, at the top of the right-hand pillar, so close to the light you could almost touch it. Feel yourself drawn upwards at the very thought of it; up into the impossibly resplendent temple of Kether.

2. White light engulfs you, pouring in through your now-permeable astral armour, dissolving it (though it will return when you descend), and filling you with divine acknowledgement. Let this be two-way; draw yourself close

to your God, however you imagine the Creative Source. Give, do not just take. Stay bathed in this refulgence for as long as you feel inclined, vaguely aware of the veils of negative existence above you, those aspects of the creation for which our minds can only draw an analogy of concealment.

3. When you are sated on Ketheric light, it is well to bring yourself back station by station. Thus you will recompose your nature and ground any energies you may be bringing back with you.

4. So, zigzag back through each of the radiant spheres. If you can do so without my prompting, all the better. To travel back by memory will help fix the positions and qualities in your mind. If this proves too difficult, then reread the process described prior to visiting Kether, and go backwards, starting with Chokmah and ending at Malkuth.

Use of the Sephiroth in Magick

Kether—Ketheric spells include those for enlightenment, and approaching or overcoming serious karmic issues.

Chokmah—For primal motivation; that is, setting spiritual forces into action.

Binah—For higher understanding, and synthesis.

Da'ath—The "Invisible Sephirah" relates to transcendant wisdom. It represents aspects of the Universe that are hidden, even to the well-versed occultist. It is particularly apt for approaching that which is unpalatable to the mundane or classically civilised mind.

Chesed—Spiritual compassion, and growth. Paternity, in its most transcendental aspects.

Geburah—Issues of conflict. Self-protection, and protection of one's nearest and dearest. Necessary anger and madness. Hex-breaking.

Tiphareth—Religious insight. Self-sacrifice for the higher good.

Netzach—Beauty, love, and nature—both as the natural world, and as fundamental spiritual/physical impulse.

Hod—For form, structure, orthodoxy, and academe.

Yesod—For astral work, magick in general, and dreamwork.

Malkuth—For issues and spells pertaining to discrimination, aspiration, and spiritual integration with the Universe.

For more information on the Qabalah of the Western Mystery Tradition, see the following titles to start: *Mystical Qabalah* by Dion Fortune, *Magic of Qabalah* by Kala Trobe, *A Kabbalah for the Modern World* by Migene González-Wippler, and *A Practical Guide to Qabalistic Symbolism* by Gareth Knight.

thirteen

The Witch and Divination

The Witch and Tarot

"A WICKED PACK OF CARDS" is as essential to the witch as her Book of Shadows and her familiars—wicked, that is, in the modern sense. There is nothing menacing about the Tarot system; it is simply a very effective way of divining what might come to pass. Best of all, the Tarot gives the querent an idea (often a very specific one) of likely turns of events in the future. From this it is possible to deduce the best course of action. Thus, disasters may be avoided, or the inevitable handled with with optimum positivity and preparation. It is a very shoddy and unethical reader indeed who delivers a message of inescapable doom to another. It is, in fact, the sign of a null-and-void Tarot reading.

It takes years of scrutiny, visualisation, and trial and error to become a real Tarot adept. The earlier one begins, the better. Packs such as the *Rider-Waite* are cornerstones in every witch's trunk of tools. They are particularly good to learn with as the Minor Arcana are individually illustrated, rather than just showing the number of each symbol as in most traditional packs. There are, however, many others worthy of consideration. The *Mythic Tarot* by Juliet Sharman-Burke and Liz Greene does such a good job of relating the Major Arcana to the Greek gods that it has become, to me at least, an excellent source of archetypal wisdom. The Major Arcana perfectly correlates the stages of the psyche with the processes represented by the deities.

The Crowley deck, the *Thoth Tarot*, is filled with incredible imagery and an energy that is unquestionable. The cards are difficult to interpret initially, and I find their energy chaotic, but I know several witches who are stimulated by this and are consequently adept at reading them. The *Tarot of the Old Path* by Sylvia Gainsford and Howard Rodway is a wonderful Wiccan pack. The *Russian Tarot of St. Petersburg* by Cynthia Giles and Yury Shakov is one of the most beautiful I have ever seen. The *Nigel Jackson Tarot* is heavily Gnostic/Blake-influenced, wonderfully rendered, and easy to read. There are literally thousands of packs available, all with their own merits; it is a question of finding what one is happiest with.

The idea of the seventy-eight cards is to illustrate the many stages of incarnational development. The Major Arcana deals with spiritual and psychological stages, and great shifts of circumstance and consciousness. The stages of this evolution are symbolised by the journey of the Fool. Detailed descriptions of each process are given below, but it is worth taking a look at the process in its entirety.

An Overview of the Tarot

The Fool is numbered zero. He is the free spirit, with a childlike lack of understanding of danger. He heads towards a cliff edge whilst chasing a pretty bubble. He is half mad, but also full of guileless wisdom, because he cares nothing for social mores. He represents the spirit entering the world, joyous and introspective, yet full of energy and wanderlust. This is our initial enthusiastically experimental stage.

The first numbered card is the Magician. He is skilled at illusion—a professional. Now, the Fool has learned how to temper his behaviour in order to appear respectable in this strange world. He has learned the art of forethought. Yet he is still attuned to his origins, and can create "magick" before the eyes of those who are less attuned.

The High Priestess brings the dawning of spiritual awareness. Confidence is tempered by the Fool's sudden conscious awareness that all is not under his control; there is also mystery. Subconscious urges are sublimated into spiritual sign and symbol. She is the first feminine influence along the journey, and she is the most powerful and mysterious of characters. The Fool is awe-stricken by the amount he does not know.

The card marked with the number three, that of the Empress, indicates the Fool's new understanding that the biologically feminine is married to the spiritual. He begins to understand that outer manifestation is a product of inner truth. The Empress is a figure of ease and opulence, of maternal love and fertility. He also understands that the present is not the only moment of reference, but that there are also processes of *becoming,* illustrated by the pregnant Empress.

The Empress's consort, the Emperor, initiates the child Fool into the world of power and prestige. Law and logic are introduced to his sphere of understanding. He is, of course, the traditional father figure, as the Empress is the mother. Thus, the Fool approaches the archetypal male and female through the Magician and the High

Priestess—symbols of the subconscious—and their expression on earth through the Empress and Emperor. The Fool is learning duality, and rules and regulations to his behaviour, as must every child.

The Hierophant is a similar stage to sending one's children to church or a religious school. Orthodox divine law and logic impinge on the Fool's original sense of absolute freedom. On a more positive note, he can again see spirit in the material world—this time made manifest through buildings and institutions. He receives external confirmation of the presence of spirit, but probably not in the form anticipated. Morality is imposed on him. The Hierophant indicates higher needs than even the Empress and Emperor can provide.

Next comes the Lovers—the choice between familiar influences and new ones. Having been sheltered by his various guardians along the way, the Fool is here faced with his first choice. He realises that he can impose his will over circumstance, and pursue his own chosen destiny. Thus he learns the art of individuation. He also realises that thought and feeling must go hand in hand, with neither in dominance. If forced to choose, however, he would follow his heart even if it meant forsaking all that the Emperor and Empress have bestowed on him materially.

Now, newly independent, the Fool tries to establish himself in the outside world. He mounts his Chariot and rushes forward, hungry for achievement and victory. He treats his subconscious and conscious fears as motivation, as do many artists and writers. They harness negative energies and transform them into progress. The Fool, too, progresses unquestionably at this point. His possible pitfall is his utter focus on the present, the rational, and his possible inability to see the situations of others. He is intent on establishing his own kingdom, and risks selfishness in the pursuit of his goals.

However, he is brought up sharp by Justice. If he has indeed forgotten the moral lessons taught by the Empress and Emperor, and the divine laws conveyed by the High Priestess and the Hierophant, he will soon get his just deserts. Justice, as impartial as her scales, represents the effect of conscience on action. Even the most committed of warriors must at times feel concern for the results of his actions on others, and contemplate those results. The Fool learns of consequences. He develops into a fairer-minded, less self-orientated member of society.

The Hermit image, which follows, takes the Fool into retreat. Having attained considerable success in the outside world, he wishes to contemplate the lessons learned. Again, he is striving for higher consciousness. His lamp casts a dim and flickering light on the terrain before him—he has only his past experience and his intuition to guide him. In quiet and lonely nooks of the world and of his own psyche, he seeks communion with the Greater Spirit.

What does he discover, but that life is a game of chance! After all of these lessons in spirituality, practicality, and morality, it seems that three fickle sisters rule the fates of men. The Wheel of Fortune represents the apparently random factors over which we as mere mortals have no control, however powerful we may seem or be. Is it all part of some greater plan, or are our fortunes and misfortunes the luck of the draw, or, worse, the work of malicious deities?

The Wheel of Fortune is ever-turning, and as the Fool finds himself beset by sudden circumstance during his meditation, he looks within and discovers remarkable resilience. Strength comes to him; he resists the temptation to curse this sorry realm, and transcends his baser urges: anger, blame, self-pity. His soul wrestles with his ego, and wins.

What on earth will happen next? Life seems like a roller-coaster ride for the retreating Fool at the moment. Perhaps he should not be a hermit after all, but return instead to the busy world of men. At least there he might be able to be of some use to others. After all, what is the point of being strong and spiritual in isolation? He feels the urge towards some humanitarian act or process; a need to counter his self-interested escapades in his Chariot, and the intense introspection of the Hermit, Wheel, and Strength phases. What should he do though?

The Fool returns to society in a newly self-sacrificial mode. He is cautious now, waiting for exactly the right circumstances in which to express his new philanthropy and spiritual ideals. As the Hanged Man, he becomes a conscientious objector. Contemplative and passive, he trusts his inner calling. He suffers to learn.

Eventually, a transformation occurs. The referents he has become accustomed to—his tree, the rope, the sky—all change. The bough is shaken by cold autumnal gusts. The leaves turn and shrivel, eventually falling dead to the ground. The Fool knows that it is time to move into the Beyond. He may be unable to assess what lies ahead of him, but it is time to face risk. The still small voice within tells him that change is illusion, and that eternal truths exist, including the truth of our actions on earth. Our lives are our legacy. As we cross beyond the veil of Death, all illusions of the ego are shed, leaving only the pure spiritual essence. The Hanged Man unties his feet and falls to the ground. In his delirium, he imagines that he is dead; but it is just a fantasy, and now he must arise and recreate himself. The scythe cuts away his past—a painful process, but he welcomes it. He feels lighter and brighter without carrying the burdens of all that had become obsolete to him.

He begins to walk; not an easy feat after so long suspended from the Tree of Knowledge. He stumbles, veering from one side to the other. He cannot seem to keep his balance. Until, that is, he meets the radiant angel Temperance. She stands with one foot dipped in a river, the other on dry land. In her hands, water flows continually from one flagon to another. She is an impressive juggler, for sure. Smiling mildly at the stranger, she offers him guidance.

The cold dark skies are scintillated by rainbow hues at this kind offer, and warmth touches the Fool for the first time in what feels like aeons. The harshness of Death seems illusory thanks to the solicitude proffered by Temperance. She represents sublimation after spiritual quest. She is the stage at which suffering begins to reap rewards; but the Fool knows not to be self-congratulatory. He still has much to learn—at least eight major lessons to go. The reward is Temperance itself: the ability to accept fluctuation and change, whilst remaining inwardly steadfast; a gentleness of nature that comes from knowledge of Divine love; and the ability, therefore, to shine this light into a dark world—and boy, can this world be dark, as the Fool is about to discover.

Everything has its equal and opposite reaction, and that of Temperance is chaos—here, personified by the Devil. He is, of course, the dark twin of the Angel, and they are cut of the same cloth; but what a different atmosphere! Suddenly, the Fool is surrounded by music, revelry, temptation, and all he has been taught by the High Priestess and the Hierophant to see as sense-slavery. Yet he finds himself deeply interested in it. Surely now that he has passed so many tests he deserves a bit of a party?

The winged, horned Lord passes him a chalice of green elixir. It tastes divine, and brings on good visions. He lights a cigarette and makes inspired notes in his journal. He touches on truths he has never encountered before, and has insights that he would never have received without the Devil's potent influence. This is not delusion—there really are fruits to be picked when this card comes up. The Fool knows that he must go with the flow, just as Temperance has taught him. There is a time for everything. He must simply avoid going overboard.

The first few weeks the Fool spends with the Devil are the best of his life. Both are charming, witty, and attractive in the extreme—and the Fool reaches psychospiritual peaks he had never dreamed of before. He is happy to be released from the captivity of responsibility he had imposed on himself; he figures he is due some relaxation. He fancies himself a dashing figure as he regales the Devil's women-in-waiting with his travel stories, attracting their affections with his naïve earnestness. They adore him right back. Sometimes he cannot tell whether it is day or night in this palace—or is it a tavern? He's drunk so much absinthe now he can barely define between dusk and dawn.

He begins to wake up with headaches and aching lungs from all the tobacco and opium he's smoked. Time to move on, he tells himself. A shock over the bathroom mirror has brought this conviction daily, but still he remains. He attempts to remove the ribbons by which a playful wench has tied him to his bedstead, and finds that the more he moves, the more they knot. They begin to cut into his wrists. He calls for help, but hears only a cruel laugh. The laugh is like a bucket of water over his poor woolly head. He tries harder, and harder still. Struggling, he breaks free of the pretty, silky bonds.

Grabbing his journal, he runs outside, rejoicing in the freshness of the air and aware that he has had worthwhile experiences that will make him a more empathetic person in the future. His child within has enjoyed being naughty and breaking the rules a little. He is fatter than before, but also more jittery. He congratulates himself for his Magician-like forethought in escaping when he did.

The Fool continues along the path, anticipating the sixteenth stage of his epic journey. What could it be? After all he has experienced so far, he feels that nothing could surprise him.

However, complacency never lasts for long. For the next thing he knows, the building in which he is residing for the night is struck by lightning.

The Tower is so tall that when it crumbles, the stones and inhabitants have further to fall than had they resided in a less impressive building. His vanity enlivened by his escapades with the Devil, the Fool had built himself an ego that he believed was protected and indomitable. All of his Chariot feelings flooded back to him: the world was his oyster it seemed, and he the infinitely wiser, more experienced, spiritually refined master. Suddenly, out of the blue, he finds himself escaping from his edifice in fear not just for his life, but for all that he had perceived as unquestionable. Perhaps those lines around his eyes are those of vice rather than wisdom? After all, he certainly gave that old Devil a run for his money.

The Tower brings changes that shake us to the core. We are, quite frankly, left feeling bereft.

Is there any hope out there? The Fool gazes up into the sky. His journal has been lost in the fire; he feels he can remember little of the wealth of information he had accrued along the journey. Wormwood is nibbling at his brain—too much absinthe! He sighs and slugs down another shot, his dark eyes searching the skies for some solace, some little glimmer of celestial solicitude. How he misses Temperance and her gentle, knowing ways! But he is too far down the other route now to stop and relocate her.

Eight stars shine in the sky—one is particularly bright. They reveal a body of water, which reminds him of the fact that fortune necessarily ebbs and flows. A small bird perching in a tree brings to mind the lofty aspirations of the Hanged

Man period. Perhaps there is hope after all. The Fool decides to follow the bright Star, feeling naked before the gods. His vanity is truly stripped away.

He struggles through the starlit terrain with a slight return of optimism. Gradually, the Moon appears, recalling his childhood with the High Priestess, and filling him with awe at the mysteries hidden in nature. He is just beginning to relax, when a terrible howl rends the night asunder. Adrenaline shoots through his veins, and he instinctively ducks for cover in a nearby bush. He wishes that the Empress, with all her maternal radiance, was here to comfort him, but he is alone. He watches nervously from the shadows.

He sees before him two wolves intent on the Moon, howling up at it. A cloud passes over, and they turn and pad up to him. They are domestic dogs, and they lick his hands and promise to be his guides and companions. The cloud clears, and their eyes turn savage again. He shrinks back in fear.

Memories of the Tower torture him as he prays for the sun to rise. All of the power of the subconscious is unleashed during the Moon phase, and the exhausted Fool is ill-equipped to handle it. He settles into a bower and, unsure as to whether he is awake or dreaming, is prey to nightmares until dawn.

When the Sun rises, he begins to sleep. By the time he awakes, the Sun is high in the sky. The Emperor has returned! Childlike with relief, he strips off his blackened clothes—the legacy of ruined fortune—and notices that his limbs and face are not as haggard as he had feared after his experiences with the Devil. The tenuous hope of the Star seems to find affirmation in the brilliant, energising light of the sun. He celebrates life as if reborn. He realises that he is protected by a wall, and has been all night, if only he had recognised it. In his secret garden he is free to play and to reassess his long journey. Surely this is the end? He wants it to be—he wants to stay. A white horse grazes nearby. It notices him and, attracted by his now-relaxed aura, trots over to him, nuzzling his outstretched hand. He mounts it.

For a short while, they frolic together, the Fool feeling as if he has reinherited the world. He thinks of the gifts proffered by the Emperor, and wonders whether he should return to his father—a prodigal with so much more to offer now that he has undergone so many initiations. No sooner has he thought it than his steed begins to move on. He attempts to direct it, but he no longer has reins. Still, enraptured by the beauty of the passing scenery, and by his inner narrative in which he relates all around him to his previous experiences as if living in pathetic fallacy, he has little will to dismount. He is too self-absorbed to notice that the walls have vanished.

They enter a cemetery. It contains the tombs of all his former personae, all of his stages of progress along the way. He dismounts and looks around a little, engrossed.

He is tired, he realises. Perhaps living in the Sun is not enough after all. He yearns for something greater—that indefinable thing that has compelled him to continue throughout his journey.

Another huge sound rents the air asunder, but this time it is not a howl. No earth-based creature could create a sound so sublime. It sounds familiar, yet transcendental.

Above him, the angel Gabriel appears, trumpet in hand. A flag hangs from it, reminding the Fool of his allegiance to the spiritual realms. The revelry he encountered with the Devil and in the Sun now seems irrelevant, trivial even.

Around him, his previous personae start to rise from their graves, arms stretched up to Gabriel. They are celebrating the final calling—a true vocation, the sum of all past actions. The Fool rejoices, and prepares to ascend. His journey is over.

With the World, we find that all of the lessons of the Major Arcana have been learned and assimilated. Earthly and spiritual powers have been attained—now is the time for a quantum leap of consciousness. The Fool finds his mind elevated, and for a while he enjoys this new state of being.

However, his number is zero, and he emerges again at the end of the Major Arcana cycle. He is reborn, he has developed in every way possible, but there is always room for evolution. After a while, the Fool will decide to make the journey anew. It is not merely a journey, it is a pilgrimage to all the sacred sites of the soul. The Fool—the soul—is never complacent enough to rest for long.

The four suits of the Minor Arcana give details on the minutiae of life, which are important to our daily existence. Pentacles represent earthly conditions such as material well-being, business projects, family ties, and wealth. Cups, naturally relating to the watery qualities, are concerned with emotions, creativity, the lesser psychic arts, and also with luck and love. Swords are related in one tradition to fire, and to air in another. They symbolise thought, conflict, restriction, and expansion; often uncomfortable processes. Wands indicate endeavours and aspirations with more than a financial goal in mind. They relate (corresponding to either air or fire, depending on personal proclivity) to impulse, energy, and creativity that can be directed almost anywhere. (See below for further explanations.) One must complete all ten stages of each of the qualities represented by the Minor Arcana, and avoid or learn from the pitfalls indicated by each process when ill-aspected (or, in the case of some Sword cards, when they are simply present!). Each is an element of life, with an important strength to confer once the code has been cracked.

The *Mythic Tarot* again does a wonderful job with the Minor Arcana. The same characters appear throughout each elemental process, but this time they are heroes from mythology striving with their quests. Cups tell the story of Eros and Psyche. Wands involve the saga of Jason and the golden fleece. For Swords, we have the dilemma of Orestes, which is a brilliantly apt parallel as Orestes is in a no-win situation, as sometimes we mortals are. (Orestes is ordered by Apollo to kill his mother, who has killed his father, but is threatened by the Furies, who avenge matricide.) Swords being a suit of strife and mental agonising, this fits perfectly. Finally we have the adventures of Daedalus representing the Pentacle processes.

When I read my own Tarot (which, contrary to some opinions, is extremely effective so long as I am calm!), I see the images as comic-strip projections of my own future. I try to enter the image and look around a bit—what options are there, and what can I do in the present to prepare myself for this stage? "Entering" the images of your chosen deck(s) is an effective way to learn them. A good pack will have a definite atmosphere to each card, as the symbolism will prompt your subconscious into creating a specific scenario.

In the Western Mystery Tradition, Tarot cards have been used since the advent of the Golden Dawn as astral doorways—often to points on the Qabalistic Tree of Life. There is much potential for entering deep states of collective consciousness when meditating with Tarot. In the unlikely event that you attempt this and feel uncomfortable, simply come back. You may well find that you have a guide anyway, if you enter the image effectively. There is quite a bit of traffic up there, and newcomers are catered to. This is the point at which the inner realms become the outer reality—a key point to the operation of magick. Tarot is probably the most powerful visual tool that we as witches possess.

The Major Arcana

O—The Fool

The mythology surrounding the wise fool is immense. Because he operates outside the norm, attuned to the spiritual quest, he bears the eternal digit zero. He is equally at home at the beginning and the end of the Tarot cycle, in which all human experience is encompassed.

The *Nigel Jackson Tarot* Fool is dressed in green, with asinine, belled ears attached to his hood. We are reminded of the Golden Ass into which Lucius Apuleius's picaresque hero is transformed in Thessaly in his spiritual journey towards redemption through the goddess Isis. The ears, and the ass, represent the gross physicality of the body, which the Fool, with his golden aura, is optimistic of transcending.

Nigel Jackson's Fool carries a stick and bag on his back, which represents his minimalistic worldly goods. In his other hand he bears a thyrsus, the wand of Dionysus, which bears grapes. These represent mystical inebriation—the divine madness of the spiritual seeker, which will be fully discovered later with the Devil. He smiles, confident in his convictions. The fact that his next step will carry him over a cliff—from earth to air—bothers him not in the least. He smiles as he observes the butterfly of his hopes, dreams, and intuitions. The butterfly also represents the psyche—and it is this, rather than his logical mind, that the Fool is pursuing. The cat at his heels confirms the validity of his intuition. Most packs depict a dog, representative of convention, yapping at the feet of the Fool.

Here, the Fool is blissfully unaware of any bounds to his aspiration. He innocently pursues his dreams, like a child chasing a bubble. He represents the powers of the intuitive creative urge and random impulse, especially when combined with the Wheel of Fortune. He has the confidence to take a gamble and to attempt to turn it in his favour. He feels so attuned to the Universe (though in fact he is callow) that his faith in himself is boundless.

Meaning—When the Fool appears in any reading, he represents new cycles, spontaneity, and divine inspiration. It is the card that appears when old employment is abandoned in favour of a vocation, or convention is flaunted in order to experience greater adventure and satisfaction. He always represents a risk, but one rightly undertaken.

Reversed—Needless to say, when this card appears in the negative (either reversed, or in the "Obstacles" position), it represents folly and lack of control of the faculties. It is often the bane of the creative person to undergo this flip side; it is when risks are taken for the sake of hedonism, or without true spiritual backing. Inspired musicians who go off the rails spring to mind—Jimi Hendrix, Janis Joplin, and Jim Morrison, for example. For these, the new cycle is entered into on another plane altogether.

II—The Juggler/Magician

The Magician represents the full use of the faculties. He is, however, like all stage magicians, a master of illusion, his thoughts complex. The Fool has learned to dissimulate. He can now amaze others with his prowess rather than his folly. Nigel Jackson's Juggler indicates this by keeping three balls suspended in air simultaneously. Other versions of the Magician stand behind an altar on which a wand, pentacle, sword, and chalice sit. These represent the qualities of each Tarot suit: emotion, intellect, creativity, and normal human endeavour (observance of the laws of nature, and of respect for material concerns). No aspect of human life is overlooked or overemphasised; the system is in perfect balance. He is attuned to the elements of water, air, fire, and earth in equal measure. This allows the Juggler, or Magician, to act in perfect harmony with his environment. He has the properties of every element at his fingertips. Because of the Fool's essential purity, he has control of the elements, both within himself and (thus) externally.

He wears the wide-brimmed hat of Hermes, indicative of his eloquence and trickster skills. Hermes was able to disappear and turn himself into a breeze at will, thus allowing him to sneak into the homes of others and steal or disturb, if he so wished. He is mischievous in the extreme.

On the other hand, his white robe represents detachment from worldly concerns, while his coloured cloak represents self-sacrifice and self-protection. The Magician or Juggler will strive for what he wishes to attain. He is perfectly confident that he is composed enough to call upon higher levels to aid him. The white aura emanating from his head represents his pure, cerebral ability. His sleight of hand and ability to appear and disappear at will (just like Hermes in Greek myth) assure his success.

Meaning—This card represents cerebral skills, and their articulation; its recipient cannot fail to charm and convince. All of the powers of air are indicated: swift, precise communications, and the ability to overview a situation in its entirety and move strategically in order to attain one's ends. Everything is present that is needed to succeed.

Reversed—When reversed or in a negative position, the Juggler/Magician indicates cunning, deceit, and trickery. A salesman who uses his "gift of gab" to manipulate the old and infirm, for example, would receive this card reversed as his significator.

II—The Popess/High Priestess

The High Priestess is usually an Isian figure sitting between the pillars of the conscious and subconscious (though she is infinitely more aligned with the latter). These pillars also have Qabalistic relevance as those of Mercy and Severity. She is enthroned at their centre, aligned to the Middle Pillar where all coheres and balance is attained.

The *Tarot of the Old Path* depicts the Maiden Goddess, the fresh face of divinity in nature. However, as Robert Graves points out in *The White Goddess,* she is beautiful but also cruel. Her hints at greater meaning in life are not always comfortable to receive.

The *Nigel Jackson* pack shows the High Priestess as Pope Joan, a Christianised version of the goddess Juno Lucina, who represents the higher self, inner guidance, and intuitive skills. As all High Priestesses, she sits before the sea, a crescent moon shining onto the book of ancient wisdom she holds in her lap. The peacock at the feet of the Popess confirms her affiliations to the Queen of the Heavens (peacocks being sacred to Hera/Juno) and the many eyes with which she sees into the night. Physical light has no bearing on the feminine insight depicted by this card. She represents the wisdom of the ages.

The blues and purples in which the Popess is attired affirm her affiliation with the eternal cerulean and the purple of self-sacrifice and spiritual insight. There is pain inherent in this card, just as the sephirah Binah in the Qabalah represents pieta, the sorrow of the mother for the sacrificed child. The Popess/Priestess knows what it is to "suffer to learn." From her vantage point of divine wisdom she observes the follies of mankind and suffers with them. She longs to connect with the lost souls of earth and bring spiritual understanding and development. She may represent an older woman—a mother or grandmother, for example—whose counsel is in the querent's best interest. Her thought-provoking presence is a positive influence, whether it comes from a human mouth or from an inner voice.

Meaning—The Popess/High Priestess shows the influence of higher psychic and spiritual activity. When she appears in a reading it is safe to follow one's intuition, especially in nonworldly matters or those that pertain to creativity and true fulfilment. For anybody studying occult arts, no greater affirmation of progress may be attained through Tarot than the presence of the High Priestess herself.

Thus, wisdom, guidance, and "going with the flow" are key meanings of this card.

Reversed—Superficiality is indicated, along with pretension to spiritual ideals, gossip, and slander.

III—The Empress

The Empress presents an image of fertility and abundance. A round-bellied woman relaxes in her natural environment, a promise of continued growth and procreation in her heart; she is the very essence of the biologically feminine. Roses embellish her shield and staff, flowers sacred to Venus and the Netzach in the Qabalah. This is an Orphic sephirah, a state of progression through music, dance, and nature. The positive, therapeutic properties of natural behaviour are emphasised. The Venus Mount is visible behind Nigel Jackson's Empress with a sacred stream running through it; this is the womb of life. A bundle of corn in her arms and sheaflike plaits in her golden hair confirm the Empress to represent Demeter, Rhea, Aphrodite of the golden aura, and all other female deities whose properties include agriculture, propagation, and love.

Here, we find the spiritual (encountered earlier as the High Priestess) married to the material. We perceive a process of *becoming*—and the satisfaction of growth. The Fool moves from the inward sphere into the outer, still under the wing of the ultra-protective Empress. She may become stifling in later years, but for now, the querent/Fool is happy to be under her aegis.

Meaning—When the Empress appears in a positive context, there is certainly no need to worry about sustaining sufficient means to attain one's ends. Everything the querent desires will be given with a generous flourish. Creativity will flow, particularly when one is in natural surrounds. Love is the keynote, and the beauty that love brings to all lives. On a physical level, pregnancy is possible. The person who receives this card must pledge to enjoy the gifts of Venus/Aphrodite, for she promises all that is good in life.

Reversed—When reversed or in a negative position, the Empress represents sterility, and those traits of motherhood that can be negative: overprotection, mental and physical dominance. It can also represent frustration, and the stifling of creativity.

IV—The Emperor

The Emperor represents authority on earth perceived to be given by divine right—that of the pharaoh or pope, for example. His orb and sceptre confirm this. Golden, fiery light surrounds him, and his robes are the red of proactive power. However, his energy is material rather than celestial; he is the just ruler of earth who establishes and maintains dominion over lands and their peoples. His rule is one of justice and harmony. The number four by which he is represented indicates his rulership over the four elements. The Juggler/Magician uses the power of air, earth, fire, and water to further his own spiritual quest; the Emperor uses them to maintain control of his vast earthy kingdom. He is authority and paternal power at its strongest. In the positive, this indicates wise and solicitous guidance; solid foundations from which the individual is able to flourish. The establishment of a promising future is also represented; one is "standing foursquare" in the face of any opposition, ready to meet it with confidence and strength.

Meaning—The Emperor card indicates leadership and authority gained through experience. He is like Ulysses returning to reclaim his wife and lands after his adventures, his right to rule both legal and moral. He represents martial skill (not necessarily literal), active power, and a masculine force to be reckoned with. With the Emperor as a backer, all the physical and hierarchical power needed will support the querent.

Reversed—The dominance of a male authority figure is indicated: physical and social bullying, the abuse of power, a fiery temper that cannot be controlled. In this sense, the card represents the Qlipothic face of the Qabalistic Geburah: mindless force and pointless destruction.

V—The Pope/Hierophant

On this card, the *Mythic Tarot* shows the centaur Chiron, the wise, wounded teacher of Greek mythology. This is an apt image as the true spiritual leader is both empathetic and disciplined. He seeks to sublimate his own experience and pain through helping others—the ideal aim of any spiritual mentor. He combines the body of an animal with the insight of an elevated spiritual being.

The traditional image for the Hierophant is of a pope enthroned before two acolytes, his hand raised in benediction. The crossed keys on his breast represent the means of entering the astral and spiritual realms. The equilateral crosses in Nigel Jackson's pack signify, along with the pentacle, control of the four elements—earth, air, fire, and water—and the ability to channel the fifth, Akasha. The Pope is draped in Akashic purple, while astral clouds billow behind him, representing spiritual planes and possibilities. He sits again between the two pillars of Mercy and Severity, day and night, in perfect balance in the state of duality. With all the power of the orthodoxy behind him, the Pope brings ritual spiritual awareness into the heart of the material world.

The ray of light emanating from his head represents insight and spiritual genius. Just as the Qabalistic lightning flash travels down the Tree of Life between the Pillars of Duality carrying the properties of every other sephirah into Malkuth, so does the Pope bring forth the qualities of loftier spheres. He is their representative on earth.

Meaning—When the Pope/Hierophant card appears in a reading, it signifies the influence of orthodox religion and ceremony on the querent. This could range from attending a moving church service, to reading the Zohar or Bible (for example) and receiving flashes of inspired thought. Doctrine and long-established ceremonial patterns are emphasised. Teaching, knowledge gained through quiet suffering, and the ability to heal and be healed (particularly on a spiritual level) are also indicated.

Reversed—When reversed or in a negative position, it follows that the querent is suffering from religious red tape and overbearing dogma. Religious cant is also indicated. Here we witness the seeds of many wars.

VI—The Lovers

The Lovers card represents the harmonious union of opposites. Usually it is depicted by a man standing between a mature woman (his mother) and a young one (his chosen partner). He is clearly facing a decision—in the *Marseilles* pack his body is inclined towards the young woman while his ear is bent towards his mother. He must make a choice between that which has nurtured him and become familiar, and what he really wants out of life when standing on his own feet. This is a process of individuation.

In the *Mythic Tarot,* Paris's enforced choice between Athena, Hera, and Aphrodite is depicted. Strength and justice, power, or sexual beauty—which is most worthy of the prize golden apple? He is in a no-win situation, which perhaps detracts from the true meaning of the card—that is, the situation can indeed be won, and not merely temporarily. However, in the mere act of making a conscious decision that will have external repercussions, he is developing. Courage of his own convictions is necessary, despite the whispered prompts from other, often familiar quarters. Nigel Jackson describes it as the "Alchemical Wedding"—the joining of masculine and feminine principles in sacred marriage. This is the marriage of the subconscious to the conscious as much as anything, for what else does Paris or the Lover figure have to go on but his intuition? The rainbow colours that surround the Lovers in most packs signifies the joining of heaven and earth through sacred and intimate communion.

Meaning—The meaning of this card is not difficult to deduce: partnerships, romantic love, the move from childhood (or a situation of childlike security) into one of equal responsibility for another. Choice is always indicated by this card, usually between two options. The querent is capable of attaining the best of both situations. Infatuation, and blossoming sexuality, are also indicated.

Reversed—It follows that the Lovers card reversed indicates the termination of a partnership. Disharmony, and the pestilence of bad temper and cruel words are also indicated. The querent will have to take action to prevent what she has established from falling into ruin.

VII—The Chariot

The Chariot is always good to see in a reading, as it indicates unstoppable progress. The motivating factors may be negative, such as when one is propelled into action by depression or adverse circumstance. This is represented by the sphinxes that drive the Chariot: Phobos, Fear, and Anger. These negative energies are being transformed into fuel for progress.

It is also sometimes said that Anger (personified as Ares, perhaps—the Greek god of war) drives the carriage. Seven is a number regarded in ancient magick as sacred to Mars (Ares) and Apollo. It also relates to Pythagorean theory of the self-moving soul migrating from one sphere to the next—the number of this process is also seven. This is the interstellar chariot.

Meaning—When the Chariot appears in a reading, it may be taken for granted that progress will ensue, enemies and obstacles will be vanquished, and full control will be taken of the situation.

Reversed—When it appears reversed, it can mean anything from a car/transport problem or accident, to erratic circumstances that are difficult to bring under control. Obstacles are also indicated when the card appears reversed.

VIII—Justice

Justice depicts Athena as goddess of rightful order. She sits enthroned with sword and balancing scales in hand, judging all with absolute objectivity. When she appears in a reading, she indicates balance and the natural result of past actions. In some respects, she is the ultimate card of karma.

Gazing impassively from her throne, Justice is a symbol of conscience. If our success hitherto has not been honest or fair, she can indicate the stirrings of self-scrutiny. Being an orthodox figure, she represents the conscious. Here, we attempt to take control of baser instincts and subconscious urges. Justice represents the process of striving towards higher goals.

She can also represent legal proceedings: upright, the judgement goes in the querent's favour or at least is overweeningly fair; reversed, the result may be less favourable for the querent. When appearing in a reading for somebody with no legal issues at present, she represents the tides of justice in one's life. The way we treat and are treated by others is an issue of Justice. It could be an issue as apparently irrelevant as a friend getting the wrong end of the conversational stick and retaliating unfairly. These little things make up our lives. It could also mean that we are about to reap the consequences of our own actions.

Meaning—Justice represents equilibrium, conscience, and balance between conscious and subconscious; also contracts and agreements, legal proceedings, a fair verdict.

Reversed—When reversed, this card can represent a miscarriage of justice, an inability to be objective, unfairness, or punishment for past actions.

IX—The Hermit

The Hermit represents the inner search, the need to travel inward and seek a spiritual path in life. The theme of self-isolation is paramount; the fripperies of daily life are abandoned in favour of solitary meditation. The material world has been rejected, at least temporarily. He is the pilgrim on his own path of self-discovery. However, what the Hermit seeks is greater than himself—the staff, reminiscent of a wand, and the lamp, both represent a striving towards greater spiritual truths. Union with the life-force would be the ultimate aim. The light cast by his lamp symbolises his faith; despite the snow that covers the ground, and his drab clothing, it provides the image with a warm glow. The Hermit, with his long grey beard and bent, cowled head, is seeking spiritual rejuvenation.

The pace the Hermit works at is the antithesis to that of the Chariot. Now is the time for measured response, minimal action, and maximum reflection. Individuality is also emphasised. The querent receiving this card is moving away from the mass emotion of society into a self-contained sphere. His or her effect on others will also be minimal at this time (unless the card is reversed). This person may, however, dazzle the herd with brilliant insights when he or she finally returns to the fray. This will not be for some time, however.

Meaning—Upright, the Hermit signifies solitude, personal learning processes without recourse to family and friends, and caution. It may also mean wise advice from an older person, or reclusive behaviour to serve a higher, possibly creative purpose.

Reversed—When reversed, this card represents excessive solitude, neurotic self-exclusion from the world, or materialism hiding beneath a spiritual veneer. The false guru fits into this latter category—all of the trappings of spirituality without the actual practise, coupled with base desires.

X—The Wheel of Fortune

The Wheel of Fortune represents the vicissitudes of Fate, and always indicates a change, whether for better or worse. In some ways it is the strongest card in the pack, answering the most common question, "Will things improve or decline?"

Some packs, such as the *Mythic Tarot* (based on Greek mythology), depict the three sister Fates spinning, weaving, and cutting the fortunes of their subjects. No matter how successful or secure a person may seem, he or she is always vulnerable to bolts out of the blue. This card represents our awareness of this, and our everlasting inability to come to terms with it. Mankind has struggled since consciousness was attained to understand and take control of the Wheel of Fortune—this is the whole purpose of magick.

The lesson of the Hermit is freedom from mass consciousness; the next stage, that of the Wheel, is that even the most personally enlightened being is vulnerable to higher forces. In many packs, a sphinx sits atop the Wheel, smug and cryptic, impossible to fathom. Here, we accept that life is a riddle. We can attempt to turn the Wheel in our favour through steadfast effort, but the final push belongs to the Morae/Fates/Norns.

Another lesson of the Wheel of Fortune is that we are never satisfied with what we have achieved. There is always the urge to undertake risk in order to attain higher goals. As well as symbolising our ultimate inability to control our destiny, the card represents our innate need for challenge. We do not actually desire status quo—the urge of humankind is towards progress. If it were not for the Wheel, we would stagnate. Gambling with Fate is part of the evolution process.

The Wheel is not merely material. The richest, healthiest person in the world might get the Wheel of Fortune in a reading and suddenly find him- or herself questioning all that has been established in this incarnation. Influences one might consider random or irrelevant come into play when this card appears. These can be simple shifts of consciousness, but may leave the querent devoid of psychological foundation. The theme of feeling like a plaything of the gods is also tantamount.

Meaning—This card represents a change of circumstance, usually tied in with the destiny of the soul; also incarnational crisis (usually highly productive), loss of complacency, and risk-taking. Upright, the results are likely to be favourable.

Reversed—When reversed, this card represents karmic backlash, ill fortune, and a bad time to take risks; a sudden downturn in the affairs of the querent.

XI—Strength

A beautiful, delicate young woman stands with her hands on a lion. In many packs he has his jaws open, sharp teeth exposed. She remains serene and in control.

Here, we find the "feminine" aspects of the psyche taking control of the baser instincts such as aggression, anger, and fear. She also subdues the lust for power and all other worldly ambitions one might expect to be represented by the king of the jungle.

The woman carries no implements; weapons and even magickal paraphernalia are conspicuously absent from her person. Where, then, is the source of her Strength?

In the *Tarot of the Old Path,* the woman rides naked upon the lion's back (admittedly, in this instance, carrying a caduceus), an image reminiscent of Durga in Hindu mythology. In the case of Durga, she is also beautiful and delicate. However, her control is absolute. She has attained a state of unquestionable control on the inner planes, and thus can qualm the raging beasts of instinct. She has come to terms with Death.

In Tarot symbolism, the Fool meets Strength on his journey before Death. This is one point I might consider changing were I to create a pack of my own. Yes, Strength is required to withstand Death, but a knowledge that Death is not the end might come in handy when facing a lion. The Christian martyrs had it, and allowed themselves to be torn limb from limb in the coliseum with inner serenity. Similarly do yogic masters look death in the eye (meditating in cemeteries, for example) in order to reattain life. Shamans undergo initiatory death experiences in which they are astrally savaged by wild beasts; they are eventually recomposed, bit by agonising bit, and consequently reborn. They *then* attain Strength.

The lion is an obvious symbol of the ego. Anyone who knows a Leo will be able to see that prestige is an important issue to many born under this sign. This is often self-esteem as much as external, but the route to attaining it is usually via the affections and opinions of others. Here, the greater consciousness—represented by the lady—quells the obvious with her subtle tact and intuition. She does no harm to the beast—she understands and feels compassion for it. It is, of course, part of her own psyche. She has simply outgrown it.

Meaning—This card represents the ability to face difficulties with fortitude; seeing through a façade and finding oneself able to empathise with what lies beneath, whilst preventing it from affecting one's judgement. Also, strength in the face of sound and fury; control of the instincts.

Reversed—When reversed, this card represents battling for dominance unnecessarily. Also, excessive self-control—an inability to "go with the flow." Lassitude, inner torment; lack of courage.

XII—The Hanged Man

This image is often perceived as menacing by those not accustomed to Tarot imagery. However, the character is hanging by his foot rather than neck, and his face is serene and often surrounded by a halo. The sacrifice made by the Hanged Man (who might more aptly be named the "Hanging Man") is willing. Temporary suspension is indicated—of circumstance and progress.

Ray Buckland's *Romani Tarot* contains the novel and effective image of a rabbit hanging outside a Gypsy wagon. The only snag with this is that the rabbit is dead, which the usual character is certainly not. However, the rabbit is a symbol of fertility in its own right, and the theme of sacrifice is underlined. Like the usual Hanged Man, the rabbit's feet form a cross—a symbol of the sun and thus mystical self-sacrifice and rebirth. As Buckland points out in his explanations, the Romani do not kill for sport, but only through necessity, and the rabbit is a symbol of reincarnation and the perpetuity of life, rather than of death.

The Hanged Man is waiting in limbo for outer and inner conditions to change. He is often compared to the self-sacrificial gods, and especially to Odin hanging from Yggdrasill, the World Tree, in Norse myth. In the beautiful *Russian Tarot of St. Petersburg,* the Hanged Man, dressed resplendently and smiling contentedly, is surrounded by falling apples shaken down by a bird of paradise. The rewards of this situation will far outweigh any personal inconvenience or discomfort.

An obvious meaning then is having the courage of one's convictions. Rational thought begins to align itself with the intuition. The Hanged Man is moving aside from convention and taking a risk in order to attain a coveted goal, often of a humanitarian nature. He therefore undergoes a spiritual initiation in the tradition of the "vision quest." He has no external support—except for the structure he has created for himself—for the Hanged Man has certainly hanged himself rather than been hanged. Therefore he can only rely on his own abilities, past as well as present and future. He has performed a leap of faith, and is caught midway.

Meaning—This card represents delayed decisions, temporary inaction, but mental flexibility. Also, accepting one's own inner judgement; the willingness to adapt to new conditions; willing sacrifice for a greater good; long-term perspective.

Reversed—Reversed, the Hanged Man can indicate fear of upsetting the status quo, and procrastination.

XIII—Death

Again, this is a menacing image for those unaccustomed to Tarot. Death, however, is welcome to many who suffer. Life without death would be unbearable, on this plane at least. Death means change, transition. There are very few who would wholeheartedly wish to remain stagnant.

Fear of Death is simply fear of loss. We may value what we have—our bodies, our pleasures, and the pleasure we gain from the lives of others. Death is infinitely worse for those left behind than it is for those who have "passed through the Veil." We also fear the process of dying, and admittedly, this can be harrowing in the extreme. However, witches and all others with spiritual beliefs see Death as an initiation—one of many through which we pass on our Fool's journey of consciousness.

As a species, our experiences of death come in two categories: animal and agricultural. With animal death (which includes human), we observe the sudden removal of a body from this world, apparently on a one-way ticket to oblivion. The sense of vacuum when a person or beloved animal dies is not, however, specifically related to that being—it is intimately interlinked with our own perceptions. Of course, we will miss the interaction we previously enjoyed, but this does not mean that the being concerned has expired completely. He or she has exited this consciousness, sure. Yet it is commonly believed by the "unscientific" religiously inclined that they have moved into another realm of being. However, this optical and sensory illusion of departure accounts for nihilistic theories.

With agricultural death, however, we observe the translation of the dead into new life; the Corn King dies in order to feed the populace, and to allow new growth in the coming year. Biological debris breaks down and becomes an essential base for fertility, again, feeding new life; thus, the first inklings that perhaps it is the same for humans too. After all, the sun sets, vanishing throughout the long night, and then rises again from another angle in the morning. Could the human essence be similarly reborn?

Witches believe in reincarnation, as do Hindus, Buddhists, and a variety of other groups. There is no Death, but simply "Transformation." In the *Tarot of the Old Path,* Karma (Judgement) plays a similar role to Death in "The Close," even looking rather like him as Justice stands with her scales over souls in various stages of death and rebirth. Death is the initial step onto a new and higher level; the Judgement stage defines how successful one has been in learning the lessons allotted before birth.

Death is the great leveller, as the mediaeval populace was so keen to indicate in their philosophies and artwork. The Grim Reaper calls us all in at one stage or another, regardless of all physical and social referents. The image reflects this—in most packs, a variety of people of all ages and degrees of worldly success are subject to the utterly objective scythe.

Death is by no means a negative card to come up with in a reading. Upright, it means transition; possibly the death of all that has previously seemed unquestionable.

However, actions from the past continue to be of relevance—as our legacy, if you will. Those subjected to this card inevitably undergo a process of mourning; life before Death strikes seems naïve and carefree. The changes involved are radical, but the end result brings an improvement, not the least of which is an understanding of the fundaments of life.

Meaning—This card indicates a sudden change, with strong karmic implications. Also, the shedding of all that has become obsolete; spiritual progression; possible loss of material status.

Reversed—When reversed, the Death card can indicate possible physical death (depending on surrounding cards). Also, an inability to adjust to change; fear of mortality and thus of progress; atheistic beliefs.

XIV—Temperance

An angelic-looking figure stands before a body of moving water, one foot dipped into it. He or she holds two chalices, between which water is flowing. The winged character is serene and absolutely in control. In the *Rider-Waite* pack, a mountain is visible in the background, a radiant light shining from its peak. Irises flourish in the foreground.

The chalices held by the Temperance character represent opposites; here, they are synthesised by the fluid flowing between them. They are united in change. Fluctuations of specific circumstance are irrelevant. Temperance has the overview.

Approaching life with temperance is a difficult task indeed. It means far more than the avoidance of extremes (often construed as the result of drink, drugs, etc.); here, these extremes have been experienced and assimilated. Temperance is wise rather than naïve. This card heralds the understanding that life is necessarily comprised of both positive experiences and negative. The trick, which the character in the card symbolises, is to rise above both and maintain a serene spiritual and psychological stance.

The river in which the angelic foot dips itself is seen, in the *Rider-Waite* pack at least, as the Styx. Thus are life and death united. Awareness of mortality informs but does not inhibit progress. In the *Mythic Tarot,* the meaning is represented by the goddess Iris. She is a messenger of the gods to mortals, and her symbol is the rainbow, the bridge between the sky and the earth. Thus are high ideals calmly and beautifully brought to pass on the material planes.

Diverse energies are synthesised through the process of Temperance. The image represents intelligence in conjunction with "going with the flow." It can indicate the need to be less proactive in one's life; any action should be taken with a philosophical overview.

Meaning—This card indicates balance, overview, and understanding that life is a state of permanent flux, and that this is good as it allows for progress. Also, calmness, tranquillity, and insight.

Reversed—When reversed, Temperance indicates bipolar responses—ecstatic one moment, depressed the next. Also lack of control of one's situation; a need for solitude and calm reflection; outside interference.

XV—The Devil

Again, this is a card that causes alarm in many unaccustomed to Tarot imagery. The image has been updated in several packs (the *Mythic Tarot*, for example) to that of Pan, which is more appropriate to the modern meaning than the Baphomet image of the *Rider-Waite*. Admittedly, it represents excess in either case, and the dominance of hedonism over sensible action and sometimes over free will. The Waite pack depicts a horned, winged Devil with two subjects chained to his throne—chained loosely, but chained nonetheless. These are willing captives, entranced by the gifts this card has to offer: excess leading to enlightenment. This often comes at the risk of insanity and public disgrace. Thus it is the perfect card to represent the "sex, drugs, and rock and roll" lifestyle—one that often leads to enhanced creativity and occasional spiritual breakthrough, but which might equally end up as choking to death on one's own vomit, or accidentally overdosing. A scenario such as this, however, would usually be accompanied by cards such as the Tower.

However, the Devil can also be liberating, and this is what the Pan figure represents. Sexuality and sensuality are emphasised. In the *Russian Tarot of St. Petersburg,* the Devil has eyes in his nipples. This is possibly a reference to Ayin, the "eye" of Hebrew language and symbolism associated with the twenty-sixth path (between Hod and Tiphareth) of the Qabalah. This is the "Renewing Intelligence" because it moves one from dogmatic thought to mystical perception. Similarly, the virtues of the Devil card elevate the querent from a mundane, hide-bound lifestyle to relaxed and creative altitudes. The eyes in the nipples also represent vision through animal nature. This, however, can only come healthily when the subject is already intellectually and psychologically developed. Otherwise, it is merely the type of base instinct fought on the Fool's journey at the Strength stage.

Whenever the Devil appears in a reading, a type of chaos is indicated. This is symbolised in the *Rider-Waite* pack by the inverted pentagram at the Devil's brow.

Usually, spirit is indicated by the topmost point, and the other four essential elements are below it; thought and spirit over matter. Here, however, matter takes precedence. This can indicate the emergence of neuroses, which find their vent in hedonistic pursuit. Repression is released in a healthier manner than might be found later in the Tower card. If utilised properly, this stage is a blessing—an opportunity to escape convention and thus nip future problems (anger, suppressed sexuality, fear) in the bud. The Devil may be approached and found to be less of a monster than one might previously have supposed. "Pan"-ic subsides when the horned beast is approached fearlessly, and eventually understood. This relates especially to the suppressed libido—thus, bisexuality and homosexuality are also indicated. This is not in a negative sense, but rather as a release of previous fears and inhibitions.

Another theme of this image is that of informed morality. It is easy to be sanctimonious when chaos has not touched one's life. This card represents human understanding of the biological organism—mind and spirit are included, but temporarily held on a back burner. It is impossible to operate as a well-rounded human being unless the Devil has been experienced in some form—even simply as temptation. In the *Tarot of the Old Path,* the card is given this very name. Trauma, and the questioning of previous social/psychological mores, is therefore inevitable when this card appears.

Meaning—This card represents the facing and eventual acceptance of impulses previously considered "base." Also, experimentation; release of repressed urges, often in an unpredictable manner.

Reversed—When reversed, the Devil indicates strong attraction towards potentially harmful activities. Also, matter ruling over mind—sensuality, sexuality in dominance; lack of self-control.

XVI—The Tower

This card is also known as the Falling Tower or the Lightning-struck Tower. We may deduce from this, and from the image itself (in which bodies fall from a crumbling edifice), that a sudden, shocking event has taken place. What had seemed powerful and imposing is suddenly reduced to rubble.

The Tower could be construed as the ego. It has built itself up in the outside world, and though necessarily confining, its walls have been both protective to those inside, and impressive to those outside. Out of the blue, disaster strikes. All that has become familiar and unquestionable becomes unstable and unsafe. The most obvious parallel in modern history is the collapse of the World Trade Center in New York. It seemed impossible and surreal to contemplate the destruction of such a building—two Towers—but it happened. Complacency is shattered when the Tower appears.

People build towers to make a point. They are the most visible and imposing structures we can create, reaching up into the heavens with a type of hubris. The conscious mind dares to stretch out into the realms of the gods and erect a monument to rationale. In most packs, the people falling from the Tower are fully clothed, often dressed in cloaks and even hats—all of the paraphernalia of social prestige. In the *Rider-Waite* pack, one of them even wears a crown. As with Death, all are levelled by the processes represented by the Tower.

The Tower, however, is not entirely negative in import. It represents a massive quantum leap in consciousness. This will be positive to the querent in the long run, though during the immediate impact he or she will feel as if the ground has been whipped away from underfoot—which it may well have been, quite literally. On a mundane level, household disaster is indicated. The crown of our creation is blown from its pinnacle. We are forced to reform and reassess. Isolationism of any sort, especially elitism, is explosively eliminated.

Meaning—The Tower indicates a shock event; violent upheaval; the destruction of all that has previously seemed safe and sure. Also, insight and sudden enlightenment; a wider view, usually reached through suffering; loss of social prestige, which will eventually lead to something more worthwhile.

Reversed—When reversed, this could represent an accident, grief and intense suffering, or loss without immediate comfort. Also, the need to allow the spirit to shine through. The Tower can be a friend if personal courage is accessed; either way, a life-changing cataclysm.

XVII—The Star

Like Temperance, the character in the Star card holds two water containers, but this time, both are being tipped out—one into a pool or stream, the other onto the earth. She is often depicted naked, with a tree in which a small bird perches behind her. Unlike the characters in the Tower card, she has been stripped of signs of social prestige. She is her inner self. The bird represents intuition and aspiration.

Eight stars shine in the sky, one of which is especially bright. This is the star of hope. This woman, completely mortal (unlike the winged character of Temperance) is naked before the gods. She is no longer under any illusions as to her personal status. The water she pours, symbolic of emotion and of the subconscious, goes half to its source (she is therefore intuitive) and half to earth, the other element to which she belongs.

The Star therefore represents the synthesis of conscious and subconscious, and life lived in balance with no pretensions. External influences are irrelevant; she is alone, but carrying out a ritual beneath the blinking eyes of the gods. She is inward-looking and positive. With the Hermit stage, the Fool was seeking affirmation of a greater power; with the Star, the energies are now focussed on following personal beliefs, much as the Hanged Man was, but with less social prejudice in effect.

Meaning—The Star represents optimism—following the Star of hope to a greater goal than already attained; honesty, intuition.

Reversed—When reversed, the Star indicates lack of joy, lack of hope, inhibition, and fear of one's own intuitions.

XVIII—The Moon

In the *Tarot of the Old Path,* this card is called "Illusion," which emphasises the tenuous nature of its messages. Here, all becomes symbolic and impossible to fathom with the conscious mind. Intuition is called for, as well as the same faith that brought the Fool through the Star episode. The signs could be genuine prompts of the subconscious, or they could be mere tricks of the imagination.

In the *Rider-Waite* and many other packs, two pillars are shown, between which the Moon shines. Dogs howl at the lunar orb, driven to distraction by the effect of the full moon. It is difficult to define their nature: are they wolves, or actually dogs? Are they friendly, faithful guides, or wild, dangerous animals? Likewise, our intuitions during the Moon phase. This process is widely recognised as mind-bending; witness the numerous horror films in which the moon is full. Not only do humans and animals respond instinctively to the nocturnal illumination, but this is the time when it becomes easiest to contact the "other side"—both of our psyches and the Veil. Hence the esbats, or full moon celebrations enjoyed by witches.

The moon in mythology represents the feminine, intuitive side of the collective unconscious; at this time, it becomes possible to cross the conscious with the subconscious. It is a time of moods and instinct. The twin pillars, the two dogs, and the other images of duality to be found in the card symbolise the union of these opposites. If unbalanced—lacking in solar, active, rational qualities—the mind will tip over at this time, and fall prey to violent upheavals of the imagination. Only by synthesising the two will clarity be achieved.

In the foreground of the card is a river (or the edge of the sea), out of which a crayfish or crab crawls. This is the sign of Cancer, and again emphasises the product of the watery traits: emotion, imagination, spirituality. Sometimes we crave spiritual affirmation so much that we are glamoured by absurdities, and distracted by creatures from the depths of our inner selves. At other times these feelings and images are valid prompts. Here, discrimination is called for. The crustacean is by its very nature armoured; we cannot fully attack it with rationale. It has its own set of referents in which it is completely valid. It may seem as surreal as Dali's lobster telephone when we first encounter it, but with the Moon phase we learn again of different levels to life.

Magickally, this card is auspicious, especially when coupled with the High Priestess. However, as in the Qabalistic Yesod to which this card most relates, astral light and the "treasure house of images" (Gareth Knight's name for the Tarot itself) must be treated with caution. The card is a gateway to much we don't need or probably want to know. Just as those exploring past incarnations can find themselves utterly traumatised by revelations received, it is worth approaching the river clad in a wet suit of reality. Otherwise we may be chilled and swept away by the currents.

In the *Russian Tarot of St. Petersburg,* a man paddles along the river. He looks a lot like the Hermit. He casts his oar with trepidation into the swirling waters. He is, however, in control. He has been initiated into solitude; now he is touching the very essence of his own life-source. It takes absolute control to ride the currents with success. He stands upright, indicating his mastery of the situation. Thus, the learned mystic is able to define which subconscious currents are safe to ride.

In the same pack, a telescope sits atop the left tower pointing at the moon. The moon, complete with visage, stares right back. The moon has a face in many packs. This emphasises the personal nature of the objective at this time. Patterns are sought, and all is perceived through personal experience. The telescope indicates close scrutiny both of the natural, "outside" world, and the natural inner self. How are they interlinked? This is the question of the Moon card.

It is said in the Charge of the Goddess, "Whenever you have need of anything, *and better it be when the Moon is full* [emphasis added], then shall ye assemble in some secret place and adore the spirit of Me Who am Queen of all Witches. There shall ye assemble, ye who are fain to learn all sorcery, yet have not won its deepest secrets; to these I will teach things that are yet unknown." The timing is indicative of every meaning of this card. The "deepest secrets" of the subconscious and other planes are indeed revealed at this time.

Meaning—The Moon represents imagination, emotion, and spirituality fused together. Also, difficulty in discerning between truth and illusion; the need for caution and discrimination. Self-scrutiny is essential at this time—question all motives, especially subconscious. This is a tall order, but it is backed up by the strength of intuition at this time.

Reversed—When reversed, the Moon indicates deception, madness, and hormones out of control. Also, a dire need for logical thought.

XIX—The Sun

After the intense, self-questioning night of the soul represented by the Moon, the sun rises, bringing warmth and comfort. Even in the negative (or ill-aspected), this card is barely bad; the worst it can augur is pleasant laziness, or childishness. The characters in most packs frolic, often atop a pale horse, in front of a wall. They are blissfully excluded from danger—both from the outside universe, and from their own imaginations. The phantasms of the Moon have been dissipated; now is a time of unbridled happiness.

In some ways, this card represents a return to the mentality of the Fool; innocence and childhood fancy are indicated. However, we must not be duped by the diminutive nature of the character concerned. A baby or naked child in Tarot imagery is a reincarnated being, complete with all the natural wisdom so often accredited to the child (witness Annie Besant and Charles Leadbeater's apotheosis of the boy Krishnamurti). The idea is one of wisdom without guile. The introspection of the Moon card has been processed; now is the time to shine light back into the world.

This is a card of delight, and of disposal of self-doubt. However, a wall is still required. In order to break out completely, the Fool, innocence regained, will have to break through into yet another process of discrimination.

Meaning—The Sun means happiness, revitalisation, and a return of energy. Also, the gods and the Universe smiling on one; safety.

Reversed—When reversed, the Sun means laziness—feeling that one has struggled and deserves an indefinite rest. Also, the misuse of energy (hedonism rather than self-development/helpfulness to others).

XX—Judgement

Figures young and old—entire families, in fact—rise from their graves, arms upstretched to greet Gabriel, who blows his trumpet from the skies. In some packs he stands on a crescent moon, imagery concomitant with his role as lunar, water angel. Every aspect of the psyche—anima, animus, and the child of the Sun card—is brought into play here. There are no walls, just open tombs and great stretches of sky in which mountain peaks may be seen. This is clearly a time of renewal and of aspiration. The sky is not the limit, it is the invitation!

The fact that these characters are rising from the earth confirms the aspect of aspiration—in this case, spiritual. However, it is a far greater spiritual aspiration than that indicated by the other ultraspiritual cards in the pack—the High Priestess, the Hierophant, and the Hermit—because the consciousness has now been merged (through the Moon and the Sun) with the Universe. Samadhi, or mergeance with all, is now possible, the ultimate goal of the ascetic mystic. This has been attained not merely through solitude and introspection (though these have played an important role), but through interaction with all that life contains. The Minor Arcana elaborate on the details; the Major Arcana give a title to the larger spiritual, developmental process.

Here, the Fool once again chases his dreams, but this time they are not self-conceived—they are universal truths. Judgement is a process of reaching for perfection.

In the *Tarot of the Old Path,* this card is called "Karma," and looks a lot like Death. Characters are shown as the soul exits the dying body and rises up to greet long-lost loved ones, or enters the womb ready to be reborn. So, this is a time for assessing all that has been achieved, and for plans as to how spiritual evolution may be improved. Judgement is not a symbol of punishment but rather—as the Scales of Justice held by the Karma figure indicate—of impartial and necessary balancing. Coming just prior to the rebirth of the World card, this process (and the wonderful image that represents it) summarises the state of being following a particular cycle of development.

On a more mundane level, then, the card represents release from captivity—from the apparent bounds of mortality and physical circumstance. The call of Gabriel's trumpet is heralding and vocational rather than compulsory, as many Christians are tempted to construe the image. Judgement does *not* mean separating the wheat from the chaff of religious paths, or the sudden elevation of "God's Chosen." We are still free to decide whether to follow, or whether to return to our "tombs" of self-perceived circumstance. However, should we choose to follow this strong inner calling, we could well find ourselves en route to incarnational completion. Judgement represents a spectacular opportunity if we have the courage to leave that to which we have become accustomed.

Meaning—Judgement indicates challenge in the cause of achievement, or the dramatic opportunity to attain a desire often hidden and long-suppressed. Also, rejuvenation; spiritual callings.

Reversed—When reversed, Judgement represents a lack of courage to follow through with convictions. It also refers to other mortals rather than to the Divine plan. The querent may have a need for quiet meditation in order to establish priorities.

XXI—The World

An androgynous (or sometimes female) figure dances in the midst of the cerulean, no ground beneath her feet, and usually inside a laurel wreath. Heads or figures representing the four angels of the elements appear around her surrounded by cloudy ether. In her hands she holds two scrolls. She is a sky-dancer, calm but joyous. In some packs, a globe appears behind her.

The scrolls represent knowledge attained and assimilated. The laurel symbolises achievement. It was also the tree whose leaves were burned by the ancient Greeks to make their Pythias, priestesses of Apollo, oracular. Thus, divine wisdom and the ability to teach are also represented. The character is graduating from one stage of cosmic consciousness to another. In the Crowley *Thoth* pack, the card is named "The Aeon," which perfectly sums up this upgrading of understanding. The card symbolises spiritual evolution.

The angels of the cardinal points and four elements indicate the presence of all qualities—and of all qualities sublimated. The fact that the figure itself is usually androgynous shows that gender barriers have also broken down. The dancer has achieved what she needed to learn; the fruits of the Fool's journey are hers to pick. Of course, there will be a new cycle opening up after this, but successful completion of one important cycle is certainly indicated.

The figure is wrapped in a scarf—part naked, part revealed. All has not become totally clear; there are still certain mysteries to the cosmos and even to the individual that will never be understood. We may attempt to align ourselves with the subconscious, but by its very nature it can never entirely be understood. For example, this image is ideal to represent reincarnation. When delivered into a new body, the soul has amnesia, and the mind picks up more immediate stimulae than inner knowledge. However, as the person begins to grow, certain memories and responses will be triggered. The previous incarnation(s) may be hinted at, but they will never fully be known through necessity; there is no point in flooding the present with the past. The whole point is progression.

Meaning—The World card indicates great achievement. Also, understanding, cosmic consciousness; unity of physical, spiritual, and mental energies; the end of one cycle and, inevitably, the beginning of another.

Reversed—When reversed, the World represents stagnation, or being stuck in a rut. It can sometimes indicate important plans and aspirations turned upside down; certainly, a loss of inspiration and joy.

The Minor Arcana

The four suits of the Minor Arcana represent the four qualities of normal life: material well-being and sensation (Pentacles), inspirational energy and creativity (Wands), thought and strife (Swords), and the emotional life (Cups). Together they describe normal human circumstance, from interference to confusion to attainment of a cherished goal. As in witchcraft, each suit represents a cardinal point and its qualities: earth for Pentacles, fire for Wands, air for Swords, and water for Cups. Thus a reading with many Swords will represent mental strife, and one filled with Wands will indicate an excess of ideas.

There are also court cards for each suit, which symbolise both people and various areas of concern. The King of Pentacles, for example, could be a generous, paternal, dark-haired man, or he could represent a new project coming close to fruition. They tell a smaller story than do the Major Arcana, but one that is of more immediate relevance to our daily lives. After all, when most people come for a Tarot reading, they are more concerned as to whether they will find a new job soon or whether their partner will leave them than about their state of progress spiritually.

The court cards signify different stages in the evolution of their assigned element. In the Page, an idea is conceived, discussed, and proposed. In the Knight, it is vigorously projected—and the affairs of the querent are faithfully protected. The Queen shows the querents' creative fruition, and the King their standing in the material realms. There is much more to each court card, of course, but these factors act as guidelines.

Each number also has its own significance. Aces indicate beginnings—each proving a powerful impetus. They are very good news when upright, and reversed, they can represent negative extremes.

With the two, we develop the idea or project. Information is accrued from outside—the impulse is no longer merely internal.

Threes represent planning. Just as the figure in the Three of Pentacles sits studiously at his desk, forethought comes into play here.

With the four, we begin to see the fruits of our labors. Complacency (as in the Four of Pentacles) is to be rigorously avoided, however. Despite the balance and security it provides (the idea is now accepted and set into motion), the rewards are still distant. Further energetic input is required.

The five brings questions—all seems unbalanced when the fives appear. Is reason or chaos the true ruler of our lives? The entrepreneur fears for his enterprises. External influences inflict themselves on us. We are tested.

The six brings renewed equilibrium, though certainly not complacency. Success is becoming visible, but factors from the past may still come into play. (The Six of Cups, for example, represents extreme nostalgia, and a psychological return to a childlike state.)

The seven of each suit indicates choice. The Seven of Cups is a prime example of this; seven chalices are on offer, each containing an entirely different quality, but the querent must discriminate and ultimately choose among them. Options are apparent, which is good, but they are not clear, which is a headache. Inner tranquillity is required in order to facilitate a correct decision.

With the eight, we begin to take control of the situation. An attempt is made at organising all of the relevant factors into groups that can be logically (and intuitively) dealt with. This is man fighting against Chaos. In the case of the Eight of Swords, it is necessary to recognise conscious choice in the situation. One is bound by circumstance, but still has the power to change it, despite depression. This is the hero's quest, and there is no place for self-pity. Swords teach strife (as do the other suits, in their unique ways), but it is rarely insurmountable physically, and never spiritually.

The nine brings affirmation. There is still no complete relaxation—which is rare in this life—but there is a definite feeling of pending success. In the Nine of Wands, for example, we witness a character fending off other Wands—but who is also surrounded by them. These are the rewards of past striving. The querent has established a scheme or project, and now, just a little more vigilance will bring it to pass.

The ten represents completion—at least, of a temporary nature. The Ten of Cups is joyous indeed—home and family are established, and there is room for much growth. The Ten of Pentacles underlines this—the strength of history, legacy, and blood-ties seems unquestionable. Of course, there is always the play of the Major Arcana to consider; for example, the Ten of Pentacles aspected by the Devil may indicate hereditary vice, as in the dissolute aristocrats of old. The Wheel of Fortune could send established families tumbling from their vantage points. The Ten of Cups combined with the Hierophant reversed may show an excess of bureaucracy, red tape, or even religious guilt overshadowing an apparently happy union/family scenario. The Ten of Swords, with its violent, back-stabbed imagery, represents a culmination of negative circumstance. However, with the ten, a certain small cycle has come to completion.

For more specific interpretations of each card, see below. I have used the *Rider-Waite* pack for reference, as it is the most influential of all Tarot decks, and many sets are based on it.

Ace of Pentacles

A wonderful opportunity on the material planes. Sudden, unexpected income. A new idea that will bring future recompense.

Reversed—Problems getting plans off the ground. Mundane considerations. Loss of wealth and potential.

Two of Pentacles

Juggling with circumstance. High seas and stormy weather financially, as indicated by the heaving ocean waves in the background and the seasick-looking figure to the fore. Borrowing from one source to pay another, but certainly in good faith. Ventures are launched, but their future is uncertain. Stoicism. The sort of card a student will get when broke but working hard at school. Long-term projects seem like a good investment, though their fruits are distant. Drunkenness may ensue, as a comfortable antidote to immediate concerns—this can be as much on aspiration as on liquor. Either way, an attempt at establishing balance.

Reversed—Mindless hedonism, lack of foresight, unstable ventures.

Three of Pentacles

Apprenticeship, skilled craftsmanship that is appreciated by others. Two robed men, one of them a monk and the other a possible sponsor, stand and comment on the work of a mason. He accepts both their instruction and their praise.

This image represents the opportunity to learn a trade or craft (particularly relevant to skilled manual work), probably directly from a master of the art. Encouragement, and possible sponsorship. When this card appears, it shows that endeavours are well-omened and should be continued.

Reversed—Shoddy work, or effort that is not bringing its due rewards.

Four of Pentacles

A smug, sometimes avaricious man sits in the middle of the card, clutching four pentacles. In the background, a built-up city is visible.

This man is clearly a materialist, literally clinging to his possessions, status, and so on. Thus, limited views are shown—there is security, but no creativity. Even in its positive aspect, this card warns of mental stagnation. A solid foundation has been established, but progress could be hindered by unwillingness to take a risk or to accept new ideas.

Reversed—Complacency, arrogance, avarice, blinkered views.

Five of Pentacles

Two vagrants, one of them on crutches, hobble their way through the snow. They are passing the stained-glass window of a church or castle. Light and presumably warmth exist on the other side, but these two are outcast. Wealth belongs to others, and they stand no chance of accruing any for themselves, except perhaps by begging.

Although times are very hard when the Five of Pentacles appears, there is companionship in adversity. Friends are indicated, who are able to offer little (if any) financial help, but who will be there for the querent to talk to, and to give psychological support. However, there can be no avoiding the fact that, when this card appears, times are difficult.

Reversed—Financial disaster. Very strenuous times. Extreme caution is required in business matters.

Six of Pentacles

A robed man holds balancing scales in one hand and dispenses money to beggars with the other. His status and affluence are unquestionable.

When this card appears, it indicates philanthropy, usually given and received in equal measure. Also, the balance of income with expenditure—possibly with a little more given than received, but all in good cause. Financial clout and conscience combined.

Reversed—Irregular income, and an excess of red tape in financial/material matters. Stagnation in material matters, most likely due to lack of resources.

Seven of Pentacles

A man leans on his hoe and gazes idly into a bush. On it are represented the fruits of his previous labours. He cannot, however, be bothered to tend to them right now. He is bored.

The obvious theme here is feeling lackluster about one's own achievements, and not having the will or energy to follow them through, thus risking all that one has established before. It is important to continue making an effort, otherwise the fruits might wither on the vine. Sustained effort is essential.

Reversed—Laziness, ennui, lack of attention to details. Depression and failure.

Eight of Pentacles

A craftsman sits on his workbench, happily hammering away at a pentacle. Others are on display before him, and another waits to be crafted.

This is an excellent card for all work projects and artistic, creative endeavours, particularly those for which one will be paid. Effort is steady and easy because the task in hand is one actually enjoyed. Enthusiasm, assiduity. Continuing in this vein will guarantee success.

Reversed—The possibility of having chosen short-term rewards over long-term aspirations. Misuse of energy. Not a bad card even reversed, but choices regarding work and financial return may need to be reconsidered.

Nine of Pentacles

A comfortable-looking woman in fine robes stands in a flourishing garden, a hawk at her wrist. The card is predominately yellow, indicating wealth, health, and happiness.

Ease has been attained by this stage, which is one of well-being. There is no pressure, except perhaps for an excess of social engagements! Life is good, one has time to relax, and even to consider new ventures. It is important, however, to keep ethics in mind, and not to become elitist, as do so many whose fortune is good.

Reversed—Ill-gained wealth, the well-being of one based on the misery of many; exploitation. A clique mentality.

Ten of Pentacles

A family group is shown in the homestead, which is a castle. An old man watches his children and grandchildren with satisfaction. He is proud of them, and he knows he has set them up nicely. He has achieved all any parent can ask for; he has worked hard in order to give them a good life. They will want for nothing.

Family ties and inheritance are key to this card. Wealth and tradition have been established, and are unquestionable now. All that the material plane has to offer is available to be enjoyed. Money and legacies are certainly indicated, as are inherited traits and discoveries regarding family.

The Crowley *Thoth* deck has the ten coins arranged in the shape of the Qabalistic Tree of Life, each "sephirah" marked by an individuating sigil. The card bears the title "Wealth." This wealth is clearly not just material, however. Each coin represents an entire sphere of experience and understanding. So, this is wisdom accrued over years, just as the head of the family in the *Rider-Waite* card has worked steadily for years in order to establish his own homestead, and with it lessons, rules, and regulations, and rewards and punishments. The ten shiny coins in the *Thoth* deck sit atop a heap of duller ones, which lie chaotically beneath. The mind, through experience, has created order, and the brightness of insight shines above the apparent randomness of the universe. Crowley also implies the use of wealth for positive spiritual progress, which is likewise hinted at in the *Rider-Waite* illustration. This is most definitely of a more orthodox nature than Crowley's!

The patriarchal set-up is not quite perfect, however. His children may be compelled to act in a stereotyped way, and there is considerable restriction on freedom of choice. Others must be taken into account and even consulted first. However, generally, this is a card of well-being.

Reversed—Stagnation, frustration, and restriction, most likely caused by family affairs or orthodox institutions. Not a terrible card, but one that indicates a need for greater adventurousness.

Page of Pentacles

This card represents a dark, affable youth. He is a steady worker, good with the practical and/or logical, with aspirations that are most likely to be "sensible." He is a boy who knows his place and works happily in that context.

The Page of Pentacles can also indicate the initiation of a business endeavour.

Reversed—A lumpen youth unwilling to free himself from his own narrow perspective. A venture that cannot get off the ground for lack of initiative.

Knight of Pentacles

This is the card of a loyal young(ish) man, a steadfast friend, and a permanent good ally—usually fraternal in implication, or a son. He is most likely to be dark-haired. This card represents somebody who can be trusted, or issues pertaining to that person.

Also indicated is the successful launching of a project.

Reversed—A dull-minded male who cannot see beyond his own material and psychological comfort. A selfish materialist. The spoiling of an endeavour through diminished inspiration and/or lack of funds.

Queen of Pentacles

This is the card of a mature and well-grounded, dusky woman. She is a positive and nurturing maternal influence; the Empress on a minor scale. As a character she is likely to be creative—especially good with home-making—though not experimental with her lifestyle. She is often a woman who has followed conventional paths all of her life, but who is now open to fresh concepts, though only within the contexts she has set for herself. She is cautious with herself, but often generous to others.

The Queen of Pentacles can also signify the near-completion of a creative project; a stage at which ideas and inspirations are still applicable.

Reversed—As an opponent, the Queen of Pentacles brings jealousy and small-mindedness into the arena. The influence of the mundane, deadening to the aspiring spirit. Possible double-crossing and unseen psychological influences. Problems aligning the inspirational with the practical.

King of Pentacles

This card represents a mature man well-established in the material world, especially in the familial sense. In looks he is likely to be dark. As a character he has his "kingdom" already up and running, his vested interests and concerns as a steady foundation to his personality. He is a minor expression of the Emperor card.

When the King of Pentacles occurs positively in a reading, he is a paternal or fraternal influence—a person who is likely to impart good sense and steady support to the querent. He may also represent the successful progress of a project that is likely to bring material rewards.

Reversed—Opposition from the orthodoxy; the inability to attain spiritual truth and direction over material concerns; a man as described above standing in one's path. Stubbornness and lack of imagination. Materialism and fear of losing out financially.

Ace of Cups

An image of abundant and effervescent joy. A chalice, archetypal symbol of the feminine, overflows into a pool on which lilies float. A dove flies into its centre, carrying in its beak a disc marked with an equilateral cross, a solar symbol and indicative of balance at the middle of the Tree of Life. Thus, despite the excess of emotion present at this stage, there is also an inner equilibrium that prevents the situation from getting out of control.

When this card appears, happiness is definite. Nor is it a case of complacency—there is no place for stagnation in this scene. Pleasure may grow from tranquillity—as do the lilies—but all here is active. The chalice is ever-creative, pouring forth waters from an apparently fathomless source. So joy, abundance, creativity, and spirituality are all indicated.

Reversed—Happiness spilled or wasted (especially if combined with the Five of Cups). Barrenness of mind and possibly body. Loss of love; possible secret or unspoken factors interfering with the emotional life.

Two of Cups

A man and a woman stand facing one another, their chalices nearly touching. A caduceus topped by a winged lion springs from between them, the wings of the lion hanging protectively over them.

These characters are clearly friends. Their bodies face one another directly—theirs is an honest relationship. The caduceus represents similar interests; the snakes of their thoughts intertwine gracefully. The lion represents the heart, so there is also affection here. The wings show potential, and swiftness of thought and communication.

We may deduce from these signs that a harmonious relationship is indicated. Male and female traits are balanced, and there is pleasure as well as mental stimulation involved. Empathy is assured. So, this indicates an important friendship, and possibly a partnership; balance and understanding. A good card in any situation.

Reversed—Disenchantment with a relationship. Betrayal and loss. A rift in a loving relationship and a loss of ability to communicate effectively.

Three of Cups

Three women dance, their chalices held aloft. Flowers are visible in their hair and on the ground around them. Clearly they are mid-celebration. A wedding, a conception or birth, or simply a party for close, loving friends—whatever the cause, this is a celebration of life, and their hearts are filled with joy. Sometimes this can be as simple as a drink with friends—it is the feeling of joy and belonging that is the important factor. Similarly, a union is confirmed. When it appears in a reading for a querent who has recently become involved in a relationship, the card gives a very positive indication of happiness. The union will prove fruitful on every level.

Reversed—Confusion, unbalanced emotions. Difficulty in deciphering the nature and potential of a partnership. Misplaced optimism.

Four of Cups

A bored-looking chap sits at the foot of a tree, his arms defensively crossed. Three upright chalices stand before him, and out of the ether, a hand proffers a fourth chalice. He does not notice it.

When this card appears, ennui is indicated. One is so busy looking inwards that new offers are ignored or not even noticed. Thus, there is a strong possibility of missing out on opportunities that are right under one's nose. Energy is required, and a change of attitude. In relationships, complacency may have infringed on pleasure. Some success has been enjoyed, but more of the same is unlikely if new ideas are not brought into play. Dissatisfaction is imminent if ideas are not bucked up.

Reversed—Stagnation, boredom. Loss of love because of these factors. Dissatisfaction with the familiar, but an inability to detach from it. A need for change.

Five of Cups

A man dressed in a cloak of melancholy black stands with his back to the reader. Three cups lie to his left, their contents spilled; two stand upright to his right. A river and a bridge lie before him, but he is looking at the ground at his feet.

This is a card of emotional loss and pessimism. The querent believes that he or she has lost more than can ever be gained; future endeavours seem futile. In fact, there are great possibilities ahead, if only one has the heart and mind to pursue them; but the querent does not. He or she can think only of opportunities lost, optimism spilled on barren ground.

This is a card of unhappiness and a lack of motivation, despite positive developments being in the offing. It indicates a need for emotional resolve and closure.

Reversed—Trauma; a feeling of being beleaguered by bad luck. Intense pessimism. Things can improve, but only with a radical change in attitude.

Six of Cups

Two prettily dressed children exchange chalices filled with flowers. A yellow background confirms that happiness and health are ruling the day here. A shield with an X on it appears in stonework behind one of the children. This is Gifu, the rune of affection and love.

Childhood allegiances appear here in the most positive of senses. The atmosphere is one of love and affection, and also of nostalgia. This is the only possible downside of this card: an excess of retrospection. A good friendship is indicated, and positive influences from childhood. The mood is gentle and appreciative.

A beloved friend from childhood/early significant stages is of relevance. Thoughts relate to the past; established rapport. This card indicates pleasure, and childlike affection.

Reversed—Idealism of the past, and an inability to get on with the present and future. A split in a cherished long-term friendship.

Seven of Cups

Chalices appear swathed in swirling mist; the hands that proffer them are invisible. Each contains a different, often fantastical image: a fairy-tale castle, a dragon or chimera, a snake, or a levitating, glowing being. A man stands before them poised as if he has just conjured them out of thin air; or is he choosing among them? It is difficult to discern whether the images are real possibilities, or illusory. So, discrimination is called for—as well as an awareness of motives behind any offers received—when this card appears.

Emotionally, many paths seem possible; each leads to potential riches. Options are given regarding relationships. There is no great need to choose yet—they can simply be enjoyed until the situation becomes clearer. There is the possibility of a mystic experience through attraction and love.

Reversed—An excess of options, and difficulty in discerning which are best. Confusion, overoptimism, self-delusion. A need to find a quiet place, allow emotional hyperactivity to recede, and wait until circumstances are less clouded by subjectivity.

Eight of Cups

A man walks away from eight chalices, his head bowed. A stream already lies between him and his previous emotional situation, represented by the cups. His cloak is red, a colour of both warmth and of pain. He is doing the right thing and knows it, which gives him strength, but the situation is a sorrowful one. What has become obsolete is abandoned in favour of a brighter future. This card is the "Death" of the Cups suit—creating a fertile environment for new emotional experiences.

Reversed—The situation being approached is not necessarily better than that being left. Changing relationships/partners for the sake of it, perhaps through boredom. A need for thought rather than emotional response.

Nine of Cups

A smug man sits with arms crossed before a crescent of nine uplifted chalices. His arms are folded, not with self-defense, but as a gesture of ease.

Here, the emotional life is well established, and happiness is almost complete. This does not necessarily mean being in a relationship—the key is in "whatever makes you happy and is right for you." The recipient of this card is undergoing (or about to undergo) emotional harmony and satisfaction. Pleasure is strong and productive. Help may be given to others, with no loss of personal equilibrium.

Reversed—Smugness; the emotional equivalent of the avarice in the Four of Cups. Being a dog in a manger in a relationship (for example, hanging on to somebody because you cannot bear the idea of him or her being happy with anyone else). Dissatisfaction, moodiness.

Ten of Cups

A classic family unit—father, mother, boy, and girl—are clearly blessed by good fortune. The parents raise grateful arms to the rainbow above, while the children dance felicitously in the foreground. A house is visible amidst the verdure, and a stream flows past it.

It does not take an occult genius to interpret this exuberant imagery. All that is good in life is held here: security, mental engagement, new opportunities (symbolised by the stream), love, and pleasure. The rainbow indicates harmony on the emotional planes, but also, importantly, the bridge between the worlds. This card is not merely one of emotional and material satisfaction, it is one of spiritual connections and developments too. Obviously this situation will not last forever—nothing ever does in Malkuth (the material plane)—but it is cherished while it lasts, and is positive for all who are nurtured by it.

Appearing in a reading about a relationship, this card represents complete happiness.

Reversed—A situation that has been outgrown and has thus become oppressive. Alternatively, the pointless upsetting of a family home (such as when a parent has an affair, or a teenager causes pointless arguments). A need for reassessment, honesty, and development. This may require the removal of a person from the home, and certainly augurs emotional upset.

Page of Cups

This is the card of an intuitive, poetic young person; one with creativity and sass, but who is very self-aware. In some respects, this is the archetypal introspective teenager. The Page of Cups also represents the creative process.

Reversed—A waster—a nice one, but a waster nonetheless. Likewise with projects dreamed about, pored over, but never set into action. Somebody (or an idea) that needs to be defined and grounded in order to make any real impact on the outside world.

Knight of Cups

This card represents a friendly young man with the ability and desire to empathise. A positive exchange of experiences is indicated; for example, in love issues, the genuine emotions of a/the male. A relationship is getting off the ground.

Reversed—Misunderstandings in friendships and love. Communication between the genuinely affable going awry and offence being accidentally caused. Giving or receiving "the wrong idea." Superficial bickering may be indicated as a result of this.

Queen of Cups

This card represents a sensitive, psychically aware woman—one with many secrets she is unlikely to reveal. She is a gentle and creative soul, very much attuned to the astral levels; a minor expression of the High Priestess. As a friend, she is one who is likely to bring valuable insights and intuitions to the querent. This card also represents the discovering of these qualities within oneself.

Reversed—A paranoid, malicious woman prone to calculated gossip. An insecure feminine influence that may throw the querent off balance psychically. The draining of one's energies into pointless social scenarios. Flippancy, narcissism, and the inability to "go with the flow" and appreciate the value and beauty of those of a different nature.

King of Cups

This is the card of an introspective, deep-thinking (though this may not be obvious), mature man; a creative dreamer. He is one with high aspirations in love, which he generally fails to fulfil to his satisfaction (possibly undergoing numerous intense obsessions and idealisations of his partners). In looks he tends to veer towards the fair. This man is very much an individual, and highly skilled in his own areas. He can be complicated, but is often a charmer.

As a general situation, this card represents something that is yearned for, and possibly felt as "absent," even though it can be difficult to define what that thing is. It is most likely to be a secretly longed-for emotional scenario.

Reversed—A hopeless idealist who consistently fails to recognise the practical issues necessary to bring his dreams to pass. Somebody who thinks he or she is profound, but whose actions appear superficial and possibly spiteful. The impossibility of gaining any practical purchase on an issue or aspiration.

Ace of Swords

A powerful new concept or idea, or the beginning of a significant new cycle in the querent's life. Because of the passion indicated by the Ace of Swords, this can mean the start of a relationship. Either way, swiftness and acuity of thought, and great energy are indicated. It is an excellent time to initiate new projects.

Reversed—Wasted energy, stagnation. Abuse of power, unkindness. A need for reassessment and change.

Two of Swords

A woman sits blindfolded holding two swords balanced in her hands. The sea and a crescent moon are visible behind her. She is dressed in white.

The impetus of the Ace has been assimilated and set into motion. The querent is unsure as to how the new venture will go, but is balanced in his or her approach. Intuition has been brought into play, symbolised by the sea and moon. The latter is a crescent because the project is still in the early stages. The white robes represent purity; so far, no *x*-factors (such as worry or self-doubt) are contaminating the situation.

Reversed—Lack of balance, a mental block, using ideas to bolster the ego rather than actually carrying them through. The temptation to abandon something once the excitement has worn off. A need for perseverance.

Three of Swords

Three swords pierce a heart, while thunderclouds and rain form a grey background.

Needless to say, this is not a happy card to receive in a reading. Heartbreak, sorrow, delay, and absence of a loved one are indicated. It can also indicate sterility, miscarriage, or abortion—it is the virtual antithesis of the Three of Cups.

However, no card is entirely bad, and this one shows that problems can be overcome with kindness and patience. Project-wise, bridges need to be gapped, and agreements reached. Communication is essential, and, properly executed, can lead to the proper development of a project.

Reversed—Discord, cruelty, pain. The negatives mentioned above. It must be remembered that, in every life, a little rain must fall. A sense of humour would be greatly beneficial at this time, though one is unlikely to be able to access it. Depression, self-doubt, and dark nights of the soul.

Four of Swords

A man lies supine, hands folded in prayer. He is, in fact, a statue atop a tomb. Three swords point down at his body, another lies parallel to his spine. A stained-glass window showing a supplicant being blessed is the only colourful image in the card.

When this card appears, a need for solitude and respite from work is indicated. The character may look dead, but he is in fact travelling inwards, as his hands closed in prayer indicate. He seeks aid from a higher source, as does the character in the stained-glass window. Spiritual guidance is indicated, especially if the Four of Swords is accompanied by the Temperance card. The appearance of this card indicates a need for physical as well as mental rest—sometimes, it can refer to hospitalisation.

This card indicates relief and rest; the healing process is enabled to take place. Also, there may be balance, agreement, and/or compromise in a business endeavour.

Reversed—Solitude to the point at which it becomes a psychological problem (possibly not receiving enough attention from others). Anxiety, hyperactivity with no real benefit to the querent. Inability to express one's own true desires.

Five of Swords

A spiteful-looking character with red hair smirks at a retreating figure and another with his head in his hands. He holds their swords as well as his own in his hands. Jagged grey clouds streak the sky.

This is a card of conflict, easy anger, jealousy, and revenge. Tempers are frayed, and petty causes are blown out of all proportion. Emotional chaos rules the day, especially if coupled with the Devil and/or the Tower.

On a more cerebral level, a new problem may arise that snags the smooth running of a plan or venture. Lateral thinking is required to carry the original plan off.

This card means self-control is required in adverse circumstances. One should be aware of conflicting interests and the competition of others; motives are not clean-cut, and deliberate deception may be the result. It indicates the need to think around problems rather than lunging in with an immediate emotional response. There is a danger of short-sighted anger.

Reversed—Similar to above, but in greater measure. The danger of a crime of passion taking place unless the temper is checked. Quarrels, conflicts, unworthy emotions.

Six of Swords

A man rows a woman and child—presumably his own family—from one shore to another. The woman's head is cowled and bowed as if in sorrow. While she huddles into her cloak, the man adeptly steers them forward. He is overcoming emotional and practical obstacles, represented by the water, by facilitating a change in circumstance. This is the process rather than the goal—times are still hard, but respite awaits.

The Six of Swords indicates progress and improvement. Difficulties lie more in the past than in the present, but there is still some emotional strain such as sorrow, regret, or nostalgia. Change is inevitable when this card appears.

Reversed—Change that seems not to be for the better. It may still turn out to be, but the process is painful and a great deal of regret may be involved. It can represent continued struggle, and remedial action falling through.

Seven of Swords

A man sneaks away from a military camp with five swords in his arms. He looks over his left shoulder and creeps on tippytoe.

The atmosphere of this card is clearly underhanded and unconventional. Lateral thinking is indicated—at its best, finding an unorthodox solution to a problem; at its worst, theft and treachery. This can be of ideas as much as anything tenable.

It is essential to think a plan through before acting, from every angle, including moral. A bad decision at this juncture could prove disastrous. Also, be alert to the actions of others—they may be thinking and doing things behind the scenes that could spell ruination for you. Make sure that those in your vicinity are being frank with you. If you are at all suspicious, confront them (with tact, of course).

On a more positive note, the Seven of Swords represents lateral thinking at its canniest; a good time for coming up with alternative approaches to any situation, especially intellectual or business-related.

Reversed—Secret opposition and loss. Theft, or the painful results of others acting behind the querent's back. This is often unavoidable and is best dealt with employing fresh resolve rather than anger or regret.

Eight of Swords

A woman stands blindfolded, hands tied behind her back, amidst eight swords, their points buried in the ground. The tribulation has run its course, as the earthed swords represent, but the woman, unable to act or see, must employ her intuition to sense whether danger has entirely passed before she releases herself. So she stands there, dressed in the red of sorrow, on a patch of water that represents her leaking emotions. That she is crying internally we cannot doubt.

It is time to liberate oneself from restrictive circumstances, but this takes courage and faith. Things seem terribly bleak, but improvement is possible through steadfast effort and optimism. A steadfast strategy is the best way to tackle the situation. Formulate one, and go!

Reversed—Pessimism, a sense of entrapment, and sorrow all define this card in its negative aspect. Possible nervous problems. Therapeutic aid, either professional or from friends, may be required. One is not in as bad a predicament as it seems, but thoughts have become so black as to render this impossible to see. An epiphany is required, and will come as soon as the querent allows and wills it.

Nine of Swords

A man sits up in bed, his head in his hands. Nine swords hang against a black background behind him. The top of his body's profile cuts through them. He is clearly haunted by bad dreams and waking fear and despair.

This is a card of depression. Those of us who suffer from extreme emotions will receive this image fairly frequently in regular readings, as it depicts the process that leads to ultimate lows—usually, the dark before the dawn. Some of it is circumstantial, yes (a normally steady person who receives this card is certainly undergoing a negative situation), but it is more a card of mental/spiritual torture than actual physical adversity. If one stops to think logically, there are ways to improve the situation and much may be salvaged. However, it is difficult to be rational when undergoing despair.

At its most subtle, this card represents pangs of conscience and hidden, possibly self-denied discomfort with one's actions and situation.

Reversed—Discomfort, caused by no really tenable factor. A niggling feeling of discontent and anxiety.

If the querent has been depressed, this card indicates the approaching end of the negative part of the relevant cycle.

Ten of Swords

A man lies face down in what appears to be a pool of blood, ten swords sticking out of his back. He is alone before a body of water, beneath a black sky in which the dawn is just beginning to break.

On closer inspection the "blood" is actually a red cloak or blanket. However, that this character is in dire straits cannot be denied. His head points towards the rising sun; things can only get better.

The querent's good fortunes are at their lowest ebb. Combined with the Tower, a sudden terrible shock is indicated, followed by shattering grief and possible depression. With Death nearby, or various other cards (such as the Four of Swords), bad health can be indicated, though divination is unlikely to be necessary if the card appears in the present; the querent is bound to know what the problem is, as it is far from subtle.

So this card indicates a bad situation from which resurrection is inevitable. The human spirit is strong and will prevail despite incredible odds. There is the closing of a cycle and a potential birth of another (especially when accompanied by the World, Death, and/or the Fool).

Reversed—The pending of a new and better cycle. After the lowest ebb, a testing of one's resources at the deepest level. The initiation complete, the querent moves on with strength redoubled and lessons learned.

Page of Swords

This is a more diplomatic card than the others of this suit! This youth is always open to debate, intelligently aware that the facts are not necessarily set. This person is a good communicator. This card represents a person or situation that brings useful messages and information. On a mundane level, it represents phone calls, e-mails, and lively discussion.

Reversed—Misinformation, slyness, unnecessary complications. A person who brings these influences to bear. Communication systems going awry.

Knight of Swords

This is the card of an impulsive young man likely to fly off the handle or go careening into situations with full "sound and thunder." He is a sharp and intelligent youth with many ideas, and a firm belief in his own rights. This card also represents emotions and actions of this ilk; impetuosity and belligerence/defense.

Reversed—Flying into situations without gaining the facts beforehand. Hot-headed action. Arguments and unnecessary damage. A person or situation bringing these influences into the querent's life. Anger.

Queen of Swords

Here we find an independent, mature woman—one who has learned much through experience and pain. She is a person on her guard, but who can be an excellent friend once her trust is won. She is also a person who is admired, but often deemed formidable. She is a widow—even if not literally. This card represents the sublimation of adversity into a practical psychology. Thus, it represents lessons learned, and now let's get on with it.

Reversed—An embittered, damaged person, usually female. One who is suffering, and inflicts this pain on others. A sadistic personality. An adversary who must be approached on his or her own terms rather than through any attempt at friendship, which will only elicit disdain. Respect must be won through skilful challenge.

In general, intense and complicated thought motivated by pain and loss.

King of Swords

This card represents a powerful mature man, highly skilled at communication. He is one with his ideas already very well established, and likely to impose them on others. Intellectual and witty, this man is often a figure of authority, such as a father or employer. He is a superb tactician and totally focused. He knows exactly what he wants and can sacrifice much—including the delicate feelings of others and ethical scruples—in order to get it.

This card can also represent a powerful enterprise such as a business that has "taken off."

Reversed—A despot. A cruel man with no regard for the concerns of others. An endeavour gone awry through negative psychological and political influences. Powerful adversaries.

Ace of Wands

A burgeoning wand is held aloft by a hand bursting from the clouds. The landscape below it is verdant and unspoiled. One castle in the distance represents the establishment of structured life in the area.

A primary meaning of the suit of Wands is creativity. Wherever a Wand appears there are ideas galore, and the means of putting thoughts and inspiration into action. The Ace also represents communication, high energy, new ideas, and the initiation of new creative projects; a sudden bolt from the blue that can change one's entire life. It is a propitious time to launch new ideas of almost any sort. Also, fertility is indicated—physical as well as mental. (It depends on the nature of the reading. Coupled with the Empress, for example, and the Three of Wands, a joyous potential birth may be indicated.)

Reversed—Sterility, or misguided energy, perhaps being grounded before it takes off. One might have all the fine plans and ideas, but they rarely progress beyond the initial high of conception; being all talk and no action or effect. Possibly dissipating energy by applying oneself to too many projects; it would be better to choose one and stick to that alone.

Alternatively, lethargy and lack of inspiration.

Two of Wands

A man stands between two wands, which act as a gateway. He surveys a wide expanse of land and sea, and holds a globe in his hand. He is well dressed in the manner of a wealthy merchant. The mood of the card is abundant and optimistic, but by no means complacent. This man is thinking about his next venture.

This card indicates new ventures, carefully planned and logically assessed. There is a creative spirit in conjunction with good business sense. Travel is possible over water, or there may be ventures in new territories. This is a very positive card so long as effort is steadfastly applied.

Reversed—Bad planning of a project, or the inability to get the support required to launch it. A lopsided view of the world. Intuitions about creative/business projects should therefore not be trusted when this card appears in a reading reversed.

Three of Wands

Another wealthy-looking merchant surveys a sea coloured golden by the sun. Three of his vessels sail away on this sea of gold. He holds relaxedly to one of three wands that surround him. The atmosphere of the card is opulent, but the quest is far from over.

This is a card of the successful launching of new projects. Communication is essential to keep the project afloat and progressing, but all is looking highly auspicious for seeing dreams become reality. Trustworthy workers and honest dealings are indicated. Rewards should arrive in due course.

Reversed—Delays and snags in one's business and creative projects, and unnecessary complications. Possibly a sudden change in circumstances that upsets plans. A need to check the details that keep the venture afloat. Sudden fear and pessimism replacing inspiration.

Four of Wands

Two figures hold bouquets of flowers aloft in a gesture of celebration and welcome. Four wands, festooned, provide a gateway to their homestead. The card is predominantly golden-yellow, reflecting health, optimism, opulence, and joy.

Happiness and blessings in the home are indicated. There is a temporary cause for celebration, such as the realisation of a coveted goal, or a significant stage in this process. The successful launching of plans and projects are also represented by this card.

Reversed—Being too stuck-in-the-mud to progress as one ought to. Restriction coming from habit and tradition. A need to break out from the comfy norm and take a few creative risks. Fear of speculation, breeding unhealthy complacency.

Five of Wands

Five frantic-looking characters are involved in a wand fight. Each participant in the fray looks dishevelled and confused.

The Five of Wands is a card of confusion, many differing opinions, and no real structure to one's thoughts. The querent may be going through the motions emotionally and creatively with no real understanding of one's motives. He or she may be acting on impulse when self-discipline would be a better course of action.

Hidden enmity is also indicated by this card. It will take steadfast application and great skill to negotiate one's way through this frenzy of thoughts, emotions, and circumstances. Minimalising the influences on one's affairs would be a good place to start.

Reversed—Many factors opposing one's plans. These are difficult to predict and are likely to cause confusion. The best remedy is to sit down with pen and paper and try to disentangle these influences and combat them individually. Otherwise one will be unable to see the wood from the trees. It is also important to employ rationale rather than spontaneous action, which could prove unwise or even perilous at this time.

Six of Wands

A man rides a white horse, and holds a victory laurel aloft on his wand. He is surrounded by supporters who travel by foot.

A minor victory is indicated, complete with elevation above one's peers. There is a recognition of the querent's virtues and skills; effort is paying off. Finally one's efforts seem to be producing the desired effects. Thus, this card represents a sense of relief and renewed optimism.

Reversed—A feeling of loss or discomfort that is difficult to fathom. It is essential to remain alert to all influences and not to count one's eggs before they have hatched.

Seven of Wands

A man stands with a staff or wand in his hand, defending himself from encroaching wands. We cannot see who brandishes them, so we know he is elevated above his aggressors. He is in a position of strength, but must remain alert in order to maintain it.

As one might suspect from the image, the querent is shown to have attained some success, but he or she is still required to fight (or at least put a lot of effort in) in order to maintain it. So, a time of relaxation is out of the question. If pleasure can be taken in all activities, especially those that are the most strenuous, success is assured.

Energy and resolve are indicated—one is far from the end of one's reserves.

Reversed—Fighting against the odds. Possibly draining energies by misapplying them. A need to look at why one is fighting the tides, and perhaps to wait for a more auspicious moment to see aspirations realised.

Eight of Wands

Eight wands descend from the sky. Numerous options are obviously available, but it is impossible to see where each one ends. Still, this is a time when ideas and possibilities abound.

In order to sift through these options, it is important to prioritise, assess long-term goals, and how they are best attained. The querent may be involved in too many things to allow proper concentration on any. This is a propitious time to make a choice—and things will certainly be much clearer when a decision is made.

Reversed—Procrastination is a fatal flaw at this time. If the querent has options, he or she should make a decision now. Otherwise a choice may be forced on one— probably not the best of the options.

Nine of Wands

A man stands, wand in hand, before nine other wands that form a fence behind him. He has a determined, solid look about him, and is obviously alert to any interlopers on his plans and position.

Attainment, and the ability to maintain it, are represented by this card. There is self-confidence, energy, and at least the beginnings of external status here; a practically unassailable position. Strength, and powerfully positive influences aid the querent.

Reversed—Efforts may be rewarding, but they are something of a strain in some other way. This may even boil down to a mere vague feeling of malaise. Perhaps new forms of enjoyment are required; something to take one's mind off its accustomed themes, even if these are perfectly happy, positive ones.

Ten of Wands

A man carries a bundle of ten wands, his back bowed beneath their weight. He appears to be transporting them to a jolly-looking homestead in the distance.

This card often indicates a literal change of abode. Another possibility is excess of success—being burdened by one's own achievements. A coveted goal brings with it an excess of work and commitments. The querent is reluctant to let any of these go, but it will take great effort and endurance to complete all commitments satisfactorily.

Reversed—A bad move involving much unnecessary strain. The querent is likely to be completely overburdened with commitments and activities. As with many of the Wands cards in reverse, it is important to prioritise.

Page of Wands

This card represents a fairish young person who is talkative and alert—one who enjoys life and its social aspects. This is a card of fun and frivolity; possibly an invitation to a party. It can also represent a bringer of news, or messages and new ideas.

Reversed—Malicious gossip, emotionally confused information. Confidantes that turn out not to be trustworthy. Petty annoyances.

Knight of Wands

The Knight of Wands is a possibly eccentric young man; certainly one with innovative ideas. Interaction with creative persons or processes is indicated, as well as impulsive action. It can also represent the positive influence of an inspired, dynamic male.

Reversed—Slipshod planning; ventures that go up all the wrong paths (but with the potential of them working under the right circumstances, with the right backup). Hostility from a young man as described above.

Queen of Wands

This represents a warm, natural woman with an artistic flair, likely to be fair/reddish and, often, a great lover of animals. She is a pleasant friend who is very much preoccupied with "her own": her family and close, established friends. She is an intelligent lady with a strong practical streak. This card also represents artistic ideas being successfully developed.

Reversed—The influence of one who is being selfish for what he or she believes to be all the right reasons. Communications failing. Lack of faith and foresight.

King of Wands

Here we find a fairish man who is both practical and artistic. As a paternal figure, he is one who gives leeway to his charges. He is a nature-loving individual who is self-aware and tries to be open-minded. This card also indicates the successful launching and fruition of a creative project.

Reversed—Wasted energies, futile endeavours. A stubborn man who prevents real progress by fixating on one idea and finding it difficult to proceed to an alternative. A situation that has become this way.

Of course, nuances vary from pack to pack, and some Tarot decks feature new systems and meanings. However, the above gives a good idea of some of the most traditional meanings of each card. It is up to the witch, however, to employ her intuition in conjunction with the clues offered by the cards. This is true divination.

Tarot Magick

With this wealth of arcane symbolism invested in them, Tarot images act as obvious doorways to the astral plane, and can be integrated into visualisations for specific purposes. The cards and their import can also be used in spells, as this simple spell for justice indicates.

JUSTICE SPELL

No prizes for guessing which Tarot card we will be using, but they can also be selected according to specific types of strength needed. For example, Temperance and Strength may provide the most helpful vibrations in issues of conflict or overcoming bad habits or unruly opponents. They can also be chosen with reference to one's astrological sign; for example, Gemini relates to the Lovers, and that card could be used for a spell relating to having the courage of one's convictions and life choices.

However, Justice is the obvious choice.

Take this card from your favourite pack, and place it on your altar along with candles of suitable colours. Justice relates to sky blue and white, but these may be a little too passive to allow energy to build. My choice would be red, yellow, and orange, if the issue is redressing an unfair balance. If the exercise is simply for balance, calmer colours are certainly better.

You may wish to play inspirational music to empower yourself psychologically as you prepare.

Pick the card that represents you as you are now with regards to your problem. Cards such as the Eight, Nine, and Ten of Swords are likely candidates.

Then select another card that represents you positively dealing with your problem, such as Three of Pentacles, the Magician, or whatever is most apt to you. Then take a card that signifies the best possible outcome. Place them in a silk cloth the colour of your own sign (see Table 1). The problem should be at the bottom, the process of solution in the middle, the end result on top of that, and your significator (the card that represents you) on the very top. Now add a sprig of lavender and one of sage and say:

TABLE 1
Star Signs and Corresponding Colours

Aquarius	Pale blue
Pisces	Aqua through to blue
Aries	Red
Taurus	Brown or green
Gemini	Red or yellow
Cancer	Blue through to white
Leo	Red, orange, or gold
Virgo	Grey
Libra	Sky blue
Scorpio	Brown or black
Sagittarius	Indigo or blue
Capricorn	Terracotta or black

Note: Colour correspondences vary. These, however, are the ones I tend to use myself.

Spirit be with me
Spirit be around me
Spirit be above me
Spirit be beneath me

Repeat five times, increasing the volume of the chant with each round. Then, kiss the cards, and say:

With these cards, I spell my Fate

Bind them with a purple ribbon, wrap the silk scarf around them, and put it beneath your pillow. After one night's sleep, return the cards to the rest of the pack.

The Witch and Runes

The word rune means "to whisper." Through this sacred system of divination, the Teutonic races listened to the whispers of the gods that told them about their past, present, and future. This was usually done by breaking off a branch from a fruit-bearing tree and slicing it into strips. A rune was inscribed on each; then, no doubt with solemnity and ritual, the runes were cast onto a white cloth. The fate of the caster was interpreted by the seer. Runes can also be inscribed on rocks and pebbles, though it is important for all to be of regular size and shape.

The runes are used for more than just divination, however. They are a potent magickal alphabet, as well as individual sacred sigils that may be used in many types of magick. Runes have become increasingly popular with witches over the last decade, and in many cases are a preferred system of divination to Tarot. They are often used as script, and can provide a good form of privacy to the witch who suspects that her magickal diary is not safe from prying eyes. I used to write mine in Seax-Wiccan runes (devised by Raymond Buckland), until I realised that it was taking me hours to read back over a few sentences!

As far as divination is concerned, much depends on the seer's own skills of interpretation; the meanings differ greatly according to the proximity and implications of the surrounding runes. The basic interpretations, however, are as follows.

Feoh/Fehu ᚠ

This is a rune originally connected with cattle and animal husbandry; so, the concept of "breeding wealth." Great luck, especially in business; financial increase, and attainment of coveted goals. Enterprise paying off. Concerns over self-esteem and pecking orders, but in a positive sense. Hierarchical improvement. Fehu is ruled by Venus and the moon, and thus has romantic and intuitive connotations also.

Reversed—A need to stand guard over what you have attained. The possibility of misplaced trust. Do not be discouraged—keep at it despite possibly feeling discouraged, and it will pay off.

Uruz/Ur ᚢ

Casting off old patterns. Energy, as in the Tarot Ace of Wands. Fertility, imagination, instinct. Good physical health. Self-confidence and capability.

Reversed—A time to forge ahead regardless of any reticence you may harbour. Do not be a shrinking violet—be a big roaring lion! Uruz's planetary ruler, Mars, offers you all the strength and energy you require.

Thurisaz/Thorn ▷

As the shape and name of the rune suggests, this represents protection. Its planetary ruler is Jupiter, so this protection is likely to be patriarchal in nature—either from an individual with authority, or from an institution (even simply the orthodoxy of everyday, structured life, especially when working for a large business). A possible warning not to become complacent. A need to listen to advice and be wary. Self-discipline and humility in adversity.

Reversed—It is important to assess the past in order to progress in the future. The querent needs to learn from the mistakes of others too. It may well be that advice is offered. Take it, and act with great caution.

Ansuz ᚠ

Communication, movement, and thinking about (rather than making) journeys. New information. Sudden change. Balance, fairness. Ansuz brings all of the qualities of the Libran scales of justice despite fluctuations in the external (and internal) worlds. The rune is ruled by Mercury, so all things swift and new. Visits. Karma. A good time for making informed decisions.

Reversed—Bad advice. Lack of objectivity. Perhaps too much reference to parental/familial advice, when the querent really ought to grow up and think for him- or herself.

Raido/Rad ᚱ

Opposites reconciled. Issues from the past coming together fruitfully. A significant stage in one's life path, with spiritual encouragement and protection available. A fruitful, pleasurable journey. Raido is ruled by Mercury and the North Node, representing messages given indirectly—in modern terms, by e-mail or telephone. It represents a good time to act and make journeys for what one really wants, especially if this involves educational issues.

Reversed—Confusing messages and signals. A need for rationale. Think before you act. In travel, inconvenience and unexpected obstacles. A bad time for negotiations of any kind, especially business.

Kano/Ken ᚲ

Kano, belonging to Mars and the sun, represents fire. So, passion, illumination, and creative action. Good health and vigour. Recovery from all types of negative situations. Protection. An excellent time to initiate new projects.

Reversed—A possible extinguishing of hope and faith in a situation or person. Change; an ending rather than a beginning. Fortitude and self-belief are required in order to extricate the querent from a situation (or relationship) that has become defunct.

Gebo/Geofu/Gifu ᚷ

Freedom within a relationship (not necessarily personal—Gebo could relate to business partnerships and projects in which there is emotion involved). Ruled by Venus, Gebo also indicates lover's tokens, gifts of the gods in the form of affection, love, and deep peace. Satisfaction, pleasure in progress. Rewards. Sudden windfalls.

Reversed—No reversed position.

Wunjo/Wynn ᚹ

Ruled by Venus and Saturn (in its most positive, unrestrictive aspect), Wunjo represents joy, understanding, success, sudden epiphany. A good omen for business—particularly of the artisan—and pleasure alike.

Reversed—Lack of energy and inspiration. Fear of failure, feeling pressured by the expectations of others and oneself. Possible third-party interference in projects. It may be best to postpone projects for the time being.

Hagalaz/Hagal ᚺ

Hagalaz is ruled by Saturn (in passive aspect). Thus it represents events, the natural effects of circumstance and karma, coming out of the blue, and possibly having a short-term negative effect. However, also possible is the sublimation of ideals into a plan of action. Goals are still far from tenable, but at least they may become coherent at this time.

If close to negative runes, this indicates change, often of an unexpected nature. In some respects the same message as the Tower and Death cards of Tarot—extreme discomfort leading to eventual improvement. Spiritually, a significant time over which one has little external control.

Reversed—No reversed position.

Nautiz/Nied ᚾ

With Saturn in his negative aspect at the helm, Nautiz inevitably represents a time of misfortune and hardship. The possibility of ill health of the degenerative nature. The negative effects of mortality (e.g., physical restriction). A need to transcend old, destructive patterns in order to effect positive change.

Reversed—Strength and self-control in adversity. Displacement. Inappropriate action or situations. Tranquillity of mind is the best response to any situation.

Isa/Is ᛁ

Delays, but possibly helpful ones (Jupiter's passive but protective influence rules this rune). A feeling of stagnation, though things will change eventually (of course!). When shown in a negative light by surrounding runes, a need for caution with what you make known to whom. Again, obstacles in your path. In amorous situations, possibly too much negativity has taken place for the situation to continue. Separation and bad feeling is indicated.

Reversed—No reversed position.

Jera/Jara ᛃ

Effort paying off. Change, new cycles, the first signs of payoff for effort made. The need to continue striving and not to relax at the first sign of recompense. Jera can also indicate marriage, in its positive aspects, or the dissolving of a marriage or partnership if it appears surrounded by runes in their negative aspect. Jera is ruled by Mercury (in its neutral aspect).

Reversed—No reversed position.

Perth/Peorth ᛈ

A good time for esoteric studies and divination. Good luck. Ruled by Mars and the South Node, Perth signifies a fortuitous time to further one's causes. Also, sexual passion (if appearing in conjunction with runes that suggest this); a closely guarded secret.

Reversed—Perth reversed suggests disappointment, possibly because of some hidden factor. Possible new cycles being initiated. If these are of an esoteric/spiritual nature, it is important to be better informed before embarking on them. The tenable results of effort, especially esoteric, but not as the querent would have wished. A need for humour and perspective in any situation.

Eihwaz ⌇

Positive repercussions despite a negative-seeming scenario. Learning from conflict. Venus and Jupiter rule this rune—the former infuses it with positivity and healing. Jupiter extends a protective influence, making it a symbol of optimism, insight, and potential success.

Reversed—No reversed position.

Algiz/Eolh ᛉ

Protection and victory in a cherished project or aim. Clarity is required; with it, you are insuperable. Keep hold of your moral perspective no matter what challenges it.

Reversed—A need for self-protection, including physical (even simply making sure you get those early nights when you need them!).

Sowelu/Sigel ᛋ

All of the blessings of the solar orb that this rune symbolises: victory, success, positive energy, power, activity, fertility, health. If close to negative runes, honesty is essential, not least self-honesty. Look at the real emotive facts in the situation and act with intelligence rather than on impulse.

Reversed—No reversed position.

Teiwaz/Tir ↑

Martyrdom (or self-sacrifice) for a just cause. A rune ruled by Mars in active aspect—therefore the querent in this situation is strong, warriorlike, and prey to impulse rather than rationale. The forces of reform are at work, but caution is needed to avoid a just cause deteriorating into fundamentalism. On a more muted note, enthusiasm and boundless energy for a project. Romance and passion are also indicated.

Reversed—The need to take your time in all decisions and actions. This is the only way to get things right. Possibly a lack of enthusiasm and general malaise, maybe even depression. This will soon clear. A hint of ill health; check the other runes in the reading to confirm or refute this.

Berkana/Beorc ᛒ

Regeneration, nurturing, and infancy are referred to by Berkana, the rune represented by a birch tree. With the moon and Jupiter ruling over it, it represents maternal influence, protection, and good fortune. A cause for happiness within the family is clearly indicated. A need for caution, but otherwise all looks good in the realms of health, fertility, and progress.

Reversed—A need for greater open-mindedness. Irritations and arguments between kith and kin (usually temporary—unless the rune is surrounded by several others in the negative aspect). Possible infertility or problems with pregnancy. Worry over children and young people, who may be coming under negative influences.

Ehwaz/Eoh ᛖ

Movement—possibly of your abode, to a different location. (The symbol of Ehwaz is a horse, and it is ruled by the active aspect of Mercury.) A propitious time for making decisions.

Reversed—A bad time for making decisions and movements or journeys. Stay put for now.

Mannaz/Mann ᛗ

All things familiar are of relevance right now. Blood and emotional ties concern you. As long as you keep your feet on the ground, all issues will be successfully tackled. Mannaz also indicates independence, humanitarian issues, especially those that are essentially duties, and/or a helpful professional person.

Reversed—A need to break away from social and imposed mores for the sake of others as much as yourself. How precisely to act would depend on the other runes surrounding Mannaz, but clarity of vision—and objectivity—are essential at this time.

Laguz/Lagu ᛚ

A rune of water and the moon, with all their implications. Emotion, psychism, spiritual fluidity, and receptivity are indicated. Also hidden guides and protection.

Despite confusion, if you stick to your intuitions, you will be safe. Strength, especially for a woman. A good omen for learning, education, creativity, and all things psychic/occult.

Reversed—Possible indiscretion and/or misapplication of talents. Psychism for the wrong reasons, meddling, and confusion. Seduction (by a woman), female power-over.

Inguz/Ing ᛝ

Fruitful labour. Completion. Inguz is ruled by Venus, and therefore by beauty and bounty. Enjoying the process rather than just the rewards. Positive action on many levels.

Reversed—No reversed position.

Dagaz ᛞ

An influx of positive new influences. Optimism and inspiration. Dawn after the darkness. Increase, growth, all that is suggested by daylight and its properties. Ruled by the sun and the North Node, Dagaz signifies optimism, self-confidence, and having learned from trying circumstances in the past.

Reversed—No reversed position.

Othila/Othel ᛟ

All things concerned with traditional values and what has been firmly established is being questioned. Family ties, issues concerning those with whom you are intimate. Material wealth, possessions, possibly being restricted by these. Hereditary ties— heirlooms, wills, and so forth. With Saturn and Mars ruling Othila, the circumstances of gain may be difficult. Also, inherited traits, which may be a source of both strength and restriction.

Reversed—As usual, when runes are reversed, a need for caution, especially in the matters mentioned above. Do not presume. Delay; patience is needed. Help may be available, however, from old ties and acquaintances.

fourteen

A Brief History of Witchcraft

IN ANCIENT TIMES, THERE WAS animism. Life and deity were perceived everywhere. From this grew pantheism, with its celestial as well as terrestrial gods. First there were native deities, then new tribes and societies brought their gods with them. The Greek and Roman pantheons, for example, were worshipped in many foreign climes, including British. These tended to be more sophisticated than the basic nature and hearth deities they replaced or merged with.

A type of witchcraft—sympathetic magick—was practised by most, if not all, early societies. It is thought that cave paintings showing fat game being trapped by man are an example of this—the desired result is drawn and willed, which attracts success. This represents man as a minigod: designing his future, and overcoming the obstacles presented by his environment.

Sympathetic magick was not used simply to obtain food. Love and revenge have always been popular causes too. Images were made of wood, stone, or vegetable, donned with individuality courtesy of carving, paint, hair, nails, or blood, and diminutively subjected to the desired processes.

Sorcery has long been confused with old-fashioned witchcraft. Indeed, it bears some resemblance to this "dark art," except that many sorcerers were charlatans, and most witches were genuinely wise in herb and folklore. Sorcerers of many societies flourished on fear, while witches sensibly went out of their way to avoid causing it, the results of persecution being familiarly dire.

The old Pagan gods were female as well as male. Both types of energy were recognised as essential, and respected and worshipped. Nor were they confined to gender clichés. In ancient societies, we find sun goddesses such as Inanna, and moon gods such as Chandra.

There is no point in idealising Paganism—in its original form, it was brutal. Human sacrifice and sometimes torture did indeed exist, though there is not much to choose between this and the habit of the later Catholic church of walling up the "Anchoress." I have visited a church in Shere, Surrey, that is famous for its mediaeval anchoress, Christine Carpenter. She was incarcerated in a tiny cell attached to the church wall in her early teens, her sole job to pray for the salvation of the inhabitants of the parish. She was fed through a small hole in the wall. In her twenties, after much desperate work on the bricks of her prison, she escaped. She was free for a few days, and became pregnant. Then she was captured and, baby delivered (what happened to it I know not), returned to her cell. She died there in her nineties. So, clearly, early Christianity has much to answer for on the personal cruelty front too. This idea, however, came from Pagan roots. Individual souls were often used to consecrate sites and bless rituals, usually through their death. The Romans, despite having some excellent godforms based on the Greek pantheon, are infamous for their cruelty to man and beast alike. Christianisation stopped some of the more extreme Pagan brutalities, but of course, produced some new ones of its own.

A society accustomed to worshipping female as well as male deities, and to following the agricultural year and sacrificing or celebrating accordingly, needed some encouragement to pay its respects to a new, male god and his son. Pope Gregory knew this, and directed that Christian worship should take place in the old Pagan sacred sites. Archaeological research is continually unearthing Pagan phalli under altars, chalices under fonts, and other ancient symbols of the gods and goddesses of old. Combined with the fact that Christian high days and holy days "coincided" with the old Pagan ones, the transition became easier.

There is some controversy about the origins and continuity of the Craft. Some say that pockets of people continued to worship the old nature gods and goddess, and have passed down an unbroken line of Pagans and practising witches—that is, those who practised seasonal-based magick as well as worshipping the gods of earlier times. Others say that the resurgence of interest occurred as recently as the 1960s. Certainly, it took off then, but we need only to look at literature across the ages to see that the old gods and goddesses never lost their grip on the popular imagination. Shakespeare's work is riddled with them, not least Hecate, the goddess of witches. The staid, utterly Christian Victorians filled their art and literature with the classical gods and goddesses beloved of their own queen, the head of the Church of England. I am not suggesting for one moment that all of these writers, artists, and readers were openly or even privately worshipping the old gods, but some were. They must have been. They were writing paeans to the demigods, and where man's imagination wanders, his spirit follows.

There were always occultists too. Look at John Dee and Edward Kelley in the court of Queen Elizabeth, invoking angels, raising the dead, and reading the constellations for information. Though only elements of these factors relate to witchcraft as we know it now, the impulse and legacy are the same. It is man engaged in magick.

Needless to say, once Christianity took over the orthodox forms of worship, the old religion was seen as "evil." Nature-worshippers were confused with demonic entities, and the image of the Circe-like witch reemerged, though often with considerably less beauty. The archetypal image of the scheming, evil woman—the enchantress—became associated with those who did not worship the Christian god, and thus, in the new laws of duality, were necessarily evil. Those who did not pay heed to the new creeds were Devil-worshippers, an entirely novel idea to Pagans, who hold all energy to be neutral. The moon and the night—symbols of the Goddess—became representative of evil. The Christianised wicked witch was born.

Many historians put the witchcraft charges of the Middle Ages down to mere hysteria, illness, and the effects of Christianity on a superstitious, death-haunted populace. Coven meetings of this era, if they are believed to have existed at all, are depicted as nothing more than a reversal of Christian ritual, an attempt to win back power from an oppressive church. Of course, Black Masses happened and were participated in, but the thesis of many modern witches, especially hereditary, is that the Craft was alive and kicking throughout history in a much healthier form; that of worshipping nature, the God and the Goddess, and living thus attuned.

So, alongside the topsy-turvy renditions of Christianity, there reputedly existed a much gentler, much older form of real witchcraft, which paid heed to the land and her gifts of herbs for healing and food for nourishment, and worshipped accordingly. Many Gypsies follow a religion similar, if not identical, to this more realistic view of magickal living, and it seems almost inevitable that at least some pockets of society, however small, would revere the Goddess and nature deities at any given time. Dr. Margaret Murray published theories on this subject, most notably in *The Witchcult in Western Europe* (Oxford University Press, 1920) and *God of the Witches,* which were popularly used as back-up by witches in the fifties and sixties who wished to prove Wicca to be an ancient religion. However, a great deal of Dr. Murray's work is hypothetical, and most academics and witches today agree that many of her theories are charming but unrealistic. It is no longer a popular belief amongst practitioners of the Craft that a "Silver" or "Goddess" Age once existed, as Murray suggests, from which Goddess-worshipping, magick-practising witches and Wiccans are descended. However, witchcraft is, of course, the adoptive daughter of Paganism, worshipping the dual powers of male and female energies innate in nature and as represented by specific archetypes or god- or goddess-forms.

The history of witchcraft as it is commonly perceived bears little relation to the real Craft. Rather, it chronicles the descent of a society (whether this be in Britain, Europe, or America) terrorised by the ever-present threat of mortality, propelled into hysteria by rigid ecclesiastical creeds, and into wanton mob violence and vengeful cruelty. In some cases, hallucinations are to blame (for example, ergot poisoning from rye crops causing visions similar to those induced by LSD); in others, sane persons were genuinely convinced that the evil eye was upon them, and in panic, went to those who said they could help. That somebody might have to be tortured and killed to facilitate this was, well, arbitrary. Fear is a major killer.

The latter statement is the root of Voodoo as it is perceived in the West—an aspect of magick worth mentioning because of its immense power over the human imagination. This hybrid combination of African/West Indian magick and Catholicism took a strong hold in the new white worlds thanks to the slave trade. Entire tribes were imprisoned and exported like objects to England and America, though, curiously, the effects of this inhumane treatment seem to have been of far greater magickal import in America than in England. If we look at the history of New Orleans, for example, we witness the spread of this branch of Voodoo to such an extent that the city is world-famous for its Hoodoo past. Slaves who had no other expression, their civil rights being initially nonexistent, created and projected the most violent of thoughtforms, their only outlet against terrible oppression. Outwardly, the slightest hint of rebellion or insolence would result in a beating or in death.

My great-great-great-uncle Benjamin Henry Boneval La Trobe (popularly Americanised as "Latrobe") tells of what he witnessed of the cruelty to slaves in New Orleans in 1819, about fifty years before the Voodoo cult took off in the city. Reading his journals (published by Yale University Press, 1980), one is unsurprised at the terrifying occult backlash that beseiged both Creole and white thereafter:

> In going into Davis' ballroom, and looking round the brilliant circle of Ladies, it is impossible to imagine that any one of the fair, mild, and somewhat languid faces, could express any feeling but of kindness and humanity. And yet several, I had almost said many, of these soft beauties, handle *themselves,* the Cowskin, with a sort of savage pleasure, and those soft eyes can

look on the tortures of their slaves inflicted by their orders, with satisfaction, and cooly perscribe [*sic*] the dose of infliction, the measure of which shall stop short of the life of their property.

Mrs Tremoulet—why should I conceal the name of such a termagant?—is one of those notorious for her cruelty. She is a small mild-faced creature, who weeps over the absence of her daughter now with her husband in France. She has several servants, one a mulatto woman, by far the best house servant I know of her sex, famous also as a sempstress, and for her good temper, so much so, that she can at any time be sold for $2,000, and Mrs Tremoulet actually asks $3,000. In six weeks, I have never seen in her conduct the smallest fault; she is modest, obliging, and incredibly active. A few days ago, she failed (because it was impossible) to make a bed for a stranger, at the hour prescribed. In consequence of this fault Mrs Tremoulet had her stripped quite naked, tied to a bed post, and she herself, in the presence of her daughter Mrs Turpin (the mother of three beautiful children), whipped her with a Cowskin till she bled. Mrs Turpin then observed, *'Mamman, vous etes trop bonne; pourquoi prenez vous la peine de la fouetter vous meme; appellez donc Guillaume'* (Mamma, you are too kind; why do you bother whipping her yourself; why don't you just call William?) William was called and made to whip her till she fainted. This scene made a noise in the house, and the blood betrayed it. Poor Sophy is ill, and constantly crying. I shall leave the house as soon as is convenient to me.

Madame Lanusse is another of these Hellcats. Her husband is a very amicable Man, president of the bank of Louisiana, whom she had driven to seek a divorce, but the matter has been compromised lately. She did actually whip a negress to death, and treated another so cruelly, that she died a short time afterwards. Mr Nott, a principal merchant of this place stated the facts to the Grand Jury, but it was hushed up, from respect to her husband.

Mrs Kennedy my Land lady, a sensible Irish woman, saw through the fence preparations making by Madame Conrad to punish several of her negroes. A ladder was brought and laid down, and a naked man tied upon it. She was so shocked, that she left her house for several hours, and did not return, until she supposed the execution was over.

There are many other equally horrifying observations of the predicament of the black slave in Benjamin's journals. Some of these victims had been Christianised, and revenge was probably the last thing from their minds. However, naturally, in some cases this would not be so. On the inner planes, there was nothing to stop the beleaguered black from recalling his village witch doctor and magickal practices, and employing them to the best of his ability. When slaves were finally allowed to meet in groups—several decades of despicable treatment later—they obviously wished to counteract their captivity, and, lacking the physical or legal means, communicated their ideas in terms of primitive magickal revenge. Thus was this aspect of Voodoo born—to punish and to terrify.

There are many stories of young ladies in New Orleans (for example) discovering gris-gris beneath their pillows, or conjure-balls complete with samples of human hair and flesh in their gardens. Many Voodoo fetishes were intended to kill. Their power came from a variety of spirits, including some Roman Catholic saints, but the major deities are snake-related. Slaves would gather, once meetings were permitted, around blazing fires on the shores of Lake Pontchartrain, strip, and clad themselves in red knotted handkerchiefs. To the compelling thud of the drums (beaten with bones), the Voodoo Kings and Queen would dance, and their subjects with them.

The altar would feature an elaborately decorated box containing Vodou, the holy serpent. Pledges, promises, and curses issued from the mouths of those present. Before very long, the Queen would be possessed.

The Voodoo Queen is the High Priestess, and she enjoyed a position of authority very unusual to women of this era. She came to be treated differently by the whites also, through fear both of magickal attack and of a mutiny amongst the slaves if this one concession were not made. By the mid-nineteenth century she was naturally free—usually a woman of great beauty as well as magickal prowess. She was expected to take lovers at will, and her word was authority. This malignant queen bee was said to be the true governor of the city, despite her colour and gender.

The most famous New Orleans Voodoo Queen is Marie Laveau. She seems to epitomise the combination of beauty and terror that inspires the practitioners of Voodoo. The popular books of Robert Tallant—*Voodoo Queen* and *Voodoo in New Orleans,* both recently reissued by Pelican—give a highly readable if somewhat old-school look at the religion as it was practised (and perceived by nonpractitioners) in New Orleans. (Other sources should be sought for its true philosophy and contemporary practise.)

The tradition of Voodoo Queens was the herald of both feminism and black liberation in the South. Fear and dark magick were the only ways of convincing the arrogant whites to respect their slaves. No doubt there were many plantation owners who disbelieved Voodoo, or who relied on the power of Christ to preserve them, but if there was anything likely to cause a mutiny, it was a slighting of the religion and its priestesses.

Voodoo hammered another nail into the coffin of white complacency. With its conviction in supernatural powers and punishment to any who might slight a voudoin, it symbolised the Afterlife. Though many slave owners believed they were performing a social good by taking tribes from their own countries and Christian-ising them, Voodoo represented punishment of the most unpleasant sort. Many people, both black and white, are reported to have suffered Voodoo illness and even death, and the threat was enough to cause hysteria and psychosomatic symptoms through either plain fear, or the pricking of a guilty conscience. Some people are reported to have fallen into a speechless trance the moment they discovered a fetish aimed at them. The shock would weaken the constitution, and fear and self-starva-tion would do the rest—as would the magick, of course.

Voodoo as a religion is still practised in Haiti, and no doubt in many pockets of the world where African/West Indian and white have mixed. Voodoo is as eclectic as modern magick, and has absorbed the Christian saints into its practises. St. Expe-dite is a particular favourite, but there are many others. It is a complex religion with far more to it than the performance of revenge magick.

Modern Pagans might point the finger at Christianity in the above scenario. It is certainly true that Christianity has imposed its beliefs on a great many cultures, sometimes savagely. However, we do well to remember that the Romans, for exam-ple, did exactly the same, as well as concocting the most revolting and cruel deaths for both public entertainment and to worship their gods with. Millions of men, women, children, and exotic animals were tortured and slowly executed in pre-Christian Rome; it was not until the empire was Christianised that the atrocities stopped. Also, the Celts and Nordic tribes so popular today were violent savages. However, it does indeed cut both ways.

This is intended to be a positive book, and there is no need to dwell here on the atrocities committed against Pagans and women by now-orthodox religions. Most witches have read or seen Arthur Miller's *The Crucible,* and know of the *Malleus Maleficarum* in all of its infamy. We are aware of the rampant chauvinism and occult-paranoia still evident in certain fast-growing religions—yes, even in this "enlight-ened" era. We resolve never to let anything like slavery or the Inquisitions happen again in our domain, and to counter it in others, as much as is possible. Against so-called heretics, against witches, or against any creed, race, or species, even.

Of modern witchcraft, there is much more of positive import to be said. As it has progressed into popular consciousness, the "occult" has lost a great deal of its previous negative aura in the perceptions of nonpractitioners. There is a good reason for this: it has changed, and become positive. Ethical occultism arrived with the Victorians, influenced as it was by Hinduism and Buddhism. With the Theosophists it ceased to be a bag of selfish tricks, and became a search for truth and enlightenment. This knowledge, largely transferred by Helena Blavatsky, Annie Besant, and Alice Bailey (see the next chapter, "Who Influenced the Witching World?"), was employed by magickians such as Crowley, Leadbeater (a Theosophist also), and the wondrous Dion Fortune. The former, Helena Blavatsky, had a powerful effect on British and American spiritual consciousness. Dion Fortune, though predominantly of the Western Tradition, combined the intellectual and spiritual elements of Eastern and Western esoteric practise in a brilliant and ethical manner. This became incorporated into witchcraft practise in the 1950s and '60s, which changed aspects of the Craft from mere nature- and Goddess-worship to focused, intellectual magick.

The Victorian High Magickians Eliphas Levi, Samuel Mathers, and Aleister Crowley contributed a system to the Western Mystery Tradition that has infiltrated many aspects of modern occultism and witchcraft: the Qabalah (see chapter 12, "The Witch and Qabalah"). The ancient Jewish system of Kabbalah was made compatible with an enormous body of non-Semitic belief, such as ancient Egyptian religion (always popular with occultists), astrology (not that Jewish lore lacks astrological and astronomical reference, but this system was specifically more magickal), and even Tantra. This represents the dawn of the eclecticism—or perhaps one should say, the ability to embrace all valid beliefs—that typifies modern magick. Until Helena Blavatsky and these magickians hit the scene, paths were very much differentiated. From the Victorian era onwards—largely due to the increased ability to travel (albeit voyages abroad were long and uncomfortable)—it became possible to make relevant cross-cultural references.

Major occult schools grew out of the Victorian/Edwardian era: Theosophy, the Golden Dawn, the Society of Inner Light, the Servants of the Light, and the Temple of Thelema, to name some of the most prominent. Each had a different bent and a different aim, but the modes of thought and belief were similar, and all involved the combining of Eastern and Western religious practise. Victorian ladies would meditate on their chakras and chant mantras; gentlemen of diverse professional backgrounds would invoke Ra and Horus in powerful High Magick ceremonies.

The mid-twentieth century brought the founders of modern Wicca: Gerald Gardner and Alex Sanders. Each has been considered both by followers and by themselves the "King of the Witches." Gardner brought witchcraft into rebirth in a new form, and Sanders perpetuated it.

There are two main "sects" in Wicca other than Gardnerian (following the teachings of Gerald Gardner) and Alexandrian (those initiated by Alex or Maxine

Sanders, or by one of their initiates): these are Traditional and Hereditary. Followers of the Traditional Path work robed, and their practise, as far as I am aware, varies very little from that of the other groups, except that it is less high magickal than the Alexandrian path, and less "skyclad" than the Gardnerian. The Hereditary witches, of course, claim to come from a long line of practising witches, and tend to keep themselves very much to themselves. As Stewart Farrar points out in his book *What Witches Do,* the more "modern" branches of Wicca tend to court publicity, believing of occult knowledge, "He that hath ears to hear, let him hear."

Certainly this is a modern trend in all paths of occult knowledge. Since Israel Regardie spilled the beans of some of the key Golden Dawn rituals, everybody has been spelling and telling. This has meant public access to a vast amount of esoteric lore. Nowadays, it is not necessary to be a member of an occult fraternity (or sorority) or a Hereditary witch in order to experience the keys to esoteric practise. This, of course, coheres with the concept of an Aquarian era in which all are free to ascend by whatever path they feel to be the most appropriate. The access to hitherto "secret" principles represents humanity's evolution from a state of fear and divorce from God to something more positive and progressive.

Gerald Gardner was the first "publicity agent" for witchcraft, which he referred to by the less emotive term "Wicca." He claimed in his book *Witchcraft Today,* published in 1954, to have encountered a group of witches (descended from those hunted down in the Middle Ages) in the New Forest in England, and to have been initiated there by a witch named Daffo. He explained that the Craft was, in fact, a tool for good, and listed its possible uses as crop protection and propagation, healing, and general beneficence. It was fundamentally a form of nature worship, he claimed, giving it the title "The Old Religion." The Mother Goddess and the Horned God had been continuously worshipped by Hereditary witches since pre-Christian times, according to Gardner.

Though Gardner's often rather imaginative explanations of Craft history did indeed boost its profile and change the minds of many who had previously feared it, his activities also caused a counterreaction, for he used ritual nudity and light, symbolic flagellation in his ceremonies.

Naturally, Gardner had excellent arguments to back up this apparently fetishistic behaviour. To go naked was to be "skyclad," or open entirely to the elements. As those of us who have worked naked in the great outdoors will know, there is much in this philosophy. The earth beneath your feet, the wind in your hair, and the air caressing your body as it dances and perambulates the Circle is an amazing sensation indeed. What better way to connect with the Mother Goddess than to go as naked as a newly born babe? (With the exception of ritual jewellery, that is.) Then, the body truly feels attuned to the elements. And as to the flagellation: it was light, and symbolic—a process of cleansing.

All very well, but we witness here the scope for much abuse of such a philosophy. It is as unlikely that Gardner's motives were entirely spiritual as it is that his histories of witchcraft are entirely historically correct. Bearing in mind that Wicca is largely a fertility religion (by Gardner's own terms), a sexual overtone is to be expected. However, assuming his tenets were created in all innocence, it cannot be ignored that many men have been attracted to the Craft because of the other element promoted by Gardner: sex within the Circle. "The Great Rite" is usually performed symbolically using a chalice containing red wine to represent the female and a ritual dagger to signify the male. When they are conjoined, the magick climaxes. Gardner, however, though he barely hinted at it in his books, was keen for the flesh vessels of male/female polarity to be united within the Circle. It is true that this is very powerful magickally (when properly executed), but the idea of it being in any way perfunctory is horrific. It also attracts precisely the wrong type of people to what ought to be an ethical, religious path.

Many of Gardner's theories seem to be drawn from the works of Margaret Murray, Crowley, Montague Summers, and other idiosyncratic anthropologists and magickians. His rituals were influenced by a variety of sources (not that this renders them less effective), and were poetically revived by Doreen Valiente, giving them increased psychological impact. Though many follow the teachings of Gerald Gardner today, it is hopefully not blindly. Most witches recognise this man's limitations as a spiritual guide, but have adopted Gardnerian Wicca in order to form a meaningful relationship with the Earth, the Mother Goddess, the Horned God, and the cosmos. The channel may have been flawed, but much of the creed, when properly and ethically employed, is of value.

Gardner's life spanned the repeal of the Witchcraft Act in Great Britain in 1951. This anti-witchcraft act was repealed because the government decided that to maintain a ban on the practise of magick was to acknowledge its existence. As the world moved towards scientific cynicism, Gardner took full advantage of his era, and Wicca was born.

Patricia Crowther, English witch and author, asserts in her book *Lid off the Cauldron* that Gerald Gardner was "of the blood," and that a reliable Hereditary witch friend of hers had stated as much. This, of course, backs up his argument about witchcraft lines, both genealogical and spiritual. Crowther, who knew Gardner in his twilight years, spurns the criticisms of those who never met him. Naturally, she has a point here. It is indubitable, however one might view the man as an individual, that he was the pivot for the witchcraft revolution—that is, for its infiltration of public consciousness in a nonhysterical sense. And there are times when one ought to be judged by one's works.

One of Gardner's most important contributions to the development of the Craft was the idea of the Priestess-Oracle acting as a channel for the currents of the new aeon. Certainly Wicca has brought a great deal of energy from the lunar spheres (mainly), but this needs to be activated by solar energy, which is often underemployed in Wicca. Also, the energy invoked must be directed towards world good, rather than absorbed in its entirety into a coven project. Having said this, the assumption of godforms during ritual, and the involvement with higher (at least astral) spheres and archetypes, has done much to shift heavy, mundane energy from the last era. Anyone working with more refined concepts and magickal currents is helping to alter world consciousness, and facilitating the eventual transformation of these planes, or humanity's "ascent."

Gardner was guardian of the Museum of Witchcraft in the Isle of Man before he died in 1964. Its contents were later sold to America. It displayed the knives of which Gardner was so fond, boxes of relics he claims to have been given by Hereditary witches (containing items belonging to Matthew Hopkins, Witchfinder General, apparently), and incredibly kitschy displays of people performing magick (nubile women lying on altars, for example). Some of it is the imagination of a concupiscent old man. However, much of Gardner's legacy is of value. Witches discriminate and adapt in every aspect of their lives, including in the teachings of the Craft. It is, after all, supposed to be a path to the Light, rather than a network of delusion.

Alex Sanders, the next "King of the Witches," was born nearly forty years after Gardner, and is likely to have been heavily influenced by his writings. Claiming to have been initiated by his grandmother at the age of seven, Sanders declared that he came from one of the very few families of Hereditary witches in England. His matriarch/High Priestess taught him witchcraft skills over the course of his childhood and adolescence. He was a "natural," which prevented him from being traumatised by finding his grandmother stark naked in a Circle and being instantaneously initiated. He also claimed to have been introduced to Crowley by his grandmother at the age of ten, and to have participated in "Rites of Horus," which presumably made him a magickal protégé of Crowley as Osiris (or Seth?). Sanders admits that, as a young man, he decided to use his powers to attain money and sex. Instead of the predominantly wholesome Path taught by his grandmother, Sanders deteriorated into black magick—that is, the abuse of power in order to attain personal ends.

One of the manifestations of his spellcraft, allegedly, was the appearance of a wealthy couple who claimed that he looked just like their deceased son. They took him in, bought him expensive clothes, and gave him money. Eventually Sanders asked them to buy him a house and give him a regular allowance, which they duly did. Sanders used his flashy clothes and luxurious accommodation as bait for girls, as young men are wont to do. He led the life of Riley for a while, attempting to ignore the flashes of conscience that told him that what he was doing was terribly wrong.

We may deduce from this that Sanders was either a very young soul, or one that had been out of circulation for a while. His lust for life and its luxuries and his use of magick to procure them indicate the lack of both humility and wisdom—the former being an essential tenet of the latter. However, the fact that he confessed to these ethical errors says much for the learning process that inevitably followed. Several members of his family were struck down by the disease that eventually killed Alex too: cancer. One of his favourite lovers committed suicide. However, having been well trained by his grandmother, Sanders appreciated the symbolism of sacrifice. He had taken and taken from the cosmos without giving anything at all back; now it was his turn to be taken from.

As the Wiccan Rede announces, we "Suffer to Learn." Sanders took the hint and began to purify himself through ritual and through his daily actions. He resolved to use his knowledge positively, to initiate others into the Craft, and to ensure (as much as possible) that they did not experience the same pitfalls. Consequently, he created many covens in his hometown of Manchester, and later, in London. He married Maxine Morris, a strikingly attractive blonde who became his High Priestess.

I have met several of those initiated by Alex or Maxine Sanders, and all of them comment on the amazing charisma Alex had, despite his diminutive, somewhat gaunt appearance. Because of this, and the controversial nature of his work, Sanders received considerable media attention between the late '60s and '90s, when he died. This includes the recording of some of his rituals by A&M, and their production as a record. Listening to this soundtrack is highly recommended. The lilting, soft tones of the witch's invocations, the chanting, and the sound of the bells are extremely effective if one wishes to visualise an early Alexandrian ritual in its entirety. Many of the phrases he uses have now become classic Wiccan liturgies.

One of Sanders's most important contributions to Wicca was the introduction of higher magick than was commonly practised—hence the integration in the '60s of

Qabalah into the Craft. By the time he progressed on to the next plane, Sanders was so important to witchcraft that his name had been used to define his particular brand of magick: "Alexandrian."

Another major influence on modern magick in Britain and America was the era of the 1960s. With Flower Power came Eastern gurus reminiscent of those talked of by the Theosophists, but incarnate; the legacy of the American Indian, courtesy of American writers such as Carlos Casteneda; and with the latter, shamanism. The concept of "walking between the worlds" suddenly seemed not so impossible. The quantity of drugs consumed in this era also helped, as a group mind became more willing and able to accept new possibilities.

Suddenly, it seemed viable that the Christian Devil might be a mutation of the Horned God of the Old Religion, as Murray, Gardner, and Sanders all claimed. It was a tenable theory that the Virgin Mary might be a distant cousin of the original Great Goddess. These were ideas that would have seemed absurd and been condemned as blasphemous before the mass quantum leap of consciousness in this era. Perhaps it really was more than coincidence that Christmas coincides with Yule and the winter solstice, and Easter with the ancient fertility festival of Oestara.

Wicca has progressed immensely over the last thirty years, and many of the taints of the Gardnerian/Alexandrian *modus operandi* have been eliminated. There are many highly respectable priests and priestesses in modern Wicca. However, there is also a fundamentalist Wiccan element; all successful religions inevitably become orthodox in the end.

Stewart Farrar was a journalist sent to interview Alex Sanders. It was 1969, the year that the film *Legend of the Witches* was released, which was a follow-up to the release of Sanders's biography, *King of the Witches,* by June Johns. Sanders invited the journalist to attend an initiation the following Saturday. Farrar, a "Christian-turned-atheist-turned-interested-agnostic," was so impressed by Alex and Maxine Sanders, that he ended up joining their coven and being initiated by Maxine. He started working magickally with his wife Janet, and they wrote many books together, including *Eight Sabbats for Witches* and *What Witches Do.* During Stewart's lifetime, the couple became celebrities within the Craft, long queues forever forming outside their tents at various Pagan and Wiccan festivals. Again, they did much to improve public perception of witchcraft.

Other positive influences include Doreen Valiente, Patricia and Arnold Crowther, Marian Green, and John and Caitlin Matthews. All of these have written books. The most popular mode of communicating ideas about Wicca, witchcraft, and esoterica in general has become the published work. The Internet is a close second, with websites such as www.witchcraft.org and www.witchvox.com creating virtual communities and making the sharing of information quick and easy (see "The Cyberwitch" section in chapter 16). Much of the secrecy has been taken out of the Craft, as has much of what might seem threatening to nonpractitioners. In its most basic form, Wicca has become respectable ecological awareness, God/Goddess worship, and the will and ability to heal.

Wicca has helped parent an enormous legacy of New Age self-help books. By pointing to the relevance of mythology and magick, of ritual, and of visualisation, the ideas of Gardner and Sanders spilled into the psychotherapy arena. There are thousands of books available today that give little or no mention of religion or spirituality, but which employ magickal techniques. There are also many that openly embrace the "Age of Aquarius," and cover subjects as diverse as attuning to the Earth and contacting beings on other planets or stars.

Most of the above can be defined as the "right-hand path." If "right-hand path" is informed by the rede "An' it Harm None, Do As Thou Wilt," "left-hand" might be surmised by Crowley's edict (on which the Wiccan Rede is no doubt based) "Do What Thou Wilt shall Be the Whole of the Law." The occult studies encompassed by this philosophy include Thelema, modern Enochia, Chaos Magick, and branches of esoteric experimentation too numerous and complex to go into here. All are of value, and I regret that I am unable to explore the so-called "left" path in this book. Suffice it to say that there are thousands of schools of magick and witchcraft extant today, as one might expect in an age of enlightenment—whether we call it that of Aquarius or the Aeon of Horus.

fifteen

Who Influenced the Witching World?

THE FOLLOWING ARE IN CHRONOLOGICAL order.

Moses de Leon

Moses ben Shem Tov de Leon was born in Muslim Spain near Castile between 1240 and 1250. His exact background is obviously hazy, but we do know that in 1264 he commissioned a copy be made of the *Moreh Nevukhim* (*Guide of the Perplexed*) by Moses Maimonides. This suggests that de Leon was born closer to 1240 than 1250—unless he was a child prodigy and rich enough to afford a hand-copied text into the bargain!

The mystical young man was well placed to pursue his interests. Not only did he have the potent Jewish lore that was his birthright, but Sephardic Spain was a centre of Moorish philosophy and Islamic mysticism. Maimonides (1135–1204) had studied both in a rationalistic vein, and his work deeply influenced that of his spiritual acolyte, who was less rationalist. De Leon's primary attraction was towards Kabbalah, the mystical Judaic system of correspondences, which was purported to have been delivered to Moses by the archangel Metatron in ancient days. (See chapter 12, "The Witch and Qabalah," for the relevance of this system to the modern witch and occultist.)

Moses de Leon eventually synthesised his mystical perceptions, largely based on the *Midrash ha-Ne'elam* (*The Mystical Midrash*), in his work the Zohar, which was written in an idiosyncratic form of Aramaic. It has been posited that the book may have been written in a trance state, like automatic writing. This is not a surprising theory considering the nature of the text. However, de Leon was educated enough for it to be his conscious work. The text, which he certainly edited for publication, includes dramatic narratives, parody, humour, pseudepigraphical passages, allusion to other mystical systems, analysis, and creative fantasy. It is said that the Zohar, like the Torah, "hides more than it reveals." Like magick, its key is imagination. This enlivening force is the key in the mystical lock, for God can only be "known and grasped to the degree that one opens the gates of imagination."

Whilst living in Guadalajara, de Leon copied sections of the Zohar for serious students of the Kabbalah, and they began to make use of it. It was first quoted by Isaac ibn Abu Sahulah in his own writing in 1281. Moses himself continued to write and to teach Kabbalah. Eventually he moved to Avila, where he lived very modestly with his wife and daughter until his death in 1305.

De Leon is relevant to contemporary occultists because his work has become incorporated into the Qabalah of the Western Mystery Tradition. This influences most magick and, thanks to Alex Sanders and later eclecticists, much Wicca too. His work was also studied by H. P. Blavatsky, and therefore influenced Theosophical teachings, which in turn had a profound effect on the Order of the Golden Dawn, and thus on much modern esoterica.

Cornelius Agrippa

Cornelius Agrippa von Nettesheim was born in Germany in 1486. His book *De Occulta Philosophia* (1531) is a compilation of mediaeval magick and its symbols, including astrological ones that are still in use today. In his collection of occult lore, Agrippa adopted and "improved" some of these emblems, and his work was so widely used for reference by other occultists that his improvisations stuck. Thus he affected the mediaeval-based studies of Wynn Westcott and Samuel MacGregor Mathers, whose work provided the founding principles of the Golden Dawn, on which most modern magick is based—a considerable achievement for one who died in 1535.

John Dee

John Dee, born on July 13, 1527, in London, was an alchemist, astrologer, and mathematician. From an early age he was regarded as an academic genius. He invented the word *Brittania,* with relation to the British Empire, and developed a comprehensive plan for the British Navy. What has this to do with being a witch, you might ask?

In those days, gentleman scholars, of which Dee was indubitably one, were not confined to one subject. Indeed, they were expected to be well versed in many, including the metaphysical. Dee was an astrological expert. His mathematically brilliant mind leant itself to many endeavours. Having translated Euclid's works, he built the instruments to apply these principles to navigation, trained others to navigate, and made important developments to early maps. He also conjured and spoke with angels—all of this in an era in which some church members believed mathematics to be a form of black magick.

Working with his friend and accomplice Edward Kelley, Dee discovered (or "channelled") the system and language of Enochia, a highly complex collection of tables and guttural angelic calls (see the section "Enochia" in chapter 18). Dee, who was logically brilliant, reputedly had no mediumistic abilities. The main purpose to which Dee put Kelley was that of divination. Having successfully cast the horoscopes of Elizabeth I and Mary Queen of Scots, Dee enjoyed temporary favour with the former as "my Nobel Intelligence." He correctly predicted that Elizabeth I would be released from house arrest in Oxfordshire and become a powerful Protestant monarch, while the Catholic Mary Queen of Scots would perish. Dee's motivations were indeed noble and intelligent, despite practising what was essentially regarded at the time as divine treason (because the ability to predict inferred the ability to affect). The motivations of his partner were not always as "Noble," however—Kelley tried to extract money from the spirits, but as any witch who has ever attempted to elicit money from spirits will well know, they care little for mortal currency and never help.

Dee was sometimes ambivalent about the spirits channelled by Kelley, whose own character left much to be desired, but he believed he may be being "tested." Kelley on his part feared that they might be demons in disguise. With their cold, beautiful, Apocalyptic speech, and their wont to become suddenly flirtatious and sly, it is easy to understand his reservations about these contacts. Yet their predictions were proved correct time and time again, and soon Dee found himself following their every instruction. There were seventy of these celestial entities in all, though their main interaction was with Madini, a particularly coquettish "angel" who ended up instructing Dee and Kelley to wife-swap (the idea being, presumably, to encourage them to shed all mortal vanities and inhibitions). They went so far as to sign a pact, with Dee recording in his diaries: "I offer my soul as a pawn." He was prepared to risk not only his marriage, but hellfire itself, so great was his desire for Cosmic Truth.

However, the act proved the death-blow to the magickians' friendship, especially as John Dee's wife became pregnant by Kelley and gave birth to his son. The situation forced the esotericists to part ways, but not, however, until they had undergone many intense and bizarre scenarios together.

Dee had been philosopher and court magician to Queen Elizabeth I of England, and fell in and out of favour with those in power according to the political tides of the moment. Many considered him dangerous, and wished to assassinate him. The "angels" issued warnings and advice accordingly. He was jailed, but released—a scenario that would haunt him for the rest of his life. He spent much of his life fleeing the persecutions that ensued as he gradually revealed his magickal ability. As Elizabeth I's horoscope-caster (the regent dubbed by Spencer "The Faery Queen," and not without reason), he determined the most suitable days for major events such as fighting the Spanish Armada (which he is said to have hexed), and the queen's very coronation date. He was the founding member of the Rosicrucian Order (the highest section of the Freemasons), and was learned in alchemy, Hermeticism, Qabalah, and all aspects of the occult. He provided the blueprint for Shakespeare's "Prospero" in *The Tempest*. He was also key in changing the Julian calendar to the Gregorian one that we use today.

Dee and Kelley worked together at Mortlake, England, conducting their esoteric experiments. They gathered an extensive library of tomes magickal, scientific, and cartographical. Their aim, which was especially pressing for Dee, was to discover the key to the Universe. This became symbolised as the Philosopher's Stone; the men experimented tirelessly with alchemical formulae, and tried to turn base metal and mud into gold, literally. Nowadays, it is more or less accepted that the Philosopher's Stone is spiritual rather than material in essence, but we must remember that Dee was a master Scientist, and he operated as such—always seeking the material manifestation of his religious beliefs and practises.

In 1583, John Dee published his book *Monas Hieroglyphica,* in which the fundamental symbols of equilateral cross, arc, circle, and point are analysed. He related these to the elements, the moon, and the sun, respectively (the point appearing at the centre of a circle—the esoteric solar symbol to this very day). His ideas were assimilated by the occult groups budding in his day—especially the Rosicrucians—and have thus had a vast influence on contemporary esoteric lore. Many proficient magickians, especially those influenced by Crowley, are able to operate in Dee's language of Enochia.

Dee and Kelley were instructed by Madini to leave Mortlake to go to Poland, where further revelations were promised. They obeyed, and as soon as they departed, Mortlake was mobbed and ransacked by those who believed them to be meddling with devilry. They arrived in Poland, abiding there until they were told by their Angels to—wait for it—visit the king of Bohemia, the Holy Roman Emperor Rudolf II in Prague, and to deliver the message that his Path was wrong and that "God . . . rebuketh your sins. If you will not hear me, you will perish ruthlessly."

Dee and Kelley heroically followed these logically suicidal commands. The two British occultists, no doubt shaking in their boots, obtained an interview and told the almighty Rudolf exactly what they believed God to think of him. Rather than having them executed on the spot for impudence, as one might reasonably expect, Rudolf, who like many of his era was fascinated by magick and alchemy, set them up in Prague with their own alchemical laboratory.

Word spread amongst the rich and powerful, and soon the tsar of Russia was courting Dee and Kelley. Elizabeth I caught wind of the exploits of her "Most Noble" one, and strongly desired that the occultists return to England immediately to "make gold" for their own regent. However, this was impossible at the time, as political adversaries in England would surely have had them killed if they returned.

Pope Sixtus V sent spies to Prague to investigate. He saw Dee as a dangerous enemy. Dee and Kelley were duly summoned to Rome, but they refused the invite. The pope then forced Rudolf to expel them. Once again, the dynamic duo found themselves and their families on the run in fear for their lives.

Luckily, a local Czech count shared the interests of his peers and regent, and offered the magickians refuge in the Rosenburg castle, one hundred miles south of Prague. Here is where the terrible wife-swapping Pact took place. As author Ronald Hutton amusingly put it in the U.K. channel 4's *Masters of Darkness* series, "They thereby became 'Not just Swingers—Sinners.'"

However, the angelic conversations ceased. Kelley was made a baron and became a master hedonist. He eventually died trying to escape from prison, into which he was inevitably and eventually thrust.

Dee returned to England, dying there of "natural" causes in 1608. He never realised his aim of discovering the "Key"—indeed, he struggled to decipher Enochia itself—but his work has had a profound impact on magick as we know it today. His work has acted as a stepping stone to many others who have sought the Truth—as to those who seek it still.

Robert Fludd

Robert Fludd was probably the most proficient and innovative occultist of the seventeenth century—in Britain, at least. Born in 1574, he was profoundly influenced by the work of John Dee, and many of his mystical theories were expounded in complex diagrams still extant today. One of these correlates the Music of the Spheres with Pythagorian harmonics, for example.

Fludd studied the relationship of man (microcosm) and spirit (macrocosm) in a highly intellectualised and mystical manner. Like many of his era, he saw the human body as a set of symbols with elemental and planetary correspondences. Like the Qabalists, he attributed the heart to the sun, the genitals to the moon, and so on. He saw human life as entirely sustained by the cosmic force, as do most occultists. An inspired Rosicrucian, he experimented in both medicinal and alchemical fields. The essence of his beliefs is conveyed in his book *Utriusque cosmi historia.*

In the manner of many of his educated, spiritually inclined peers, Fludd was a polymath with a great deal of alchemical knowledge and understanding. He departed his body in 1637.

Jacob Boehme

Jacob Boehme was a Protestant Lutheran mystic. He was born in 1575, and started his life as a shepherd. Perhaps pastoral contemplation set him on the road to inner awakening. Boehme became a master cobbler after that, and from these humble origins sprang a visionary still revered today.

Boehme underwent thoughts and perceptions of mystical unity (despite the conviction that God existed beyond the stars) long before he ever spoke of them. "I saw in myself the three worlds—the Divine angelic world; the dark world, the original of Nature; and the external world, as a substance spoken forth out of the two spiritual worlds." For twelve years after his first experience he contained his thoughts, but eventually he began to set his theosophy to paper. *Aurora,* his first book, was written in 1612. His Christian mysticism bears many resemblances to Qabalistic cosmology (by which it was influenced, along with astrology and alchemy). Boehme greatly influenced William Blake (see below) and Hegel and Kant's inquiries into metaphysical contradictions and their solutions.

Boehme believed that the harmonious balance of opposites might be attained through self-sublimation. This meant committing all to God rather than living selfishly.

What is most interesting about the mystical experience of "all being" is that it occurs in a similar, if not identical form for people of completely different cultures, religions, and countries. In his *Autobiography of a Yogi,* for example, Paramahansa Yogananda describes one such experience:

My sense of identity was no longer narrowly confined to a body but embraced by circumambient atoms. People on distant streets seemed to be moving gently over my own remote periphery. The roots of plants and trees appeared through a dim transparency of the soil; I discerned the inward flow of their sap.

Yogananda had long surrendered himself to the Divine Will, and thus achieved Boehme's goal by harmonising opposites and aligning his consciousness to that of the Creator—and this in India, 350 years after the German Protestant Boehme.

Witches likewise understand that all is connected, and all is sacred. Traditional witches do not cast Circles in which to work, as they believe all to be sacrosanct by nature. Many witches undergo a feeling of divine unity, especially during ritual or close to the major sabbats. A key point is that the body is not the limit, but that our single lives are a microcosm that contain aspects of all polarities, and are astral doorways, or a unified means of spiritual elevation.

Boehme lived and died in the seventeenth century, but like Blake later, his mystical and metaphysical insights live on. Both presented radical and intellectual religious viewpoints, which may be boiled down to the basic clause that God or the Divine is within us all and within nature, and can be accessed and interacted with as such. No witch or magickian could possibly disagree with that.

William Blake

The astonishing illustrations and words of William Blake are known and loved by many a modern witch and mystic. The image of Urizen bursting from the skies in the painting *The Ancient of Days;* the flea, in which Blake sees an entire character (very much like a familiar) in what to his waking vision is but a speck; and his Biblical etchings are both accomplished and mind-boggling. His "Proverbs of Hell" speak volumes of truth, and are widely used in modern literature. "The cut worm forgives the plough"—does it? Each statement poses a philosophical argument. "The road of Excess leads to the Palace of Wisdom"—a philosophy followed by many in the sixties on their psychedelic search for truth.

Born in London in 1757, the author of the poem/hymn *Jerusalem* was one of the first Christian mystics to re-present a world of gods, demons, living myths, and mysticism in a straight-laced, newly industrialised era. He created entire cosmologies, painting and writing about them in immense detail, each with philosophical significance. Jung later interpreted these and of course described them as "archetypes," which indeed they are. Blake wrote that "All Deities reside in the human breast," which is exactly what most modern witches believe. Personal interaction with the Divine in its many forms is not just possible, it is a human right, as Blake realised and stated over three hundred years ago.

Blake was a philanthropist as well as a mystic; he sought to identify the primal causes of both suffering and joy. His poems *Songs of Innocence and Experience* explore the pain and epiphanies of the human condition. He saw the world as "fallen" in a classically Christian manner, and held a similar view to Paramahansa Yogananda on creation in that it is cast in "Error." God and his lost created ones must therefore be reconciled, which comes through the power of "Jesus, the Imagination"—that is, the Christ-force of redemption through the ability to visualise and interact with the Divine. Thus, the intercessor and Saviour lie within each of us, and are not confined to one religion or religious path. Blake, like the modern witch, respected all paths to the Truth, saying: "The Religions of all Nations are derived from each Nation's different reception of the Poetic Genius," and that "All Religions are One."

The immensely prolific genius that was William Blake died in 1827, but his work remains alive and continues to inform and progress spiritual seekers of many disciplines. The Pre-Raphaelites and W. B. Yeats were amongst those influenced by Blake's Gothic imagination and radical outlook, which might be summarised by the aphorism: "Prisons are built with the stones of Law, brothels with the bricks of religion." His writings are worth meditating on, and his paintings and etchings are a boon to any mystic's insight and inspiration.

Eliphas Levi

Alphonse Louis Constant was born in Paris in 1810, and had a staunch Roman Catholic upbringing. He was ordained as a deacon at the age of twenty-five, but never entered the priesthood. Instead, his love of mysticism and ritual led him to study the thaumaturgists Cornelius Agrippa, Raymond Lully, and other magickally inclined authors. He noticed that all powerful religions contain the same symbols and techniques, stating in *Transcendental Magic* (Rider, 1923), "Occult philosophy seems to have been the nurse or god-mother of all intellectual forces, the key of all divine obscurities and the absolute queen of society in those ages when it was reserved exclusively for the education of priests and of kings." As he also perceived, "Fable abounded in its miracles, and history, attempting to estimate this unknown power, became confused with fable." Here we have the roots of modern occult

Figure 3—Eliphas Levi

practise, in which the study of mythology has become a potent magickal tool. The modern witch and magickian are adept at understanding and correlating mythologies, seeing them as sets of symbols representing various underlying esoteric currents and ingredients. Jung stated the same thing decades later, seeing the world and all in it as archetypes and their variations. This is now common practise amongst esotericists, psychologists, and mystics. By correlating the world as such, we draw closer to the original source of creation. It is not a matter of pigeon-holing, but rather of understanding or growing to understand the essential ingredients that comprise the Universe and its inhabitants. The magickian always seeks patterns, believing that there is a larger Divine plan, within which we operate with the red herring of free will as a tool for spiritual judgement. This in no way contradicted Levi's Christianity. The latter did mean, however, that he was often reluctant to practise the techniques he expounded.

Eliphas Levi was never wealthy, and the need to eat, whilst hopefully pursuing his magickal interests, led him to London in May 1854. A failed marriage to a much younger woman now behind him, he hoped to encounter "sympathique" minds in the British capital, but was sadly hindered by his knowledge only of

French and Hebrew. Certainly Moina Mathers would have been able to talk fluently with him had he visited a few decades later, but she was still between incarnations. Unfortunately for Levi, those souls who were drawn to his teachings later in the century were not around to greet him when he visited. Instead, he found himself almost obliged to produce "party-tricks" for wealthy patrons, something that must have grated terribly on his integrity as a priest and magus.

Still, at least one of these experiences turned out well for Levi, as he relates in *Transcendental Magic*. One day when he was in London, a card arrived at his hotel asking him to meet its sender "Tomorrow, at three o'clock, in front of Westminster Abbey." He did so, and "soon recognised [an aristocratic female friend of Sir Edward Bulwer Lytton, one of his patrons,] as an initiate, not exactly of the first order, but still of a most exulted grade." This anonymous Lady provided Levi with "magical vestments and instruments," and somewhere to stay to prepare a ritual of spirit evocation. The spirit to be interacted with was that of "the divine Apollonius" of Tyana.

Despite the "last-minute nerves" of one of the proposed triad of evokers (the other being the Lady in question), the working went according to plan, with Levi operating mostly on his own, until, "I beheld distinctly, before the altar, the figure of a man of more than normal size, which dissolved and vanished away." He recommenced the evocation, which he now described as an "invocation," and saw a spectre in his magickal mirror. "When I looked again forth there was a man in front of me, wrapped from head to feet in a species of shroud, which seemed more grey than white." The apparition gave Levi a shock, "and did not altogether correspond to my preconceived notion of Apollonius," causing him to gather his mage's resources and command it not to alarm him. It vanished, and he commanded it to reappear. He used his ritual sword for this, but "divined that the sword displeased the spirit, and therefore I placed its point downwards." This is one of the many lessons that eventually became a creed for some, such as Dion Fortune: simple manners in ritual. One would not approach a stranger on the street for directions or information wielding a weapon of threat, and likewise for a spirit who has been dragged over to the earth planes for questioning.

Levi became overwhelmed, unsurprisingly, and "fell into a profound lethargy, accompanied by dreams" in which the questions he was obliged to ask were answered mentally.

Like all effective magickians, Levi analysed the experience afterwards for subjective (and objective) influences. Also like all effective occultists whose aim, after all, is to explore and discover rather than proselytise, he announced, "I state the facts as they happened, but I would impose faith on no one." However, his own belief (through personal experience—the only type that is of true relevance) has led to significant developments in ritual magick, particularly its relationship to Qabalah. Esoteric philosophy has changed because of the work of this founding father of modern magick.

Eliphas Levi was one of the first modern authorities on Qabalah, and essentially brought it to the Western Mystery Tradition. He preached extreme mental and moral caution in occult matters, and was aware of the distinction between the sacred and the profane to a far greater degree than are many practitioners today. The aim of magick is not to command personal power, or wealth, or the glorification of the transient ego, it is to draw closer to the Divine—the source to which we will all eventually return, sooner or later, depending on our decisions and practises during each life.

In 1854, Levi returned to Paris where the author Adolphe Desbarolles (*Les Mysteres de la Main,* 1869) helped keep Levi's body and soul together with practical aid. Levi taught Qabalah, continued his studies of Tarot, and furthered occult understanding through a variety of lateral studies. He died in 1875, having spent his entire incarnation dedicated to the study of the Mysteries. His books, such as *The Key to the Mysteries, Transcendental Magic,* and *The History of Magic* are still in print and widely used today.

Crowley, the best known of modern magickians, claimed Eliphas Levi as one of his own incarnations. Whether this is true or not, both men shaped the face of esoterica as we know it today.

Helena Blavatsky

Helena Blavatsky was the founder of the Theosophical movement, and her writings continue to influence modern occultism in many subtle ways. She is rarely directly credited, but she was an esoteric nonpareil. Despite allegations of fraudulence pitted against her by those threatened by her feminism, her strength of character, and her amazingly detailed spiritual tracts, she is responsible for uniting Western and Eastern magickal practise in the esoterically vibrant Victorian era. This continues to affect every practising occultist in the Western world today.

Helena Petrovna Blavatsky (nee von Hahn) was born into the Russian nobility in 1831. She had a privileged and somewhat undisciplined childhood characterised by a fiery, independent Leonine spirit in conjunction with strong literary influences (her mother was a successful novelist). Later she married General Nikifor V. Blavatsky, a man old enough to be her father, or even her grandfather.

Figure 4—Helena Blavatsky

The wealth of Helena's childhood and social status meant little to this turbulent, aspiring soul. After a mere three weeks, she abandoned "old whistlebreeches" (as she called her husband) and travelled to Constantinople, Egypt, Paris, and Asia. From the age of seventeen, Helena devoted herself to geographical and spiritual exploration. She improvised in order to survive, and turned her hand to everything from piano lessons, to riding horses in a circus, to experimenting with the spiritualism so popular in mid-nineteenth-century Europe and America. She is reported to have been a passionate, Bohemian woman with a roll-up cigarette ever burning between her fingers. Her skills as a medium were never far from the surface.

In 1851, having journeyed from Asia to London, Madame Blavatsky found herself in Hyde Park in conversation with a tall Hindu, one of the Ascended Masters that characterised the group she eventually founded, the Theosophical Society (see the section on Alice A. Bailey for a similar encounter). In this sense, she continued the work of the Rosicrucians (some claim that Blake was also a natural initiate of this order), who had earlier expounded the idea of a spiritual Brotherhood, whose aim was to help mankind evolve.

The expression of Helena's developing beliefs was eventually aided by Colonel Henry Steele Olcott, whom she met in 1874, and who facilitated the publishing of her experiences and ideas. *Isis Unveiled* is a major work in which "the images of the past are ever marshalled before my inner eye" (John Symonds, *Madame Blavatsky: Medium and Magician*). This concentration on Goddess energy was deeply unusual in the Victorian era. "The fair good goddess" delivered a great deal of intuitive and magickal information to her acolyte, which was duly transcribed. Blavatsky's notoriously confused manuscripts, full of inspiration and spiritual insight but with the pages rarely numbered, proceeded to change the face of spirituality in the West.

The impact of the Theosophical Society on modern magickal thought cannot be overestimated. Blavatsky's groundbreaking work brought the influence of Asiatic religions—most notably Hinduism—to the West. Words and phrases that we take for granted in modern occult practise (*Akasha, maya, astral planes,* and *prana,* for example) were improvised from Sanskrit and brought to the Western tongue by this remarkable woman.

A key concept vaunted by Blavatsky is that of Ascended Masters; that is, advanced souls who guard and guide mankind in our search for spiritual Truth. These are not only beings with whom it is possible to gain inspirational contact, but they are energetic, positive entities working in a sacrificial mode for our advancement and liberation from the realms of matter. Her emphasis was on service to these Masters. She taught that, through the "hierarchy," it is possible to understand "The Plan"; that is, the means to ascend to closer proximity to God.

Nowadays, it is commonly accepted amongst occult and "New Age" circles that spiritual teachers exist in realms other than our own, and may be approached for guidance. We are quite accustomed to encountering books about accessing higher intelligences, and manuscripts written through "channels." Jane Rogers's "Seth" books have been of great value to many readers, and influenced writers such as Gill Edwards, author of *Living Magically* and *Stepping into the Magic* (Piatkus, 1994). Ivan

Cooke, channel for "White Eagle," has produced work of great value such as *Healing by the Spirit* (The White Eagle Publishing Trust, 1955), and the books of Sanaya Roman and Duane Packer, channels for "Orin" and "DaBen," may be found in virtually any bookshop with a "Mind, Body, and Spirit" section (for example, *Opening to Channel,* H. J. Kramer Inc., 1986). However, at the time that H. P. Blavatsky began to interact with her guides, the concept was unknown in the West. Only one Master was recognised, one whom Blavatsky includes in her Hierarchy. The Master Jesus is identified in her cosmology as a "Sixth Ray" teacher (this level being directly connected with world religion), one of ten lofty entities working for the good of mankind.

Blavatsky's cosmology is complex, and would take a much longer book than this to abridge it with any accuracy. However, a skeletal summary of her beliefs follows below.

Each level of consciousness is defined as an "Ashram"—a spiritual group with a mentor and disciples, as in Hindu practice. These Ashrams, however, are not confined by physical specifics. The Masters concerned have ascended out of the material planes, but make themselves accessible to potential luminaries on the earth plane.

The First Ray Ashram is led by the Master Morya, and is concerned primarily with political and occult matters.

The Second Ray Ashram is presided over by Kuthumi [pronounced *koot-humi*] and Djwhal Khul, also known as the "Tibetan Master." This level is concerned with love, wisdom, and philanthropy. It is Kuthumi who visited the young Alice La Trobe-Bateman (later Bailey) in her grandparent's home in Surrey, and inspired her to strive towards spiritual service and to unite her Christian beliefs with Buddhist and Hindu teachings. "The Tibetan" later dictated many of her books (see section on Alice A. Bailey). The key point of this Ray is education.

The "Venetian" Master is the major mentor of the Third Ray Ashram. This is concerned with philosophy and major movements of humanity—the rise and fall of civilisations, and the impact of different cultures on humanity.

The Fourth Ray Ashram is the home of the arts—those that inspire us to greater spiritual expression and understanding. Music, art, and literature, particularly drama, are accessed and produced here. The Master Serapis presides over this process. The Masters "P" and Jupiter, apparently the oldest of all the Masters, are implicit here also.

Science is the key note of the Fifth Ray. Hilarion is the Master of this Ashram. He is said to have dictated *The Voice of Silence* to Helena Blavatsky, and *The Light on the Path* to Mabel Collins.

The Sixth Ray, as already mentioned, is that of the world's religions. Included in its Masters, then, is Jesus. Because this Ray is concerned with the communication of spiritual and ethical ideas, language is one of its particular properties. The Sixth Ray works against the babel of mindless chatter that characterises our realm. The fact that world religions have often deteriorated into rhetoric and cant is indicative of the strong force of matter (which Blavatsky termed as *maya*, or delusion and distraction from the true spiritual path), and certainly not of the purity, humanity, and discipline of their original concepts. This is a plane that produces the essential tenets of all true religions.

The Seventh Ray Ashram is concerned with the translation of the material into spiritual expression. The Master Rakoczi presides over this process. He is credited with many former incarnations, including Christian Rosencreuz (fourteenth century), Francis and Roger Bacon (seventeenth century), and the Comte de St. Germain (eighteenth century). He is particularly relevant to witches and occultists as Master of ritual magick. He aids the process of external conceptualisation.

The charisma and power of Madame Blavatsky were unquestionable. Even those who scorned her unorthodox methods (mediumship, and producing matter out of thin air, for example) were unable to explain away her occult prowess. Her writing is replete with spiritual correspondences and insights, and influenced even the most necessarily staunch defenders of Christianity, such as Queen Victoria's poet laureate, Lord Tennyson. Helena Blavatsky's Theosophical teachings were even admired by the great Hindu ascetic, Mahatma Gandhi.

Eventually, as Helena Blavatsky's notoriety spread, her manifestations were investigated in England by the Society for Psychical Research. There is some confusion over the conclusions. Though she was suspected of producing mediumistic effects artificially (with the use of dummies, for example), the symbolism inherent in these acts may explain her apparently parodoxical description by the Society as "One of the most accomplished, ingenious and interesting imposters in history" (John Symonds, *Man, Myth and Magic*).

There seemed to be a general acceptance in esoteric circles of Helena Blavatsky's work, especially following her next magnum opus, *The Secret Doctrine*. This respect and awe remained, despite the negative repercussions of any "stage effects" that may have been utilised in her practical expressions of spirituality at certain points. She may have been trying to make a point, or perhaps she was taking the mickey out of the earnest "spirit-seers" around her. We know that she had a strong sense of humour and of social realism. The English elite may well have irritated her—it is quite possible that she used dummies and other gimmicks as a joke. Unfortunately, this backfired and cast a slur on her character that has endured (she would have cared nothing for this, however).

Even if the aspersions were true, such a wealth of information exists in Helena Blavatsky's books that most witches, magickians, and spiritual seekers (and all Theosophists, of course) find it impossible to place any human failings in higher priority. We are also aware of the rampant cynicism of this plane, and of the enthusiasm with which the unusual is slandered by disbelievers.

Madame Blavatsky died in 1900, but her work is still widely available. It speaks for itself. Eliphas Levi influenced it, Mahatma Gandhi read it, Crowley read it, Dion Fortune read it. Krishnamurti was bred on it. The Theosophists are still going strong, as is their splinter group, the Lucis Trust (see the section on Alice A. Bailey). There is no branch of modern occultism that has not been influenced by Helena Blavatsky. The best test is to read it. This is dense work, and must be digested in small quantities, but its value is immense to those with eyes to see. Without it, modern magickal practise would be very insular and mediaeval indeed.

Annie Besant

Anne Wood was born in 1847 in London. Like many young ladies of that era, she became passionately involved in religion as expressed by the orthodoxy of the time; in her case, High Anglican. She flung herself into it with all the fanaticism of a repressed psyche, rather as Alice Bailey did in later years. Also, like the woman who was later to become her mentor, Helena Blavatsky, she found herself engaged to a man she did not love—the Reverend Frank Besant, whom she married at the age of twenty.

Disillusionment with the church ensued. Having written her first pamphlet, *On the Deity of Jesus of Nazareth,* she joined the staff of the National Reformer, a freethought, radical journal. This brought her into touch with like-minded spirits, and quelled her feelings of being at odds with the world, whilst also offering the intellectual stimulation she required.

By 1877, Annie Besant and others in the society were being prosecuted for atheism and obscenity, having advocated birth control in one of Besant's classic texts, the paradoxically entitled *Gospel of Atheism.* One of the key persecutors was her husband, the Reverend Besant, who used his position as "guardian of Christian morals" to keep their children from Annie.

Undeterred, Annie Besant continued to promote humanitarian and feminist causes with gusto. She met George Bernard Shaw in 1884, and joined the Socialist Fabian Society in 1885.

Despite her reaction against orthodox Christianity, Besant did not lose the religious urge. She reviewed a copy of Helena Blavatsky's *The Secret Doctrine,* and was deeply impressed by it. In 1889, the two women met for the first time. By 1891, when Blavatsky died, Annie Besant was appointed leader of almost the entire Theosophical movement. She had swallowed its teachings whole, and proved herself remarkably proficient on all levels. Like Blavatsky and Bailey later on, she "heard the voices of The Masters" (see Blavatsky section for more on this).

In 1893, Annie Besant arrived in India, the spiritual home of Theosophy. Working with C. W. Leadbeater, author of *The Chakras* and several other books on the occult, and ex-clergyman with a dubious reputation, Annie Besant concentrated on developing the Theosophical Society and on increasing her own psychic abilities. The influence of Hinduism became naturally stronger as she abided in India and studied its native texts.

It is at this point that the Theosophical movement became divided, with Annie Besant and Charles Leadbeater at the helm of a peculiar conviction. One of the key beliefs of Hinduism is in avatars, or incarnations of divinity upon earth. Annie Besant became convinced that the great god Vishnu was due to be reborn at any minute. Leadbeater agreed, homing in on a pretty Brahmin boy named Krishnamurti, who was adopted by the pair. They decided that Krishnamurti was the new incarnation of the Hindu deity, and that it was their duty to raise and look after him.

Krishnamurti had divinity duly thrust upon him, along with the best education money could buy (though he proved academically ungifted) and world travel such as no ordinary Indian (or even English) boy could have dreamed of at the time. Reared in the precepts of Theosophy, and sometimes believing them, Krishnamurti toured the world under the aegis of Mrs. Besant and Mr. Leadbeater, lecturing to the Theosophical Society and other interested parties. For years, he bore the burden of their expectations, sought this apparent godliness in himself, and strove to live up to this vast and unreasonable task that had been laid on him since boyhood. Eventually, Besant and Leadbeater declared themselves the "disciples" of the young man they had raised.

Krishnamurti, meanwhile, suffered greatly under the pressure of self-doubt. He was an honest, conscientious individual with enough self-knowledge to doubt that he was indeed an avatar. In 1929, he shocked the Besant-Leadbeater school of Theosophy by announcing, "The moment you follow someone, you cease to follow Truth." After years of being set up as a leader, he finally renounced it, saying:

Because I am free, unconditioned, whole, not the part, not the relative, but the whole Truth that is eternal, I desire those, who seek to understand me, to be free, not to follow me, not to make out of me a cage which will become a religion, a sect . . . No man from outside can make you free; nor can organised worship, nor the immolation of yourself for a cause, make you free; nor can forming yourself into an organisation, nor throwing yourself into work, make you free. [Mary Lutyens, *Krishnamurti: The Years of Awakening*]

Good advice for us all.

Krishnamurti's affection for Annie Besant seems to have remained, however. He called her "Mother," and managed not to become embittered by what can only be described as a spectacular error of judgement on her and Leadbeater's part. An otherwise sensible, humanitarian lady, her attachment to and belief in Krishnamurti were utterly genuine. She believed him to be Vishnu, and was willing to serve and to worship him in every way possible.

Despite her protégé's eventual renunciation, the Theosophical Society grew stronger thanks to the work of Annie Besant. It still continues today, and its influence on modern witchcraft and esoteric practise is subtle but vast (see the sections on Helena Blavatsky and Alice A. Bailey for more on this).

Annie Besant died in 1933 at the grand old age of ninety-five.

Wynn Westcott

Wynn Westcott is the founding member of the Golden Dawn, and his influence on Qabalistic studies within the Western Mystery Tradition is vast.

He was born in England in 1848, and was orphaned by the age of ten. He was then adopted by his uncle, and became involved with medicine. As is natural for an educated, professional man with interests in the occult, Westcott gravitated towards Freemasonry. He became a full-fledged member in 1871, and by 1874 had become a Worshipful Master of the group. Living in Matlock, he worked as a doctor for nine years and became involved in several other lodges, including the Orders of the Temple, the Red Cross of Constantine, and the Ancient and Accepted Rite. The Masons were certainly active and interesting in those days.

Alongside Westcott's external Masonic activities, he developed an active interest in many of the practises hinted at in its ceremonies and symbolism, not least Alchemy, Hermetic Magick, and Qabalah. Westcott's research into the latter, particularly, was to influence the workings of the Golden Dawn at a root level within the next decades.

Another society of vast occult influence, of which Westcott became a member, was the Rosicrucians. He also joined the more Eastern-influenced Theosophical Society, though he allied himself more with the later Christian branch of the order. Westcott had a finger in every esoteric pie, so to speak.

He was therefore the most appropriate person, perhaps, to receive what was later known as the *Cipher Manuscript,* a collection of ritual initiations passed on to him by an elderly Freemason. Scribed in sigils that Westcott understood from his esoteric studies, the manuscript allegedly originated from one Fräulein Anna Sprengel, an elevated esotericist belonging to a German lodge, but there is much doubt as to whether this person actually existed. Westcott claimed to have corresponded with her—albeit briefly—but he may have been using her fake credentials for the script he hoped to put into action in the "Society of Eight," an organisation that never quite happened but which provided a blueprint for the Golden Dawn.

Along with two of his friends from the Masons and Rosicrucians—Samuel MacGregor Mathers and Dr. Robert Woodman—he worked on these mysterious pages. Out of this emerged the ritual structure for the Golden Dawn. The magickal triumvirate kicked off in February 1888, with the seeress Moina Mathers as their first initiate. She was to be the first of many.

In the spring of 1892, the Matherses moved to Paris and established the Ahathoor Temple. As Woodman had died in 1891, Wynn Westcott became the chief of the Order in England. This continued until 1897, when he accidentally left some of his grimoires and scripts in public, and his activities became known to the police. He was forced to resign from the Golden Dawn, establishing Florence Farr to take his place. His role was now as mentor rather than as an overtly active member—a position he repeated with the Rosicrucians even after moving to South Africa in 1920. This well-respected and apparently liked grand esotericist died in 1925, leaving works such as *An Introduction to the Study of Kabalah* and a translation of Moses de Leon's *Sepher Yetzirah,* a study of "the two and thirty most occult and wonderful paths of wisdom" and their sephiroth.

The contents of the latter are worth mentioning here, as they are key to the development of the Golden Dawn. See chapter 12, "The Witch and Qabalah," for a more hands-on approach to this mystical system.

"He created this Universe by three Seraphim: Number, Writing and Speech"; so reads Westcott's 1887 rendition (facsimile; Robert Fryar, Bath) of the *Sepher Yetzirah*. Number, letter, and sound—these are the creative principles referred to in many creation myths, not least Hindu. The power of writing is reflected not merely in syntactical meaning, but in the letters themselves that, "like scintillating flames," contain the key to dimensions closer to the Creative Source. The power of speech includes its intonation and rhythm—its mantric and vibrational essence, another portal. And in number is structure and essence symbolised. So, the magickian and mystic seek to understand and utilise the information of which life as we know it is comprised—"Ten are the numbers, as are the Sephiroth, and twenty-two the letters, these are the Foundation of all things."

The letters—Hebrew ones, of course—begin with the Three Mother Letters, *Aleph, Mem,* and *Shin.* Their qualities include "Heat, Cold, and a Temperate Climate, and the temperate state from the spiritual air which is again the equaliser between them," and they correspond to the head, the stomach, and the chest. We see here how the macrocosm becomes microcosmic in the occultist's perceptions. The whole Qabalistic system is a series of such correspondences through which information may be gleaned.

There follows seven Double Letters, each having two possible sounds. Within the diagram of the Tree of Life, these represent the seven vertical lines. Again, each has cosmic properties, which Westcott summarises as such:

> *Beth*—Predominant in Wisdom.
> *Gimel*—Predominant in Health.
> *Daleth*—Predominant in Fertility.
> *Kaph*—Predominant in Life.
> *Peh*—Predominant in Power.
> *Resh*—Predominant in Peace.
> *Tau*—Predominant in Beauty.

From these seven came the Seven Worlds, Seven Heavens, Seven Seas, Seven Deserts, and so on. Likewise, from the qualities represented by the twelve Simple Letters sprung the constellations, the twelve months of the year, the twelve essential organs of the human body, and the "twelve limits of the Universe."

These Simple Letters, or "Elementals," being associated with the constellations, have obvious astrological significance. Each is also related to a primary human function, as follows:

> *He*—Aries—Predominant in Speech.
> *Vau*—Taurus—Predominant in Mind.

Zain—Gemini—Predominant in Movement.

Heth—Cancer—Predominant in Sight.

Teth—Leo—Predominant in Hearing.

Yod—Virgo—Predominant in Labour.

Lamed—Libra—Predominant in Sexual Desire.

Nun—Scorpio—Predominant in Smell.

Samech—Sagittarius—Predominant in Sleep.

Ayin—Capricorn—Predominant in Anger.

Tzaddi—Aquarius—Predominant in Taste.

Quoph—Pisces—Predominant in Mirth.

The Qabalistic system is vast and complex, but it provides a basis for much occult activity and analysis today. Ironically, its "outing" by such people as Israel Regardie in the twentieth century has caused it to lose the taboo from which Dr. Westcott suffered when he left his papers in public. Today, these "secret keys to the Universe" may be bought from any good bookshop. This is thanks to the founding fathers of translation and information, of whom Wynn Westcott was most certainly one.

Samuel Liddell MacGregor Mathers

Samuel Mathers was born in 1854 in Hackney, London. His father died young, and Samuel lived with his mother in Bournemouth until she died in 1885. He was interested in Freemasonry, and became a Mason in 1877. He became a Master Mason in 1878. In Bournemouth he met Frederick Holland, a mystically minded student of Judaism and particularly Qabalah. Mathers's natural love of symbolism and ritual were stimulated. He became a Rosicrucian in 1882, and ascended fast within its ranks. Despite his esoteric interests, Mathers had to live. He had no means, unlike many members of the early Golden Dawn, and thus embarked upon a military career. In 1884 he wrote a book entitled *Practical Instruction in Infantry Campaigning Exercise*. He was a muscular as well as intellectual young man, with skills at both boxing and fencing under his belt. He was also a committed vegetarian and supporter of feminism.

He married Mina Bergson in 1890, a friend of Annie Horniman, the thespian, esotericist, and tea heiress. The latter provided the impoverished Mathers with the means to exist.

Under Wynn Westcott, Mathers became a chief of the new Esoteric Order of the Golden Dawn, which was founded on March 1, 1888. The Isis-Urania Temple accepted his wife Moina as its first initiate. Mathers himself adopted the motto *"S Rioghail Mo Dhream,"* Gaelic for "Royal is My Tribe," and the same name he had used in the Rosicrucian Order. In the same year, he published a book on the *Marseilles* Tarot deck entitled *The Tarot: Its Occult Significance, Use in Fortune Telling, and Method of Play.* His best-known books are *Book of the Sacred Magic of Abramelin the Mage,* and *The Key of Solomon the King.*

The Golden Dawn concentrated on magickal theory rather than practise until 1891. Then Mathers created and became chief of the Second Order, in which magick was actively practised. Mathers and his wife excelled in creating dramatic ritual by incorporating esoteric information gleaned from long hours studying ancient manuscripts in the British Museum in Bloomsbury, London. They also formulated a comprehensive training program, dispensing esoteric theory and practise in lessons that allowed the initiate to move through a carefully constructed series of initiations. Their approach was learned and conscientious, and opened the doors of consciousness with utmost attention to ability and detail.

In May 1892, Moina and Samuel relocated to Paris and established the Ahathoor Temple of the Golden Dawn. As well as working in the Inner Lodge, they performed Isian rituals publicly.

The Golden Dawn itself ceased to exist in 1903, but its teachings and practises continued through the Orders of the Stella Matutina and the Alpha et Omega.

Samuel MacGregor Mathers died in 1918. Moina carried on their work until her own demise in 1928.

W. B. Yeats

William Butler Yeats (1865–1939), primarily known as an Irish Nationalist (along with his long-term lover, Maud Gonne) and literary figure, was also an eminent occultist. He was initially involved in Theosophy, and became personally acquainted with its founding member, Helena Blavatsky. Through this group he learned the principles of Eastern esoterica, and a little about Qabalah and similar mystical systems. He also became acquainted with the Ascended Masters and the concept of universal correspondences (similar to Jung's collective unconscious, but expressed by Blavatsky as "the Akashic Records"). (See the section on Helena Blavatsky above, and on Theosophy in chapter 14, "A Brief History of Witchcraft.")

Helena Blavatsky formed the more practical "Esoteric Section" of the Theosophists partly at his request, for Yeats was keen to put theory into practise. He did this with gusto, but was disappointed to find that his experiments nearly always failed. His faith in their essential viability still in tact, he left the Theosophists and became a member of the Order of the Golden Dawn. The Order was far more Western-based—Qabalah and myth and legend providing a significant chunk of its teachings. It was also heavily influenced by Masonic and Rosicrucian beliefs and practises (a fact that caused the politically aware Maud Gonne to quit the Order eventually). Yeats was greatly influenced by MacGregor Mathers, Wynn Westcott, and Dr. Woodman (the Golden Dawn triumvirate), and his esoteric investigations affected his writing. Best of all, the Golden Dawn was practical, involving highly thespian ritual that brought tangible results. Yeats's migration to the Golden Dawn was a brilliant move, as the Order was in its heyday at this point, and provided him with the ideal scenario in which to meet other talented, highly educated occultists. Among their number was the love of his life, fellow Fenian, and literary diva Maud Gonne.

Yeats's search for magick and mysticism lasted throughout his incarnation. As he put it in his essay simply entitled *Magic,* "Whatever the passions of men have gathered about, becomes a symbol in the great memory, and in the hands of him who has the secret it is a worker of wonders, a caller-up of angels or of devils."

Moina Bergson Mathers

Mina Bergson was born in 1865 to Irish Jewish parents in Geneva, Switzerland. They moved in order to counteract the anti-Semitism that hounded them. Mina's brother Henri, later a famous philosopher, was deposited in Paris under the aegis of a scholarship, and Mina and her parents moved to southern England. In 1880, Mina, a talented artist, went to study at the Slade School of Art in central London. She naturally gravitated to the nearby British Museum, where she encountered MacGregor Mathers (as he called himself), a clerk from Hackney with a brilliant mind. He had recently translated Knorr von Rosenroth's *Qabalah Unveiled,* and was involved in several other intellectual and esoteric projects that would provide the foundation of the Golden Dawn system. The young Bohemian artist and the erudite esotericist fell in love. Mathers had known and learned from Helena Blavatsky (see her biography above), and had been a founder of the Hermetic Lodge of the Theosophical Society, an organisation that has affected many aspects of magickal and New Age practise as we now know it.

Together, Mina (now known as Moina, a more Celtic equivalent) and Samuel MacGregor Mathers devoted themselves at every level to occult progression. Their combined efforts, along with those of Wynn Westcott, created what became the Order of the Golden Dawn.

Figure 5—Moina Bergson Mathers

Moina was initiated into the Golden Dawn on March 1, 1888, its first entrant. She took on the magickal motto *"Vestigia Nulla Retrorsum,"* which translates as "Never to retrace these steps." Her faith was absolute. Ritual enactment, complete with full costume and paraphernalia, was a primary technique they used to forge a closer link with divinity. There are several wonderful photographs still extant of the couple dressed and posing in such personae as "The Hierophant Rameses and the High Priestess Anari." Celtic and Egyptian ritual—including rites of Isis, which they enacted publically on stage in Paris—gave added impact to their living imaginations. They certainly believed the adage "Prepare the Temple, and the God will come."

Moina was a devoted, faithful priestess, despite her striking looks and the poverty she shared with Mathers. Their relationship is legendary for being chaste. Occult studies were of optimum importance to them. Moina was a talented seeress, as W. B. Yeats records. A total belief in reincarnation informed her perceptions, as is normal practise in esoteric realms.

When Wynn Westcott and Florence Farr took over the London Lodge, MacGregor Mathers and Moina went to Paris to begin that branch of the Order. In 1896 they worked on Celtic Mystery rituals with Maud Gonne and W. B. Yeats in the

Paris Lodge. When her husband died in 1918, Moina became head of the Paris branch, but eventually she returned to England. She initiated Dion Fortune in London, but there was a natural antipathy between them for some reason, as Dion Fortune's books attest. Fortune believed Moina Mathers to be blocking her progress through jealousy, and because Moina believed Fortune to be revealing some of the secrets of the Order in her book *The Esoteric Philosophy of Love and Marriage*. According to Dion Fortune, Moina Mathers went as far as to expel Fortune from the Golden Dawn because "certain symbols failed to appear in her aura"—a charge that Dion Fortune summarises as "unanswerable." It is a terrible shame that two of the most talented esotericists, living in the same era and place, did not get along, for they had a great deal in common. Instead, the accusations flew.

In 1927, Moina's health began to suffer, and she stopped eating. She was perhaps undergoing one final purification before progressing into the Greater Initiation, which she did on July 25, 1928. More is known of Dion Fortune than Moina Mathers because of Dion's numerous books, but Moina was without a doubt one of the most talented magickians of the Golden Dawn and a magickal force to be reckoned with.

Aleister Crowley

Aleister Crowley—the man who bridged the gap between Oscar Wilde and Adolf Hitler.

—Cyril Connolly

Soak me in Cognac, C★★t and Cocaine.

—Crowley, from a wall painting at his home in Cefalu, Sicily

Despite his infamy, Crowley's contribution to occult studies cannot be overestimated. His flamboyant character, his avid involvement in magick and its fraternities, and his renowned eccentricity all acted as major catalysts on esoteric developments in the late nineteenth and early twentieth centuries. His Tarot pack, illustrated by Frieda Harris, demonstrates his extensive cross-referencing of the religious symbolism of numerous cultures (epitomised by 777, his table of correspondences). Its rendering also demonstrates a futuristic outlook unusual in esoterica, which is often retrospective. The Knight of Swords, for example, has the look of a man-(and horse-)powered helicopter, both mediaeval and ultramodern, and his Hermit is almost abstract. Crowley and Harris were very much in tune with the artistic and magickal avant-garde.

Figure 6—Aleister Crowley

Edward Alexander Crowley was born in Leamington Spa, England, on October 12, 1875. His father was a wealthy gentleman of leisure, and both of Crowley's parents were evangelical members of the Plymouth Brethren. As a child he was preached to about the imminent end of the world and the salvation only of the faithful (and morally strict) Brethren—factors that undoubtedly sculpted his psyche into one of extremes. Threats of hellfire surrounded the youthful Crowley. It is small wonder that he became, in later life, violently anti-Christian. He tested the implications, and with every failure of God to strike him dead, another (or potential) neurosis seemed to be eliminated.

Crowley was a terrible snob throughout his incarnation, but paradoxically he attempted to eliminate his sensations of "caste" through "debasing" himself in a complex and magickal way. He was attached to his ego to an unusual degree, yet periodically he attempted to eradicate it in order to find enlightenment. This occurred only in a magickal context; in the mundane world he was so habitually arrogant that he alienated many who would otherwise have found empathy with his quest.

As his work indicates, Crowley received an excellent education, leaving Trinity College, Cambridge, in 1898 after three years. Whilst there, he was introduced to the work of the Decadents—Beardsley, Wilde, Huysmans, and the French Symbolists—and developed his own hedonistic, self-indulgent nature. He was acutely aware of mortality, and pleasure seemed to be the call of the day. His magick reflects these traits combined with genuine erudition.

Poetry and bombastic verse were Crowley's first modes of self-expression. However, he soon found this inadequate (though he maintained to the end that he was the finest poet of the century). He read whatever magickal texts he could get his hands on, and eventually, through his interest in alchemy, was introduced to the Hermetic Order of the Golden Dawn (see sections on Samuel MacGregor Mathers and Florence Farr). He was admitted into its ranks as Frater Purdurabo in 1898. His earlier interest in Kabbalah was then revitalised by the work of other members on the subject—most notably Wynn Westcott (founder of the Order) and Samuel Mathers. With the eclecticism typical of the Golden Dawn (which has influenced all modern occult studies in the West, including Wicca), Qabalah was cross-referenced with Tarot, alchemy, Hinduism, Freudian and Jungian psychology, Theosophy, and many other scholarly areas of psychological and spiritual endeavour. For Westcott, Mathers and Crowley were undoubtedly scholars, spending much of their time in the British Museum reading and translating manuscripts of mediaeval and ancient magick.

W. B. Yeats was also a member of the Order, though his relationship with Crowley was stymied by Crowley's belief that Yeats was jealous of his poetical prowess—a conviction that cumulated into the belief that Yeats had hexed him because of it. Just as Mathers, a bank clerk, convinced himself that he was chief of a Scottish clan, Crowley believed his own hyperalliterative, deliberately unsubtle verse to be of immeasurable literary value (though, to be fair, some of it is accomplished, and some breathtaking). If others did not accept this, it was due to their own lack of discrimination. Crowley's self-belief seems never to have wavered as far as his own genius is concerned.

Initially, Crowley affiliated himself with Mathers, who elevated him fast within the Order of the Golden Dawn. There were about a hundred members at the time of Crowley's arrival, and several lodges, the main two being in Paris and London. The Golden Dawn initiates were highly educated, intense, politically aware, and idiosyncratic individuals, and Crowley's arrogance did not go down well with some of them. When Florence Farr (see biography) objected to Mathers's swift elevation of Crowley, her London Lodge became estranged from the newer Paris Lodge, of which Mathers and Crowley were key members. Much back-biting and intrigue ensued, which may be read about in Francis King's *The Magical World of Aleister Crowley* (Wiedenfeld and Nicholson, 1977), or Colin Wilson's *Aleister Crowley: The Nature of the Beast* (Aquarian Press, 1987), to give but two examples.

In 1899 Crowley moved into Boleskine House on the shores of Loch Ness, Scotland, in order to work the rituals of Abra-Melin the Mage (as translated by Samuel MacGregor Mathers). The aim of this ascetic six-month magickal endeavour is to contact one's Holy Guardian Angel, but the discipline required proved an unsurprising obstacle to the pleasure-loving Crowley. He most probably rebelled against the same factors that had beleaguered him in childhood—this time in the form of Judaism rather than Christianity. Much humility is required to work the rituals effectively, and this was not Crowley's strong point. He quickly tired of everything that became a "duty," and six months of chaste living and self-prostration were not appealing, Guardian Angel pending or otherwise. The community itself, which was disturbed by Crowley's goings-on and became superstitious about his abode, infuriated him with its parochial atmosphere.

Crowley was a wildly melodramatic character with immense magickal aspiration, but, as Colin Wilson points out in *Aleister Crowley: The Nature of the Beast,* he lacked "self-dedication." He grasped the concepts required for such an act as the Abra-Melin ceremonies, but was by now a compulsive womaniser and hopeless braggart. Yet these were points he was proud of, and others were free to either take him or leave him, usually with a string of curses behind them.

One of the few people with whom Crowley did not compete was a friend from the Golden Dawn, Allan Bennett. The latter was deeply influenced by Hinduism and Buddhism, and his effect on Crowley was immense. Crowley had always been a traveller, both physically and spiritually, and Bennett led him towards Eastern disciplines, including yoga, which was later to be transmuted into the more Crowley-friendly practise of Tantra. Crowley's book *Magick* gives detailed explanations of the principles of yoga, much of which he learned at the feet of Hindu gurus, and into whose secrets he was initiated.

Following a great deal of womanising, Crowley eventually married. However, as usual, it was no conventional scenario. The woman concerned, Rose Kelly (the sister of a friend from Cambridge), had been having an affair with a married man, and was the object of the affections of several suitors. Crowley married her to help relieve pressure from her family for her to make a choice. Both were soon surprised to find themselves in love. Crowley began to use Rose as a seeress.

In March 1904 in Cairo, the most significant event of Crowley's magickal life took place. Via the mediumship of Rose, he was contacted by an extraterrestrial being called Aiwass, who delivered *The Book of the Law,* a text heralding the New Age or Aeon of Horus and, as the title suggests, setting out the means of attaining suitable states of spiritual reception. "Do What Thou Wilt" is a key command. The "insights" contained seemed to confirm everything Crowley had hitherto believed. Rather like Blake's "He who desires but acts not, breeds pestilence," came the adage "The word of Sin is Restriction," and lateral declarations. However, Crowley trod the "Road of Excess" to much further extremes than did Blake, nearly always in a serious and magickally experimental manner. He shocked his contemporaries with his active bisexuality (and may be one of the causes of the anti-homosexual statements found in the works of other magickal writers of his era, such as Dion Fortune), and he took so much cocaine and heroin that by the time of his death, he was obliged to inject himself daily with the latter. He even obliged his Goddess/Whore of Babalon, at that time Leah Hirsig, by eating her excrement. At least we can see here that he lived what he preached.

In the same year, Rose gave birth to the first of many of Crowley's short-lived offspring. The little girl was named Nuit Ma Athanor Hecate Sappho Jezebel Lilith, an appellation that pretty much sums up Crowley's hopes for the New Age. Not only is it violently anti-Christian, but it also resonates with mystery and unexplored depths: "Nuit" means "night," and "Nut" means "the sky." The sky was not the limit as far as Crowley was concerned, and, as "Every Man and Every Woman is a Star," the idea was to claim our rightful place in "Nuit," and be our magickal selves to the best of our ability, fearlessly.

Fear was not a trait Crowley allowed himself to harbour, but his craving for excitement was relentlessly indulged. Even the birth of the New Aeon was put on hold while he went to Nepal to climb mountains, popped over to India to shoot as many animals as he could aim a gun at, and took Rose and Nuit to China. There he abandoned them in order to visit an ex-mistress in Shanghai; during this time, his daughter died of typhoid.

In 1907, Crowley wrote *777,* a table of magickal correspondences of immense value to any occultist. Many of the correlating images are highly subjective, but such is the nature of magick. Now, they have been so widely employed that they have become truths in themselves. Much of *777,* however, is accurate cultural cross-referencing, and again illustrates that Crowley, hedonism included, was very serious about his subject.

In the same year, Crowley formed the "Argenteum Astrum," an alternative occult group to the Golden Dawn, who had refused to accept him as their leader. Victor Neuburg became involved, with whom Crowley had an intense magickal homosexual relationship. Rose, meanwhile, became alcoholic. In 1909, he divorced her "for her own sake."

Crowley's wild living led him into severe financial straits. He dramatised some of his rituals in order to earn a little money; some were well received, others not so. His reputation as a sodomite offended some of his less-experimental friends, and, as he had always intended, attacked the social mores of his era. He was always delighted by publicity of any sort, and loved to shun the "ignorance" of conventional society. However, he needed money in order to live.

New lovers and sponsors were not difficult to find for one as charismatic as Crowley. In Cefalu, Sicily, he rented a villa, which he named "Thelema" after Rabelais' "Theleme," emulating the utopian ideals of his novel *Gargantua*. The creeds of *The Book of the Law* are known as "Thelema," and there are many "Thelemites" around today who follow Crowley's magickal practises.

The idea of Theleme was to create a new society. Since Crowley had by this time acquired two "wives" (one actual—Leah Hirsig—and the other a nanny picked up along the way) and two children, one of which was his own, it seemed that the New Aeon was in the making. Other interested "disciples" came to stay, some finding enlightenment (usually in a completely unexpected form), and others being utterly revolted by the debauch on display there. One unfortunate disciple, Raoul Loveday, allegedly met his death through drinking the blood of a cat he had sacrificed with Crowley during ritual (polluted water may have been the real culprit, however). Loveday's wife wasted no time in contacting the press about Crowley's practices. He then attained the title that has haunted him ever since—that of "The Wickedest Man in the World."

The rest of Crowley's life, which terminated in 1947, might be summed up as a long string of lovers, drugs, infamy, and unpaid debts. However, that would be missing the point. His search for ultimate truth was carefully chronicled, and his magickal manuscripts are of great value to the discerning occultist, whatever one might think of his personal behaviour. These include: *Magick in Theory and Practice, Equinox of the Gods, The Holy Books of Thelema, Konx Om Pax: Essays in Light, Liber Aleph Vel Cxi: The Book of Wisdom or Folly, The Book of Thoth* (Tarot divination), *Gems from the Equinox,* and *The Book of the Law.*

Aleister Crowley's influence is still very much felt by the modern witch and magickian. His followers aim to de-condition themselves, shed imposed reactions, and to become their true selves. This involves rejecting all personae that have been imposed on one by others, for the way that we perceive ourselves is often through the eyes of others. Crowley tried to fight this, as do his spiritual disciples today. It is a complex process unlike modern psychotherapy only in that it often involves a shock-factor; that is, enacting what, to the individual and the group concerned, challenges their standards. In this sense alone it is "demonic"—the useful aspects of what is bad and unacceptable are faced and processed. It was for purposes of psychospiritual progression that Crowley "debased" himself. Eating Leah Hirsig's excrement, for example, was a carefully chronicled magickal operation.

Crowley's famous definition of magick is "The Science and Art of causing Change in conformity with Will." Will is the key; as far as Crowley and his followers are concerned, will can move mountains and more. In this respect, his beliefs do not differ from those of many religions in that mountains may be moved by the striving soul of man. The difference is faith. Crowley advocated that no humility, no intercession is needed. We can do it all ourselves, through our own spiritual power. The "Change," of course, involves manipulation of the physical plane via the etheric level. Otherwise "magick" would be no different from any other intentional act.

Because he was such a strong and controversial figure, there is no wholly objective biography of Crowley available, and there probably never will be. John Symonds's *The Great Beast* (now entitled *King of the Shadow Realm*) seems to be accurate historically, but indicates no empathy for Crowley's motives or aims—indeed, it seems thoroughly adverse to them. *Magical Dilemma of Victor Neuburg* by John Overton Fuller contains some insights and is less stilted by contempt. Recent additions are Martin Booth's *A Magick Life,* and Lawrence Sutin's *Do What Thou Wilt* (St. Martin's Press).

Alice A. Bailey

Alice A. Bailey is a name known to many of the older generation as a one-time Theosophist and later founder of the Lucis Trust. She helped spread the concepts of Theosophy and spirituality through her numerous books, and wrote *A Treatise on White Magic* in 1934 when the word *magic* still sent shivers down many a conventionalist's spine. Her work is abstruse, but has had enough of a founding influence on modern occult practises to be worth a witch's study time. She also has a fascinating personal history as a spiritual seeker, as revealed in her *Unfinished Autobiography* (Lucis Publishing Trust, last reprinted in 1994).

Alice Bailey was born Alice Ann La Trobe-Bateman in England in 1880. Her aristocratic, religiously inclined family provided her with an educated, disciplined childhood, which, though she did not enjoy it much at the time, benefitted her greatly when she came to write the twenty-five books on occult philosophy still in print today. She spent her childhood after the age of eight, when her father died, living with her grandparents (my own great-great-grandparents, as it happens) at Moor Park in Surrey, where she and her sister Lydia were taught the graces expected of conscientious ladies of leisure. Both girls strove for greater things. Lydia became one of the first women ever to graduate from Edinburgh University with distinctions in science, leading her to become an expert on both tropical diseases and cancer treatments. Lydia remained an orthodox Christian throughout her life, while Alice explored many spiritual paths and wrote books on esoterica.

The stifling orthodoxy of her childhood religious upbringing—High Church Anglican and Scottish Presbyterian by turns—and the tedious social mores of her class combined to make Alice spend much of her adolescence pondering over whose soul was saved and whose was not. This trait ran in the family—several of Alice's great uncles were Moravian ministers and missionaries. She was keen on charity work, thanks partly to the *noblesse oblige* attitude of her Victorian upbringing. Alice, as a privileged young lady of the upper class, was expected to help the sick and the poor. As she admits in her *Unfinished Autobiography,* this may be an example of aristocratic paternalism, but it instilled good habits in her.

At the age of fifteen, Alice had her first mystical experience. She was sitting in her library with none but the servants in the house when a turbaned man walked in. She was more alarmed by his headwear than by his sudden appearance, never having seen such an item before. He told her that he had important spiritual work for her to do, but that she had to improve herself first. He was, she says, the Master Kuthumi [pronounced *koot-humi*], one of ten members of the cosmic hierarchy whose primary aim is to aid humanity in its evolution. We can only imagine what a turbulent effect such a visitation must have had on a young Christian girl.

More spiritual introspection ensued, during which time Alice seems not to have liked herself much. She was frustrated by her wealth and social status, which seemed to have no real spiritual meaning for her. She asked herself continually, "What's it all about?" She was earnest in her Christianity to a degree that may well have grated on others. Despite being painfully self-aware, she was helplessly sanctimonious in her youth. Lacking further visions or visitations, she became a Christian missionary and preached to soldiers in Ireland and in India.

On her way to India, Alice learned an important lesson. There was a man on the ship who offended her Christian sensibilities greatly. He was the "life and soul" of the voyage's social activities, gambling and drinking whiskey all the way across the

Atlantic. Surely he was the Devil's own spawn? She had never before witnessed such shameless dissipation! A God-conscious, do-gooding Purist, Alice observed him with disdain and no doubt prayed for his "lost" soul.

When they arrived in India, Alice found herself having to make her own way from the Bombay railway station to the missionary project in Quetta. The smells, sights, and sounds of India, the lack of personal space, and the continual staring of the Indians—not to mention the strange language and customs—overwhelmed her. Even in this day and age, a solitary foreigner would most likely find this a daunting prospect; for a naïve English lady, it was terrifying. Alice was desperately afraid. Suddenly, a familiar face appeared, offering to escort her. It was that dreadful man from the ship, and she not only accepted his offer with gratitude, but learned an important lesson about sanctimony.

From this point onwards, Alice became much less of a snob. She still carried with her the expectations she had been reared with, of course, but she learned to take each individual according to his or her spiritual worth, rather than judging the person by actions and referents of which she had been taught to disapprove. Much later on, she was to rely on the friendship of workers in a sardine factory in America—a world away from that of her family—but, as she admits in her *Unfinished Autobiography,* without these strong, humble companions, she would never have pulled through in desperate times.

Alice spent several years in India preaching, helping the sick, and transforming spiritually from a rather prim and proper young lady into a compassionate tour de force. She departed due to the dilapidation of her health, and, once recovered in England, set out for the States, where she married an Englishman she had met in India. The marriage proved to be yet another test of her endurance, and she was ultimately forced to extricate herself and her three daughters from it, owing to the physical and emotional violence of her husband.

In America, in 1919, she received her next visit from "the Master." It was a long wait, but this time the apparition changed her life. He told her that he wished to write books through her. Alice balked. Was she worthy? Was she deluded? He gave her time to decide. True masters never force their disciples.

After further self-scrutiny, Alice decided that this was indeed her true purpose on earth. Thus began a life-long career as a "psychic secretary." Nowadays, we call it "channelling," though this is not to be confused with some of the nonsensical claptrap that many New Age advocates now claim to have received through the channelling process. The proof of the pudding is in the eating, and the books written by "The Tibetan Master" through Alice speak for themselves. They contain complex cosmologies and a wealth of objective wisdom. Nearly all of the books attributed to Alice A. Bailey, other than her *Unfinished Autobiography,* are the channelled work of either the Master Kuthumi or "the Tibetan," Djwhal Khul. She was, she claimed, merely the pen-pusher.

The teachings Alice received have been an important contribution to Theosophy and to world spirituality. They are summed up in the final line of *The Great Invocation,* a prayer-spell for world peace still used today by many: "Let Light, and Love, and Power restore the Plan on Earth."

What, however, is "the Plan"? Here, the cosmology becomes rather more complex. The interested reader is directed to Alice A. Bailey's books for an in-depth explanation, but the key points may be summed up as follows:

1. The approach of the Hierarchy—that is, the ten Masters of Wisdom who aim to help humanity in its spiritual evolution.

2. The return of the Avatar. This is usually referred to by Alice as "the Christ," but the term is generic—she means the spirit of positive redemption. The phrase has recently been updated to "the Coming One," as it is not religiously specific, and is as pertinent to Jews, Muslims, and Wiccans as it is to Christians.

3. The science of the Seven Rays, in which human and spiritual consciousness are categorised according to seven different (but equally valid) levels, each represented by a colour and by many other specifics. These are energy levels on which we operate "as ensouling entities," and by which "we shall find ourselves able to co-operate more wisely with the Plan as it is seeking expression at any particular time." This system is seen by many as the psychology of the future.

4. The importance of goodwill and right human relations. Though Alice Bailey has been vilified by some Jews as anti-Semitic, such an attitude would clash completely with her belief that humanity is One, that we are all striving towards the Light, and that every soul on earth is free to ascend by its chosen means. All religious paths and impulses are respected within her cosmology.

5. A system of prayer and channelling of positive energies through the use of "Triangles." This involves three people (not necessarily physically present in the same place) building a "Rainbow Bridge" (or *Antahkarana*) from the

mundane to the spiritual. The colours of the Seven Rays reflect this imagery. It is facilitated through the meditative use of the *Great Invocation,* and by the beliefs outlined above.

Many of these principles will be familiar to those involved with Aquarian consciousness. Alice Bailey (through the Tibetan Master) pinpointed this era as extremely relevant to the ascension of humanity, particularly in the West. The spiritual energies manifesting here will climax, according to the Tibetan Master and his psychic secretary and aide, "between the years of 1965 and 2025." That's us!

The Arcane School, based on Theosophical ideas and practises, was founded by Alice A. Bailey in 1923. Its principle function was, and still is, to train its members in meditation and spiritual self-improvement. It is possible to participate in group meditations *in absentia* through focussed workings at particular times. Usually this occurs with two others, thus forming a "triangle" of psychic energy.

As well as individual development, the Arcane School is deeply concerned with "the Plan"; that is, the progress of humanity as a whole, of which Alice Bailey writes in her "Great Invocation":

From the point of Light
Within the Mind of God
Let Light stream forth into
The minds of men.
Let Light descend on Earth.

From the point of Love
Within the Heart of God
Let love stream forth into
The hearts of men.
May Christ return to Earth.

From the centre where the
Will of God is known
Let purpose guide the little
Wills of men—
The purpose which the
Masters know and serve.

From the centre which we
Call the race of men
Let the Plan of Love and
Light work out
And may it seal the door
Where evil dwells.

Let Light and Love and Power
Restore the Plan on Earth.

Because of its somewhat old-fashioned references to "Christ" returning to earth, some have misinterpreted this prayer and invocation as anti-Semitic. In fact, Alice and her group are entirely nonsectarian, and the "Christ" to which she refers is the Christ principle of the sephirah Tiphareth on the Qabalistic Tree of Life. It is the Mystical Ray, not, as some have understood it, part of some "Plan" to eliminate the Jewish or any peoples or creeds from the planet!

Indeed, Alice's teachings are largely Buddhist, and much of her work was dictated to her by the Tibetan Master. The idea is to spread universal love and understanding through self-discipline, ethical living, and compassion. Practical esotericism is key to its teachings—the mystical experience is part of the proficient student's daily life. Occult meditation, study, and service to humanity facilitate this. As the School itself declares, "Sincerity of purpose, purity of motive, and persistence in the face of all obstacles and difficulties are required in those who voluntarily undertake this self-training in the esoteric science of the soul expressed through discipleship living." In other words, it provides a series of internal initiations in what Alice was the first to term "The New Age," the well-known Age of Aquarius. This is brought to pass through discipleship, the main tenets of which are, "To serve humanity, to cooperate with the Plan of Hierarchy as he sees it and as best he may, and to develop the powers of the soul, to expand his consciousness and to follow the guidance of the higher self and not the dictates of his threefold lower self."

The hierarchy in question is, of course, that of the Ascended Masters (see the section on Helena Blavatsky for more on this).

The essential aim of the Arcane School, as of any effective occult path, is spiritual evolution.

The work of Alice Bailey (who married Foster Bailey, a fellow spiritual seeker, in the 1930s), is perpetuated today by the Lucis Trust, which she and her husband founded in America. Though many of her books are highly complex, they contain a huge body of spiritual wisdom that is extremely relevant to those studying esoteric science in this era. As an initial introduction, I recommend Harold Balyoz's *Three Remarkable Women* (Altai Publishers, 2000), which charts the contributions of Helena Blavatsky (a huge influence on Alice Bailey, and on many other spiritual seekers), Helena Roerich, and Alice Bailey herself.

W. E. Butler

Walter Ernest Butler was a key founding member of the Society of the Inner Light, a major Western Mystery School. He later went on to found the Servants of Light, which is now run by Dolores Ashcroft-Nowicki.

W. E. Butler was born in Yorkshire in 1898. As a child he was insatiably curious, and receptive to the spiritual. He suffered terribly from pneumonia and bronchitis, a fact that laid him out for several months a year.

Dion Fortune, with whom Butler was later both friend and colleague, describes her fictional and asthmatic character Wilfred Maxwell as extra-psychically perceptive because of his frailty. Wilfred has his first "communion with the Moon" following an attack: "As I lay there, doped and exhausted and half hypnotised by the moon, I let my mind range beyond time to the beginning. . . . with the weakness and the drugs the bars of my soul had been opened." It is possible that Fortune was thinking of Butler when she wrote this, or at least that he had shared the fictional Wilfred's experience.

At a very young age, Butler was moved to offer up a "sacrificial fire" to the gods, following the ancient examples of which he had read. As he tells Janine Chapman in her *Quest for Dion Fortune* (Samuel Weiser, 1993), "Quite suddenly, the sky began to darken. It was as though an impalpable veil began to build up between me and the sun, and, though it was a brilliant summer day, I was cold. . . . I *had* proved to myself—that there was something beyond the material."

The young seeker found an early mentor in Robert King, who was speaking at a local Spiritualist church. This, and the Theosophy movement to which King introduced him, provided an early occult education. He joined the Liberal Catholic church in 1915. Butler travelled to India after serving in the First World War, where he applied to join the Inner Section of the Theosophical Society. He was rejected, which upset him greatly. He learned much from the Hindu yogis he encountered in India, and was shocked by the physical deprivation he encountered in some areas. Years later, Dion Fortune identified the cause of his rejection by the Theosophical Society: it had been because their Path was Eastern and his own Western.

He had travelled to Glastonbury to meet Dion Fortune after reading one of her articles in *Occult Review*, and became an active and devoted member of her lodge, the Fraternity of the Inner Light. He later founded the Servants of the Light. His major works are *Apprenticed to Magic, Magic and the Qabalah, Magic: Its Ritual, Power and Purpose*, and *The Magician: His Training and Work*. He wrote several other books on psychism and the Western Mystery Tradition.

Florence Farr

Florence Farr was born in 1860 in Kent, England, and named after her father's friend and fellow hygiene reformer, Florence Nightingale. Daughter of an educated, liberated family, Florence Farr was one of the new breed of independent women that characterised her era. She was also fascinated by the occult.

Florence was a natural thespian, and became an actress in London's West End, marrying a fellow actor. Through her acting she met George Bernard Shaw, and embarked upon an affair with him. Florence's husband was absent. In June 1890, Florence was initiated into the Golden Dawn under the magickal name *"Sapientia Sapienti Dona Data"* (meaning "Wisdom is a gift given to the wise"). The activities of the Golden Dawn occupied her thoughts even more than her acting, though with the High Ritual of the Order there were many similarities between the two.

It is barely surprising that Florence Farr found the Golden Dawn so stimulating at this time, for it was at its most potent. Annie Horniman, Moina and MacGregor Mathers, Maud Gonne, W. B. Yeats, and Wynn Westcott were all members, with all but Westcott still in their twenties and thirties. The British Museum was just down the road, and with its extensive reading rooms filled with magickal manuscripts, they were able to read the works of mediaeval alchemists, Qabalists, and magickians collected from the world over. The group experimented and the psychism flowed.

Between acting and practising her arts, Florence taught classes in magick and wrote books on subjects ever popular with Golden Dawn initiates—Egyptian ritual and Renaissance alchemy. She was an expert skryer, as were Moina and Annie, and all of them acted as seeresses with astonishing accuracy (at least according to sources such as W. B. Yeats). In 1894, she became head of the London branch of the Golden Dawn. Wynn Westcott had retired and the Matherses had moved to Paris to begin the Paris Lodge. Farr was in her element, and anything seemed possible. On May 13, 1896, she and three helpers materialised the spirit "Taphtharthareth."

Florence also worked in "the Sphere Group," which was dedicated to concentrating on various Qabalistic sephiroth, their qualities, and symbols, in order to achieve visions and information.

The Golden Dawn flourished for several years with Florence Farr at the British helm. In 1898, Aleister Crowley joined, and progressed swiftly up the grades. At first he and Florence got along, but soon she became aware of his "moral depravities," and blocked his progress. MacGregor Mathers disagreed with her decision, and continued to initiate Crowley through his Paris Lodge. Florence Farr resigned. She remained involved with the Order, but the Golden Dawn was thrown into disrepute when a couple of charlatans named Mr. and Mrs. Horos (amongst other self-fabricated titles), operating under the name "The Hermetic Order of the Golden Dawn," were found guilty of the rape of several minors and duly imprisoned. They had used manuscripts stolen from MacGregor Mathers to formulate pseudospiritual rituals, and seduced these youngsters with promises of occult and spiritual progression. The public was scandalised, and the real Golden Dawn suffered accordingly. Florence quit the order for good in that same year, 1902.

Florence continued to write and enact dramatic rituals based on her occult knowledge, and became increasingly involved in the literary circles of the day, including that of Yeats. She focused on the magic of sound, and in 1909 wrote a small book on it (*The Music of Speech: Containing the Words of some Poets, Thinkers and MusicMakers Regarding the Practise of the Bardic Art, Together with Fragments of Verse Set to its own Melody*).

More books followed. Eventually, in September 1912, this remarkable woman moved to Ceylon to become headmistress of a school of over eight hundred Tamil girls. She was determined to teach spiritual principles through compassion and personal involvement, which she did, successfully, until March 1916.

In Colombo in April 1917, Florence Farr died. Her faith in and practise of spiritual and occult principles accompanied her to the end of her incarnation, and no doubt beyond.

Austin Osman Spare

In 1904, when Austin Osman Spare was only eighteen, the Royal Art Academy in London proclaimed him a genius. They may perhaps have failed to appreciate the already proficient occultism apparent in his work, but his skill as a draughtsman was indubitable.

Spare's adult life thus started as one of adulation and opulence. His first solo exhibition was held in 1914, by which time he had already published his *Earth Inferno: A Book of Satyrs* and *The Book of Pleasure (Self Love): The Philosophy of Ecstasy*. *Anathema of Zos* followed in 1924, by which time Spare's personal politics were coming into conflict with those of the culture-vultures that surrounded him. Turning his back on a life that could have kept him in luxury until his death in 1956, he retreated to South London to live the life of a poverty-stricken bacchanal. Here he experimented further with esoterica and art, narcotics, and bisexuality, and was amazingly prolific.

Spare claimed to have been initiated into the esoteric by one Mrs. Paterson, an aged hag who features heavily and rather obscenely in his artwork. "Hag-ridden" he certainly was, pushing the challenges of his conscious mind to ever-further extremities. Like Crowley, Spare flew in the face of convention, including aesthetic (though, unlike Crowley's, Spare's work is often remarkably beautiful and subtle). The two met, became friends, and then underwent one of the horrific rifts for which Crowley was infamous in occult circles. The details are hazy, but intense antipathy developed in Spare against his fellow magickian and hedonist. Possibly, Spare was not keen enough to accept Crowley as the Divine Overlord he believed himself to be.

Part of Spare's quest to expand his consciousness and magickal knowledge involved the technique of sigilisation (see relevant section in chapter 18, "Magickal Techniques and Spell-casting"). He incorporated this into many of his artworks, whose theme was often astral and invocational. The paintings are vibrant with Spare's life-energy, which William Reich would call "Orgone." Even the briefest glimpse at the originals is enough to see that they are still very much astrally alive.

Spare, like Florence Farr and Crowley, worked on and developed techniques of concentrating magickal will. His aim was simplicity. The sigil created was intended to be burned onto the subconscious, stimulating it to act on the magickian's behalf even when he or she was completely consciously preoccupied with other matters. This often took a strong sexual charge, and always a significant emotional one. It was essentially a species of subconscious Pavlovian response, and it worked for Spare, though often erratically. Like its representative Pan, whom Spare adored and illustrated copiously, the sexual urge is capricious, and Spare underwent many unexpected results courtesy of his intense magickal workings. One famous example is when he attempted to create the aroma of roses in his home, and the sewage drains overhead burst, creating quite the opposite olfactory experience. He referred to the energy thus created as "atavistic resurgence."

Spare attempted to confront his inner demons—or "The Dweller on the Threshold" as it is known to like-minded esotericists—and to initiate himself into higher internal "grades" through the catharsis of death-in-life, a technique widely employed by mystics worldwide. Unlike some of these, however, he often went into trance to do this, adopting what he called the "Death Posture" and undergoing the exquisite agonies and ecstasies of spiritual death and rebirth therein. He believed also that the gods were alive in each intelligent human, and that the Divine could be accessed within. He employed the Golden Dawn Qabalistic system to help him explore this and other esoteric issues.

The best way to learn of Spare is to meditate on and thus experience his artworks. The colour paintings seem to be sadly neglected by many who have studied Spare and written about him, but for me anyway, these are the most astrally vivid and active. However, all of his artworks have a spirit of their own. This is because each contains a genuine fragment of the soul of Austin Osman Spare.

Dion Fortune

Along with her contemporary, Aleister Crowley, Dion Fortune is probably the best known of modern occultists. Her book on Qabalah, *The Mystical Qabalah,* is still a major touchstone for many on the path of the Western Mystery Tradition, and her novels, particularly *The Sea Priestess* and its sequel *Moon Magic,* still delight and fascinate their many readers. Her many other publications, from *Aspects of Occultism* and *Practical Occultism in Daily Life* to the more obscure *Mystical Meditations on the Collects* are still to be found in bookshops across the globe, over fifty years after her death. People remain fascinated by this enigmatic lady of whom so little is known, as exemplified by Janine Chapman's *Quest for Dion Fortune,* written in the '70s and published by Samuel Weiser in 1993. Two other biographies are extant: *The Story of Dion Fortune* by Charles Fielding and Carr Collins (Star and Cross Publications, 1985) and Alan Richardson's *Priestess.* Gareth Knight recently contributed *Dion Fortune and the Inner Light* (Thoth Publications, 2000), which throws more light (and, delightfully, includes a new photograph) on its elusive subject. Yet there is still a hunger for more personal and practical information on this magickal woman.

Dion Fortune was born as Violet Mary Firth on December 6, 1890, in Bryn-y-Bia, Llandudno, Wales. However, she always described herself as a Yorkshire woman (her father was from Sheffield). She bore strong affiliations to Norse and Viking mythologies, her physical vehicle being of this stock. Her family had attained modest wealth through Sheffield Stainless Steel; several places in Sheffield are still named

Figure 7—Dion Fortune

after the Firth family. Her *nom de plume* and Golden Dawn name came from the family motto, *"Deus Non Fortuna,"* or "By God, not Chance."

Violet's parents were Christian Scientists, and their philosophies doubtlessly had a huge effect on their growing daughter. Christian Science teaches faith over the physical, a belief that remained with Violet throughout her life. It was mind and God over matter from the word go.

In her twenties, Violet went to work in an agricultural college, where, incidentally, she discovered the joys of the soya bean and its milk, now much-vaunted, but never attributed to her. She also underwent the shattering experience of being psychically attacked by the college warden, who had learned mind-control techniques in India. Others at the college seem also to have come under the influence of this malign lady. The latter was furious when Violet attempted to leave her post without statutory notice, and retaliated by concentrating on Violet and repeating, hypnotically, "You are incompetent, and you know it. You have no self-confidence, and you have got to admit it." (See Fortune's *Psychic Self-Defense* for further details.) This mantra continued until Violet's psychic barriers were destroyed and the warden's work complete. This precipitated a nervous breakdown coupled with complete physical exhaustion.

Fortune's involvement in the occult began with an active interest in psychology, which she studied at London University following her recovery. One imagines that the violence of this onslaught also stirred up memories and occult intuitions. Her interest certainly became acute from this point. Working as a lay psychologist, which was easier to do in those more experimental days than it is now, she encountered many phenomena that she identifies as having psychic root causes. Working beneath one Dr. Moriarty, Violet encountered psychic vampirism, past incarnational issues, and elemental influences in her clients. These provide the themes for her wonderful book of occult short stories, *The Secrets of Doctor Taverner.*

In 1919 she became a member of the Order of the Golden Dawn, and in 1922 she established the Fraternity of Inner Light (now the Society of Inner Light). However, she did not believe psychic ability to be the sole province of the deliberate occultist. She attributed natural psychism to involvement in "mediaeval witch covens" and such in former lives, or to natural sensitivity and intelligence: "Given these two things—a right judgement as to the nature of a problem and ability to concentrate, a great deal can be done, even by the uninitiated and untrained" (*Practical Occultism in Daily Life,* Williams and Norgate Ltd., 1935).

She was a great believer in the powers of the mind, as her training in psychotherapy and her encounter with her dreaded college principal had taught her. Indeed, she echoes this experience in *The Demon Lover,* when the unlikely heroine Veronica Mainwaring (Fortune's heroines are often unlikely, except for the wealthy, glamorous, and beautiful Vivien Le Fay Morgan/Morgan Le Fay of *The Sea Priestess* and *Moon Magic*) is hypnotised by her new boss, Mr. Lucas. He wishes to use her as a trance medium in order to attain Words of Power he requires for his magickal purposes. His progress in the occult lodge to which he belongs had been blocked by those who rightly feared that he would use his power selfishly. To facilitate this, he employs Veronica Mainwaring as a "secretary" in residence in his house, a significantly half-starved and very naïve young woman. He hypnotises her and makes great use of mind-control techniques on his victim, as does the evil magickian Astley on Ursula Brangwyn in *The Winged Bull.* Mona Wilton in the *Goat-Foot God* is also semistarved; in both cases it makes the women more psychically perceptive. As Fortune says of her leading female in *The Demon Lover,* "She floated rather than walked, and saw grey ghosts about her instead of men and women." In *Psychic Self-Defense,* Dion Fortune rightly points out the converse effect as a useful technique—to ground oneself and cut off psychic perception, simply eat.

The unlikely hero of *The Sea Priestess,* Wilfred Maxwell, attains his initial communications with the moon courtesy of asthma and "a large dose of dope." This allows him the mental freedom to travel beyond his usual boundaries. The moon being analagous with spirit and femininity, Maxwell lies in bed "wondering what the dark side of the moon was like, that now man has ever seen, or ever will see." He is gradually led into his subconscious, where he encounters Vivien Le Fay Morgan, his ancient lover, femme fatale, and competent Priestess. She soon materialises in his conscious life too, leading him from the confines of a conventional incarnation into one that enables him to "trace my lineage to the stars." This condition would not have been possible were it not for the weakening of his physical constitution through asthma, hunger, and drugs. These elements are all utilised in shamanic activities too, of course.

Many of Dion Fortune's fundamental beliefs and practises are summarised in *The Sea Priestess* and *Moon Magic.* In the first paragraph of the introduction to the former, she declares, "All women are Isis, and Isis is all women." She seeks the Priestess within every woman and the Priest within every man. The two go hand-in-hand in Fortune's books, creating the circuit of force through which the gods may be made manifest. As Vivien Le Fay Morgan tells Wilfred in the text, "Do you not know that at the dawn of manifestation the gods wove the web of creation between the poles of the pairs of opposites, active and passive, positive and negative, and that all things are these two things in different ways and upon different levels, even priests and priestesses?"

Fortune saw herself as able to establish these circuits of healthful, spiritual energy, and to identify and eliminate other psychic problems. Her novels lead the reader through a series of occult initiations—through hint and symbol as well as through explanation. She brings us face-to-face with archetypes both human and divine—a tactic that was quite deliberate on her part, her aim being to improve the psychic health of the nation. As she says in the introduction to *The Sea Priestess,* "The psychological state of modern civilisation is on a par with the sanitation of the mediaeval walled cities." She then offers her works as tributes to Cloacina, goddess of hygiene.

Dion Fortune's interest in the state of evolution of the species extended itself to sociological as well as spiritual enquiry. In June 1925, she published a book under her real name of Violet Firth, entitled *Psychology of the Servant Problem.* This gives an interesting indication of the compassion and insight with which the Priestess Dion Fortune faced the world both on the inner and outer planes. Of the employing classes, she says, "They are so habituated to the presence of a being from another sphere who is credited with a blissful freedom from human feelings that it is a shock to them to find a human nature akin to their own concealed by a servant's apron." The same would apply to her approach to spirits and spirit helpers—she looked at every being as a sensate entity, and saw those with power as responsible for the well-being of their charges. As she says of the servant, "The labourer who works very long hours ceases to be a man and becomes a machine. The old-time farm hand was hardly to be distinguished from the animals he tended: his outlook was little wider than theirs; the next meal, the night's sleep bounded the horizon of both." She beseeched the ruling classes to treat their servants with sensitivity and respect, just as she advocated that all entities be rightfully treated in magick.

The servants in Dion Fortune's novels are sometimes the subjects of affectionate jest—such as Silly Lizzy in *The Goat-Foot God*—while others are quietly acknowledged for their discretion and loyalty—such as Mrs. Astley in *The Demon Lover,* who declares, on being asked about her master, simply that "Them as knows most tells least."

Dion Fortune's attitude to the material planes was the same as that of most occultists and spiritually minded persons—that it is "the end result of a long chain of evolutionary processes that have gone on in the subtler planes, the realms of spirit, mind and astral ether." In other words, we are spirits in a material world, and everything here "will have a kind of soul, as it were, composed of factors from each of these levels of manifestation." Individual, racial, and global karma each have their effect on spiritual, mental, astroetheric, and physical modes of being. So, though individual choice is certainly possible, there are many minds guiding our hands, seen and particularly unseen. Concentration upon "selfless dedication to the highest ideal that can be conceived" was Dion Fortune's key principle. This set her aside from fellow magickians such as Crowley, whose aims included glorification of the mundane persona. In *The Demon Lover,* the anti-hero makes the drastic mistake of attaining power he has not earned. His presumption causes terrible side effects on many innocents, and on himself and the only woman he loves. Lessons about the destructive power of the ego are never far from Dion Fortune's subtexts.

Positive thinking is also of utmost relevance. "Fear," she says, "is entirely the product of the imagination." Yet, she knows the power of the imagination as a live force, as does any magickian. In *The Goat-Foot God,* for example, the hero Hugh Paston follows the technique of Ignatius Loyola, founder of the Jesuits, by visualising his ideal, and performing "composition of place." He thinks the scene, and it comes alive. He may then interact with it in a manner that affects change on other planes. Wilfred Maxwell does the same in *The Sea Priestess,* as he lies drugged and dreamy after a bout with asthma. He is able to reconstruct his former incarnations and set profound psychological and magickal forces into motion by freeing his imagination. This is a fundamental skill of any witch or esotericist.

Positive thought creates "glamour" in the useful sense. Preempting the techniques of many modern New Age psychologists, Fortune writes that "Nothing succeeds like success." She can be a little harsh towards the compromised person—as are most with such beliefs—seeing misfortune as karmic, and obstacles as self-created manifestations of inner blockages. Of the wife of a bad husband, for example, she says that "there must have been something unworthy in her to have been attracted to such a mate." Whether she would have continued to state this after her own failed marriage is unknown (though her own husband was far from "bad"). However, she acknowledges that the natural flow of our spiritual lives—personified by the Lords of Karma—involves the "Good" rather than the "pleasant." Life is a struggle, but we may surmount it through selfless effort. The anti-hero of *The Demon Lover*—the "Demon" himself, Justin Lucas—is eventually redeemed by choosing his own eternal pain over the compromise of his one beloved. Through this sacrifice, he is given a new chance, and is resurrected. In this case, he achieves ascension via the Qabalistic Dark Angel "that stands behind his left shoulder, becomes an initiator and shows him the Path."

Despite being Christian fundamentally, Dion Fortune did not fall into the all-too-destructive Christian ideal that "the meek shall inherit the earth." She believed this attitude to "enhance the vices of the coward," but, informed by the Qabalistic principles of balance, she also recognised that "courage and energy render more dangerous the vices of the bully." Chesed (mercy) and Geburah (destruction, or deconstruction) were always counterbalanced in her philosophy. Qabalah, with its sephiroth, or spheres, representing each of ten major psychological and spiritual states (and the paths representing twenty-two processes of becoming) was a major touchstone. Too much Hod (form, protocol, ritual) requires that one meditate on Netzach (nature, impulse, the creative urge), and so on.

At one with the theme of polarity, Dion Fortune has much to say on the subject of the male-female relationship. Her book *The Esoteric Philosophy of Love and Marriage* (first published in 1930) sounds hopelessly naïve today, but it had the Golden Dawn in such a spin at the time according to Dion, that Moina Mathers accused her of revealing secrets into which she had not yet been initiated. Moina, a staunch monogomist and wife of the High Priest Samuel MacGregor Mathers, allegedly resented the revelation of statements such as "The male needs the female physically, female needs male etherically." Yet the psychospiritual implications of sex had always fascinated Dion Fortune, as her 1928 publication *The Problem of Purity* reveals.

This latter book is another that seems terribly outdated now. For example, she suggests that the archangel Michael is visualised "drawing a flaming circle of protection round the bed with a fiery sword" to prevent "evil" thoughts of sexual self-gratification arising at night. Yet we have to remember the post-Victorian era in which she was writing. Fortune also firmly believed in the cross-dimensional prop-erties of sexual impulse and enactment, with which no magickian would disagree. The difference lies in her essential belief that a high degree of "unchanneled" sex-ual energy will attract Qlipoth (demons or vampires). She was big on "circuits of force"—the Priest needs the Priestess to channel his psychic and physical energies wisely, and the Priestess needs the Priest to give form to her imagination and spirit. Without the other, each is flat; together, new vistas open out. In solitary confine-ment, each is prey to the potentially vampiric forces that Dion Fortune saw all around. There is much sense in this, as any psychic will know, but most modern occultists now believe, as Crowley did, in eliminating infringement on liberty that is social rather than psychic. In other words, society has moved on, and "purity" is in many ways no longer the virtue it was construed to be in Dion Fortune's day.

Despite such classic statements as, "The sex force within us does not belong to us, it belongs to the race, and we are only trustees of it, and . . . use of it for personal ends such as physical pleasure, . . . is as if we were misappropriating trust money" (*The Problem of Purity*, 1928), Dion Fortune was far from a prude. In *The Goat-Foot God,* the entire theme is that of letting loose "the Pan within," and calling upon "the Great God Pan without." Freedom from repression—including sexual—is the whole point of the text. The hero and heroine are unlikely lovers—both are plain as pikestaffs in the mundane world, and from very different social backgrounds, but they gradually become able to draw out the "magnetism" from one another, until both come alive spiritually and emotionally. Hugh Paston, in shock after the death of his unfaithful wife, stumbles across an old bookseller in London who has studied the mystic arts. The latter takes Hugh, on the verge of nervous collapse, into his home. Hugh immediately gravites towards dark magick until the bookseller's niece, Mona Wilton, helps guide his energies. They have shared previous incarnations, as have most of Fortune's main characters, and the key to Hugh's emotional cure lies in invoking Pan, a god connected with an incarnation they shared in ancient Greece.

Mona Wilton reflects Dion Fortune's own views on sexuality: "Remembering Freud's dictum that cure proceeds via transference, she faced the possibility of having to become Hugh's mistress for a time, and concluded that it wouldn't kill her if she had to. Mona cared nothing for convention and had her own ideas on the subjects of morals." The next statement shows that, where psychological and magickal health are concerned, Fortune believed in "Do What Thou Wilt": "She was not a sensual woman, but she would give herself for love, freely, and under whatever conditions she saw fit; and oddly enough, she would also give herself out of pity if the need were great enough." Rather than *The Problem of Purity,* the text should perhaps be called *The Problem of Unwanted Psychic Interference*, as *The Goat-Foot God* and others of Fortune's works amply demonstrate that sexual energy is seen as the key to the Inner Mysteries. This does not have to involve the actual act, although Fortune does not balk at that either: "At the climax of the Mysteries of the Earth Mother all the lights went out, and the High Priest and the chief Priestess descended in darkness into the crypt and there consumed a union that was a sacrament just as much as eating the Body and drinking the Blood."

Like Crowley and the Theosophists, Dion Fortune believed in the existence of Occult Masters on the inner and spiritual planes. While the Theosophists followed an Eastern mystical path, Fortune adhered to a Christian, Western tradition, and her technique was practical occultism. Crowley united the two, but his morality was anti-Christian. These three very different schools all shared experience of the "Hidden Masters" of the "Great White Lodge," and received channelled writings from them. Fortune's main experience of this was whilst writing *The Cosmic Doctrine*, a complex cosmological text written to "train the mind" rather than to "inform" it.

The Cosmic Doctrine was written following a ten-day inner quest to encounter these Masters. Fortune had a powerful dream, obviously an astral projection, in which she encountered the Master of the Hermetic Ray, the Most Wise, and the Master of Compassion, Jesus, the Most Holy. Having been instructed, Fortune returned to her body with what she claims are memories of a religion taught to her in many previous lives. *The Cosmic Doctrine* was thereby produced over a mere three days.

Dion Fortune died on January 8, 1946, but continued to guide the Society of the Inner Light from the astral planes. When she died, her novel *Moon Magic* was still incomplete. The last two chapters were dictated to one of the Society's mediums. No change in style, syntax, or authorship is apparent.

Her many esoteric books include: *Applied Magic, Aspects of Occultism, The Esoteric Orders and Their Work, The Training and Work of an Initiate, Mystical Meditations on the Collects*, the famous *Mystical Qabalah, Psychic Self-Defense, Through the Gates of Death, Sane Occultism, The Circuit of Force, The Cosmic Doctrine, The Esoteric Philosophy of Love and Marriage, Glastonbury: Avalon of the Heart, An Introduction to Ritual Magic, Machinery of the Mind, Magical Battle of Britain, Practical Occultism in Daily Life, Principles of Esoteric Healing, Principles of Hermetic Philosophy*, and *Spiritualism in the Light of Occult Science*.

Fortune also authored *Psychology of the Servant Problem, The Problem of Purity*, and her horticultural classic, *The Soya Bean*. Her novels are *The Sea Priestess, Moon*

Magic, The Demon Lover, The Goat-Foot God, and *The Winged Bull,* though she wrote others under the name Violet Steele. *The Secrets of Doctor Taverner* is her only book of short stories.

Gerald Brousseau Gardner

The father of modern witchcraft was born in 1884 in Lancashire, England. He first travelled at the tender age of four, when he was taken to warmer climates for health reasons—young Gerald was asthmatic. He continued to travel widely, and worked as a tea planter in Asia. He eventually became a customs officer until he retired in 1936.

Gardner claimed to have been initiated into a coven in the New Forest by "Old Dorothy Clutterbuck" (Daffo) in September 1939. He always argued that there was an unbroken line of witches reaching back to ancient days, and that "The Old Religion" had been consistently practised by Hereditary witches over the centuries.

In 1949, Gardner published the fictional *High Magick's Aid* using the *nom de plume* Scire. Following the repeal of the Witchcraft Act in the U.K. in 1951, Gardner was able to publish *Witchcraft Today* (1954), a "non-fictional" account of modern witchcraft. He became head of a revivalist movement, initiating new witches and covens all over the country. He authored *The Book of Shadows* ("Ye Book of Ye Art Magical"), a pseudoarcane magickal text.

Gardner was not a particularly honest man, as Doreen Valiente confirmed when she approached the University of Singapore, whom Gardner claimed had given him an honourary degree owing to his archaeological discoveries. His friend and cowriter found that the University of Singapore had not even existed at the time Gardner had specified. Many of Gardner's claims are now seen as spurious at best, even by Gardnerian witches. It is a shame that the founder of modern witchcraft sullied his work reputation with falsehoods, but it does not alter the fact that many of his magickal techniques work. Whatever the credentials of this bearded, Pan-like man, he made an important contribution to modern occultism. Wicca would certainly not exist as we know it today, had it not been for Gardner's imagination. As Doreen Valiente put it:

> The big question which remains to be answered is, how much of the Gardnerian "Book of Shadows" represents the rites of the old New Forest coven and how much is Gerald Gardner's own concoction? I braved some hostile criticism from devoted Gardnerians by trying to answer this questions

when I collaborated with Janet and Stewart Farrar in their book *The Witches' Way*. I remain totally unrepentant, because I too seek the answer and shall continue to do so. There has been too much childish cloak-and-dagger business in the world of the occult, too much of what Aleister Crowley satirized as swearing someone to the most frightful penalties if they betray the secret knowledge and then confiding the Hebrew alphabet to their safekeeping.

Added to this unfortunate propensity for mistruth is the fact that Gardner was both a nudist and a fetishist of a semisadistic, voyeuristic nature. Many of the rituals still taught to Wiccan neophytes today come from the sexual imagination of a sleazy, aging man, and attempts to defend them with his original arguments—that they aim to shed sexual neuroses, and that they honour the female form—are sad indications of a naïve Wiccan community. Gardner was no angel, he was simply an imaginative man with a penchant for Goddess-worship, who contributed some interesting ideas to our spiritual search by formulating Wicca.

Gardner's *Book of Shadows* contains much food for positive thought. It apparently contains material taken from Crowley's Gnostic Mass, as perceived by Doreen Valiente, who helped Gardner rewrite the whole thing, eliminating Crowley's input. This grimoire has provided a foundation for the practise of modern witchcraft.

Shortly before Crowley's death in 1947, Gardner bought an Ordo Templi Orientis charter from the deteriorating magickian, and attempted to launch a lodge, illustrating his interest in many aspects of magick, not simply "natural Wicca." Gardner died on February 13, 1964, whilst travelling. His books, the last three of which are in print today, are: *Keris and Other Malay Weapons* (1936), *A Goddess Arrives* (1948), *High Magick's Aid* (1949), *Witchcraft Today* (1954), and *The Meaning of Witchcraft* (1959). Much more can be learned of him through the work of the late Doreen Valiente, and through Patricia Crowther's books. (See "A Brief History of Witchcraft" above for more about Gerald Gardner.)

Maud Gonne

Maud Gonne was the daughter of a British colonel stationed in Dublin, but her heart was Fenian through and through. She was introduced to the Order of the Golden Dawn by her lover, W. B. Yeats. Many of his finest love poems are about her.

A young, intelligent, and well-educated woman of independent means, she was already involved in Irish politics—namely, in Irish liberation from British rule. She was also interested in reincarnation and other "alternative" spiritual paths, and Yeats therefore arranged for her to meet Samuel and Moina MacGregor Mathers in Paris. She was initiated into the Order in 1891, and adopted as her magical motto, *"Per Ignem ad Lucem"* (meaning "through fire to the Light").

She found an immediate affinity with Florence Farr and Moina Mathers. She was deeply impressed by Moina's artistic skills, and fortuitously, Moina was translating Celtic myth and Irish folklore into French when she met Maud. Like Moina and Florence, Maud was strongly psychic, with seeress skills and the ability to skry on the astral. Some of her predictions were witnessed by others; she became known in County Donegal as "woman of the Sidhe."

As MacGregor Mathers obsessively pointed out, much High Magick is based on Masonic ritual (Mathers believed most things to have Masonic roots). When Maud discovered this, her Irish political sympathies obliged her to resign from the Golden Dawn as such, though she continued to work with her friends from its ranks on a nonritual basis. She felt unable to be involved in a thing that in any way represented the oppression of her beloved Ireland.

Maud Gonne was one of the several strong, educated, experimental women who had more than a small influence on modern occultism. For example, long before the modern revival of Paganism, she enacted Pagan ceremonies that attuned her with nature and aimed to heal it, particularly in Ireland. She was possibly the first active Neo-Pagan. She founded the Daughters of Erin, a group intended to preserve the Irish language and culture, and worked consistently throughout her life for humanitarian causes. She was imprisoned several times for inciting violence through her political speeches. She lived to the age of eighty-six.

Annie Horniman

Annie Horniman, heiress of the Horniman Tea Company, met Moina Mathers at the Slade Art School in London, and the two women bonded immediately. Moina became something of a counsellor to Annie, whose heart was broken after a fruitless love affair. Annie was involved, like many of the early members of the Golden Dawn, in theatre. She also became an adept astrologer and practitioner of magick. She was known by the magical motto *"Fortiter et Recte"* ("bravely and justly"), and was an extremely exacting personality by all accounts. She may have seemed a rebel to the Old School, but Annie had a sense of rectitude strong enough to risk alienating herself from others by criticising and keeping moral watch over them. This eventually led her into difficulties with the less-judgemental Matherses.

She was extremely wealthy, and became patron to MacGregor Mathers, George Bernard Shaw, and William Butler Yeats. Again, like many of our early magickal sisters, Annie was a feminist who flouted convention by smoking and wearing an early form of trousers. She travelled widely, often cycling. She rebelled against the many restrictions placed on her by her gender and social status.

Annie was the first Inner Temple initiate, and due to her close relationship with Moina and Samuel Mathers, consecrated the Parisian Ahathoor Temple. However, Mathers and she eventually clashed over an issue of esoteric sexuality—she believed a member to be indulging in unethical behaviour, and Mathers disagreed. In so doing, Mathers took a considerable financial risk. He and his wife always struggled—indeed, Moina died in poverty—but it is clear that they stuck to their beliefs no matter what.

When the old Order of the Golden Dawn split for good, Annie worked with W. B. Yeats to form the Stella Matutina. She entered into communication with an entity she called "the Purple Adept," apparently a secret chief such as Helena Blavatsky, Alice Bailey, and Crowley also acknowledged.

Annie continued as patron to Yeats, but was eventually superceded by another of Yeats's keen financial suitors. She transferred her patronage to other young talents, and did much to encourage and create modern drama as we know it. She died in 1937.

Israel Regardie

Israel Regudy was born in London in 1907 to poverty-stricken Jewish parents. The family altered their name after an elder brother was mistakenly referred to as "Regardie" by the Army during World War I.

When he was thirteen, the Regardies emigrated to America, settling in Washington, D.C. As a young man, he was fascinated by literature, and became particularly attracted to Theosophy and Hinduism. He also learned Hebrew, a skill of great use to the occultist in the early days of Qabalistic rediscovery. He joined the Rosicrucian Order in 1926, and moved swiftly up its ranks. At around this point, he discovered the works of Aleister Crowley, who was then living in Paris. Regardie contacted him, and the latter offered him a job as his personal secretary. Regardie accepted willingly. Unfortunately for the keen neophyte, Crowley did not pass his occult knowledge on to him. Regardie therefore pursued his own magickal studies until Crowley was deported back to England for crimes against public morality. Regardie did his best to defend Crowley against the many allegations for which he is infamous by coauthoring the eulogistic *Legend of Aleister Crowley*. Eventually,

Figure 8—Israel Regardie

however, Crowley's rough treatment of Regardie caused an irreparable rift between the two. Regardie was to live under the shadow of the "Great Beast" in people's perceptions for the rest of his incarnation.

In 1932, Regardie published two cornerstone books on Qabalah and magick with Rider & Co., London: *A Garden of Pomegranates* and *The Tree of Life*. Amongst the appreciative audience of Regardie's books was Dion Fortune. She defended him in the *Occult Review* against those who still found him contaminated through association with Crowley, and in 1933, invited him to join the Stella Matutina. He made prodigious progress, but was dissatisfied with the lust for power and prestige he witnessed amongst its members. He left in 1934, and in 1937 caused a huge occult frisson by publishing many of its rituals in his book *The Golden Dawn*. In so doing, he paved the way for occult practise becoming available to all, and shaped the "Mind, Body, and Spirit" sections of every bookshop extant today. Names of power and magickal techniques that would once have risked an astral hell-hounding for their premature revelation (see Dion Fortune's *The Demon Lover*, for an example) are now available to the uninitiated. Many members of the Orders found this to be a terrible betrayal, and some, such as Maiya Trenchell-Hayes, cast off and buried their ritual robes in disgust. Regardie was no doubt responding to years of working for Crowley and being denied information despite his aptitude to receive it.

In 1937, Regardie returned to the States, and published *The Philosopher's Stone,* a book on alchemy as the title indicates. He attempted it in a practical sense, but found it of little significance until later on in his life, when he was again drawn to it. *The Middle Pillar* was published in 1938, another book explaining Golden Dawn practise. In America, Regardie studied psychology and psychotherapy, becoming a lay analyst in 1941.

In 1947, he moved to California to practise Reichian counselling and therapy. We can see here further sympathetic parallels between Israel Regardie and Dion Fortune. They were also equally prolific. Many books flowed from Regardie's self-consecrated quill after this on talismans, meditation, divination, and of course, the Golden Dawn rituals.

Towards the end of his incarnation, Regardie retired to Sedona, Arizona, where the clean air and red rocks refreshed his lungs (troubled by an alchemical experiment that backfired) and spirit, respectively. He died in 1985, but his texts remain key source material to all aspiring witches and magickians.

Alex Sanders

Alex Sanders, after whom the Alexandrian tradition of Wicca is named, claimed to have been initiated by his grandmother in 1933, an emergency measure after he caught her stark naked inside a magickal Circle. Oaths duly sworn and scrotum duly nicked (presumably allying his procreative capacities to the Old Path—appropriate, as he grew up to "father" many covens), the younger hereditary witch was trained by the elder.

Sanders also claimed to have been taken by his grandmother to meet Crowley at the age of ten (see also "A Brief History of Witchcraft").

After the death of his grandmother, Sanders took to using his magick to gain sex and money, but, losing several close ones through a cancer he deemed karmic, desisted from corruption and took to Wicca. He clearly based a huge amount of his work on Gerald Brousseau Gardner's, but to it he added the Qabalah and High Magick that gave it constructive as well as Pagan power. In other words, in the hands of Sanders, Wicca ceased to be simply a form of worship and Netzachian interaction, and became a more Hod-like, practical magickal path.

During the early 1970s, Sanders met Maxine Morris, twenty years younger than he, who became his High Priestess. They married and had a child. The marriage did not last, but Maxine's love and admiration for Sanders seems to be alive to this day, though she has reverted to Catholicism. There is not the world of difference between some Wiccan and high magickal practise and belief and orthodox High Church that many deem extant, though clearly there are significant discrepancies psychologically.

Because of his era—the late sixties and early seventies—Sanders was caught in a tidal wave of interest in the Craft, followed by media exposure. He was interviewed in national newspapers and on radio, and an album of his rituals was released on vinyl by A&M. He was largely responsible for bringing witchcraft to the forefront of public perception. Not so very much earlier, the Witchcraft Act had remained unrepealed in Britain simply because there was believed to be no such thing as a witch. Sanders certainly changed that misconception, whilst also creating many other witches.

After his death in 1988, Sanders's work was continued by many of his initiates and followers, not least Janet and Stewart Farrar, who contributed many useful, and possibly definitive books on the subject of Wicca and witchcraft.

Doreen Valiente

Doreen Valiente is author and poet of much modern Wiccan ritual. Her wonderful verse was incorporated into Gerald Gardner's *Book of Shadows,* which has become a classic Wiccan text.

Doreen Edith Dominy was born in Micham, South London, in 1922. She was raised in the West Country by Christian parents, but at the age of seven, had a Yesodic experience during which, she says, "I saw the world of force behind the world of form." This is, of course, the fundamental mystical experience.

As a teenager and throughout her twenties, Doreen experimented with magick, as do most on the Path. She was initiated at the age of thirty-one by Gerald Gardner, to whom she was apparently introduced by a witch named "Daffo," the same "Old Dorothy Clutterbuck" who had allegedly initiated Gardner.

Gardner showed his new initiate his mainly pseudepigraphal *Book of Shadows,* and she instantly spotted alien sources such as Aleister Crowley's work included. Gardner challenged her to do better, claiming that those extracts were merely included as padding, and to include information lost over the centuries. Doreen rose to the challenge. The result was the compelling chants and interesting proverbs so many Wiccans use and love today.

Doreen Valiente's books are *An ABC of Witchcraft, Natural Magic, Witchcraft Tomorrow,* and *The Rebirth of Witchcraft.* She was much more discreet in her ways than was

Gardner, and lived quietly, aside from the attention caused by her publications (she made one or two appearances on TV as a result of her achievements).

Doreen Valiente remained an active, valued, and popular member of the Wiccan and Pagan communities until her death on September 1, 1999.

Gareth Knight

Gareth Knight is a renowned authority on the Western Magickal Tradition and Qabalistic symbolism. His book *A Practical Guide to Qabalistic Symbolism* (two volumes, Kahn & Averill, 1998), written in 1965 and containing much of the work of the Society of the Inner Light on the subject, is a cornerstone of most occultist's libraries.

He was born in Colchester, England, in 1930. His childhood interest in magick, mysticism, and myth led him to join Dion Fortune's Society of the Inner Light at the age of twenty-three. He progressed fast and was initiated into the Greater Mysteries in 1959, also becoming the Society's librarian.

In 1962, he became editor of an esoteric magazine, *New Dimensions,* its principal subjects being Dion Fortune's unpublished work, and Knight's own. The two are still intimately linked today, with Knight having recently published *Dion Fortune and the Inner Light* (Thoth Publications, 2000), an engaging biography of Fortune that presents a great deal of new information and analysis on its subject.

Knight parted ways with the Society of the Inner Light in 1965, and in the early seventies was involved (with W. E. Butler) in setting up a group based on the same principles, but less Christianised: the Servants of the Light. His students now received copies of *Quadriga,* a hand-typed booklet that had replaced *New Dimensions* by this time.

Gareth Knight is one of the most prolific writers and practitioners of magick alive today. The depth of his knowledge and the clarity and intelligence with which he writes make his books a "must-read" for aspiring witches and occultists. These include: *A Practical Guide to Qabalistic Symbolism, The History of White Magic, Dion Fortune and the Inner Light, The Magical World of the Inklings* (about C. S. Lewis and his peers at Oxford), *Principles of Hermetic Philosophy,* and *The Treasure House of Images* (one of his books on Tarot).

sixteen

The Witch in the Arts and Media

MOST OF US ARE FAMILIAR with the lumpen, toothless hags painted by Goya during a particularly disturbed time of his life. Cannibalism, geriatric and bestial sexuality, and Devil-worship are the image of witchcraft portrayed by this master painter.

The Witches' Sabbat depicts a crowd of amorphous uglies, eyes bulging with vice as they view the arrival of their master in the form of a black goat (Eliphas Levi's later *Goat of Mendes*). In a reversal of the pastoral idyll, the goat guides the flock of willing humans, and the results can only be diabolical. The painting reflects both the religious paranoia of the era in which it was committed to canvas, and the artist's evident fear of female power and independence. The entire coven is female, and the allure they evidently feel towards their capricious master reflects an almost eugenic fear. Will they couple with the man-goat in black? Of course they will—they are his slaves, and what could better reflect Puritanism upturned than rampant bestiality? What will be their spawn? Goya uses the witch analogy to represent his fear of several things: one, mankind's innate vice; two, inescapable evil, such as that of the mother to the child; and three, the future of humanity. With so much vice breeding vice, the painting says, what is the hope for the redemptive purity of the species?

Goya's *Scene de Sorcellerie* confirms the latter point. Now brought into colour—into real life as it were—the figures become fewer and more defined; the evil has become specific. A young mother, babe in arms, is touched by the black leg of an upright, wreathed goat, who is clearly the coven's prime mover. A withered harridan holds an equally withered infant to the attention of the master. We are struck by the incongruity of a baby with the physique of an ancient. The young mother's

323

mouth is open—is it in protest, or in praise? Is the baby to be sacrificed, and if so, is the mother willing to hand her child over?

Either way, the painting points to travesties of nature. Veiled figures, almost forming part of the landscape, may be seen in the background—all are women, all as indefinable as protoplasmic guests at the moot. Other women, their skins orangered with—one assumes—the tincture of hellfire, look pensive as they observe the ceremony.

The wreath of leaves on the goat's head recalls Dionysiac ritual, and though no wine is in evidence, several sprawled figures suggest intoxication by vice of some sort. Another infant lies watching, his ribs sticking from an unnurtured body. Has he been neglected by his mother in favour of the goat-god, as in the Bacchanalia of the Greeks, or has his innocence simply been sucked dry by sorcery? Thoughts of candles made of baby fat bubble in our minds. As an advertisement against witchcraft as Goya perceives it, this picture is pretty effective.

How does Goya perceive it, exactly? We know that during his "Witch" phase he was having a psychological crisis, haunted by hallucinations and so forth. Perhaps he felt out of control, perhaps he was angered by his increasing age, and the mortality of the flesh. His hags represent, in part, the horror of aging, especially in an era (prenineteenth century) when many diseases were incurable, and symptoms of mortal demise were written all over the flesh of its victims. His etching of two old hags fighting, their naked legs wrapped around one another as they spin in evil spirit-infested space, perfectly summarises this revulsion. Both seem desperate, yet both stubbornly persist in employing their dwindling strength against one another. There is nothing solid to help them; no chance of relief. Conversely, a bestial wraith reaches out an ugly paw and uses it to pull the strawlike hair of one of the harridans. A depressing scene indeed.

Goya's paintings clearly represent a great many of his personal issues, not least fear of being overwhelmed by evil, and fear of physical as well as spiritual demise and death. As far as his attitude towards witchcraft is concerned, he was a child of his times, full of anxieties propagated by Christianity. Hell seemed as indubitable as the wrinkles of the hag.

Austin Osman Spare (see also "Who Influenced the Witching World?") emulated Goya's draughtsmanship, and many of his images are highly reminiscent of Goya's own. However, the two artists could not be coming at the subject from more diverse angles. Spare was an occultist, and an artist of the Edwardian era, in which Victorian religion and morality were being rejected as obsolete. The light of speculation was falling on everything, and Spare cast his on observing the spirit and elemental realms. Satyrs, nymphs, undines, and sirens populate his works, each emitting its own enchanting frequency. He is renowned for the technique of "sigilisation," the condensation of magickal will into glyph form. The monogram, then, acts as a stimulus for subconscious confirmation of the sorcerer's intent, reaffirming it every time it is glimpsed. Many of Spare's paintings were spells and ritual workings, and many feature the sigils characteristic of his enduring bond between art and magick.

This bond is, of course, as old as the caves. Primitive man depicted himself capturing bison in an attempt to will it so. Sympathetic magick is native to many diverse cultures, as a cursory glance at "The Golden Bough" or other anthropological works will show. Ritual sprang from this principle; we have long realised that, if something is strongly visualised, it may be enhanced into being. An occultist would say, create the form on the astral or Yesodic planes, invest it with the relevant energies (coming down from beyond the causal, possibly even Ketheric), and then will it to solidify in Malkuth, the earth plane. Spare knew both how to paint what he had seen, and to experience what he chose to paint. A magickal lodge or coven externalises the process by using symbolic paraphernalia to represent what is understood as truth by its members, and then arranges these symbols through ritual acts into a pattern that embodies the group intent. The idea travels down through the planes, gathering energy and matter en route. Finally, when the working is complete, it is made manifest, as intended.

Spare's paintings change with the magickal tides. Any painting is invested with the spirit of its creator, but how much more so when the piece is executed in full magickal consciousness! Spirits have had their essences caught in the works of Spare. With the phases of the planets, stars, and moon, and with the viewer herself, the emphasis shifts, and the tonality changes. These are pictures cast in full magickal subjectivity. The paintings are especially proof of this.

Spare's *Book of Ugly Ecstasy* expresses the same conceit as Goya, but from an entirely different standpoint. Spare is not revolted by the demise of the flesh, because he understands the immortality behind it. His baddies are "daemonic" rather than "demonic." Like the ancient Greeks, he accepts the darkness as a necessary ingredient to the whole. Yes, he also becomes fascinated and side-tracked by the darkling souls, but why not? He is an occultist and an artist; his duty is to record creation as he finds it. He does not filter the unpalatable out; he assimilates it into a balanced worldview. He crosses boundaries; he is sexually beguiled by an aged harridan—his patron, Mrs. Paterson. His ecstasy may be ugly, but it is a doorway nonetheless, and probably all the more potent a portal for contravening social mores.

The Australian artist Rosaleen Norton worked in a view similar to Spare's. Her myth was self-perpetuating; she lived in a manner self-consciously Dionysiac, whilst promoting her magickal thoughts through her drawings. Filled with elfin faces, spritely forms, and significantly geometric shapes, her work is an extravaganza of the fantastical and the occult. It does not, to me, carry the finesse and weight of Spare's prolific hand, but as a 1950s artist and live bacchante, she is worth a mention.

A popular depictor of witches and wizards is the Victorian artist Arthur Rackham. His enchanting watercolours and etchings have enlivened many a child's book of fairy tales, and he is famed for his work on the stories of the Brothers Grimm. Some of his work is a little too twee to be mentioned here, but his painting *The Wizard* depicts the Goya-like idea of the practitioner of magick as motivated by vice. The wizard's beady eyes are avaricious, his oversized hand is a grasping claw. He clutches his little bag of possessions and tricks in the most miserly of manners, clearly intending to receive rather than to give. A small, wicked smile plays about his pursed lips. Birds—familiars, perhaps—regard him over ugly, greedy-looking beaks. As he walks through the forest of spindle trees characteristic of Rackham's imagery, the wizard is definitely bad press for the magickally inclined!

Another format in which the witch has been amply depicted is that of the comic book. An obvious example is Vertigo's *Witchcraft* (DC Comics, 1996), a rollicking tale of wicked witches and deeds avenged. However, the fantasy format in which the book is styled preempts and eliminates the element of prejudice. This is artistry, archetype, and fun; perhaps even nostalgic for an era in which things such as witchcraft were commonly believed in.

The *Death* comics depict a funky, witchlike Reaper—not grim, but a little tragic. Her sister "Delirium" is more akin to what we have grown to expect of a witch typically portrayed. Of course, the subject of sorcery and magick provides an ever-replenishing source of inspiration to the fantasy writer.

Popular demand for a tamed version of the arts magickal (for everybody loves the idea of them) brings us such characters as Jill Murphy's "Worst Witch," the sweet academy schoolgirl who just can't get it right. I can't help but relate to some of her magickal accidents. It's always difficult when first practising to avoid accidentally turning one's best friend into a mouse, or some such thing.

Roald Dahl's *Witches* is an enthralling classic of witchphobia. The queen witch is beautifully portrayed in the film by Anjelica Huston—and when I say "beautifully," I mean it. For a children's film, the pronounced sexuality of the "Madame" witch intelligently and provocatively demonstrates the allure—even to those of her own gender—that a powerful and magickal woman can have. The children involved are so irritating that one barely sympathises with their plight as potential witch-fodder. Of course, Dahl, the king of children's nightmares, is playing on the ancient idea of witches feasting on the flesh of infants. This contravenes the most fundamental law of nature—that the females should nurture and protect their young. We are getting into Lilith territory in this entrancing tale; the women concerned are selfish, barren, and interested in power. Naturally, they must be destroyed in the end—all but the one who was good, really (underneath, that is). Otherwise, how would our little darlings sleep at night?

The Pre-Raphaelites depict enchantresses of many sorts, one of the most effective to my mind being John William Waterhouse's *Circe Offering the Cup to Ulysses*. This stunning portrait of the pale siren was used very appropriately on the cover of Rider Haggard's classic novel *She* (Wordsworth edition). Haggard's journey into Africa in search of the ultimate powerful and terrifying woman perfectly describes the archetype Waterhouse painted.

Another favourite is Lord Frederic Leighton's *Spellbound*. The deathly white beauty of his painting stands before a mirror in a state of narcissistic hypnotism. She towers over her page boy like a column of deathly enticement, threatening to damage the hearts and lives of men wherever she goes. These Pre-Raphaelite and Symbolist beauties are femmes fatales whose flipside is the Qlipothic hag so feared by Goya. They are therefore archetypally lunar and female (at least, to the eyes of men)—terrifying in their magickal ability to glamour, and to switch incomprehensibly from Brightside to Darkside.

Coleridge's "La Belle Dame Sans Merci" poetically describes this same scenario. "Christabel," with its hints at lesbianism, crosses yet another boundary, running again into Lilith territory, or the fear of the autodidactic female. Christina Rossetti's "Goblin Market" does the same, but from a female standpoint. Here, two sisters join forces against the sensual goblins that are, in Rossetti's eyes, essentially men.

Baudelaire's poetry is rife with reference to witchery and vampirism, along with the langorous sensuality that defines his work. Baudelaire was no esotericist, more's the pity, but he abided (like Poe and other Symbolist and Gothic writers) in the Yesodic realms, channelling his astral encounters into his work. Drug-, love-, and syphilis-stricken, he talks of being attached to his "Vampire" *"Comme au jeu le joueur tetu, Comme a la bouteille l'ivrogne, Comme aux vermines la charogne"* ("Like a gambler to his game, Like a drunkard to his elixir, Like vermin to a corpse"), and curses her for it. Again, we encounter the archetypal entrancing and laterally repulsive witch.

In ancient Greece, this aspect was perhaps epitomised by Cybele—the all-consuming Mother Goddess, flesh-tearing and frantic and utterly uncivilised, the antithesis of the Apollonian ideal. In the cumbrous Cybele, intellect and rationale are overruled by primal impulse. The Hindu equivalent is Kali, though her portal of bloody death leads to assimilation with the Divine. The Egyptian parallel is Sekhmet, whose blood-cravings cause havoc in the realm of mortals. Yet she, too, is beautiful and sleek, and one's natural urge in her presence is to please. She is a cat goddess, bringing to mind Baudelaire's poem on the subject: *"Amis de le science et la volupte, Ils cherchent le silence et l'horreur des tenebres"* ("Friends of learning and of ecstasy, They seek peace in the terrors of the dark"), and, significantly, *"Leurs reins feconds sont pleins d'etincelles magiques"* ("Their fertile loins are full of magic sparks")—yet the word for "sparks" is similar to the word for "needles," which brings an uncomfortable touch to the person who wishes to find refuge therein.

There are countless other examples of the uncomfortable relationship between the magickally inclined and the mortal in art and literature, particularly when the magickal person is female, or a witch. Balzac's lugubrious "Cousin Bette" is a "primitive peasant"—feral in her scheming ferocity, and of the chthonic sorceress archetype. Charlotte Bronte's novel *Wuthering Heights* touches on the male equivalent, Heathcliff, though he finds his match in the equally obsessed and supernaturally proficient Kathy. Dion Fortune's novels often describe the awakening of the magickally unconscious person by an occultist of the opposite gender. Her own archetypal witch is Morgan Le Fay, the Sea and Moon Priestess who entices the unlikely heroes Wilfred Maxwell and Dr. Rupert Malcolm with the brilliant reply to the question:

> "How many men have you tried this with, Morgan Le Fay?" (Said I.)
>
> "A very great many, Wilfred Maxwell," said she. "And from all I have got something, but from none have I got everything . . ."

In both cases, the men end up happily married, but not to the woman they truly love, because she is eternal, and cannot be pinned down or made mundane. She is the Goddess, but her Priestess is discovered within the "ordinary" female. Herein lies the rub for every witch and magickian—the ability to become a channel for the Divine forces that are greater than all of us, yet to be discovered microcosmically within every live, pliant psyche. It might be added that Goya, with his contemporary fears and loathings, completely missed the point in this respect. Every proficient witch and magickian knows that the initiation is to face the fear, assimilate its terrors, and cross the psychological (and psychic) boundaries into the great Beyond.

The Media Witch

The way any group is represented in the media has an immediate effect on the way they are treated by the general public.

Witches used to be anathema—ugly, old spiteful things like the Wicked Witch of the East in *The Wizard of Oz.* Now, however, the legacy of the '70s sitcom *Bewitched* is bringing us a new generation of glamorous young sorceresses. Who can resist the tight-topped trio in *Charmed,* or fail to be entertained by the antics of svelte Buffy? Nowadays, a Book of Shadows seems to be essential to every girl's school locker or home attic.

The film *The Craft* was not as good an explanation of Wicca or witchcraft as one might have hoped. Instead, it represented magick at its most pernicious. A precocious teenager and her gang get their sticky little mitts on Words of Power—sometimes, unfortunately, similar to our own—and use them to satisfy the most immature of impulses. The shot of Nancy floating across the room, scraping the points of her shoes on the floor, however, made it worth wading through the rest of the film. Reminiscent of the vampire-child scratching at the window in *Salem's Lot,* the image was provocatively spooky in that gravity-defying kind of way. The rest of the film, however, was disappointingly clichéd.

Okay, so the Charmed Ones have to enact some pretty cheesy encounters with warlocks and windigos and so forth, but at least they're what their name suggests— charming. Plus, *Charmed* is well researched (the producers consulted Llewellyn Publications regarding some of the content of the series). "An' it Harm None" is a constant consideration before the sisters act. Their main preoccupation is the protection of "innocents"—quite unlike the teenage disgruntlement portrayed in *The Craft,* before they get their karmic comeuppance at the end of the film.

Buffy the Vampire Slayer has taken North America and Britain by storm. What meets the eye as spoof-martial-arts-movie-meets-"Hammer House of Horror" can equally be read as metonym for wider issues; and these wider issues underline every episode. On a minor scale, we have the example of Oz's lycanthropy representing the cerebral versus the sexual, while Buffy's protection of and willingness to die for her sister Dawn symbolises self-sacrifice on a mystical scale. Somehow, this is possible despite the comic function of the series. The programme is about Good versus Evil, but the boundaries are blurred, as in our own reality. Angel, the love of Buffy's life, is himself a vampire, whom Buffy is forced to slay—that's her job after all. In a cruel twist of fate and magick, however, Angel is "cured" just as he is dispatched into one of the numerous hells that have portals in Sunnydale, where the series is set. Buffy undergoes grief and irony in one fell swoop. She is brought even lower in the episode "The Body," in which her mother dies. This episode alone proves the simple genius of the show. Though the backdrop features rabid zombies, red-eyed demons, and undead crusaders of all sorts, it is easy to suspend disbelief and enter into the very real, emotional world of Buffy, Willow, Xander, and their grisly crew. Buffy's reaction to the death and its sympathetic filming make it a genuinely haunting portrayal of bereavement. Yet, the series has a constant sense of humour, and is experimental to boot; one episode is conducted almost entirely in mime, another entirely in song. The series veers continually from slapstick to insightful and back again.

Willow the witch is an interesting addition to the entourage. Again, we have the modern, formulaic, pretty witch referring to Wiccan lore and ethics to help herself and Buffy combat the evil that surrounds them. Willow also has Sapphic appeal, popularising the concept of Wicca as feminist and nondiscriminatory. During the course of her involvement with witchcraft, she becomes more and more attracted to the Darkside, until, intent on avenging the murder of her girlfriend Tara, she becomes so Black that even her eyes and hair turn that colour. Magickal power has a gradual druglike effect on the stripling witch; anger and loss make her downright murderous. Here, Buffy becomes the voice of principle, attempting to remind Willow of her original ethical self. The issues of Good versus Evil are never far from the surface in this wonderfully self-aware series.

At least a nod in the direction of Dario Argento is required here for his late seventies/early eighties films *Suspiria* and *Inferno* (brilliant in their lurid emotional kitsch) and Jaromil Jires for *Valerie and Her Week of Wonders*. The latter is my all-time favourite film, a baroque and gothic extravaganza of vampires, witches, and High Church Christianity. There are many other venues for the witch in media, of course, but those mentioned here provide reasonably diverse examples.

The image of the witch as a hook-nosed crone in a black cloak has certainly developed into something more palatable to the public. Not just her image, but the portrayal of her intent has changed. The work of famous Wiccans and witches such as Janet and Stewart Farrar, Laurie Cabot, Scott Cunningham, and Silver Raven-Wolf has helped to adjust the way that witches are represented in the media.

However, it is slightly ironic that many books on witchcraft portray exactly the images that alarm the uninformed public. There are photographs in books by the Farrars, for example, that portray covens working skyclad with ritual dagger and sword. We know what is symbolised by these tools and factors, as does anyone reading the book thoroughly, but to a casual browser, the images look Satanic. One only has to observe the reactions of stripling Wiccans to such images (comments written on Amazon.com, or shared on websites) to realise that there is still a negative ability to shock with the Craft, unless we are careful and explain each process step-by-step. Though many witches and Wiccans are interested in "normalising" their image in the eyes of the public, others enjoy the melodrama of it all and lean towards blatant witchiness—possibly in order to highlight their cause by drawing attention to it. As with everything in this book, and in life in general, it is purely for the individual to decide whether he or she is happier in jeans and jumper or long black cloak. There is no point in saying that witches or Wiccans are either "normal" or "theatrical" in their dress—both exist. Gothic attire is still popular in occult circles, but, as the programmes mentioned above attest, the image of the witch is ever-changing and developing.

Physical attributes aside, it is evident that the image of the nature of a witch is changing too. Nearly all are now seen as positive role models, which of course helps explain the popularity being enjoyed by some of our sisters and brothers who have efficient publicity machines behind them. Now, we are being feted rather than ducked, but this will only continue for as long as genuine, insightful material is generated. My plea to all witches and magickians alive today is: Don't just follow already-established paths. Experiment, and be intelligent and conscientious about it. Magick is a live force, not just a case of following prescribed rituals and patterns. Yes, there is much in the archetype, but go for the ancient rather than the modern. The book market is seething with spellbooks lacking in depth and experience. The whole point of any spiritual path—and Wicca and witchcraft are most definitely spiritual paths—is to contact the Divine, both within and without. Rehashing the sabbats and a bit of folklore doesn't cut the mustard anymore. Gerald Gardner and Doreen Valiente did it validly because it was new then, Alex Sanders followed up, and the Farrars made it clearer and added many insights that were therefore also of import, but since then, not a great deal of evolution is in evidence. The key is learning, meditation, and practical application; the ability to behold the Divine within everyday life, as did the Kabbalists. Simple nature-worship and ego-tripping through spells—essentially, lower psychism—aren't where it's at; active intelligence and semiotic awareness are.

I hope that, within fifty years, the media will be taking the subject with fewer grains of salt because its bastions will be flummoxed by the amount of genuine learning and wisdom in evidence in those who have followed the occult Path. The ability to do so with impunity is a gift of this era—we have to use it well.

Willow, Buffy, and the Charmed Ones are doing a great job at keeping witchcraft in the public eye, and entertainingly so. The Harry Potter films touch on it through Hermione, though J. K. Rowling states that "Obviously, it's all just fantasy." However, if we could act as Dion Fortune did through her novels and bring the magickal to the public eye in a Cloacina fashion, all the better. We're talking spiritual and psychological hygiene here. Let's get rid of the Goya witches and the lateral Lilith fantasies and into the twenty-first century.

The Cyberwitch

The cyberwitch is the modern witch. She e-mails rather than writes her Grimoire with a quill—or, at least, participates in both. She composes letters to be sent etherically, much as the ancient magickians formulated Words of Power and chanted them with intent during ritual. She knows that her messages will directly affect the recipient—this is a type of immediate modern magick. Therefore, she selects her words and their readers carefully, and is capable of influencing another being from a great distance at the press of "Send." She networks and chats with kindred spirits, a scenario that was only possible astrally until not so long ago. The modern era is a great gift to the witch as well as to her non-esoteric peers, and she takes advantage of it.

Now, there are entire covens and gatherings who meet only over the Internet. This is far from unnatural—it is astral communication clarified. She is also able to pop in on sites belonging to like- or un-like-minded persons with similar interests, and to share her views, often anonymously. The Internet in many ways takes the danger out of magickal empathy—for, if the person with whom one is communicating is not physically present, and knows not one's physical specifics, the interaction can only be intellectual, psychic, and honest.

There are some excellent sites with many members available to the cyberwitch. For the neophtye, the Children of Artemis website is highly recommended (www.witchcraft.org). There are many young members on this site, as well as knowledgeable Elders. The more advanced occultist is advised to surf for topics of specific interest—Yahoo.co.uk and Yahoo.com are particularly good search engines for witchy topics. American readers are directed to www.witchvox.com, which contains a comprehensive guide to relevant sites, as well as many contacts. Other sites of interest, many of which relate to topics in this book, are listed at the end of the bibliography.

Part III

PRACTICAL WITCHCRAFT

seventeen

A Witch's Working Tools

Tools

A WITCH DOES NOT REQUIRE tools to make her spells work. Many witches acquire the ritual paraphernalia listed below late, if they own them at all. Improvisation is the key tool required by the truly proficient witch.

However, there are certain objects that can aid concentration and may be "charged" over years of use into truly powerful pieces of equipment. A wand, athame, or chalice, for example, will greatly enhance a witch's workings if she is so inclined. The now-traditional tools are actually far more of a legacy of High Magick than of witchcraft, except perhaps the cooking pot or cauldron. They are not what makes a person a witch—it is the mind and personal abilities that do that. However, nowadays many Wiccans and witches take it for granted that the following items are as essential as their will power.

Altar

Not all witches are able to have altars permanently operative in their homes or gardens, but some do. Most of us erect (or open) them for specific occasions.

There are many books on Wicca that give elaborate suggestions for altar arrangements, often complete with diagrams. The usual items to be found atop a witch's altar cloth are: statues of the God and Goddess, a chalice, a wand, a black-handled knife (or athame), a bowl of salt, a thurible for incense, a bell, and whatever decorations are suited to the season, sabbat, esbat, or working at hand. There will also be candles, or possibly fire in a small cauldron, depending on the size of the altar.

Other possible items to be placed on the altar include: the individual or coven Book of Shadows, a small symbolic scourge, lengths of cord for use in cord magick or to outline the Circle, a flat pentacle often made of copper or clay (to represent the element of earth and also the combining of elements—including spirit—on the material plane), a garter, and whatever other objects seem appropriate to the witch or group at the time.

Like altars in all religions, the witch's is a place of both worship and interaction with the Cosmic Intelligence. It becomes representative of the crossover between planes, and the significance of every item placed on it is magnified by this symbolism.

Athame

The athame is the witch's working knife, though it is usually used to cut nothing but air. For cutting herbs, there is the (normally white-handled) boline. However, as with everything in the Craft, the individual witch is the innovator rather than (one hopes) the slavish follower of prescribed rules. So her athame is hers to personalise and use however she sees fit.

It is always best, of course, to choose an athame with as good a history as possible. One that has been lunged into some hapless victim will not suit the work of most witches, and certainly not of any Wiccans. Yes, the dagger can be cleansed, as can anything else, using salt water and incense and strong visualisation, but the impact of a blade on most situations is so strong that the violent energies might well prove hard to shift. There are enough random pitfalls facing the novice without her new athame also contributing to them.

To symbolise that violence is anathema to the witch's way, the athame is usually blunt at the tip and sides. This also helps prevent accidents during rituals, when the athame is often used to carve symbols and portals in the air.

Most athames have black handles, and often they are individualised by artwork on the hilt and handle. Sometimes they are used instead of a ritual sword, and sometimes in conjunction. Both are ideal for channelling energy from higher planes, and for directing it. Swords look superb, but can be rather unwieldy, especially in group situations. The athame is a neat and effective representative of the element of fire or air, and of the male principle in nature.

Regarding the fire/air dilemma, some attribute wands to fire and swords to air. Others argue that, as fire burns wood, they should be the other way around. It is claimed by Francis King and Stephen Skinner in *Techniques of High Magic* that the Golden Dawn deliberately switched the correct attribution of wands-air and swords-fire in order to throw off the uninitiated. Whatever the cause of the confusion, there are witches who follow one set of correspondences, and an equal number who follow the other. I think it may be agreed now that both are valid. The main thing is to decide which seems right to you, and then stick to it.

Besom/Broomstick

This is, of course, the item most traditionally associated with the witch. Some sources indicate that it derives from use in folk magick as a symbol of fertility that would be "ridden" by the women of the village in vigorous leaping gestures, rather like the 'Obby 'oss, encouraging their crops to grow. Others suggest that the handle leant itself to use as a pessary, inserting hallucinogenic herbs and ointments into the witch, who would then become unconscious and visit the sabbat meeting astrally. The broomstick would therefore be associated with the act of flying through the air. Because of the phallic implications innate in these suggestions, some witches argue that the broom should be ridden with the bristles at the front, to represent her "riding" it in an empowered act. However, there are certainly far more images of the witch riding her broom with the bristles at the back!

It has also been posited that the broom was used to conceal another witch's tool: the wand. The idea, of course, is that one could hide one's ritual implements in the guise of ordinary household equipment.

Nowadays, many witches and Wiccans keep brooms both as an affectionate nod in the direction of the imaginative sky-faring witch, and as a handy tool to represent clearing out the old and making way for the new. Many handfasting rituals involve jumping over a broomstick. They are also kept by doorways to guard from danger.

Boline

This is the white-handled knife used to harvest herbs and to perform any cutting, such as of cords, that the witch requires. It is usually curved, originating as it does from the sickle, and its lunar associations are obvious.

Cakes or Biscuits

Included in most coven rituals is the ceremony of Cakes and Ale (or Wine and Cakes), a traditional group Eucharist of a sharing and celebratory nature. It also performs the important role of "grounding" the group, food and drink being one of the most effective means of cutting off psychic perception.

The cakes or biscuits are usually made from three ingredients to represent the three stages of the Goddess, and cut into crescent moons or into circles embossed with a pentacle or runes, as appropriate to the group or working in hand. It can be helpful to engrave the biscuit with a sigil representing the sum total of the celebration or intent of the gathering; to then consume it carries obvious significance. The ceremony of Cakes and Ale is the Eucharist of the witch. Wine or fruit juice is sipped from the chalice, which is symbolic of the blood of life.

Candles

In the days before electricity, fire and candlelight were essential to every household. They provided a gathering point for the family at which food was cooked, bonds were made, and stories told. Nobody can doubt the ambience created by flickering flames—much mystery and imagination has been destroyed by the electric light bulb. Clearly, inhabitants of the modern world sorely miss the atmospherics of the candle and open fire, as the candle industry remains huge, especially in Britain.

Flames act as foci for psychic and magickal energies. To light one atop a candle of appropriate colour enhances and refines the type of energy desired. To light one atop a candle of the right colour that has also been anointed with relevant oil, carved with conducive symbols, and magnetised, is a spell in itself (see "Candle Magick" section in chapter 18, "Magickal Techniques and Spell-casting"). A magickal working without candles or fire is only a ghost of its potential self!

Cauldron

The cauldron is another of the classic symbols of the witch. From the Cauldron stirred by Cerridwen to the modern plastic versions available in tacky shops towards Halloween, the witch is inextricably associated with this three-legged pot. As a receptacle, and with its tripod associations, it, of course, represents the blending of all aspects of the Goddess—Maiden, Mother, and Crone—and their respective influences on the potion, water, or fire contained therein.

The cauldron is in fact rarely used to brew up magickal potions, as most witches find their kitchen pans (usually set aside specifically for this purpose) a far more convenient alternative. Solutions may be put in the cauldron afterwards and sent a powerful bolt of energy, which performs the same function as brewing it in the cauldron would have done. It is blessed with the power to renew and vivify.

The cauldron represents rebirth and the melting pot of life and death that typify the seasons and human experience on this level. It is a symbol of fecundity, of the womb. Cauldrons were hidden in Greek and Roman mythology within caves, and in Celtic lore beneath bodies of water in the Underworld. These blatant references to the process of (re)birth underline the true symbolism of the cauldron—that of transformation.

The cauldron may also be used for divination purposes. Water, potions, or steam can act as props to intuition when the mood is right. *The Spoils of Annwn* (in *The Book of Taliesin*) tells of a cauldron whose fire was kept alive by the breath of nine maidens. The fumes of the cauldron were oracular, as one might expect from a chthonic symbol reminiscent of the Priestess on her tripod at Delphi, intoxicated by the fumes emanating from deep within the earth.

The cauldron may also be used as a large vase for flowers or other appropriate decorations in the witch's makeshift (or permanent) temple.

Chalice

The chalice represents the female principle and the element of water. In Tarot, it appears as the suit of Cups, signifying all that is to do with the emotions and psychic perceptions. It is also used in ritual to hold the wine, the representative of the life-force. This is the most intensely feminine of symbols.

The chalice is also the Grail—the ultimate goal for all spiritual seekers. The sharing of the cup is an important group ritual, representing the common aim of spiritual enlightenment; when working alone, it represents participation in and celebration of life in its most significant and widest sense. By drinking from the chalice, one is taking sustenance from the Goddess, thus affirming a positive life stance.

The ceremony of Cakes and Ale (or Wine and Cakes) obviously involves the ritual use of the chalice, as does the Great Rite. Because the chalice represents the Goddess, it is usually silver or silver-plated. However, once again, it is down to the individual to choose, and there are many fine pewter, pottery, glass, and even wooden chalices to be found on the altars of witches who prefer them.

Incense

None of the senses is more evocative than that of smell. For centuries the art of olfactory scintillation has been practised in religion. Herbs, gums, and resins have been carefully selected for their associations and effect on the human organism.

Witches, like others who seek experience of higher planes, use this wealth of experience to elicit particular responses in themselves and their covens. Frankincense, for example, so popular in the Christian church, has strong solar connotations in witchcraft. It is associated with the regal, with wealth, success, and honour. It is redolent of wealth, and also of spiritual aspiration. It is an incense to burn in honour of the male principle, and to aid workings concerning philanthropic or spiritual schemes and projects.

Some incenses make one alert, and others cause a trancelike state. Some are relatively smoke-free, while others create a fug. The witch learns, through practise and with the aid of the numerous good books now available on the subject, to suit her incense (usually used to represent the element of air) to the season and the purpose at hand. She can perk herself up at any time with a dab of lavender or rosemary oil, but she knows that if she burns rosemary, she is likely to become intuitive, lunar, or even oracular. Combining these properties is another art.

Some covens (and individual witches) have experienced difficulties working inside with incense, precisely because its effect and, often, its physical manifestation (pungent, billowing smoke) is so strong. If there are asthmatics in the group, or anybody who finds incense a difficulty, joss sticks are much lighter than loose incense, and may be used instead. If even these prove too much to bear, oil is an option—either evaporating it or dabbing it on the candles or the robes or wrists (diluted, preferably!). Flowers of a suitable sort are another possibility, though I have always disliked cutting flowers and thereby killing them. Potted ones might be an option.

However, nothing beats the good old gums and resins. They create exactly the right wavelength, along with a wonderful, mystical atmosphere. Leaving the disc lit for fifteen minutes or so before the incense is sprinkled on it may cut down the spitting of charcoal discs and the overproduction of incense in a short time. The discs are best placed on a bed of sand or atop a metal candlestick (ensuring that there is plenty of space around the disc, as it will crumble). When the charcoal is glowing red, it is the right time to aromatise the working.

There are many fine ready-made incenses available today. My personal favourites come from the Lotus Emporium in Bath, England (www.lotusemporium.com). It is also wonderful, if you have time, to make your own. This teaches correspondences and adds a personal touch to any ritual.

Oil

Oil is used to anoint candles and equipment, to carry influences both psychic and herbal, and to bless the initiate in Wicca. Obviously there is plenty of scope for innovation using this basic ingredient. Body rubs, magickal perfumes, and so on are often part and parcel of a witch's bag of tricks. The usual "carriers" are olive oil and grapeseed oil.

Oils are easily charged with psychic energy, and retain it for a long time. The essential oils are chosen for each spell with personal and astrological correspondences in mind. They may be mixed to produce particular effects. For example, frankincense, with its pungent, almost solvent smell, relates to the element of fire, and is used for purification and protection. Orange is also a fire oil, and brings confidence, prosperity, and friendship. Together they are powerfully positive.

Anointing oneself in oil can provide wonderful effects. However, some oils are very powerful irritants, so do a dab test before you go anointing your entire body in them. Recently I gave my boyfriend Joe a phial of "Lucky Lodestone" oil I had bought in New Orleans. It contained a lot of clove oil, amongst other things, and one dab brought him out in the most awful raised rash. Not quite the fortune-enhancing effect intended! So treat oils with caution, and especially so if you are pregnant.

Baths containing essential oils are pure luxury. Rose oil with candles around the bath is one of my favourites for relaxation; lavender after a hard day at work. If your skin is sensitive to essential oils, try evaporating them instead. This has become a popular delight—aromatherapy is everyman's occultism nowadays. Combinations such as ylang-ylang and geranium create a warm, welcoming environment. Many chemical scents are available for use in oil burners, but I would avoid these. It is worth paying that little bit more for essential oils—they really can't be beaten as far as real relaxation and magickal intent is concerned.

Pentacle

Primarily, the pentacle represents the element of earth, and thus the north. It also symbolises the binding of humankind to the material plane, as represented by the circle that surrounds it (either directly at the points, or at a wider circumference, embracing other symbols of significance). Each point of the star signifies an element: air, earth, fire, water, and spirit. The other components of the human condition are simply mixtures of these ingredients in different measures.

Many witches and Wiccans wear an upright pentacle about their person, the point at the top representing the dominance of spirit over base instinct, and will over matter. It also serves as a reminder of our place as part of the Universe—linked with everything, rather than existing separately. This obviously has environmental as well as spiritual and psychological connotations.

The shield of Sir Gawain had "a pentangle [sic] charged on it in pure gold." This was a sign "that Solomon devised of old, as a token of fidelity"—symbolism obviously appropriate to his legend of stalwart faithfulness to friendship and honour. The English call it "the endless knot," as each line of the star overlaps and locks with another to create a symbol of eternity. Gawain was faultless in five ways, and five times in each way. His five wits were ever at the command of his higher will, and the skill of his five fingers was never-failing. There is Christian imagery too in this tale, related after the succession of Christianity in England: the Five Wounds of Christ, in which Gawain placed his trust; and the Five Joys of the Queen of Heaven (the Annunciation, the Nativity, the Resurrection, the Ascension, and the Assumption). These, of course, have their Pagan parallels. Finally, there were Gawain's five personal virtues: generosity, brotherly love towards all, cleanliness (always seen as a major virtue in orthodox religions!), courtesy, and sympathy. Some of these associations are not of direct relevance to the witch, but the point of honour most certainly is. The pentacle should be worn as a symbol of high spiritual values.

In some schools of Wicca, attainment of the second degree is represented by the reversal of the pentagram, but personally I have always seen this as representing chaos, and have avoided it. Also, every disgruntled teen who likes heavy-metal music can be found with an inverted pentagram at their neck. It is a matter of choice, but this witch could live without the angst-ridden associations!

Rope/Cord

Most witches working in covens keep a set of at least three cords, each one nine feet in length. These may be used for many purposes, individually or to enhance group work. Their colours, which can be any but usually include white and red, are selected to represent particular properties and energies. The red, for example, represents blood-bonds, including the blood of birth and death. Tied together to create the "spokes" of a wheel (usually above the coven cauldron), they "fuse" a group both together and to the "Wheel of Life," which the cords represent. This facilitates the "Wheel Dance," with participants chanting and dancing deosil around the cauldron.

Cords are knotted in spells to tie energy in, which will sometimes be released at a later date. Usually this involves chanting a spell and knotting the cord accordingly—for example, by the number of the deity evoked, or using the number of relevance to the task at hand.

Sometimes the cords are used as their shape suggests: to bind. An obvious example of this is during handfasting, though the ties are always loose to represent freedom of choice. In orthodox Wicca, the initiate is bound and blindfolded. Binding is also incorporated into other workings for symbolic purposes. For example, a witch might be bound in order to represent an unwanted habit or set of circumstances. When he or she liberates him- or herself in the ritual, the tie is broken. It is simple sympathetic magick, but it is effective.

Salt

Salt relates to the element of earth, of course, but it is used primarily in witchcraft as a purification agent. Salt is a brilliant visualisation-enhancer, dissolving astral pollutants and aiding concentration. Where salt—especially salt water—lands with intent, unwanted spirits flee. Unpleasant residues are instantly removed.

The combination of salt, water, and mental intent-channelling is one of the most powerful spiritual cleansing agents known to humanity. Salt is a preservative, and was used as such by ancient magickal cultures such as the Egyptians and Celts. This has no doubt contributed to its ability to psychically cleanse and deter unwanted influences, especially those connected with putrefaction and psychic "illness."

Salt is often to be found on the altar in a small dish, sometimes marked with a pentagram, or dissolved in water. It may be flicked around a room or in any space in order to purify it.

Scourge

"Ninth, the Scourge," the Wiccan initiate is told. "For learn, in Witchcraft you must ever give as you receive, but ever triple. So where I gave thee three, return nine: where I gave seven, return twenty-one; where I gave nine, return twenty-seven; where I gave twenty-one, return sixty-three."

This lesson in elementary mathematics is delivered in the middle of the second-degree initiation in Gardnerian and Alexandrian Wicca. Then the initiate is lightly scourged with the symbolic item, which consists of a handle finished by eight threads, each knotted five times. The initiate repeats the lesson that he or she has learned—this means twenty-one blessings in return. The initiate promptly delivers twenty-one light strokes to the initiator.

And so it goes on, confirming the principle of returning all good threefold. Implied in this is the obvious fact that evil will be returned to one also threefold. The scourging itself is an act of symbolic purification reminiscent of mediaeval monks who flagellated themselves to purge themselves and the world of sin. However, its inclusion in Wicca has raised more than one eyebrow for reasons that should be particularly obvious when one recalls that this ritual is performed naked. Many covens choose not to include this "tool" now, or to use it in this way.

Sword

The ritual sword can represent either air or fire, depending on your own decision. There are schools of thought in favour of both (see "Athame" section above).

Whichever the witch selects as her correspondence, the sword acts as a wonderfully melodramatic channel for whatever energies she chooses to access. Needless to say, as with the athame, it is advisable to check out the history of the sword (factually as well as psychically) before purchasing it for magickal purposes. One that has precipitated another life into the Summerlands is probably not the best choice for inclusion in the Circle of a gentle, positive witch.

There is no doubt that he or she who holds the sword in any situation is wielding the power; likewise in the Circle. Often it is considered a tool of the High Priest, but not always. It adds gravitas to any occasion, and works well for the casting of Circles because of the increase in length of the caster's arm! On that note, light swords are obviously easier than weighty ones, but it is entirely a matter of choice.

Wand

Last, but certainly not least, is the magick wand. As discussed above, opinion is divided as to whether wands relate to fire or air. The best witch always goes by her intuition.

Wands come in many shapes and sizes to suit all tastes and magickal purposes. Phallic wands, for example (usually made of oak), are powerful representatives of the Pan-like aspects of the fecund god-force, and are thus appropriate for use in spring (at the equinox, or around Beltane). They might be used in workings concerning new projects, ideas, and enterprises, for example.

Better for more lunar magick (divination, dreamwork, psychic development) are delicate elder and rowan wands, or any with which the practitioner feels comfortable. Wands can be found, bought, or hand-crafted. One I used for ages was a plump twig I found beneath a tree at Avebury stone circle. It may have looked like a regular bit of tree to everyone else, but to me it was a perfectly magickal conducting stick, a gift of the gods. It felt right and its associations were good. This is the key to all effective magickal equipment.

The wand is used as the layperson might imagine: to channel and direct energy. It may be used to cast Circles, sometimes replacing the role of the athame. In dealing with the spirit world, the wand seems friendlier than an athame or sword, and has been described by Stewart Farrar as "an invitation" rather than "a command."

Some witches stick to the elaborate instructions given in *The Key of Solomon the King* regarding the wand. This is that only a sapling hazel or nut tree should be approached, and that the wood intended for use as a wand should be "cut from the tree in a single stroke, on the day of Mercury, at sunrise." However, many witches do not follow these instructions, this one included. The most important thing is to have a working tool that feels right. It is, after all, the witch's third arm.

The Witch's Working Week

Monday

As its name indicates, Monday is sacred to the moon. This is the time to optimise on the planetary influence most pertinent to witchcraft. Psychism, magickal enhancement, purification, visualisation, and healing spells are all performed on Mondays. The actual phase of the moon is also of relevance. Corresponding incenses and oils include jasmine, lemon, rosemary, and sandalwood. Candles should be silver, white, or indigo.

Tuesday

Tuesday is ruled by Mars, a planetary influence suitable for spells for overcoming obstacles. Fortitude, courage, and steadfast effort can be attained working on this day. Oils used in such workings include rue, ginger, pine, and wormwood. The latter is particularly effective for protection and for keeping enemies at bay. Candles should be Martian colours: red and deep orange. This is a perfect day for bracing yourself magickally for a quest, and for pouring energy into a new ambition or project.

Wednesday

Ruled by Mercury, the emphasis on a Wednesday is on communication, swiftness, precision, transport and travel, and study. This is a perfect day to pursue intellectual magickal work, or to communicate magickal ideas. The cyberwitch finds herself in blessed aspect on Mercury's day. Marjoram, clover, and mint are all suitable scents or oils. Candles should be yellow or blue to represent air.

Thursday

Thursday is the day to work on home and friendship issues, and all issues concerning expansion, including of business. If looking for a stroke of good luck, this is the day to appeal for it. Oils and incenses sacred to Jupiter include clove, cinquefoil, nutmeg, hyssop, and sage. The best colours to work with are gold, green, and royal purple. This is a good day to heal rifts in relationships and to strive towards a brighter future.

Friday

Friday is Venus's day, and thus the day to cast spells for love, seduction, beauty, and passion. Relationships should be blessed under the fair goddess's auspices. Candles should be blue or white (recalling the sea and foam from which Venus Aphrodite was born), green (for refreshing influences and new beginnings), red, or pink. Suitable oils and incenses include musk, rose, frangipani, and the gentle violet. This is a day to luxuriate prior to a working, and to feel glamourous, even if working alone.

Saturday

Saturday is a good time to focus on ambition, both intellectual and material. Banishing spells may also be cast on this day, and any other working involving barriers and closure. Oils and incenses include cypress and good old patchouli. Candles should be black, purple, white, or green, depending on the angle of your working.

Sunday

Frankincense is an ideal incense for this mystical day. Spells and workings requiring compassion and elevated insight work well on a Sunday. Gold and orange candles emphasise its regal solar connotations. Prayer, meditation, and healing are all suitable magickal activities for the seventh day. Also divination and assessment of one's spiritual progress.

General Correspondences

It is possible to cast a spell using mental energy only. Sometimes, very strong visualisations can be all it takes to cause a thing to happen. However, if a ritual is being performed, or even just the lighting of a candle (perhaps the most simple and effective technique of all!), it is good to have precise planetary correspondents worked out. It depends on your intent as to which planet rules your working. This will help determine the time of your spell, the colour of the candle, and the type of oil and incense you may wish to use.

The Sun

The sun is for issues concerning health, wealth, and status, career progression, and the acquisition of property. The sun is pertinent to expansion, social life, popularity, and free-flowing physical well-being and abundance. Unsurprisingly, the solar colours are yellow, orange, and gold, its stones yellow topaz and citrine, and its day of the week Sunday. The astrological correspondent is Leo.

The Moon

The moon rules the subconscious, and is intimately connected with psychism and magick. Laterally, it is associated with all "feminine" provinces such as creativity and dreams. Emotional issues also come under the moon's sphere of influence. Its colours are silver, white, and indigo, its gems moonstone and pearl, and its day Monday. The sign of Cancer is ruled by the moon.

Mercury

Mercury is for communication, swiftness, and precision work. Any intellectual pursuits, and the art of debate, mediation, and intelligent exchange are blessed by Mercury. The corresponding colours are yellow and silver, and the stone topaz. Its day of the week is, of course, Wednesday. Its astrological correspondents are Gemini and Virgo.

Venus

It will come as no surprise to read that Venus rules love, affection, fertility, and self-expression as manifested in the arts. Venus and her muses rule dance and all that is a natural expression of joy and abundance. Venus is the planet to refer to for attraction and love. Its stones are rose quartz and emerald, its colours the same; the day that Venus rules is Friday. Taurus and Libra are ruled by the fair planet.

Mars

Where Venus is gentle love, Mars is unbridled passion. Aggression, courage, protection, and honour come under Mars's jurisdiction. Its colour is blood-red, its stone ruby, and its astrological correspondent Aries.

Jupiter

Orthodox institutions are ruled by Jupiter, as is business expansion, favour-granting, and other sun-type areas. However, Jupiter represents an "older" energy, whereas the sun rules over innocence and youth. So, to launch a new business project, sun energies might be invoked to encourage rapid growth, and Jupiter might be employed to guarantee acceptance into the established marketplace. Jupiter is also connected with financial gain and business deals.

The colour for Jupiter is purple, its stone amethyst, and its day of the week Thursday. It rules over the sign of Sagittarius.

Saturn (Solid)

Saturn rules discipline and constraint, old age and protection. Its colour is black, its stone sapphire, and the star sign particular to it Capricorn.

Uranus (Air)

Uranus is for all matters concerning psychic abilities, especially those involving communication. Uranus also rules over sudden change, and the will to travel. Its stone is the opal, and the star sign Aquarius.

Neptune (Liquid)

Neptune rules over hallucinogenic drugs, liquids, perfumes, seafaring, and thus the launching of ambitious projects. Neptune also rules over the termination of an old regime to make way for the new. Its stone is aquamarine and its star sign Pisces.

Pluto (Gas)

Pluto rules over transformations, toxic and lethal drugs, vapours, and astral travel. The astrological sign ruled by Pluto is Scorpio.

eighteen

Magickal Techniques
and Spell-casting

SPELL-CASTING IS, OF COURSE, THE ancient art most associated with the witch. It plays a part in the history of belief in every culture, and epitomises the idea that individual will can be brought to bear on the natural world, especially if certain ritual ingredients and actions are employed.

Because modern spellcraft has grown out of so many different backgrounds, there are techniques to suit every occasion and inclination. I list some of these below.

Following prescribed spells has much to be said for it—they carry a unique atmosphere, and have been tried and tested in advance. Samuel MacGregor Mathers founded much of his magick, and thus the doctrine and practise of the Golden Dawn, on mediaeval and alchemical grimoires. Sometimes the arcane nature of a spell makes it all the more convincing—and conviction is 90 percent of any endeavour of will power. The correspondences of such tracts are still widely used in magick today, and imaginatively so. There are hundreds of spell-books available, should one wish to follow set recipes, all of them indicating this combination of proven techniques with imagination. There are Wiccan spells, sorceries, and dark magicks available from most bookshops with a "Mind, Body, and Spirit" section. Llewellyn Worldwide publishes many of these—Scott Cunningham's is a particularly good example of Wiccan spells (*The Magical Household,* Llewellyn Publications, 1987). Cunningham's books are amongst the first in an avalanche of simple Wiccan techniques and lore. Titania's velvety-covered spell-books have sold like hot cakes ever since their arrival on the shelves, as have many other pretty, fizzy compilations. Some of these books are devoid of much use bar the decorative, although as with anything, it's how you use it that counts. Many others are available to buy—spellbooks have been all the rage for some time now. In all cases, the material involves generic techniques and established correspondences applied in a new and imaginative way.

Using spells you have not created yourself has its bonuses—it would be unlikely that a spell got into print if, for example, it was fundamentally flawed, or its correspondences were incorrect—but creating one's own based on these principles can only be beneficial to the matter at hand. Therefore this book contains examples of spells for various occasions, plus the correspondences required to create your own. See also chapter 11, for the section on chakras, chapter 12 ("The Witch and Qabalah"), and chapter 17 for the section "The Witch's Working Week."

Spells begin with a self-hypnosis of sorts; we prepare the path by clearing it of cluttering doubts and fears. Feeling inspired and confident are the preliminary essentials; visualisations and ritual actions serve to enhance and confirm this positive mindset. Few people of any religious persuasion would deny that positive thinking brings positive results, even if they do not believe in witchcraft per se. This strong, clear mental energy combined with the energies of season, constellation, and lunar tide (not to mention deity, occult correspondence such as appropriate incense and colour, and spirit-helper), makes for a very strong probability of success in one's endeavour.

There are many techniques that may be employed by the modern witch to empower her work. There are also many different forms of magick, from highly diverse cultures. Some of these follow here, in alphabetical order.

Astral Magick

All magick is astral in that what occurs on the physical plane is merely intended to symbolise what occurs on an invisible level. However, adept magickians and some witches are able to set spells into motion without recourse to ritual or physical symbolism. They simply think it in the correct way, utilising the correct "doorways" and symbolism, and compound it with intense, concentrated will power. It can also occur accidentally, especially when a person is emotionally overwrought, or sexually frustrated (this is particularly relevant to young people). The psychically active person acts as a beacon on the astral plane, attracting all sorts of entities with his or her thoughts. In some respects, every thought we have is a kind of astral magick. If we spend all our time thinking about trivial things, we will barely be visible on the astral (unless a very intense inner life emerges in between). If our thoughts are compassionate and spiritual, they will attract spirits and entities of high integrity.

Most of us practise astral magick with props—a candle flame, a chalice, an athame, and so on. Of course, the magick does not stop on the astral. It is intended to filter through to the causal plane, and influence the root cause of events to come. Eventually this will have an effect on the physical. This is why group spiritual meditations (such as those effected by the Lucis Trust) are effective—the human will to evolve is conveyed to the Masters (spiritual intercessors, essentially on the astral and causal planes), refined, augmented, and returned to earth. Meditations for world peace have far more of an effect than is visible in a group of people holding hands or concentrating on one another's positive intent. We are all channels of the Divine, and to make this a conscious act greatly increases our chances of working effectively.

Astral magick can also take place during projection from the body. The Golden Dawn worked hard at this, exploring key symbols that acted as doorways to release the mind onto the astral and beyond. Many of their members became adept at accessing the astral and Akashic planes, where incarnational information (amongst other types) is stored. This type of magick may be worked at; the Servants of Light, for example, have condensed earlier techniques into an excellent training program (more may be learned of them at www.servantsofthelight.com). It may also occur spontaneously, as was my own personal experience. However, accessing such areas of the living, Universal psyche at will does indeed take work, which is why study programs exist and why adepts such as Dion Fortune spent years of their lives living in magickal communities doing little but. It is not easy for most of us to dedicate ourselves entirely to such pursuits, but a little work each day goes a very long way.

Binding

Binding is a technique that the ethical witch uses with caution. Naturally it has been greatly employed in amoral love spells since time immemorial to draw and attach one person to another, usually the spell-caster. This is classic bewitchment, in which the free will of the "victim" is overruled by the desire of the practitioner. Many a tale could be told of the unfortunate consequences of such an action, but, to be fair on the witch or magickian concerned, words and actions in love trysts can be equally binding and thwarting to the recipient, and they say that all is fair in love and war. The Wiccan, of course, would disagree, but a non-Wiccan, magickally minded person might argue that betrothal and wedlock are equally binding and often just as duplicitous. Be that as it may, a more common usage of the technique in magick is not so much to attract as to prevent interaction. The idea in this case would be to bind a person from causing harm—to oneself or others.

As with all spells, there are many ways to bring one's will to pass—the symbolism of the ritual must simply correlate with the witch's intent. An obvious form of binding involves the use of cords, but a bind-rune or other monogram symbolising the desired effect can also bring it about. Whittling away at a stick or object whilst strongly visualising the person's harmful capacities diminishing can also bring binding to pass. However, there are many people in the world with strong will power, and in order to magnify one's own to anything like the required capacity, other techniques should be used, with the bound symbol as the focal point. These include: casting a Circle to concentrate energy and create a cross-dimensional environment; lighting candles and burning incense of appropriate correspondences (a small black taper candle, for example, burnt right down, could serve to symbolise the destruction of negative potential action); undergoing a small fast before the rite (to focus one's mind and increase emotional impetus); and a huge variety of other magickal techniques as either given in this book or created by the practitioner. When working in tune with the natural correspondences—the tides of the moon, astrological considerations, days of the week, angelic hours, and whatever else the witch deems appropriate—imagination may be harnessed to powerful effect.

When binding a gossip from malicious speech, for example, every bolt of energy thrown at the person might be envisaged as landing on his or her mouth like sticky tape. The ethical witch will ensure that the gossip's mouth is freed up for essential and nonharmful speech, and of course for the purpose of eating, drinking, and breathing. When binding a person who is physically threatening or abusive (though legal action is highly recommended in lieu—fists should be countered on their own plane), that person's ability to harm can be imagined as flailing arms cut off or tied behind his or her back at each onslaught of psychic energy.

The use of dolls is obviously appropriate to binding spells. A classic scenario is the binding of one personalised doll to another in love magick, though, as previously mentioned, this is obviously unethical unless both people consent, which would be highly unlikely as most of us would choose to develop freely. An individual might be prevented from causing harm by being "bound" in effigy form in a black satin cloth, with the proviso that it keeps harmful energies in (and provocative energies out), but allows free flow to those that are not pernicious.

The effective witch is imaginative, and knows what works best for her, and what seems the most appropriate symbolism in any given situation.

Candle Magick

Candle magick is, for me, the most simple and effective of magickal techniques. It involves choosing a candle in a colour that correlates to the spell's intent, possibly anointing it with a relevant oil, and lighting it at the correct phase of the moon to set the witch's will into motion. A rough guide to colour usage follows:

Red—Strength both physical and emotional, determination, passion, sex.

Orange—Vitality, happiness, anti-depressive. A good choice for helping supplicants out of a slump.

Yellow—Emotional healing, health, prosperity, intellect. I also use yellow to bless, imagining the gentle rays of the sun represented by the colour.

Green—New beginnings, balance, growth. The paler the shade of green, the newer the project or issue.

Turquoise—Self-defense, both psychic and physical. Attunement to the cosmic will in action.

Blue—*Dark:* Calming, inspiring.
   Pale: Academe, enhances public performances.

Violet—Spiritual energy, inner vision, psychic development.

Pink—*Dark:* For fun, challenge, adventure. An antidote to the doldrums.
   Pale: Comfort, heart-mender. Ideal for those who have suffered an emotional shock or trauma.

Black—Banishing spells, habit-breaking, removing obstacles.

White—Blessing, cleansing, accumulating energy for general use.

Often, the candle is engraved with a suitable sign. For example, if a purple or indigo candle is being lit for psychic enhancement, a five-pointed star and crescent moon might be carved into it. If the witch is working on behalf of another, the supplicant's zodiacal symbol might appear in the wax, along with another representing the aim of the spell. If a love spell is being worked, a monogram might have been concocted combining the letters of the two people's names.

For an attraction spell, the candle might then be anointed with magnetising oil (usually by working from the centre of the candle to the end in either direction), or with clove oil (for luck and prosperity), or with whatever else the witch deems necessary. A catalyst might be added (as in any spell), such as mandrake (suitable for any spell) or mistletoe (especially good for love and luck).

The candle is then burned either in one sitting (for which votive or a very small taper candle are best), or lit on consecutive occasions at the same time or in the same cosmic hour (for example, the time with the appropriate astrological or angelic correspondences). The flame of the candle represents the witch's intent, and acts as a focal point between the worlds.

Obviously there are ways to enhance this experience and make it unique, as with any spell. A ritual bath may be taken beforehand, allowing the witch to cleanse her bodies (physical, astral, and causal) and anoint them with suitable influences (oil added to the bath, for example). A Circle might be cast prior to the preparation, or the ritual lighting of the flame, to concentrate the mind and protect the space. Incense of a suitable type might be left to imbue the room before the witch begins. An altar might be created to enhance the working, or objects of a suitable nature placed on the regular altar. Objects relating to the person in question (hair, nail clippings, and/or garments being particularly powerful) could be featured on the altar, as well as other objects and images that represent the aim of the spell. Fresh flowers bring wonderful vibrations to a working, and the flowers may be selected to suit the aim. It all depends on how elaborate the witch wishes to be.

Many of these techniques are high magickal, rather than Traditional Witchcraft. A Traditional witch would probably simply will the result at a suitable time, foregoing even the candle! It is entirely the choice of the individual how far she wishes to take it. One of the wonders of candle magick is its superb simplicity. It will work whether you surround it with ritual or not. If the will power is strong enough, the flame will set the witch's will into action.

Below is a typical example of candle magick at work in conjunction with other principles.

SPELL FOR ABUNDANCE

It is impossible to effectively imagine abundance if you fail to be generous to yourself, so begin this technique by treating yourself to a few things. These can be small, like a snack you especially like but don't have often, or larger, like a new item of clothing or a holiday. If money is a big problem, be generous to yourself in some other way, such as giving yourself time to devote to a particular pleasurable pursuit.

Always work for abundance when the moon is waxing. Most of us do not have time to light a candle at the same time on consecutive days, but if you can do that, it helps build a feeling of momentum. However, a single concentrated effort is just as good.

Colours pertaining to abundance include green, orange, and yellow, so choose your candle accordingly. Green is good for projects and business, yellow for health, and orange for happiness. For money, green, gold, or red are appropriate.

Sit comfortably in a room or space that to you corresponds with the idea of pleasure and leisure. Light your candle and ask the powers that be in whatever form you know them (the Goddess, God, a specific bounteous deity such as Laksmi) to be with you. Feel the abundance of the Universe—its fractal-like fertility, its boundless energy. Know that you are part of that endless procreation, part of this starburst of diversity.

Attune to this energy. Visualising it will help you feel it, so imagine it as a colour and texture, such as rich, buttery yellow with gold flashes. Mentally draw it over your head, and, just as the candle is surrounded by its own glow, surround yourself with this energy.

Bring this light in through your skin, absorbing it as if it were sunlight, feeling its warmth. Think of energy flowing in and out of you with equal ease—abundance comes when we give as well as receive. Now, make a specific mental request for what you desire, addressing it to your deity of choice.

This candle magick visualisation should pave the way for riches of many sorts.

Casting the Circle

Casting a Circle is one of the most simple and effective means of creating a potent magickal space. The classic Wiccan technique is to call up the Lords of the Watchtowers in each quarter, with their ensuing elemental energies.

The first thing required by a witch in casting a Circle is knowledge of which cardinal point is where. This is easy if you are in a field and have the sun and moon as guides, but if working in a built-up area, a compass may come in handy.

I still use the Wiccan words myself, as I have found them very effective over the years, but if you wish to write your own—the more evocative of each elemental quality, the better—go for it. Many witches also place signs and symbols of the elements in each quarter to help enhance the effect of their visualisation. Pictures, sigils, and actual incense (in the east), fire (in the south), water (in the west), and earth or salt (in the north) are to be found in most magickal Circles.

It is helpful to take a purification bath and to meditate a little prior to attempting the Circle. However, if the mood is upon you, act on it. Some of my most powerful Circles have been cast spontaneously as the magickal urge came upon me.

First, face the east, and extend either your hand or wand or sword. Visualise the Lords of Air, and greet them either with your own words or with the Wiccan evocation, "Ye Lords of the Watchtowers of the East, Ye Lords of Air, I summon, stir and call you up to witness these rites and protect this Circle."

As you do so, trace the invoking pentagram in the air.

Visualise the winds blowing through the portal you have created, air rushing about you, and the sylphs being released into your space. Keep your hand, wand, or sword aloft as you do so.

Not letting it drop, trace a quarter of a circle over to the south. Greet the Lords of Fire with your own words, or say, "Ye Lords of the Watchtowers of the South, Ye Lords of Fire, I summon, stir and call you up to witness these rites and protect this Circle."

Trace an invoking pentagram as you do so, and visualise the fiery lords leaping into your Circle.

When you have established your wall of fire, trace the next quarter of the Circle to the west. Again, trace the invoking pentagram, this time visualising the Lords of Water: "Ye Lords of the Watchtowers of the West, Ye Lords of Water, I summon, stir and call you up to witness these rites and protect this Circle."

When water is firmly established in the west of your working space, trace another quarter to the north, the realm of earth. Keeping your arm or implement aloft, use your own words to evoke the Lords of Earth, or recite, "Ye Lords of the Watchtowers of the North, Ye Lords of Earth, I summon, stir and call you up to witness these rites and protect this Circle."

Again, trace the invoking pentagram as you do so. Visualise earth in the north of your space—green rolling hills, red Arizona desert, whatever does it for you.

Now bring your arm, wand, or sword back to the east. In your mind's eye, see yourself surrounded by a vibrant circle of protective colour—I usually use blue-white. Now, turn slowly around the Circle twice more, affirming the presence of the elements in each quarter.

The next bit is optional, but I always do it. When the Circle is thrice-affirmed, point directly above yourself, and ask the Lords of Spirit to be with you. My own visualisation is of the purple Akashic egg, but use whatever symbolises spirit to you. Then point to the ground, and say (something along the lines of), "Spirit above me, Spirit below me, Spirit behind me, Spirit before me."

The idea of the latter is to bring higher influences into play. Often, what goes on in the modern witch's Circle is simple lower psychism. Evoking the Lords of Spirit should turn the proceedings into a valid spiritual experience.

Now you are standing in the middle of a vibrant, protective sphere, encased by the Elements and the Lords of Spirit. Magick can now commence.

N.B.: Invoking Pentagrams specific to each element can be used to call in the Quarters. This is not strictly necessary, but can facilitate additional elemental interplay.

When you have finished your working, it is important to close the Circle. Incidentally, the Circle (sometimes defined by cords or chalk on the floor, especially when working in a group) should not be left during the working. This can be overcome mentally if necessary by very strongly visualising the sphere extending beyond wherever you need to go. I often encompass the whole house to give myself freedom of movement (only if no one else is in it), or you can draw a doorway in its walls. The important thing to recall is that it is a sacred, protected space, and you do not want people walking in and out of it willy-nilly.

Closing the Circle involves the same process, but thanking the Lords instead of calling them up, and tracing the Pentagram of Release instead of that of Invocation. I *never* banish—not any more than I would invite somebody into my house and them throw them out as soon as I'd had enough. Banishing is rude and arrogant. There can be no harm in having the Lords around, so I always thank them and invite them to leave whenever they wish. Usually, I see them vanishing into the distance once this is said.

I always close the Circle with the words "Circle Open, Never Broken." This is as good as an "Amen" to a prayer, or a "So Mote It Be" to a spell. It confirms that the work is over and that life can now continue as usual.

There are many ways of casting a Circle (and Traditional witches do not even bother with this, as they view all spaces as sacred), but personally I love the sensation of working in a timeless sphere under the auspices and guidance of those much older and wiser. Inside her Circle, the life of the witch is magickal indeed.

Cone of Power

Within the Circle, a Cone of Power may be raised by a group. Hands are usually joined, and a circle dance participated in with a common focus of the Cone, which builds up naturally at the centre of the Circle. Meditation, chanting, drumming, and song may also be used to the same end. The energy thus raised is brought to a peak, often with the group raising their arms as the Cone grows and becomes ready to use. It is then directed towards some specific purpose, usually of a healing nature.

Conjurations

Conjurations—what fun! This corresponds to most people's idea of what magick ought to be—summoning familiars, calling up angels, commanding spirits to do one's bidding. Texts such as *The Key of Solomon the King* (translated and edited by S. L. MacGregor Mathers) give examples of elaborate Judeo-Christian rituals (mostly dating from the sixteenth century onwards) to perform such tasks as summoning spirits and eliciting information from them about hidden treasures.

However, the preparations are rather elaborate. This particular ritual involves going before dawn to the place suspected of harbouring buried or hidden treasures, when the sun is in Leo, properly prepared and dressed, and burning the relevant incense along with—wait for it—"a lamp, whose oil should be mingled with the fat of a man who has died in the month of July, and the wick being made of the cloth in which he was buried." Workmen are employed to labour alongside the spectres thereby conjured, and rather than the usual cup of tea or can of beer, are refreshed at intervals with "a girdle of the skin of a goat newly slain, on which is inscribed in the blood of the dead man" one of the Keys of Solomon the King. Thus are the spirits brought back to work for the magickian. Simple!

Naturally, no Wiccan or ethical occultist would even contemplate such an act, but it is worth knowing about. The gory details are, one would imagine, more to precipitate the magickian into a suitable frame of mind than they are active ingredients, although some might argue with this. The ritual is completely typical of Judeo-Christian sorcery.

The witch, however, being eclectic, is free to use magickal techniques of any nature, the judge at the end of the day being her own conscience. Some witches like to use coffin nails for their spells—and they certainly have a unique aura once they have been buried a while! Many witches of the "left-hand path" summon up spirits and keep them as familiars. This basically means that the spirits are enslaved to perform the witch or magickian's will. I have seen them used mostly as spies and protectors. Familiars can gather information and bring it back to the witch, or guard over magickal workings and personal property, alerting its master to any potential threat.

Some witches and magickians summon elementals in material form, which is an interesting, if unnerving, thought. The artist and occultist Austin Osman Spare was fascinated by this concept, and performed many such rituals, often with powerful but tricky results. The elementals cannot be expected to cooperate as the witch may desire—they are raw, primal energies with an entirely different set of referents to our own. However, they can exist in part in living people—there are some highly elemental persons around. Dion Fortune talks of these in *Applied Magic and Aspects of Occultism,* and explores the theme in her collection of occult short stories, *The Secrets of Doctor Taverner.* She posits that elementals are attracted into human bodies via a psychic vortex created when the parents (particularly the mother) are drunk during conception. I have certainly encountered some people in human form who are more than a touch elemental, and this theory fits them (though there can be other factors too). The magickian is just as likely to attract one of these into her sphere as to summon an entire elemental.

A popular form of conjuration over the centuries is that of forcing spirits of the dead back into physical bodies. Dr. John Dee, inventor (or herald) of Enochian magic ("the language of the angels"), experimented with this, as have many occultists over the centuries. Nowadays we normally forego such revolting practises. For a start, why not communicate with the spirit directly, rather than calling it back to its dilapidated body? (Imagine how unpleasant for the soul concerned!) Secondly, why not go higher and select an entity with greater knowledge than an individual—who is as fallible as the rest of us—could harbour? It is bad enough calling a spirit back from the astral planes, never mind forcing it back into its abandoned body! Yuck!

Ouija is a form of conjuration, but a random one. I have never used a Ouija board, as the feeling I get from the object is so negative I have never wished to. Friends who have used them appear to have attracted only the most disenfranchised and disturbed of spirits—obviously, it reaches out to those that are earth-bound. This means it attracts spirits like accident victims who have not recovered from the shock of their sudden dispatch into the Otherworld, thus they linger between planes, as well as those with emotional issues that tie them to this realm. Communicating with them is equivalent to conversing with a random group of convicts and prisoners—with no bars between you. Honest answers cannot be expected, and neither can immunity from the contacts.

It is possible to perform conjurations that are ethically sound. For example, a convocation would involve calling out to "A spirit suitable to my purpose, who is willing and able to help, while causing harm to none." There are hundreds of thousands of entities out there who might be happy to aid the occultist, rather than to serve them under duress.

The best way to perform a conjuration is to inscribe a suitable sign on the floor, using whatever magickal system you prefer. For example, an Alexandrian Wiccan, being influenced by High Magick, might use a seven-pointed star to symbolise Netzach and aid in Venusian or nature workings, and to attract a concomitant entity. If the working is for elemental or psychic powers, a pentagram may be used. This can either be inscribed on the floor with chalk, sewn onto a cloth for frequent use, or drawn astrally with the witch's sword, athame, wand, or finger. The important thing is to have it set in one's mind. It is usually easiest to have it physically visible for conjurations.

As with all spells, ritual paraphernalia are selected that suit the purpose: incense, music (if helpful), props. The correct phase of the moon is selected, and possibly the right astrological circumstances. Some times are more powerful than others; for a conjuration, pick a time when the worlds meet—dawn or dusk, close to a sabbat when the atmospheres of the worlds are merging, or the hour of the angel that relates Qabalistically to your intent.

This type of mediaeval magick—summoning spirits and angels, or creating golems/egregors to perform one's will—laid the foundations of much modern esoteric practise.

Creative Visualisation

Creative or guided visualisations can be perfect for inducing intuitive experiences and insights in the meditator. They offer the opportunity for psychodrama, a facet more safely and accurately played out in inner life than outer, where we are subject to the random, the intrusive, and the pernicious. If the experience is entered into fully and the inner journey is soundly structured, creative visualisation has much to offer the witch. It is particularly effective in the approaching of godforms.

I give examples of encounters with gods and goddesses from the Hindu, Greek, and Egyptian pantheons in my books *Invoke the Goddess* and *Invoke the Gods* (Llewellyn, 2000 and 2001, respectively). These are powerful tools either prior to or in conjunction with spell-casting. Such visualisations are relaxing and inspiring, allowing the left side of the brain to connect with the conscious mind.

Other "prescribed" inner journeys, such as the following, can create a group experience that thereby raises and directs energy. This is good for more general aims, such as promoting peace within conflict (see the section "What Can the Witch Do in Times of Global Crisis?" in chapter 2).

The following example is taken from my book *Invoke the Gods*. It is a visualisation pertaining to the Egyptian god Thoth. If you are female, do not be put off by the fact that he is a male deity. The psyche is composed of both male and female elements, as is the spirit. Women can gain greatly from interaction with godforms and getting in touch with the inner male.

VISUALISATION FOR RECALLING
LIFE'S INNER MYSTERY

Daily life is by its very nature mundane; with all the trivial things we have to do, appointments to keep, and work to perform, it can be easy for even the most magickally minded person to forget the more interesting and meaningful side of existence. Thoth, as lord of wisdom and magick, is well placed to jolt our memories as to life's higher, deeper purpose.

Take several deep, slow breaths of blue and silver light, and imagine these colours infiltrating your bodies as you do so. Very gently, feel a sense of relief being absorbed into you as your mind becomes freer to wander. Realise how fettered it has been by small concerns, worthless in the long term.

You begin to perceive a sensation of your consciousness "peeling away" from your body, an experience that brings a sense of levity and otherworldliness. Yet it is somehow more real and more permanent than the trivia-based, emotional consciousness you harboured before.

Now you find yourself in a hot land at night. There is no light, just warm dust underfoot and the heat emanating from pyramids all around—they are not visible, but you know they are there. Glyphs of consciousness hang in the ancient air, invisibly emanating a sense of arcane hierarchy and purpose. Mages have meditated here, magickians have walked in ritual procession muttering mantras of geometric precision, and many a soul has navigated these labyrinths in the quest for stellar immortality.

The only light, indeed, comes from the stars. The constellations are extra-obvious tonight—no stretch of the imagination as they have seemed before. Now the patterns are obvious: the tunic of Orion, where Osiris comes from; the dog-star Sothis, heralding the Lady Isis—a map for spirits seeking union with the eternal.

Looking back to ground level, you see before you a cave. The inside is cast in thick shadows like a magickian's velvet cape, and the mouth is faintly starlit, just enough to define it for you.

You peer inside, but the darkness thickens like a curtain. What you do perceive, however, is the muffled sound of a chant coming from, it seems, the most chthonic recesses of the deep, black cave.

Cautiously, you step inside. Edging forward one toe at a time, you feel, rather than the expected fear, a sense of awe and excitement. A frisson passes right through you and reminds you of the excitement you felt as a child when a story had reached a potential climax. The inside of the cave smells of cloves and spices.

The mantric music is getting louder, and as you approach its source quite fearlessly, you notice a new and brighter light. One-half of the cave is lit in silver-white light, the other in the golden rays of a Mediterranean midday.

The sounds and light and intense rich scents become almost overwhelming as you reach the final recess.

Looking in, you see a very tall man wearing the mask of an ibis bird, its long thin beak protruding conspicuously, and nothing else but a white tunic and an exquisitely wrought belt and neckpiece of silver. The sensation of magick and sorcery is so strong in here that you feel that whatever you think or desire will materialise instantly.

"There is nothing unique in this," booms a voice as you stand riveted at the door. "One simply has to go a little further back to find it."

This side of Thoth's profile emits silver light, and as you gaze into it, it begins to seem like moonlight on water. It ripples out patterns and mandalas of consciousness, each atom affecting the other, this silver water between everything, so that all is connected.

On his arm alone is a whole ocean of consciousness; you can see your thoughts dropping into it like pebbles, causing ripples that, somewhere, will contribute to waves.

He turns the golden side towards you, and there, in what seems like visible air on his other arm, you see pictures of sparks inside bodies, the bodies ranging from infancy to decrepitude, like a Hare Krishna picture, each with a glowing consciousness. The body becomes a skeleton, the spark detaches, then it descends again on an embryo, and the cycle repeats itself. Wave after wave of flesh breaks on the shores of the mundane, containing the divine consciousness, and all too often forgetting it. Thus another round on the wheel of dualities is necessitated.

As you think this, Thoth, still chanting, turns to face you. One eye blazes gold, the sun; the other shines in silver. Neither is outdone or compromised by the other. Both are in perfect unity.

The light from each luminary is interweaving itself down a staff held by Thoth at his beak. The staff becomes a caduceus—half the interweaving light solar, and half lunar. He hands it to you.

As you receive the staff, be totally aware of your true descent. It has nothing to do with genes and physical inheritance, but a trip down from the stars to inhabit the temporary vehicle that will best enable you to learn the intended lessons of this incarnation.

"Look for signs and symbols," intones the stentorian Thoth, "for this is how we guide you. Every situation, every chance encounter, every thing you see *when your intuition is activated* is there to signal your route."

Does this include what number bus you catch, or who's sitting beside you in a restaurant?, you wonder incredulously. Thoth catches you with his resplendent eyes.

"Not always, but when the time is right. Meditation facilitates it, as does magick. No need to be semiotically aroused all the time, or others will doubt and discredit you. Recall the Powers of the Sphinx—to Know, to Will, to Dare, and to be Silent. Speak only to others who understand you. Those who do not will only drag you into their own low vibrations, and an experience of this type shared is an experience halved. Use your own language, be unique. We can speak to you more clearly this way. Invent your alphabet of symbols, ask us to communicate with you, and it will become possible."

Needless to say, now is the time to discuss any other issues you may have brought into this visualisation. Thoth is so measured and in control that it is easy to stay as long as you wish. He is rather like a very friendly, informal doctor and teacher rolled into one, the bizarre appearance notwithstanding.

When you are ready, simply thank Thoth, and with a wave of the caduceus, return yourself to your room.

Daily meditation and magickal activity will keep you on this wavelength most of the time. However, it is worth noting that the so-called "mundane" is also important, especially when perceived in its symbolic aspect—and that all of the best masters and magickians have a foot planted in both worlds. They are never proud or haughty about their spiritual achievements, as the wise person knows how much further there still is to go. Not until we are reabsorbed back into the Creative Intelligence in a pure and eternal state have we really reached the Goal.

Enochia

What on earth is Enochian magick? This is a good question. Many witches have heard of it (vaguely)—I even had a friend who wrote her magickal diary in its script, but she was pretty advanced. For most of us it has, erm, something to do with Crowley, and—isn't it connected with John Dee or something?

Enochian magick is a form of angelic communication formulated by the Elizabethan court alchemist, magickian, and philosopher Dr. John Dee, and his close associate Edward Kelley (see chapter 15, "Who Influenced the Witching World?" for more on John Dee). Not that the magi would have admitted more involvement than that of channels; the system and language that they skried (using a crystal and clairvoyance) was channeled through them, as far as they were concerned, and originated from the angel Ave, who delivered it to Enoch in ancient days. Dee and Kelley were simply acting as medium and scribe.

The idea of this language is to lead to the discovery of the key to the Universe—an aim for which Dee worked tirelessly. It contains twenty-two letters—a number that will be familiar to all Qabalists and Tarot adepts—with its own grammar and syntax. It is similar to the Hebrew one might logically connect it with, yet it is unique. The sound is primal, a chariot for psychic force. Base emotions may be turned into astral gold via its utterances.

It is unlikely that Dee and Kelley fully used the system channelled to them—records suggest that they barely comprehended it themselves. This is not surprising when one looks at the bizarre tablets and words of evocation that constitute Enochia. However, once again we find that the British Museum plays a crucial role in the preservation and propagation of magickal knowledge. The manuscripts were found there by MacGregor Mathers, and introduced into the ever-eclectic Golden Dawn system of magick.

In 1659, some of Dee and Kelley's divinations were published by one Meric Casaubon as *A True and Faithful Relation of What Passed between Dr. John Dee and Some Spirits.* It is a somewhat sarcastic publication that echoed the thoughts of many of Dee's contemporaries—that he was at best deluded, at worst a charlatan. One wonders whether George Eliot based her equally sarcastic, megarational character Mr. Casaubon of *Middlemarch,* with his painfully rational and "labyrinthine mind," on this disdainful author.

Mathers seems to have had a boundless capacity for belief. He selected from a mediaeval codice here, an Elizabethan magickal tract there, and put them all together to create both the (Second Order) Golden Dawn system of magick, and a body of esoterica he would most likely not have employed himself for ethical reasons, but in which he had indubitable belief—*The Key of Solomon the King,* for example. He, and Crowley courtesy of *The Equinox* (1914), brought Dee and Kelley's ideas back into the public eye. Mathers incorporated Enochian magick into the Golden Dawn's Second Order Curriculum, transforming Dee's work into a potent system of practical magick.

Dee's ideas were again exposed by Israel Regardie in his four-volume epic *The Golden Dawn,* in 1937–1940. The main Enochian elements were the Four Watchtowers (elemental attributes and tables) and the Tablet of Union.

Enochia itself involves a complex language, the Twelve Zodiacal Gates, Thirty Aethyrs (spirits of air, and more), angelic calls, and an elaborate cosmology. These are revealed in *The Stegonographia,* still extant today.

The interested reader is referred to *Golden Dawn Enochian Magic* by Pat Zalewski (Llewellyn, 1994) for starters; it is a text less intimidating than many others. Many other esoteric texts contain references, direct or otherwise, to the ground-breaking and, frankly, quite perplexing work of Dee and Kelley. Yet it worked for them, as it has for others. The system is indubitably authentic and effective.

Evocation

Evoking the senses of yourself and others can be helpful in witchcraft. It is, of course, a handy prop to imagination and creative visualisation. It is also binding, as qualities such as scent and colour affect everyone concerned. Below is an example of sensual evocation used in a spell. It is one of Domestic Goddess Syd Moore's handy household tips.

WASHING UP SPELL

This spell will get your partner or roommates to be tidier around the house.

Perform this spell on a day on which all members of the household are either in or expected home in the evening.

This is a two-stage spell. The first step is to ensure the bonds between the occupants of your household remain harmonious.

If you know how to bake bread, great. If not, buy a bread mix. The point of the exercise is in the kneading and aroma of the bread rather than in the origins of the dough.

Once you have made up your dough, place it on a floured surface to "rest" for five minutes. Now comes stage two.

Take one purple candle and one white, either pre-scented, or embalmed with an appetizing oil such as orange or vanilla. As you anoint the candles, think about your aim in achieving fair distribution of labour in your household. Put one on either side of the dough, and light them.

Concentrate on the pleasure that the aroma and sharing of the bread will bring to your fellow occupants. Imagine hot butter melting onto the warm bread, turning it from something plain into something pleasurable, just as their added effort will increase everybody's enjoyment of the household. See the dough glowing with a warm, golden aura.

Knead this light into the dough. Shape it into a loaf, and bake.

Take the candles from the floured surface, and place them on either side of the sink. Put on some cheerful music.

Now wash up the utensils you have used to bake the bread. As you wash up, imagine the exotic smell of the candles combining with the delicious and wholesome smell of baking bread drifting out of the kitchen and hooking the relevant individuals. Reel them in mentally. Imagine them at the sink, cheerfully washing up, and going about the house cleaning.

When it is ready, remove the bread from the oven, and snuff out the candles. Invite your fellow occupants to join you in eating the loaf. Share it while it is still warm. They will not be able to resist.

Familiars

A familiar is a spirit that helps one on the invisible planes. He or she is also a companion and magickal colleague. It is the witch's own special worker—"familiar" because it refers to her for its instructions, and sometimes relies on her for its sustenance.

Some saints had familiars, a fact not often recognised by Christians. As William Bloom points out in his ceremonial diary *The Sacred Magician* (Gothic Image Publications, 1992):

> Jerimiah 20, x (INRI is being mocked for prophesying): ". . . All my familiars watched for my halting, saying, Peradventure he will be enticed, and we shall prevail against him, and we shall take our revenge on him." Here is admitted, for the first time, that a prophet of God has familiars.

The idea of personalised astral helpers is common to many religions, including Islam, Hinduism, and, of course, Voodoo. However, the white witch differs in her view of familiars to those just mentioned and to the magickian. She does not wish to enslave a spirit, as she believes in "harming none." She will be holistic in her view of familiars, taking the qualities a spirit offers naturally in its liberty, rather than forcing it to task. While a magickian might trap an elemental, say, and attempt to have it work for him, or another spirit such as an advanced animal (spirits on this level are often an amalgam of characteristics), the Wiccan and ethical witch will work carefully with her own cat, toad, or dog, sensing its moods, and using these as a natural touchstone. The rapport that can grow up between witch and cat is too well-known to require embellishment here.

I used to have a cat called Bagpuss, a lovely boy with black fur and a naturally sensitive soul. He was my familiar, as far as I was concerned. Then, one day, a witch friend came round—a Thelemite actually—and said of Bagpuss: "Why don't you put a familiar in him?"

I was shocked. "But he already *is* my familiar," I replied.

"No, he's just a cat," said she.

Needless to say, she wanted me to oust my lovely cat-friend and give his body to a "higher-level" spirit. I was not impressed.

This same witch had several familiars, all—as far as I could tell—under her duress. She had summoned, subdued, and imprisoned them in her power. They worked effectively for her, without a doubt, but imagine what underlying resentment was being caused every time she commanded them to a task! Not nice karma to be working up.

Still, I must admit to being rather glamoured by this witch. She reminded me of an Austin Osman Spare painting, with faces, auras, and dim outlines appearing, shimmering in the ether all around her. She knew what she was doing, which was just as well, considering the type of entities she was invoking. A Wiccan is more likely to convoke, especially when it comes to familiars. A Wiccan or white witch would rather work with a willing, free spirit than a scared or angry one. It makes for better magick in the end.

Familiars we might recognise from art and history include toads, goats, dogs, pigs, bats, and of course cats. I knew one witch who had a cow familiar (disembodied, of course!), which may sound silly, but when we stop to consider the symbolism of the cow in say, ancient Egypt (Isis-Hathor, wise and magickal, fecund and nurturing), or in Hinduism (supreme symbol of the beneficence of the Goddess), the choice becomes a little clearer.

It is, of course, possible to befriend a spirit, and work with it. There are still rules affecting the degree of our interaction, but is this a bad thing? There are laws and boundaries for reasons far greater than our small intelligence can begin to comprehend. Often, the Black Witch looks like a despotic brat to higher level consciousness. If he or she tries to bend Universal laws of balance, and treads on others' psychic toes to attain a selfish end, lack of holistic intelligence is clearly in evidence.

This is the lowest level of magick. Unfortunately, it can also be one of the most fascinating, as the results are often so immediate. Disaster usually ensues. More magick has to be brought in to counterbalance bad effects already built up. On and on it goes, until the fantasy castle crumbles and crushes its architect.

An effective witch will always thank her familiars for their services, whether this be guarding her home (familiars make excellent protectors of property), or alerting her to bad spirits or persons. As in any friendship, it is a case of give and take.

The best way to attract a familiar is to work with those you already have and who seem willing, or to perform a ritual to request a suitable spirit. Convocation is the key, rather than invocation. Do not command—be aware of it as a mutual agreement. You must give as much as you receive. The higher your motives, the higher the level of entity you will attract. I do not recommend summoning an elemental. This is possible, but not advisable until one is truly adept. The best spirits to work with are carnate or disembodied animal spirits, most of whom are a great deal more intelligent than one might expect. Simply requesting them to come forward, perhaps with a small ritual, will work wonders. Be careful, however, to specify your needs, lest you end up with every animal spirit in the vicinity in your room. I had that once, and it was utter chaos! Treat it as a job application, with you as the benevolent employer. Limit the number of "applicants" to your precise requirements.

Always remember that you are your familiar's familiar.

Fetches

One meaning of the word *fetch* in witchcraft is escort and messenger to the High Priestess. However, it is more usually a reference to the astral body sent out to perform a specific function or task. Dion Fortune makes much of this technique in her fiction, particularly in *The Secrets of Doctor Taverner,* in which Dr. Taverner and his trusty assistant frequently take to the astral plane in search of information. This, of course, relates to the section on astral magick.

Ingenuity

Ingenuity is a prime mover in much modern magick. With our ability to use ingredients from the world over both in philosophy and in practise, items such as non-native herbs and gemstones often become involved in spells. There's nothing new there, in some respects—magickal ingredients have always been exotic. Their value and rarity empowers the working.

The modern witch has the riches of the world at her fingertips. She may engage in creative magick as never before. Spells have become even more diverse, and their ingredients more eclectic. The following is one example.

SPELL FOR WELL-BEING

Bearing in mind reservations one might have about gems being mined unethically, it is still possible to pick those up that haven't been. However, as with all magickal paraphernalia, the intention is everything, and the instrument simply a prop. It is always best to improvise spells to your own ethical standpoint, and to use the props that mean something to you, or that you simply like.

This edible spell is especially effective in summer when the fruits are naturally available, but thanks to aeroplanes and international commerce (which have their good points as well as bad), it can now be performed in the dead of winter.

Take a bunch of bananas, four oranges, one lemon, and one lime. Then a little of each fruit oil, or just orange if the others are hard to find.

Every manifestation of life has its properties on the psychic planes, and these fruits and their oils represent prosperity (banana, orange), luck (orange, lemon), love (orange), clarity of thought (lemon, lime), perception (lemon, lime), friendship (orange, lemon), purification (lemon, lime), and optimism (banana, orange, lime). This is a certain recipe for spiritual, mental, and physical abundance! This simple technique is best performed on a Thursday when the moon is waxing.

Place each of the fruits in front of its relative oil. As you view each, concentrate a ray of yellow-orange light into it. Project your visions of abundance, and what that entails for you, into each fruit and oil in turn until you can "see" them glowing with your optimism.

Now take a piece of danburite (pale yellow/gold), a piece of citrine (pale yellow/orange/misty), and a piece of seraphinite (white). All of these are widely available from New Age stores. However, if you cannot find them, quartz crystal or rose quartz will do, or any other small objects that represent positive things to you. A favoured pendant will be just as good, if not better.

Still visualising the bright orange-yellow light of abundance flowing all around you with your fruits and their oils as the focus, begin to anoint the danburite with the orange oil. Concentrate on optimism, happiness, and steadiness as you do so.

Now take the citrine and anoint it with a little of the lemon and lime oils. As you do so, focus on clarity of purpose, determination, and the confidence to attain all that you desire.

Finally, anoint the seraphinite with the banana oil. Whilst so doing, consider the link between the spiritual planes and the material. Spiritual prosperity can manifest material abundance if we so direct it.

Wrap the three scented, charged gemstones in a silk scarf of bright yellow or gold and put it in your pocket.

Chop up the fruit, still concentrating your orange-gold light into it, and create a fruit salad. Add any extra fruits and ingredients you may wish to.

As you eat the salad and/or share it with family and friends, remember the abundance-bringing properties of each fruit. Make sure to eat it all up and do not leave it to fester in the fridge if you leave any! This is a symbol of the nourishment offered by the Universe, and all must be "absorbed." By taking it into your physical body, you are "earthing" its properties.

See Syd Moore's section in chapter 21, "The Witch's Cauldron," for other edible, feel-good psychic techniques.

Invocation

Invocation is a way of seeking higher aid, and connecting with a god, goddess, or spirit helper. The subject is vast, and I have covered many specific aspects of linking with the Divine in my other books.

Basically, in order to work with deities or spirits, it is best to read up on them, attune yourself with them, and select symbols and props that are connected with them. This principle can be used imaginatively, as the following example indicates.

Two of my friends were trying to conceive. After six years of marriage, they remained childless.

The husband was reading a book at the time on male archetypes: the Magician, the King, the Lover, and the Warrior (*The Magician Within* by Robert Moore and Douglas Gillette). This gave him the idea of looking for a deity who was appropriate to his needs. In response to what he felt he needed spiritually, psychologically, and physically, he identified Cernunnos as a suitable potential godform and helper.

After some meditation, he decided to get Cernunnos's image from the Danish Gundestrup Cauldron (second century B.C.E.) tattooed onto his back. Five months later, his partner was pregnant—with a boy.

We are waiting to see whether he emerges with antlers.

Music in Magick

As with verbal spellcraft, the use of music prior to or during a ritual is powerful indeed. Essentially, it is part of psyching oneself up and affecting the atmosphere with various rhythms and vibrations. For this reason, the type of music you choose as an entrée or accompaniment to your spell should be exactly suited to the frame of mind you seek to achieve. Anything you find inspirational is ideal.

Many witches and Wiccans like to create their own ceremonial music, or join together in the chanting along with bell and drum.

Music can also be used in a more specific manner—for example, relating it to the Qabalistic sephiroth. I begin to give examples in the "555" section of *Magick of Qabalah,* and one day would love to compile an occultist's CD of effective spell-casting/creative-musing music. See the chapter on Qabalah for ideas on what types of spells relate to which sephirah.

Buddhist chants have the effect of "vacuuming" the atmosphere—by which I do not mean turning it into a vacuum, but rather, clearing out what is unwanted and purifying it. Ritualistic music is obviously the best for magick, but its nature comes down to the preferences and needs of the individual witch. I am fond of baroque, and to me—though I would never use them in ritual—Pergolesi's *Magnificat in C Major,* Vivaldi's *Magnificat in G Minor,* and Handel's *Dixit Dominus* are good examples of music that can get me in the mood for higher things, give or take the odd, irritating "Gloria" and "Hallelujah." Nothing's completely perfect, I suppose, but some parts of these pieces are sublime.

For many these might be too imbued with Christianity to be helpful, though the fact that they're in Latin certainly helps. (Handel's *Messiah* loses much to me for being in English.) What we're seeking is the sacred/effective atmosphere rather than the orthodox religion itself. After all, all paths lead to the Light eventually—we simply do not wish to be bogged down by their specific correspondences.

On a more contemporary level, the darkwave genre is often favoured by occultists, including this one. With its weird or wild melodies, angst-filled dissonances, and often esoteric lyrics, it can be just the thing to create an atmosphere suitable for magick. Rhythm is also all-important. Thus, tracks such as "Cantus" by Faith and the Muse are ideal for building an inspired, ritualistic mindset, while Current 93, Dead Can Dance (or Lisa Gerrard alone, or with Pieter Bourke), Coil, and Bel Canto, for example, can be good for developing a mystical atmosphere. For getting in the mood for Geburic magick (such as protection against psychic or physical attack) and hex-breaking, nu (or old) metal bands are obviously apt, though this could equally be Wagner. It all comes down to taste.

Music in another tongue is often good, as its lyrics do not distract with logical connections. Others may prefer something more upbeat, or more extreme. Diamanda Galas's pained shriekings can also hardly fail to produce a powerful atmosphere. One of my friends immerses himself in Tom Waite's guttural and whiskey-soaked doldrums prior to ritual, yet always seems completely energised.

There is much New Age music around, apparently designed for the same purpose—chakra-cleansing, whale-song, American Indian chantings interspersed with flaky keyboard melodies. I have yet to discover one that I would like to recommend, but again, it is a question of personal taste. Use exactly what gets you feeling empowered in your cause.

In short, music in magick is a mood thing—part generic, part personal.

Poetry and Spellcraft

Bind fast the spell every time,
Let the words be spoke in rhyme.

Poetry has many virtues, as most witches will readily acknowledge. The poet casts a rhythmical, visual spell on the reader or listener. Even if the content of the poem is purely fantastical, such as the gothic landscapes of Poe or the languishing Pre-Raphaelite bowers of Tennyson, the poet creates exactly what the magickian requires: a strong visual image imbued with atmosphere and charged with emotion. By painting their scenes with the brush of pathetic fallacy, these poets have a ready-made internal landscape on which to work their magick. They are describing emotional, spiritual, and psychological states; in other words, exactly how things appear on the astral plane. Once this image is perceived and accessed, it may be altered. The witch and the writer both require the ability to visualise this realm of symbolic truth. The literary witch has a flying head-start over her sisters, knowing as she does how to manipulate sound and image and create a spell of astonishing verbal and astral power.

Verse has been used to convey knowledge since time immemorial. It was used in Druidic culture to establish magickal lore in a mnemonic format; poems such as the *Cad Goddeu* (*The Battle of the Trees*) list the esoteric properties of woods and groves, an essential body of knowledge to the ancient practitioner. Robert Graves's *The White Goddess* furnishes us with a translation roughly equivalent to the original, each verse reiterating the virtues and the vices of various dryads. For example:

The birch, though very noble,
Armed himself but late:
A sign not of cowardice
But of high estate.

The poem not only tells a story, helping to fix the facts in the minds of the listeners, but its characteristic metre captivates the attention of bard and listener alike. It is often sung, as in folk music, so the tale also attaches itself to another part of our memories. Words conjoined to music double the pleasure of their audience.

Chants, likewise, fixate the listener. They build up a majestically powerful, often spine-tingling atmosphere—a sure sign of energy rising. In ancient Greek plays, for example, the chorus and characters would chant their lines in what may well have been a low monotone with occasional crescendos; one can imagine what a menacing accompaniment this provided to the tragedies of Medea or Oedipus, for example. Rhythm and pitch are powerful ritual tools indeed.

Many ancient religions employed poetic techniques either to access divine knowledge (the Pythias of Apollo used to deliver their answers in hexameters or iambic pentameters), or to implore the gods and raise power (primitive cultures are renowned for their chanting and dancing for this purpose). A good prayer in any language is rhythmical and meditative, Hindu and Buddhist cultures having honed this fact to a fine mantric art. I once had the privilege of entering a temple of Durga during a ritual, when the Brahmans were chanting around the fires at the altar. I found myself almost catapulted onto the astral plane, so intense was the power in the room. The atmosphere was physically vibrating in exact accordance with the energy the priests were invoking. It was tense and crackling with psychic electricity. These effects are emulated by the witch.

A good working knowledge of literature and art cannot be underestimated in witchcraft. The study of the verbal/written word will prove particularly effective. Let us look now at some samples of powerful writing, the techniques of which we might emulate in spellcraft.

One of the most obvious sources of effective wordcraft is William Shakespeare. The witches of *Macbeth* chant a spell any schoolchild can remember:

Double, double, toil and trouble,
Fire burn, and cauldron bubble.
Fillet of a fenny snake
In the cauldron boil and bake;

Eye of newt, and toe of frog,
Wool of bat and tongue of dog,
Adder's fork, and blind-worm's sting,
Lizard's leg and owlet's wing,
For a charm of powerful trouble,
Like a hell-broth, boil and bubble.
Double, double, toil and trouble;
Fire burn and cauldron bubble.

What are the effective techniques used in this poetic spell? Despite being an extract of a play, it works equally, like much of Shakespeare's work, out of context. As a spell, the piece has many favourable characteristics. It is simple and methodical: the fire burns and the cauldron bubbles, then one by one, the ingredients are added to the potion. The vivid names of the herbs and parts help establish a strong mental image of the witches' intent, and chanting them helps invoke their properties. One by one, the images are added and layered, just as the listed ingredients are placed in the cauldron to contribute their formidable properties to the brew.

Rhythm is the key to all chanted spells. The one above is an example of an effective chant, as the rhythm remains consistent throughout. This allows the actress/witch to concentrate on the imagery, supported as it is by the strong skeleton of repetitive metre. Its simplicity gives it a childlike sound; it has a playground rhythm of inevitability, just as the results of the working are inevitable. The desired effects are etched onto the subconscious with this chant, promising to come to pass with startling effect. Shakespeare, of course, was employing this sense of potent menace to create dramatic effect, but the witch can use such techniques as she deems fit.

The power of the spell is thickened by the superimposition of a ritual of, in this case, malign intent on a guileless-sounding metre. However, even if the spell were positive, the device would work, adding as it does an air of absolute ease to what is in fact a contrivance of circumstance. The witch works with nature, yes, but she uses her will to manipulate its energies.

Another effective device is the repetition of key words and phrases. "Double" repeated twice at the opening of the spell establishes the aim: to augment the "toil and trouble" they wish to cause for Macbeth. The latter phrase is also repeated twice, and mutated into "powerful trouble" for extra emphasis when the witches repeat the aim of the spell. To increase this factor further, there are internal rhymes: "double" rhymes with both "trouble" and "bubble," creating an onomatopoeic boiling sound. These words are repeated thrice during the spell, reflecting the number of witches present and the three major Goddess phases: Maiden, Mother, and Crone. Roman Polanski's film of the Scottish play features a nubile alongside two hags, one of whom is blind, like Tiresias the Grecian prophet and many other "internal seers." Their performance of this spell is unnerving indeed. Three is also, of course, the number of Hecate, goddess of witches, as Shakespeare knew.

Hecate makes a direct impact in the imagery of several of Shakespeare's works, including that more uplifting play, *A Midsummer Night's Dream*. In one of Puck's speeches, we witness another example of potent spellcraft, this time describing an atmosphere rather than directly performing magick:

> *Now the hungry lion roars,*
> *And the wolf behowls the moon;*
> *Whilst the heavy ploughman snores,*
> *All with the weary task fordone,*
> *Now the wasted brands do glow,*
> *Whilst the screech-owl, screeching loud,*
> *Puts the wretch that lies in woe*
> *In remembrance of a shroud.*
> *Now it is the time of night*
> *That the graves, all gaping wide,*
> *Every one lets forth his sprite,*
> *In the church-way paths to glide:*
> *And we fairies that do run*
> *By the triple Hecate's team,*
> *From the presence of the sun,*
> *Following darkness like a dream,*
> *Now are frolic; not a mouse*
> *Shall disturb this hallow'd house;*
> *I am sent with broom before,*
> *To sweep the dust behind the door.*

Like the extract from *Macbeth,* this speech is written in rhyme with a compelling rhythm of eight stresses. It opens with fantastical imagery—lions not being native to England, nor wolves by the Elizabethan era—which immediately sets the ordinary physical referents awry; but they are picked up again by the reference to the "heavy ploughman" and "wasted brands." "Triple Hecate's team" flee daylight for the lunar realms of dreams one moment, and housework is being done the next.

Clearly we are entering a world in which dream and reality exist in equal measure; a liminal state in which fairies and humans are able to perceive one another, even to interact. However, from a human standpoint, this may be alarming. Puck tells us so with his references to the "screech-owl, screeching loud," the "shroud," and of course, the "graves, all gaping wide." Again, the simple, childlike rhythm works to highlight these references. There is no great build-up; we are told that graves gape as if it were the most natural thing in the world. We accept it, presented as it is in this guileless manner.

Spells constructed in this style may look rather gauche to those of us with a penchant for ritual flourishes, but clarity is the backbone of any effective working. It is essential to create a clear runnel for will, and for application of that will. Complex spells will merely distract, which is where spellcraft and poetry part ways. Nobody could accuse T. S. Eliot, for example, of being simple, but his poetry indubitably works. Magickally, it lacks the compelling metre we witness in these extracts of Shakespeare. It is cerebral and psychological, with emotions tightly contained in most places. Spells need to be simple and emotive. Their words of power are points between levels. Their rhythm must bring the practitioner naturally to that liminal crossover.

Another key point is lack of ambivalence. Spells will backfire if their meaning is not perfectly clear—a second argument for simplicity. Many High Magick rituals include invocations in Hebrew and Latin. The latter is easier to pronounce, but in both cases, there is much scope for error. Latin runs the risk of becoming a hollow incantation if the meaning of the words is not fully understood. Hebrew, like any other language, may be mispronounced unless one is fluent. As intonation is important in such scenarios, it is best to stick to one's mother tongue.

Written spells, however, are a different matter. The Hebrew alphabet, for example, has a wealth of relevance to Qabalistic/magickal pursuits, and it is easy to establish what means what without running the risk of incorrect enunciation. Alphabets such as runic or Enochian may also be employed.

Spells are always designed with the purpose in mind. For example, a dwindling spell might be written down as such:

Abracadabra
Abracadabr
Abracadab
Abracada
Abracad
Abraca

Abrac
Abra
Abr
Ab
A

A spell of this nature would be performed on ten consecutive nights. The first night would involve full ritual and speech, with a little less on the second day, and so on to the bare minimum of the tenth night. The words themselves would most likely be written on a piece of paper and kept as a charm by the subject of a spell. This would usually be for the purposes of combating fever or illness.

Some modern poets have employed spell-making techniques in their poetry. New Zealand poet Jeni Couzyn, for example, uses compelling commands reminiscent of much tribal magick in her "Summoning Spell for a Fish":

By the white sun's chill
By the dancing of the reeds
By the ripple's pull
Come to my hook

By the tang of your flesh
By the gleam of your skin
By your web of bone

By the shriek of my line
By the drone of my reel
By the blind maggot's spasm
Come to my hook

The rhythm urges, and the imagery creates a scenario the fish cannot escape. The fisher-poet is everywhere—and by each of these aspects, she has caught her prey. Even the body of the fish itself is infiltrated by the will of the spellmaker: "By the tang of your flesh." The spell continues with further description and commands and ends with the final word "Come."

I went to hear Jeni Couzyn read her poetry in 1987. I was a very flamboyant-looking, deeply nervous teenager at the time, extremely interested in the occult, and already attempting Qabalistic invocations and so forth on my own in my room.

I had no idea that Jeni Couzyn was connected with witchcraft or spell-making, I simply went on an excursion with the Poetry Club, of which I was a member.

I sat and listened to the attractive woman in black, who wore a silver Maori whale pendant about her neck, which gleamed in the spotlights, and fell into a sort of hypnotic trance. I was listening intently, and became caught up in her imagery and the rhythms of her words. Naturally, this should occur at any good poetry reading, but this one was different. It was not that she was reading anything overtly magickal (much of it was not), but the words were powerful—they were spells, blatant or not. At the end of the reading, to my intense embarrassment, I fainted. Nobody was more shocked than the poet herself, but I understand it better now. She represented much that was to come to me later—and I was naturally highly susceptible to the magickal influence exerted by her poetry. However, when I tried to reintegrate it into my everyday life (which was restricted and miserable at the time), I encountered a terrible culture clash that caused me to faint. Jeni Couzyn had brought into my life wide magickal landscapes and intricate knowledge of spellcraft that recalled much but was impossible to digest at the time. Never doubt the power of poetry!

There is an interesting section in Robin Skelton's book *Spellcraft: A Manual of Verbal Magic* on the work of Jeni Couzyn and Kathleen Raine and its relationship with magick. I recommend it to any interested in this fascinating aspect of the Craft.

So, spoken spells are an art worth learning. To write your own is infinitely more powerful than to quote, though there are some good ones around. The effective spoken spell contains:

- A suitable metre, which either commands, compels, augments, or dwindles, depending on the nature of the working.

- Words of power—perhaps god names of relevance to the spell-caster's intent.

- Repetition of key phrases or commands.

- Simplicity; if a child could learn it, it's good.

- Internal rhymes and other techniques to create a suitable aural environment for the spell. For example, a spell for cleansing might contain a great many sibilant swishing sounds, like water. Onomatopoeia is powerful for sympathetic magick, creating the right mental images in the mind of the practitioner.

Practical Magick, with Props

The standard paraphernalia of the witch are listed in chapter 17, "A Witch's Working Tools." However, it is possible to invest any object with magickal intent, as exemplified by the following sexual attraction spell.

GARMENT SPELL

Invest an item of clothing or jewellery with specific powers—for example, a garter, pendant, or even your favourite cardigan, jumper, or dress. This specific technique is for clothes.

When the moon is waxing or full, cast a Circle (see chapter 18, "Magickal Techniques and Spell-casting") surrounded by candles, so that you have a circle of light. These should be red, orange, and pink.

Place your censer at the center of the Circle. Burn a loose incense that includes musky, sweet, and sensual ingredients such as jasmine, rose, sandalwood, coriander, and loveage (this smells very little, but is traditionally associated with amorous attraction). As it burns, watch the smoke weave skywards. Pick up the garment, and hold it above the censer so that the smoke wraps around it and imbues it with its musky perfume.

Take a golden thread and a needle and pass both through the incense. Then thread the needle, and as you do this, think of the thread weaving out into the ether, lassoing and pulling your potential lover back towards your garment.

Using a minimum number of backstitches, embroider a pentacle no bigger than a cent in a discreet place on your item of clothing.

Close the Circle, and wear the garment for that special occasion.

Psychic Self-Protection

Dion Fortune's book of this title deals with ways to protect yourself from psychic attack. Not only that, but it gives some fascinating examples of psychic onslaughts and is an extremely entertaining read. It is recommended to any witches or practising occultists who do not already have it as a cornerstone of their library.

You may wonder, *If we are practising ethical magick, then why is psychic self-protection necessary?* It is not necessarily that we are likely to come under direct magickal attack, though there are some pretty warped people and entities out there. Still, such a scenario is unlikely. What is far more probable is *inadvertent* attack. It happens to people all the time, and the more receptive the recipient, the more damage may be done—accidentally.

One of the downsides of being magickally active, or simply an interesting, forward-forging individual of any persuasion, is the inevitable antipathy and resentment encountered at some point in others. Being a kind and loving friend makes no difference (except that one's conscience is clear); envy is a many-headed beast and can even rear up under the disguise of a well-loved, familiar face. If the friend concerned is of a witchy persuasion, and not as white as we might have thought, trouble looms. Even if he or she is not, subconscious urges may cause the offended party to "throw black" at us.

I've noticed that if I get depressed right before my period, I rarely take the logical approach—"Oh, that's all right, it's obviously my hormones affecting me." Instead, I find myself focussing on the things that are going wrong—needless to say, not a good approach. It is as if a veil descends over the inner eye, distorting all perceptions, especially psychological and "cosmic." The same thing can happen with psychic attack. Every other possibility seems more likely. You have cross words with a friend, perhaps, or give him or her news that, unbeknownst to you, he or she resents: "Did I tell you my new book's about to come out? And I'm dating this incredibly cute twenty-year-old at the moment. Everything's going really well."

A happy friend, of course, would be delighted to learn of this; but one who is down, whose self-esteem is at a low ebb, might be tempted to see it as boastful, or to project his or her own insecurities at you, thinking, "That patronising witch, she thinks I'm a failure," or some such thought. You, being innocent of all this, put down the receiver or leave the meeting-place and—bang!—things start to go wrong.

It's happened to me more than once. I like to have friends who are powerful witches—obviously—but powerful witches are necessarily emotional. We can't all float around being ever-compassionate and kind (more's the pity)—life would be easier, but it's just not the way we were created. We need negativity to elevate us, it seems. But what when depression sets in, and introspection kicks off?

Dion Fortune talks of the dangers of natural psychics in *Psychic Self-Defense:*

> Very many people who are at present psychics and sensitives got their training in the covens of mediaeval witchcraft, and for this reason experienced occultists are very wary of the natural psychic, as distinguished from the initiate with his technique of psychism. Where psychism and mental unbalance are found conjoined with a malevolent disposition, there is a strong presumption that the cult of Diablous is not far to seek.

It's easy to be too naïve in this arena; I often am. It may be difficult to believe that a person would wish ill on another (unless the person's crime totally credits it—and we're talking major issues here)—especially a dear friend—but it can happen. The person might not channel it as such—perhaps he or she has not reached the voodoo dolly stage just yet—but it is amazing what evil can be perpetuated by an occultist in a bad mood when he or she is daydreaming or sleeping—especially if the person is spending a lot of time alone.

Having negative energy thrown at one is not fun. This may occur with strangers or friends alike. People are storehouses of electricity, and the emotions govern their switches. A bolt from another person, for whatever reason, can throw us right off our balance.

There is a strong argument in favour of simply letting this be. After all, we do not want to become immune to the thoughts and feelings of others. We need practise in dealing with damage too—a sort of internal immunisation program. However, if somebody is having a continually negative effect—either being hurtful, or vamping your energy (you know those friends who leave you exhausted after an hour or two, for no obvious reason)—it is time to do something about it.

There are two simple ways to protect yourself. One is kind, the other unkind. The latter is the easiest: you mirror the energy back at the sender. That's what I've always done—it really works. There's nothing more satisfying than knowing that the sender's resentment is self-thwarting. It's not particularly nice, but I'm no angel and would never claim to be. I've tried "returning hatred with a blessing" in the past—a very Christian attitude—and found that I was simply trampled over roughshod. No, a witch needs her defense. If that's as simple as reflecting energy right back, all the better.

The other technique, if you want to be nice and save the sender from his or her own vitriol, is to stabilise yourself by using a technique such as the Qabalistic Cross, a simple self-centering meditation (such as sitting cross-legged before a candle and reminding yourself who you are, how strong you are, etc.), or whatever else centres you (a walk in the park, listening to music—you decide). You then establish a stance so loving that nothing can penetrate it. This might be envisaged as an armour of fire. It will have to be invested with a great deal of positive energy, calling upon the gods and goddesses of compassion (such as Tara, Krishna, Jesus) to fortify you against "the slings and arrows of outrageous fortune," outrageous friends, and random malice. You would then strongly visualise the streams of negativity being consumed by the unquenchable flames. If supernice, you could then transmute it into positive energy and send that back, but an elevated soul is required to really manage this. There's no point in doing that and then wishing forever after that you'd simply said your piece when you had the chance.

The best form of psychic self-defence is utter self-confidence and belief in the power of Good over Evil. I realise this sounds very Christian, but there are pernicious forces in the Universe—pernicious to "right growth and right living." There *is* right and wrong, and there *is* a moral code in the Universe.

It follows, then, that there are guardians of us poor half-blind mortals as we feel our way across the planes, and as we live our daily lives, particularly as witches and occultists. There is only so far that we are able to go wrong, psychically speaking, and actually asking for one's spirit guides to step forward increases the chances of active protection. There are books available on meeting your guides, such as *Opening to Channel* by Sanaya Roman and Duane Packer (H. J. Kramer Inc., 1986). However, practically everyone (if not everyone) has spirit guides who will help in times of crisis, asked or not. The exception, of course, is when those things happen that are necessary for personal development. Some say that these are "prearranged" before birth. This stance brings up the whole big argument about whether we can excuse bad things happening, and so on, which I do not intend to go into here. The point is, however, that we have protection even when we are not aware of it.

Much psychic attack is allowed by the victim. Dwelling on a harmful person, scene, or cycle of thoughts, of course, makes us vulnerable. Old-fashioned Voodoo revenge spells worked like this, by transfixing the mind through fear. Concentrating on one's own strength, integrity, and ability has the opposite effect. Polluting thoughts and experiences can be shed ritually with the aid of a salt bath, or simply by walking through purifying incense (such as sage) and mentally grounding the negative energy. Purification baths (or showers) are particularly effective. Taking these precautions regularly should stop undue negativity from affecting one's day-to-day life.

When working magick, the best form of protection is the Circle. I explain how to cast one earlier in this chapter. Not only does the Circle protect, but it also intensifies the energies evoked and creates a cross-dimensional sphere of activity. I believe it foolish to attempt magick without one, unless you were born into another school of magickal thought.

A traditional occult method of psychic self-protection is to enlist the aid of the four guardian angels: Raphael, Gabriel, Michael, and Uriel. Writer/occultists such as Gareth Knight can furnish the interested reader with traditional methods for this and many other operations. Alternately, you could envisage yourself surrounded by cosmic energies, as follows.

SIMPLE PSYCHIC SELF-PROTECTION TECHNIQUE

First, face the east. Send a request to the Cosmic Intelligence that your application for protection will be heeded. Do not continue until you truly feel that it will be. (This can prevent haphazard workings when you subconsciously know that the time is not right.)

Now, envisage a pillar of radiant yellow light before you. Feel how it shields you from face-on attack.

Behind you, sense a powerful pillar of blue, protective light.

To your left, a vibrant pillar of red vigilance stands your guard.

To the right, a black pillar prevents negative forces from reaching you.

Starting with the yellow pillar, visualise a ring of blue flame reaching out and catching the red pillar; let it spread to the blue and black and back to the red until you are completely surrounded by a circle of fire, keeping off the wild beasts of the cosmos and acting as a beacon to benevolent entities. Seal the tube with blue fire beneath the feet and above the head.

Another means of protection is courtesy of one's personal guardian(s). It is definitely easiest if you already know who your Inner Guides are (for example, a bona fide guru—few and far between on this plane—or an enlightened being such as an avatar of Christ-consciousness: Buddha, a Krishna embodiment, or even "the Master Jesus," if you are so inclined). I am not talking the suburban myth of these godforms, but their true, vibrant selves, very unlike the mundane expression we have constructed for them. Only you can know whether or not you have the energy, purity, and visual ability to make a true, noncomplacent link with such Great Ones. A regular godform is less effective, as these are specific to particular qualities. Only those who can be felt to have attained complete spiritual enlightenment are suitable consorts in every realm.

Never be afraid you are duping yourself, for when we create the appropriate channel, the gods come. As the magickal adage goes, "Fantasy is the ass that carries the Ark," and its asinine nature in no way detracts from the reality or potency of its load.

PSYCHIC SELF-PROTECTION II

Stand facing east, and take four deep, slow breaths, puffing out strongly and simultaneously envisaging all the tension leaving your body in dark billows, while your lungs begin to glow golden from the inside. With each breath, the glow increases until with the fourth exhalation your body is glowing brilliantly.

Now, tense and flex every muscle in your body, feeling the golden light creeping into its every tissue and bone as you do so. Soon your cells are alive with this vibrant prana.

Above you, the ceiling has turned a brilliant yellow-white; a crackling electricity has infused the room. Visualise the light strongly, so that your inner eye is dazzled. Feel the presence of the Divine Dreamer, the fusing of your two consciousnesses; feel the excitement of the vastness of this.

Imagine a door in the back of your head, in the lower region just above the neck. Now, draw the energy previously visualised down and in through this door, and wrap it right around your bodies, first on the inside, then, shutting the cranial gates, on the outside. Affirm that this energy is solid and pure, and that any negativity directed at it will bounce straight back at the sender. Visualise a bolt of black bouncing off the surface of your body-sheath. Be sure to concentrate on front, right side, back, left side, underneath, and overhead in turn. Let there be no part unprotected; let the golden light be ever renewable.

Now, unless you wish to be totally conspicuous on the Inner Planes, tone the colour and brilliance down, but maintain the resolution, leaving you armoured in dull silver-gold, with a warm feeling within.

Skrying

The word *skry* comes from the arcane verb "to escry." *Skrying* is now another word for divination. It usually involves looking into a dark mirror, crystal ball, smoke, or fire, and scrutinising the shapes and formations. This is, of course, a mere prop for intuition. Tea leaves cannot tell the future, but an adept psychic looking at tea leaves can. Likewise with Tarot and all other forms of divination. Skrying, however, tends to be less intellectual than Tarot or rune-reading; there are fewer set meanings (if any), and intuition takes the reins almost entirely. See chapter 13, "The Witch and Divination," for further details.

Shamanism

Shamanism is one of the most widely employed and famous forms of magick, particularly amongst Siberian and Ural-Altaic peoples. This tribal technique involves the selection of a medicine man or woman either through vocation, on a hereditary basis, or via a "vision quest." The job of the medicine man or woman is to travel to the spirit realms to discover the causes of any illnesses or adverse conditions affecting the community. In the astral body and persona of a totem animal such as a jaguar or bird of prey, the shaman locates the cause of the ill luck and attempts to bring change to pass. This involves entering a trance state, usually facilitated by the use of dance, rhythmic music, and drugs.

The process of initiation is key to shamanism. The vast body of knowledge that the shaman must absorb (the names and traits of spirits, healing and fighting techniques, languages of the animals, how best to walk between the worlds) is imparted by the tribal ancients in increments. This carries the potential shaman towards each process of assimilation of wisdom, otherwise known as initiation. This may manifest as a dream experience, or even of anti-social behaviour of the sort we in the West would consider neurotic. In many tribes, excessive solitude, epilepsy, fainting fits, and self-harm are all considered excellent signals of a potential shaman. Certainly it shows that the youth in question has more on his mind than the rest of the community. Similarly, freak accidents (such as being hit by lightning) are considered excellent indications of a person's special talents.

The explanation lies in the person being singled out by the spirits. The normal symptoms of adolescence—such as moodiness—are proof of a person's psychic attunement in these scenarios. So, the more extreme a personality, the better a shaman he or she will make. This facilitates an intense sense of life versus death, which is essential to the shaman. Every process of initiation is one of death and rebirth, as in other cultures. In shamanism, this often involves a period of physical sickness, in which the shaman lies for days, sometimes weeks, in a tent.

The visions involved follow a common pattern. The shaman feels that his or her body is torn apart by demons, limb by limb and scrap by scrap. Organs and body fluids are similarly removed. The shaman does battle with the spirits, and if successful, the body is gradually returned. Thus, the practitioner is literally deconstructed and reassembled, each portion consecrated by spiritual experience. He becomes fully aware of death in life, and able to operate on this side of the Veil and the other. Like the modern witch, the shaman will physically enact what he visualises astrally, interacting with the process in order to obtain a certain result. For example, if a person is ill, the shaman might wrestle the spirit of the illness or its cause, his actions reflecting this, or he might go on a quest to find the missing soul of the patient. Drumming, trance, visualisation, acting, and dance play a significant role in these processes.

Nowadays, there exists in the Pagan community many whose primary spiritual influences are shamanic. This usually denotes a relationship with tribal rather than mediaeval (alchemical, man-over-the-nature-of-the-beast) or modern (high magickal, Wiccan) magick. The latter forms are Renaissance-influenced; shamanic magick is more raw and more instinctual. However, many witches pick a totem animal and venture from their bodies in order to perform their magick, sometimes in the form of that animal, so the differences are in some ways not so great.

Sigilisation

Sigilisation is a technique expounded in its modern form by Austin Osman Spare (see his biography in chapter 15, "Who Influenced the Witching World?"). It involves the creation of a monogram from the first letter of each sentence of the magickian's intent, and the imprinting of this monogram on the subconscious through a sexual and/or emotional charge. The intent is then forgotten, and the monogram left somewhere where it will be seen by the practitioner in everyday situations. The idea is that this will act as a stimulus on the subconscious will. Obviously this is a form of self-hypnotism.

Spare frequently utilised this technique, and often incorporated his sigils with his artwork, making his canvasses living spells.

Traditional sigils are embodiments of the essence of a spirit, quality, or deity. These are often based on numerical correspondences of individual letters, which are joined to create a unique diagram believed to contain the essential nature of the entity concerned. This technique is especially popular in Hebrew-based magick.

Thus, sigils and monograms are concentrations of your desire in a symbolic form. They can be composed from magickal scripts such as runes, or from your spoken language. The normal technique is to write down your precise aim, and take the first letter from every word and combine them into a single symbol. Therefore they can be used in many ways. Below is one example.

SPELL FOR RIDDING ONESELF OF AN UNWANTED THOUGHT, MEMORY, OR INFLUENCE

If something or somebody's influence is blocking you, or you need to get over an upsetting situation, such as a split with a close friend, lover, or colleague, form a sigil out of a sentence such as "Rid me of pain I feel from _____." Take the *R, M, O, P, I, F,* and the first letter of the other person's name, and form these letters into a monogram. If any letter is repeated, only add it once.

Buy (or make) a bar of soap containing oils associated with auric cleansing, relaxation, and uplifting properties, such as lavender, orange, or rose. Carve your sigil into the soap, with your athame if you have one. Concentrate on your desire to rid your-self of this unwanted influence.

At the dark of the moon, or at night, take a bath and use the soap to cleanse yourself. As you wash your body and enjoy the scents of the soap, think about this person's influence dissolving. All the debris of your unwanted relationship and situation is sluiced away into the water. When you emerge from the bath, be sure to visualise yourself glowing with white light, having taken the first steps towards overcoming these difficulties. Repeat as necessary.

Sympathetic Magick

Sympathetic magick is the most primitive form of occult belief. The principle is that "like attracts like," so a "voodoo doll" or "fith-fath" representing a person (possibly embellished with hair, nail clippings, etc.) somehow "becomes" that person. The theory is that what happens to the doll also happens to the person concerned. Naturally this involves large amounts of visualisation, which is the essential point of creating a semblance. Pins stuck in the image are therefore believed to cause pain. Healing may be performed by "healing" the doll.

Another form of sympathetic magick involves attracting certain conditions by creating them in diminutive form. Rain magick is an obvious example, when rain-sticks made of wood filled with beans and pulses is tipped upside down to create the sound of falling rain. This is believed to attract actual raindrops—the "conditions" have been set. This principle is the root of much magick. "As Above, So Below" and vice versa—the microcosmic form takes on macrocosmic significance in the Circle (whether the Circle be literal or not).

Telepathy also plays a large part in this. The mind moves other mind-stuff, either in the outside world, or in the mind of another. If a strong psychic link already exists between two people (such as love, hatred, or dependency), sympathetic magick becomes easy. It is simply a question of causing a conducive frame of mind in the subject. The body always follows where the mind leads. This is the innate power of Voodoo (see section on Voodoo in chapter 14, "A Brief History of Witchcraft")—a fetish found under a pillow or in a garden will create hysterical fear in the mind of the victim. Belief in his or her own demise does the rest. (Naturally, this only applies when the magick is known of to its recipient. Often this is avoided, thus protecting the practitioner against retaliation from its subject or another voodoin.)

Technology in Magick

Technology can be used for divination when one has prepared the way with prior meditation and ritual, as can any medium in the search for symbols of significance. The ultramodern witch can also employ devices such as e-mail and text messaging as tools of her trade. These relate to the idea of Script of Power, particularly the e-mail, as words have an amazing impact when sent this way. There's a good reason that so many people are addicted to the Internet. E-mail has emotional clout.

E-MAIL SPELL

This is a very simple one-on-one e-mail spell. You are dealing with a specific recipient. You could use this technique for any purpose by adapting the ingredients of the potion and the colour of the light you invest in it, but this particular example is for sending positive energy, luck, and/or health to a friend. It is not a "Words of Power" spell, which is closer to verbal and written spellcraft as described in the section above on poetry.

Take a small amount of two oils that correspond to your two star signs. These can be bought ready-made from occult stores, or you could use straight oils that relate to your significator in the zodiac.

Put a few drops of the oils into a bowl. Add a pinch of cinnamon (or a drop of cinnamon oil) and a small piece of amber. Cover with a black cloth, and leave overnight.

The following day, remove the amber, and allow it to dry beside your computer.

Before you write your message, anoint your finger with the oil, and dab it on each of the four corners of your monitor. Imagine your fingertips sparkling and emitting orange/golden light. See the sparks of light crossing through your keyboard and down into your e-mail.

Choose your words carefully, and keep your message short and sweet. A simple wish of good luck or love, maybe in a large or coloured font if you are able, is the most effective.

As you press "Send," imagine your e-mail shooting down through your connection and across cyberspace like a comet, trailing a blaze of bright golden sparks and carrying your good wishes with it. Think of your friend opening the e-mail, and his or her face lighting up with the reflected golden light of the sparks. He or she will carry the warm amber light with her in her endeavours.

Thoughtforms and Telepathy

Thoughtforms are what the witch (and magickian) use to get what he or she wants from a spell. The thought, carefully created through ritual and intense emotion, becomes the receptacle of physical reality. The thoughtform embodies the desired reality. Magick would be impossible without thoughtforms.

The means of creating these astral bodies or symbols are many and various. In their most subtle form, they are merely projected by the witch mentally, with no need for surrounding ritual (though this is difficult—otherwise we would all be like Stephen King's Carrie!). In their most solid form they are voodoo dolls or fithfaths, a means of pinning the thoughtform down by sympathetic magick. This is handy as an aid to concentration. The use of photographs, hair, and nail clippings in spells performs a similar role, aligning the witch with her subject and enhancing the thoughtform.

The usual process is to acquire a very strong mental image of the subject, seal it in (the means of performing both stages are various), and then use channelled energy to envisage, and thereby cause, a desired effect. This might simply be visualised, or it might be enacted on the physical plane (for example, removing pins from a doll representing the person, which symbolises pain or disease being removed). Again, the desired effect is "sealed," sometimes by the tracing of an equilateral cross over it, sometimes simply by saying "So Mote it Be."

It is possible to create or "conceive" entities on the astral planes. This is done through rituals in which two higher selves are brought together, for example, and combined into one entity, which may then be sealed and named. It is exactly the same principle as having a child on this level, but it occurs astrally and causally rather than physically. If the entity is then tended and visited often, it will grow and develop a personality of its own. Of course, it can be asked to perform tasks for the witch and magickian.

Telepathy is part of this process. On the astral planes, the subject perceives the will power of the witch or magickian, and is subconsciously (and occasionally consciously) affected by it. Voodoo works on this principle; fetishes are placed in the victim's vicinity, which emanate this will, and when found, trigger strong psychological responses. Not only does the nasty-looking object stir up primal fears, but the victim becomes aware that he is hexed, and becomes more open telepathically. An aware subject is by far the easiest to work with. Naturally, if the subject is another employer of magick, he or she can then respond and possibly nullify or return the energies, but in most cases, a subject conscious that he or she is being worked on will be all the more receptive for it.

Telepathy is the means of communication used in all magick. It informs the subject, either consciously or subconsciously, that he or she is being targeted—for better or for ill. The energies sent to the subject are already directed to his or her particular tasks, but a mind informed that it is being willed to heal, for example, will aid the process through this knowledge. Similarly, many victims of hexes end up self-cursed, as fear takes them over and hysterical responses ensue.

Many witches experience telepathy on a regular, if not permanent basis. Obviously, being psychically active makes one aware of entities not normally perceived, and communication may be possible through telepathy. Such conversations with those who have died and are stuck here for whatever reason are common; likewise with telepathic communication with animal spirits. Mediumship of some sort is a natural by-product of the practise of magick.

Telepathy or ESP is even more regular between living subjects. All of us have experiences from time to time when we are thinking of somebody we haven't seen for a while and they call at that moment, or when we know that a loved one has been in an accident or is upset. Witches make use of this faculty by employing it deliberately. For example, if she wishes a particular person to get in touch, the witch will visualise that person strongly until she feels a living link with him or her. The witch will then telepathically convey to that person the image of him or her reaching for the telephone or sending a letter or e-mail to her. It's easy, and came in especially handy in the days before mobile phones!

Much may be perceived about a person who is physically present that gives our intuition clues as to his or her state of mind. Being perceptive to facial expression, body language, and subtle colour or tincture changes in the skin and eyes is an art anyone can master, and very handy in situations such as Tarot readings for strangers. However, telepathy should not be a guessing game, and it is most important to go with one's higher vision and "hearing," however contrary it may seem. For example, I once read for a tanned, healthy, and happy-looking woman in a park who was having a picnic with a friend. Had I gone by the physical "facts" alone, I would have said that she was in fine form. However, not only was there an almost shroud-like quality to her spiritual aura (different from the physical), but the Tower card came up in her immediate past, along with various others that confirmed my intuitive feelings, however unlikely they might have seemed. She went on to tell me that her mother had just died. Her friend was doing an excellent job of cheering her up, and she was tanned because she had been on holiday when she heard the news. Also, part of her was relieved that her mother's suffering was over, so her grief was less obvious.

Every time we think and feel, we create a thoughtform. Every thought emanates from us, and often visibly so to those who have developed their psychic faculties. Frequently experienced thoughts and images can get stuck in our auras, reaffirming habits, whether good or bad. This is one of the truths behind the phrase "Think positive!" as when we truly do, we emanate light and surety and are thus more likely to achieve our aim. Psychic and auric cleansing helps to remove the less-helpful of these shapes and traits, which arise through negative thinking.

Transference of Energies

The technique of transferring energies involves the simple expedient of moving an affliction, usually from one place to another. It is used in much folkloric magick, as the following example indicates.

SYD'S NAN'S WART SPELL

When Syd was at school, she had a wart beneath her right thumb on the palm of her hand. It grew until it was quite large, resisting the conventional lotions and potions; nothing worked.

Syd went to visit her Nan, who took her into the garden, bringing with her a very small piece of raw beefsteak. She rubbed the meat on the wart, "giving" the wart to the meat. She then buried it under a full moon along with three hairs from a black cat. Hey presto! The wart soon disappeared altogether.

A Summary of Aspects of Spell-casting

Time and place are of course key to spell-casting. A sacred space or an altar are often helpful to the matter at hand, though not essential. Casting a Circle makes anywhere sacrosanct.

Ensuring that one has the correct correspondences for the task—phase of moon, colours of candles, types of oil, and so on—aids precision in magick. Intent is also key—one should have a very firm idea of what is to be achieved.

Imagination is the wind in the witch's sails, and without it we are run aground. Visualisation (light, process in action, etc.) is the strongest vehicle for imagination; it becomes a channel to the energies that then take over. Incantation can help, as can music. Chanting and calling in the correct manner are essential when summoning spirits or approaching specific deities. Poetry may be employed in magick as another type of evocation—preferably, written specifically for the matter at hand.

Action—such as knotting, carving, anointing, picking, cutting, burning, weaving, and burying—is helpful to spell-casting. Obviously, the action should reflect the witch's intent; for example, burying something to act as secret protection, or knotting something later to be released. Weaving, on the other hand, would indicate harmonious interaction between, say, lovers.

Sympathetic magick (see section above) is often used as part of a spell. For example, in Wicca-style sympathetic magick, this would mean growing a plant or vegetable to represent your aspirations, and possibly eating the vegetable ritualistically; or, more folklorically, placing a coin in the soil or turning it over in front of the moon.

Props such as ritual tools, dolls, photos, garments, hair, and nail clippings all add greater clout to a magickal endeavour. Crystals, bags of herbs in a bath, oils, candles, coloured inks, barks, and so on are also good ingredients in a spell.

Purification prior to ritual is often helpful. My personal preference is a ritual bath with candles, oils, and music that correspond to the mood of the endeavour.

nineteen

Menstrual and Menopausal Magick

THE TIME JUST BEFORE HER period is the witch's strongest, magickally speaking. Any tension or pain she might feel may be employed to intensify the will; power becomes concentrated as she approaches her own personal reversal of tides. The subconscious is particularly strong at this time, one of the most important tools of magick. The subconscious is the springboard of the will; the more a desire or urge has been suppressed or programmed magickally (as in Austin Osman Spare's sigilisations, or through ritual), the higher and faster the will must fly. As ever in magick, any negatives may be employed to bring about positives.

When a witch is menstruating, her magick is best employed in purposes of erosion—especially if this coincides with the waning of the moon. It is simply a question of working in reverse. For example, if good fortune is required, this time may be used to combat bad habits that prohibit progress, or to remove obstacles from her path. The purgative properties of the period are employed psychologically and physiologically to banish unwanted influences and to exorcise unhelpful emotions and emotional ties. This is an excellent time to initiate new cycles, which may then be connected to the next new moon. The spell or working is best confirmed and strengthened at this point.

Though menstruation is traditionally taboo in many cultures, it is popularly employed for purposes of prophecy and divination. A woman is particularly able to emotionally and psychically access and influence others at this time; a fact probably enhanced by sheer physical exhaustion in eras and civilisations before the advent of the vitamin pill. Every witch and magickian knows that physical extremes caused by fatigue, sleep deprivation, fasting, and illness necessarily thin the Veil between realms. There are many examples of ordinary folk in extreme danger, or on the operating table, experiencing "tunnels with light at the end," or encountering family and friends who have passed up the Tree of Life, that are inappropriately named "near-death experiences" (they are, in fact, as near to real life as many people come in their incarnations!). The same goes for menstruation, when hormones play havoc with "sensible" perceptions, when the body is depleted of iron and other essential minerals, and most importantly, when the witch is attuned to her primeval femininity. What stronger link could we seek to the Goddess as Crone? (Crone rather than Mother because the process is corrosive.)

Hecate is one goddess with whom to work at such times, with her instinctual wisdom, and her ability to protect and aid the outcast. For women are traditionally outcast when menstruating; the body attests that the Darkside is not so very far away from any of us. Even in a highly sanitised society, with our ability to all but hide the effects of time and biological function and the deeper, more disturbing aspect of the primordial response to blood, few men or even women would wish to venture too intimately into another person's primitive depths. When she is menstruating or about to begin her period, every woman is essentially private; she fights for her workaday sanity (as illustrated by the number of crimes committed by women under such circumstances), and she hits psychic peaks that are perceptible—at the very least, subconsciously—to all who encounter her.

As goddess of murderesses (for, in menstruating or miscarrying, our bodies cancel potential life), of beggars and the pariah, there is no more appropriate deity to petition and work with at such times than Hecate. Hecate, as Crone, also confirms what every woman is aware of as she menstruates: that time is passing and she, as a physical and spiritual entity, is getting older. Hecate is also the goddess of witchcraft, and a woman is never more witchy than when she is menstruating. The wonderful power of flowing visibly and perceptibly with the life-force may seem difficult to celebrate (often being a pain, and at times even embarrassing), but it is every woman's right to celebrate her menses (at least privately) in a different but equally valid manner to the celebration of a potential birth. Fertility would not be possible without it, after all. Rather than being an annoyance, the witch knows that the menstrual cycle is a confirmation of life—death in life, perhaps, but this is again a cause for joy. Just as the year incorporates the death of one god and the initiation of another, and just as the Goddess progresses from Maiden to Mother to Crone in the cycle of a year, the witch experiences a microcosmic version within every month. Her creativity can be unrivalled at times when her body is apparently flagging. The earth herself is nurturing and germinating whilst she is apparently barren; she is hibernating.

Incubation is not merely a state of physical pregnancy. It occurs in every person and especially in the occultist (most aims being more consciously aimed for than by the nonpractitioner) with every new idea, when will is employed to bring it to pass. With appropriate ritual, a menstrual month may begin with a new idea, a new aim; it develops within the witch as the month progresses, waxing in intent and becoming more tenable as time passes. Eventually, it is sublimated by the shedding of blood (which may be perceived as a sacrifice), and projected into the astral realms. From there, it takes on new life of its own.

At the ultimate end of every menstrual cycle comes the menopause. Despite being expected, this can come as a terrible shock to many women, especially as the physical side effects are often so pronounced: erratic bleeding, interminable hot flushes, unfathomable and disturbing mood swings. However, this stage is again highly positive, indicating the woman's transference from the realms of social duty and obligatory caring and nurturing, into those of biological independence, psychic autonomy, and a deeper delving into the depths of her own psyche and individuality. I have seen many women transformed from deferential family care-givers into dynamic, deep-thinking individualists at this stage. Spiritual interests often become pronounced, obsolete patterns of behaviour are abandoned, and even the most conventional of women is offered the opportunity to reassess her place in the scheme of things. This is just as valid (perhaps more so, to the individual) as the process of giving birth, or of working with monthly cycles. It is an epic voyage into a new stage of being.

All of the menstrual issues relate to Yesod and Binah in the Qabalah. Yesod refers to lunar cycles, intuitive tides, the astral realms. When first menstruating, the adolescent witch may find herself catapulted into Yesod, with its mind-boggling, colourful, and symbolic imagery (usually perceived in dreams), its hints at death in life, and its psychoerotic connotations and issues of attaining divinity or elevated states through sex. With her first sheddings of childhood blood comes an attunement to Artemis as moon goddess and huntress, and a knowledge of her own strength and power and her relationship to the moon, sea, and tides of nature. It is common for the adolescent witch to astrally project (often in her sleep) following the onset of her periods, and to begin to perceive the presence of spirits around her. Visions, voices, and events of intense personal significance are likely to occur. However, because of her youth and the nature of Yesod, which is largely illusory, she may well find herself spooked and unable to discriminate between influences. The stricter her upbringing and the more intense (and thus suppressed) her personality, the more likely this is to occur.

Yesod, as a realm of oceanic waters and guarded by the Ashim, the Souls of Fire, brings with it an initiation into the mysteries of the elements. The "Souls of Fire" may also be perceived as the ability to bring new life into the Universe. This is both mental and physical conception. The young witch has already experienced earth through Malkuth, where she has abided since birth (this must be coupled with a growing awareness of her life purpose), and air (the mental and abstract mind, therefore relevant to Hod) via any academic work she has done; she begins to perceive "the Machinery of the Universe," or the bigger rather than short-term picture, with the onset of her attunement to natural cycles. She is likely to become hyperimaginative and creative, to think religiously, and begin to work her magick. In reverse to the state of menopause, she is incorporated into a wider plan, both mentally and physically. Suddenly, she is capable of giving birth—both physically and psychically.

Yesod remains with us at the waxing and onset of the menses. Halfway through, however, as in pregnancy and, conversely, menopause, we transfer to Binah. Binah, or wisdom, comes as we progress up the Tree of Life. Here, we touch a less-transient stage in female development. Experience becomes sublimated as we journey deeper into the meaning of what it is to be female (and male); the ability to bring forth from an ocean of countless possibilities. With Silence as a virtue and Restriction as a prerequisite (for, in giving tenable form to any concept, we inevitably restrict it), Binah, at the top of the Pillar of Severity, is appropriate to menstruation (a converse confirmation of potential life), to pregnancy (when spirit is fitted into an envelope of form), and to menopause (when fertility, extroverted to this point, becomes introverted, offering new modes of individuality to its subject). The results of Binah on the Malkuth plane may seem finite—how many of us exclaim "My life seems over, now that I've completed . . ."—but in Qabalistic terms (and in fact), Binah is much closer to the ultimate source than Yesod or Malkuth. A Binah stage will always seem barren and bitter in some respects, but it represents the sublimation of experience. This is what we are here for: not so much to experience, as to learn from the experience. Hedonism is justified by some as "experience," as is adversity, particularly when self-induced, but unless it is used to inform the higher mind and spirit, it is as illusory as some of Yesod's delightful but misleading flights of fancy.

Yesod is the early springtime, when anything seems possible, and Binah is the autumn, when all is reassessed, inevitably with some rancour (without opposites, we have no dynamic to work with, as the Tree of Life attests). With Binah, the Dark Sterile Mother transforms herself into the Bright Fertile Bride of an incarnation's latter-day possibilities.

The point of fertility is relevant here, especially when we look at the Tantric attitude towards menstruation. "The red goddess," or Dakini, offers an opportunity of reintegration with the life-force to both the male and female during menstruation. There is also an inevitable connection with Kali, the goddess of time, and of destruction within life. Red silk and fresh blood are used to honour her in festivals and rites. Fertility and mortality are marked out by a monthly shedding of blood, a stark reminder that life is not as sanitised as we may like or believe it to be. Like ferocious Kali emanating from the gentle Parvati, woman is not simply sedate, serene, and loving; her flip side is fierce and primeval. There is a Kali within every good housewife and every cool businesswoman, and the monthly periods attest to this.

Many images of Kali are shocking to a sanitised society: astride her husband Siva's corpse, or decapitating human and demon alike on the battlefield. Often she is depicted headless as Mahavidya Cinnamasta, holding her own head on a platter and drinking her own blood, which spurts from her severed neck in a three-way fountain. The other two streams are imbibed by two naked, sword-wielding females, while a couple copulate on the ground before her. Sometimes Mahavidya Cinnamasta is depicted in lotus posture at the midst of a circle of lotus petals the colour and shape of female genitalia.

As in all Hindu philosophy, the meanings of this image are multiple and complex. However, for the purposes of this chapter we note that blood provides sustenance and means of kinetic action (the women supping at the fountain of life-that-looks-like-death represent the *gunas,* the qualities of objectivity, desire, action, and knowing). We also note that the streams of blood represent three stages of progression from the dark inert (*tamas*) to the bright and active (*rajas*) to the radiance of being (*sattva*). The three stages are echoed by Western goddess lore: the three faces, representing the three visible lunations (the fourth being the dark, of course), and thus the stages of womanhood and of bringing forth life from nothing. The blood of Kali and of Mahavidya Cinnamasta is the blood of life, just as is that of the menses, despite its appearance of termination and death.

Aleister Crowley and some of his admirers such as Kenneth Grant make much of the Priestess's menstrual cycle, carefully cataloguing her sexual secretions for use in specific types of magick. Her fluids, both menstrual and throughout the month, are treasured for their various properties—quite a refreshing attitude after thousands of years of serious taboo. It is also one that makes perfect sense considering that we are all—and the Priestess above all others—changing every day with the planets, moon, and with age. These precious fluids are referred to by Grant as "kalas," a word with an obvious connection to Kali and thus to the concept of time. They indicate "times" when particular forms of magick will be best employed to elicit maximum response.

In *Hecate's Fountain* (Skoob Books Publishing Ltd., 1991), Grant discusses various opinions of those involved in the O.T.O., including that "the supreme secret of magickal power lies in the secret aeon (secret-ion) represented by the lunar current which manifests through the kalas of the menstrual fluids." Needless to say, there are some highly complex theories attached to this statement, and others made by Grant himself, such as, "The emissaries of the Old Ones seek nourishment of a kind that is available on earth only via the lunar kalas of the nubile human female." In other words, subtle entities feed off the subtle emissions of menstrual fluids. This opinion is not in the least unusual anthropologically speaking, and is part of the reason for menstrual taboos. Spirits both terrestrial and supraterrestrial do indeed attune to and find nourishment in the cross-dimensional miasma of a menstruating woman's aura and body, if the woman is operating on a suitable mental wavelength. The entities invoked may be either low-level or high, depending on the subject's spiritual affiliations and ritual circumstance.

The idea of the Scarlet Woman is greatly tied in with that of menstruation; Crowley's poem "The Blood-Lotus" (from *White Stains,* Duckworth edition, 1997) reflects this. In the poem Crowley refers to "The many-seated, multiform, divine, essential joys that these/Dank odours bring, that starry seas wash white in vain . . . ," a clear reference to the kalas and their ability to aid projection through time and space. The woman on whose "blood-lotus" Crowley waxes lyrical is "my harlot in a harlot's dress," the Scarlet Woman, Babylon (Babalon), "Who for man Now first forsakest thy leman, thy Eve, my Lilith, in this bower" (*leman* is an archaic word for lover or mistress). The suggestion of a Sapphic coupling between Lilith and Eve is perfectly in keeping with Crowley's character, and is also symbolic of the time when woman was accepted as one mixed current rather than split into a Judeo-Christian duo of good Eve and evil Lilith. Crowley, of course, prefers the feisty, intelligent, independent, and demonised Lilith, with her magick still intact. She is quintessential woman, while Eve is the man-formed version, full of shame at her own nature. Lilith is powerful and proud of her state of being; Eve is crippled by self-consciousness and fear of sin. Eve makes a feeble Priestess indeed.

The poem ends on a Kali-esque level: "And, at that moment when thy breath mixes with mine, like wine, to call/Each memory, one merged into all, to kiss, to sleep, to mate with death!" The poet and magickian experiences the union of opposites via his Priestess's "Blood-Lotus," a transcendence of the ordinary bounds of mortal time. Again, this is a reference to the menstrual kalas. In Wiccan ritual, the red wine held in the chalice represents the Goddess's blood of life, both birth blood and menstrual. Both attest to her power to bring forth physically and magickally.

Lilith is Qabalistically relevant to the process of menstruation. In the Zohar, she is the feminine part of the original hermaphrodite; Eve represents the separation of male and female. Lilith, when she saw God creating Eve, "fled, and she still dwells in the towns of the sea coast, where she attempts to entrap men"—a Siren-like situation that befits her role as seductress. Lilith is employed symbolically by the thirteenth-century mystic Moses de Leon to represent sexuality (along with her consort, the serpent Samael), the wages of which sin is perceived as spiritual death. She is also "the nakedness of Shekhinah," relating to the flip side of Malkuth, the Qlipothic or demonic aspect of the Bride of God. In Jewish lore, sex during menstruation is taboo, as it is thought to conceive "monsters," or Qlipothic entities. These, of course, are the "children of Lilith."

The Eve/Lilith divide may be seen in lunar terms as the cycles of waxing and waning. Eve is the bright, new moon, the time of sowing and initiating new projects, of bringing forth new life. Lilith is the dark moon, corrosive, relating to the mysteries of menstruation, menopause, and apparent physical death.

There appears to be no equivalent to Kali and the Tantric Mahavidya Cinnamasta in Greek myth, a society far too cultured and aesthetically aware to highlight goddesses of menstruation. However, Lamia, mother of the Skylla by Zeus, is a child-snatcher, which is a Lilith-like reference. To Lilith is also attributed the trait of eating her own offspring—a symbol of the menses "chewing up the flesh" of potential children. As previously mentioned, Hecate is often physically represented as either beyond aesthetic ideals (i.e., old), or triple-headed (lunar phases and powers of divination are indicated). Her staff depicts a serpent topped with a mare's head and that of a dog and lion, all of them glaring a warning, a foretaste of energies beyond the commonly acceptable. Her affiliation with murderers, outcasts, witches, and the moon deepen her connection to the powers of menstruation.

In Egyptian myth, the fiery lioness Sekhmet, again with a staff depicting a snake, is a representative of the powers of menstruation. A Tantric might detect a connection with the kundalini force, especially as Sekhmet's serpent spits fire, just as Tantric energy is forced up and emerges through the top of the spine. The goddess of the barren desert, a formidable enemy whose wrath scorches her enemies, Sekhmet exudes the indomitable will of the magickally menstruating woman. She craves blood, and creates a bloodbath of the enemies of Ra. She is only deterred by being tricked into drinking beer that is dyed red to make it look like blood. Even the gods on whose behalf she is working are repulsed by Sekhmet's ability to produce and assimilate gore.

Menstruation has been impossible to ignore ever since the first "wise wound" dripped its trail of red down a primeval leg, horrifying all. It may have been tabooed, concealed, and sanitised, but with the suppression of plain fact, the unacceptable has augmented in power. It now carries an entire mythos with it. The goddesses above are just a few examples of the magickal and mythological correspondences of menstruation.

A witch is never more powerful than just before and during her period. "Hecate's Fountain" provides her magick with a potent source of death in life. Her focus is fixed on all planes. She emanates and she attracts. To use these gifts of the Goddess to good effect is every woman's (and especially every witch's) prerogative and privilege.

Some Menstrual Spells
TO DEFINE YOUR PSYCHIC
AND PSYCHOLOGICAL BARRIERS

When you are on the verge of your period, and all the better if you are tense with PMS, decide what in your life you might change to make you truly fulfilled. If you are in a job or relationship that is getting you down, strongly visualise the best that your life could offer without it. Concentrate on the positive factors that might be unleashed if you extricated yourself from it, implications no issue.

This exorcism is best performed at night. If it coincides with the full or waning moon, all the better. However, the main factor in this case scenario is your personal biorhythms.

Stand in the middle of your favourite room, or your temple, and cast a Circle. This is important as this spell is best cast when emotionally turbulent, but you do not wish to attract negative entities. There are always plenty of them around at such times, but a bright circle of blue psychic power will ensure you immunity from them.

Standing at the centre of your Circle, articulate the things in your life that you wish to change. If these sound outrageous to your workaday self, all the better. Be as honest as you possibly can be. There is nobody here to hear you but your higher self and the gods, after all.

If you like, you may light some cleansing incense such as American Indian sage sticks or bundles (now widely available from New Age stores and, strangely, many gift shops), lavender oil, joss sticks or dried flowers, eucalyptus (a highly medicinal smell—good if you feel in need of psychic/auric cleansing), or sweet basil (good for bringing the past to a progressive conclusion).

Strongly envisage yourself surrounded by your sphere of blue, protective light. Now project the thoughts of the things you wish to exorcise from your life to the outside of the Circle. Trap them outside your sphere. Inside, maintain the image of all you wish to nurture in your life. When these two images—of what you want, and what you wish to extricate yourself from—are strong and definite in your mind, say, "I separate myself from all that is inhibiting me. I have suffered to learn. I now wish to progress in what I have learned without suffering. Allow me to tread the Path of Righteousness in the knowledge of all that has passed before in my life [or 'lives,' if you believe in reincarnation]. So mote it be." Close the Circle swiftly.

If you have undergone a particularly traumatic exorcism, complete the ritual with a salt bath containing a few drops of geranium or ylang-ylang for purification and comfort.

Either way, when you have separated yourself from the unwanted influences, and when you feel that they belong to a sphere different from your own, go to sleep in the knowledge that you have purified yourself and are heading towards a closer fac-simile of what your higher self truly wishes for you.

EXORCISE YOUR LIFE OF UNWANTED DIFFERENCES

On the first day of your period, resolve to let all of the negativity you may be har-bouring flow out of you. To facilitate this, take a piece of paper and write down the first letter of every word of every issue you wish to purge yourself of. You may use runes or Enochia if you wish, or any language that appeals; the more magickal the script is to you, the better. If any are the same letter, delete the duplicates so that you are left with a list of single letters.

Now combine the letters so that they form a monogram. Allow your creativity to flow. Get lost in the beauty of the marks; fit them together so that they are aes-thetically pleasing to you.

When you have completed your monogram, repeat it on a small piece of paper or card. Now destroy your original design sheet by tearing it into tiny pieces and throwing it away.

Take one black candle. Stroke it from centre to top and centre to base simulta-neously (you may like to use a favourite cleansing oil on your fingertips, such as rosemary or sage) whilst contemplating the removal of obstacles in your life. Think of what you will achieve when these factors have been removed.

Use a pair of tweezers or another metal object in which you can hold your spell-paper without your fingers getting burnt.

Take one final look at your monogram (you do not have to think about what you are aiming at; your subconscious will know), light the candle, and burn it in the flame, saying, "As the past month flows from me and is sublimated, so do these experiences cease to influence me directly" (or whatever words of similar import seem appropriate to you).

When the paper or card is reduced to ashes, dispose of them and retreat into your own thoughts of fulfilment and uninhibited creativity.

TO BRING AN IDEA(L) TO FRUITION

At the end of your period, or on the day after it has finished, purchase one light-green candle. Cradle it in your hands and project into it the thoughts of what you wish for. Think of yourself as nurturing this germinal concept physically, as you would a child you had just conceived.

Light the candle, and strongly envisage your thoughts filtering through from the astral to the material world. As the light of your candle touches the objects in the room you are in, imagine your concept influencing the physical aspects of your life. See it as surely as you see the flame of your candle, lit by your will.

Allow the candle to burn for as long as you can clearly project the thoughts and ramifications of your project in a positive manner. When you feel the session has reached its climax, extinguish the candle, saying (words to the effect of), "I have Willed _____ to come to pass. I will do everything in my power to protect and nurture this project. I shall guard and guide it like a mother until it takes on consciousness of its own."

Repeat on successive days, preferably at the same time, for as long as you feel is effective. Repeat for fifteen days maximum.

On the final day, take whatever is left of the candle and wrap it in a green cloth (silk is best) tied with a purple or red ribbon. Stash it in the deepest recesses of your trousseau or whatever container you use to keep the fertile debris of your spells. If you do not already have one, procure it now. Every witch should have a padlocked repository of her spellcraft. You may keep other items of emotional import in there too, but be careful to ensure that they are all pollution-free; that is, relevant to the person that you wish to be, rather than the one you feel you ought to be or habitually are. Letters and cards from obsolete ex-lovers, for example, should be kept elsewhere, as should family photographs that remind you of the person you are expected to be (rather than the one you wish to become), and so on.

Now forget about your magickal working, whilst acting on the physical planes to encourage what you wish to come to pass. You will find that, just as a newly conceived child takes care of itself in any suitable environment, your project will grow and respond to conducive circumstances.

In time, it will be brought forth into the world.

SPELL FOR MENSTRUAL STRENGTH

At any time around your period, it is possible to access the great reserves of strength inherent in Woman. This may be used for any purpose you wish—from simple self-confidence to indomitable might. Be careful with this one—it is very powerful. Try to ensure that you are at least emotionally rational (i.e., do not wish harm on anyone, no matter how much they have pissed you off today, or to perform any act that might be unhelpful to your fellow beings) before performing it.

The best aim of this spell is personal fortitude when your objective is ethically viable, which could be anything from combating prejudice, to actual physical strength, to standing up for yourself in an unhelpful, vitality-draining scenario.

First, take a bath in a combination of salt (for purification) and oak extract (for stalwart fortitude) and/or hickory (renowned for its hardness) and/or a touch of red wine or any other red substance you might be able to get your hands on. As well as reinforcing the menstrual aspect, these ingredients relate to Geburah, Qabalistic repository of might, valour, and warriorlike fierceness. Because Geburah is not indulgent, the bath should be either slightly uncomfortably hot, or slightly uncomfortably cold, depending on your personal constitution and climactic conditions. Be sure to be sensible in this; do not burn yourself or get hypothermia. It is a gesture to the power you are invoking, after all, not a human sacrifice.

Arise from your mildly disconcerting bath, dress so as to make yourself feel strong (make-up, traditionally used by warriors as face paint, is good; be dramatic, make yourself feel spectacular and fierce), and proceed to your temple or whatever room you use for your magick.

Light five red candles and place them at an equal distance from one another in the room. Stand at their centre, and take a deep inhalation and exhalation five times.

With each powerful new inhalation of air, feel yourself absorbing the energy of the Universe. Think of Kali preparing herself to combat the Asuras (demons) of Hindu mythology, of Sekhmet the Egyptian lioness ready to scorch the enemies of Ra, life-giver, and of Artemis honing an arrow with which to smite any who disrespect her.

With each successive exhalation, feel yourself absolved of personal weaknesses. Nothing matters now but you, at the centre of this five-pointed star, and your objectives. Even if they seem small in the grand scheme of things, they are important; let no small thoughts intervene between you and your perfected will.

As you stand there, stretch your arms upwards and feel the Geburic power flowing into you; you take red, you give red. You are not to be trodden down; you will ensure that your determination is insurmountable. This is all that is required to bring any desired aim to pass.

Feel your higher will (the aspect of yourself that is concerned with your personal integrity, or with that of others you may wish to help) taking command. It is made of iron. Like the blood that will flow from you, it is strong, fierce, and indubitable. Your whole being is shielded by it like armour.

When you feel entirely proactive but protected, say (or think clearly and strongly), "Elohim Gebor, Kamael, Seraphim, fill my body and mind with the fiery serpents of sure intent. Let them burn away all that is obsolete in my life, allowing my personal strength to flow. May I be Insurmountable. Jehovah Elohim, Tzaphkiel, Aralim, may my intent be Enthroned. As my body dispenses, so shall my psyche dispense. May Strength and Wisdom flow into me and emanate from me."

When you have felt your will pass into the realms of surety, thank those powers you feel have attended your ritual, extinguish your candles, and retire physically and mentally from the magickal wavelength.

Music with a strong beat is highly effective at this point (anything from *Carmina Burana* to punk or metal; choose whatever makes you want to go out and tell the world what you think)—it will ground you, but hopefully carry with it the thoughts you have set into motion during your spell.

At the first possible opportunity, go out and confront your issues. With this working and the knowledge of your personal rectitude behind you, and particularly if you are menstruating at the time, you cannot fail to win the battle.

SPELL FOR PEACE OF BODY AND MIND
DURING A PERIOD OR AT MENOPAUSE

Camomile tea is always a good calmer, but if you're turning to this spell, you probably need something stronger.

If you can procure it, get some loveage roots and/or leaves, tie them in a porous material such as cheesecloth, and filter them through your bath water. If you are unable to purchase or pick these, a rose quartz (polished gemstones are now available just about anywhere) is also effective.

A few drops of essential rose oil in the water will soothe your troubled nerves and get you thinking on a Netzachian wavelength. Allow yourself to dream of the things you did in (what you perceive as) your youth. Love and potential are probably the key points here.

Take a long deep soak in the aromatic, healing waters. A glass or mug of your favourite beverage (alcoholic is fine) is always a good idea in such situations.

Arise, towel yourself down, and make yourself comfortable. Soothing music may well help.

Light nine pink candles. As you do so, concentrate on their rejuvenating powers: wax, moist but firm, pliant and tactile; pink, youthful, optimistic, healing.

Surround yourself with an aura of pale pink. Relax into it. Do this standing or sitting, whichever you prefer.

Now say (or think clearly, depending on your situation), "This body has worked for me over the last ___ years. Through it I have learned; let me still learn from it. But now I wish to let my mind and spirit run free. Tzaphkiel, release me from unnecessary restriction. Raphael, enlighten and heal me. Let me find respite. Gabriel, fill my mind with the replenishing waters of creative pursuit."

Allow your mind to drift off into its Yesodic realms of wonder, as you did as a child or adolescent.

When you feel emotionally replete, blow out your candles and retire early to bed. Your dreams should reflect your innate hopes for your future.

twenty*twenty*

The Witch and Physical Health

A PRACTISED WITCH IS NOT only adept at knowing what heals what, she is also expert at understanding the root causes of ailments. She recognises a stress-related complaint from a mile off, partly because she can read the trouble in the aura of the patient, and partly because she understands the way in which psychic and psychological trouble manifests itself in the flesh.

Here follows a few of the most common complaints, and some of their magickal or psychological causes. Please note: these are just some of the possible root causes. They do not mean that the person suffering is necessarily suffering simply for this reason, or that it is his or her fault that he or she is ill. They are intended to give clues rather than be definitive diagnoses. Everybody is different, after all.

Acne/spots—Problems with self-image; frustrated perfectionism turning into self-thwarting behaviour; suppressed anger. Also, the inability to settle.

On a more physical level, lack of sunlight, a dysfunctional sex drive (usually too demanding), and a poor diet are also possible culprits. Skin complaints often occur when a person is placed in an environment that makes him or her feel exposed.

Asthma—Feeling out of place, or displaced. Desiring perfection, but feeling unable to achieve it. Stifled creativity. Wanting too much at once—impatience. Issues relating to self-worth. Lack of faith in the Universe providing.

Backache—Feeling put upon, unsupported. Burdened by work. Martyrdom.

Colds—Being desperately in need of reattunement. Having to do what you do not want to do. The world seems hostile. Also, the obvious point of needing a break and a little self-nurturing.

Ears—Ear wax, ear infections, and even getting things stuck in your ears indicates the will to "shut off" from the outside world. Feeling harangued by a partner or close relative.

Eye problems—*Blurred vision:* Wanting to tune out of this reality. Detachment.
   Short-sightedness: Not wanting to face up to the future. Concentration on the mundane.
   Sties: Feelings of inadequacy. Acute self-depreciation.

Foot problems—*Athlete's foot:* Not enough rest, not enough time to yourself. Refusing to face important issues. Not taking care of the details that together create the whole of our lives.
   Bunions: Hyperactivity, not enough pure rest.
   Corns: Not listening to your inner self. Putting the opinions of others before your own.
   Footache: Lack of confidence in your own abilities. Feeling inferior, even outcast. Not enjoying one's everyday role in life.

Headache—Feeling trapped. Often denotes the power of another person over you, his or her influence being negative. Difficulty in untangling problems.

Kidney complaints—Lack of discrimination. Being out of control.

Lactose intolerance/allergy to milk—Unresolved issues relating to the mother-figure. Inability to feel that the Universe will sustain one. Lack of trust.

Liver trouble—The liver has long been perceived as the seat of anger. Alcoholics attempt to drown their anger by numbing the liver. Problems related to it indicate unresolved emotional issues, frequently from childhood.

Migraine—Being caught in a negative situation that makes the victim unable to act as he or she would wish. Often, this is karmic and very difficult to extricate oneself from. When the migraine victim finds freedom and happiness again, his or her debilitating headaches will cease.

Stomachache—One of the best-known psychosomatic complaints! Usually caused by nervousness and extreme insecurity, the victim requires soothing and reassurance, and possibly a less-agitating diet.

Throat—A sore throat usually indicates stress, and an excess of options. Inability to make a decision. A dilemma.

Cure-all

Common sense is the main ingredient to any healing spell, especially self-healing. Analysing the psychosomatic causes is obviously a great help. If a problem is recurring, a change in lifestyle—even a small one, such as cutting a particular ingredient out of one's diet, or meditating, or sleeping more (or less)—may be required. Unlike many witches, I am not against orthodox medicine. Yes, it has its drawbacks, but it is part of human evolution and has much to offer us nowadays.

One of my friends, a French witch, was diagnosed with cancer but eschewed conventional treatments. She meditated, performed self-healing rituals, and improved her condition with the help of others. She outlived the doctor's predictions, and died happy and whole. However, it is indubitable that her incarnation would have been prolonged had she accepted the orthodox treatments offered to her originally. She chose not to, and that was right for her on her spiritual journey. It is not right for everyone, however. We have many options at our fingertips, and it would be foolish not to consider them all.

The best cure-all is to look at the problem from every angle. First, physically (in the case of illness), is there anything we can sensibly do to prevent the problem? They are often self-caused. Second, aurically, what is it in our thoughts and actions that is perpetuating the ailment and allowing it to affect us? Finally, spiritually, what can we learn from it, and why is it happening to us? The latter is especially relevant to life-threatening conditions. Many who have suffered from heart attacks, cancer, and other serious complaints have reassessed their lifestyles and beliefs and recovered accordingly.

Ritual is a great help in such scenarios. Group work can give an essential sense of support, so long as it does not make the subject feel like a victim. Knowing that one is doing everything one can to fend off the ailment also gives essential confidence, which means eating, drinking, and sleeping in accordance with the rules of nature. The body can often tell us what it needs, and we know when it is a sensible request. A box of chocolates and a bottle of wine may not always be the answer, but occasionally, it is. If the body asks for this daily, we know we have a problem. Once in a while it might be an improving, relaxing indulgence.

The witch goes with the flow, but employs her common sense in the process. She strives to be unneurotic about the body, which is, after all, simply a vehicle. She is not a health freak, nor is she a dissipated wreck. Sometimes she indulges, sometimes she abstains. She looks at the appropriateness of her actions to her aims and progress, the time of year, and the group mood. She knows that true health is spiritual health.

The Witch and Running
by Dr. Radcliffe Morris

No legs have ever outpaced my swift strong legs. Let none outpace me.

—"Artemis" La Trobe

As witches, we are aware of the power of Artemis; we call upon her when we feel the need for increased self-reliance, self-worth, and physical strength. We recognise that her strengths—uncompromised dignity, fierce independence, unassailable self-belief—are inseparable from her physical prowess, and that her ability to run and her unadulterated joy in that ability are inseparable from her strengths. Why, then, do so many of us ignore the inevitable power of the honed and tuned body? Why do so many of us turn away from another access to increased awareness? The irony of this refusal to engage with the body's physicality is that it is a refusal based upon a binary interpretation of existence: the mind/spirit and the body. This is a belief that underlies oppressive ideologies and theologies worldwide and a belief that Wicca itself rejects. If we truly believe that our present incarnation is a product of what has come before and our purpose is to learn what we failed to learn in the past, then we must embrace fully all that this incarnation offers to us. If we fail to seek to learn, if we close rather than open the doors of perception, then we are, through laziness, fear, or self-righteousness, thwarting our own existence. As we make demands upon our intellects and our spirits, we must make demands upon our flesh. If we believe that this incarnation is not mere chance, but that there is an order and meaning to the universe, that we have a responsibility to ourselves and to humanity, then we must commit without reservation to improving the body as well as the mind and spirit. In short, you must exercise. You must train your body with the same diligence that you train your psychic and intellectual self.

Are you resisting this concept? If so, ask yourself why. Answer honestly. There are multiple reasons for shying away from physical assertion: inertia, fear, embarrassment. However, I would like to suggest that the most likely reason is cultural. We are a part of a spiritual and social community, and like any community, we have our own symbols, signs, modes of dress, and rituals of interactions. We recognise each other through not only psychic emanations, but also through the pentagrams around our necks, the paleness of our skin, the blackness of our clothes. Because we are a part of an infringed-upon community, existing in a world that worships wealth and possessions, that sees beauty in blonde conformity and mass-produced style, and that finds religion in self-righteousness, we must work to protect ourselves as individuals and as a subculture.

One way we tend to do this is to follow our own conventions and to distance ourselves from the conventions of the society that encroaches upon us. Mainstream society touts exercise and diet as the solution to all personal problems (assuming one also has money and marriage, of course); join a gym, society claims, and you will become attractive and desirable—you will become a success! While we need to protect ourselves from the vagaries of the world in which we live, we need also to protect ourselves from reactionary responses. Our psychic integrity is not diminished by our decision to put on a pair of running shoes. Most people who exercise may do so for superficial reasons, but it does not follow that all people who exercise must be similarly driven. In other words, the fact that the majority of people who exercise do not link that exercise to their spiritual lives has no bearing on the existence of that link. If we allow the image of witchlike behavior to prevent us from pursuing new knowledge and experience, from embracing all that is in this incarnation, then we are no better than the conformists of mainstream society and our community is no less oppressive.

Necessary Equipment

While it might be pleasant to daydream that we could run barefoot through the woods, servants of Artemis, the truth is that properly fitted running shoes are a necessity. In fact, if you are currently thinking about your bad knees, chances are that any exercise you have previously engaged in has been in ill-fitting shoes. The percentage of people who are genetically incapable of running due to knee and/or back physiology is extremely low, while the number of people who erroneously believe they have some physiological incapacity is as dramatically high. Properly fitted shoes are the only financial investment that you need to make in order to run. However, you must make it. While you may find the cost unappealing, consider that if you spread the cost of the shoes over the months it will take you to run the 300–400 miles each pair of shoes can withstand, this cost is quite reasonable. For example, if you buy a £60 ($96) pair of shoes and run three miles a day five days a week, it will be six months before you need to replace your shoes. How much did those shoes cost you? 33p (53¢) a day!

Failure to invest in the appropriate shoes will result in injury such as knee, iliotibial band, ankle, back, or hip problems. It is not necessary to buy expensive running shoes, but it is necessary that the style you wear is suited to your body and gait. Unfortunately, you cannot just go to any sports merchandise shop and be sure you have bought the right shoes for you. Many of the popular sports stores do not require their sales assistants be trained in the fitting of running shoes or even be runners themselves. If at all possible, go to a running specialty shop, where you will be guaranteed a proper fit. Because these shops are always small, independently owned businesses, the shoes may cost you 5 to 10 percent more than they would in the other stores; however, consider this money well spent—it is the cost of pleasurable, injury-free running.

If you do not have access to a specialty running shop, you can perform a rudimentary analysis yourself to arm you against the shop assistant looking for a quick sale. Stand barefoot with your lower leg visible, your back to a full-length mirror; hold up a vanity mirror and examine your ankles. Your ankles will be either rolling inwards (pronating), rolling outwards (supinating), or angled straight (standing neutral). This test does not replace the expertise of the trained fitter, but it will allow you to know which of the three following types of shoes you require:

- Cushioned shoes are made for neutral feet that do not roll inwards. These feet often do not absorb shock particularly well and therefore require a more cushioned ride.

- Motion control shoes are made for feet that pronate, or roll inwards. People who pronate need shoes with medial posting, a denser CM-EVA foam, polyurethane foam, or TPU device that curbs pronation and allows the runner to strike the ground straight. Runners who pronate are in danger of giving themselves knee and iliotibial band problems if they do not wear shoes with medial posting.

- Stability shoes fall between the cushioned and motion control shoes. They are suitable for mild pronators who like a more cushioned ride.

All of the major shoe companies—Brooks, Adidas, Asics, Fila, Nike, Saucony, Mizuno—produce high-quality products that fall into these three categories. Choose a model that meets your biomechanical needs and feels good on your feet; do not buy according to colour!

Caring for your shoes properly will guarantee their full life. Never wash them in a washing machine, no matter how dirty they may be. Instead, remove dirt with a damp sponge, pull out the insole, and stuff the shoes with newspaper. You should stuff your shoes in this way any time they are wet or damp.

While the right shoes are crucial to healthy running, the right clothes are crucial to comfortable running. Choose clothes that allow you to move easily but which do not surround you in swaths of material. There are technical clothes available that wick the sweat away from your body; they are wonderful but not necessary (other than in hot climes). However, you should avoid dressing too warmly, which results in unflattering and very annoying pieces of clothing tied around your waist, and avoid carrying anything in your hands, which results in alterations to your form. I strongly advise against running with a Walkman, CD player, or MP3 player for two reasons. The first is practical: you will not be able to hear cars or people approaching you and will therefore be putting yourself in danger. The second ties back to my argument in the introduction: running should not be just a physical activity for you; use this time to experience a heightened sense of your physical incarnation.

Routine/Programme

You must make a commitment to your physical body, which not only includes a commitment to exercise, but also, for some, a commitment to limit alcohol intake and to quit (or at least greatly reduce) smoking. Your desire to smoke will decrease as you continue to run and you become increasingly aware of how smoking compromises your physical strength and stamina (knowledge an inactive person never fully comprehends). However, a decision to curb smoking will be necessary in the beginning. If you feel you lack the strength to make such a decision, turn to your Craft for help, meditate on how smoking corrupts and violates your body, and examine the weakness you exhibit by making your will subservient to nicotine. There are no redeeming qualities to this poisonous habit that breeds pestilence within you—take control.

Commit to two weeks of running at a time, concentrating on the rigors and rewards of each cycle outlined below. Write down what you achieve daily. Most people find it easiest to establish a routine, such as always running in the early morning or directly after work, but some prefer to retain a more flexible routine, varying their running time according to the day of the week, the lunar cycle, or the weather. Providing that you always consider the placement of your run in each day, any organisation of routine will work. Keep in mind, however, that you should not run on a full stomach (I recommend running not less than two hours after a meal), a completely empty stomach (our muscles require fuel for the work they will do), or if dehydrated. Unless you are already exercising regularly, you must ease into your exercise routine. I suggest the following patterns:

Novice: three days on and one day off (two days off a week)
Intermediate: four days on and one day off (one day off a week)

In order to follow the programme below, both the novice and the intermediate runner must run at least four times a week. If you decide to run less than this, you must reduce the progression rates of each cycle, all of which are based upon the above frequency patterns.

For the first eight weeks, the novice should exercise for thirty minutes a day. For weeks 1 and 2, you will walk at a brisk pace for four minutes followed by a one-minute run. Please note that you should not be sprinting; instead, you should concentrate on making and maintaining a comfortable if not effortless pace. Relax your upper body; make sure that your arms, rotating from the shoulder, are moving back and forth and are not crossing your body as you run. Avoid shuffling by lifting your knees a little. Feel your blood coursing—you are life!

By weeks 3 and 4, you should be ready to increase the time spent running from one minute to two minutes, and reduce your time spent walking from four minutes to three minutes. Make sure to walk and not stroll your recovery. Decrease your running pace if you find this configuration impossible to complete; after all, completing the daily schedule to the best of your ability is your aim.

Your third and fourth cycles, weeks 5 to 8, will involve a steady build-up of running intervals. Your runs for weeks 5 and 6 will consist of two minutes of walking and three minutes of running; by weeks 7 and 8, your intervals will consist of a one-minute walk followed by a four-minute run.

After eight weeks of consistent exercise, you will be strong enough to run for extended periods of time and distance. Start with a two-mile run, broken at one mile by a two- to three-minute recovery walk if necessary. Once you have run two unbroken miles per day for a two-week cycle, you may, if you wish, increase your mileage, but do so by no more than 10 percent per week. Vary the lengths of your

TABLE 2
Running Programme

	Weeks 1–2	Weeks 3–4	Weeks 5–6	Weeks 7–8	Weeks 9+
Novice	30 minutes: (4 min. walk, 1 min. run) 6 times	30 minutes: (3 min. walk, 2 min. run) 6 times	30 minutes: (2 min. walk, 3 min. run) 6 times	30 minutes: (1 min. walk, 4 min. run) 6 times	2 miles w/ 10% increase per week allowed
Intermediate	30 minutes: (2 min. walk, 8 min. run) 3 times	30 minutes: (2 min. walk, 13 min. run) 2 times	30 minutes: unbroken	30 minutes: unbroken	3–4 miles w/ 10% increase per week allowed

runs and also the routes that you take. Choose tarmac over concrete, but whenever possible, run on grass or trails that provide natural cushioning for the body. An equally important consideration is that running in direct contact with the earth allows for greater spiritual and psychic connections and experiences. After three to four weeks, your fitness level will increase and you will begin to notice an increase in your pace, regardless of the distance run. You may also experience days of tired legs, a result of the cumulative miles you have run; these days indicate your diligence and will always punctuate your running to varying degrees. The intermediate follows a parallel cycle to that of the novice, but one that begins at a slightly higher intensity.

We must each find our own reason for being, and each make and take responsibility for the choices that we make. It is most important to remember that even when it seems we are deprived of choice, choice is always present, no matter how hidden from immediate view. As Hegel tells us, only the willing can be enslaved. Strengthen the body and you will strengthen the spirit and the mind, you will strengthen the power of your will, and you will never be enslaved, even if held motionless by ropes or chains. Learn from your body. Train your whole being to be strong.

In asking you to reexamine your attitudes to the witch and exercise, I am asking you to recognise that the power of Artemis, reachable through the body, will enhance all aspects of this incarnation. While there are multiple ways to exercise, it is running alone that aligns us with the Goddess, that connects us to the earth, and that empowers us physically and psychically. All exercise is positive, but not all exercise speaks to the character of the witch. I hope that I have swayed you to come to Artemis; if not, if asking you to embrace a lifestyle that is not commonly associated with the spirit seems too alien still, I hope that my own life will succeed where my words have failed. After all, while the advice of people who do not practice what they preach is often worth following, advice from those who live their theories is always more compelling. I speak from experience. We all contain and come to understand our own symbiosis of mind, spirit, and body, but this is what I know is true for me.

This is why I run: I run for the pleasure found in the power of the body, to feel my muscles working, my blood coursing as my feet fly over the ground. Thoughts sometimes come rapidly—a problem solved, a plan formed—but more often I am released from the mundane chaos of everyday life; freedom of spirit, freedom of soul. I run for the burning sensation in my lungs directly after a hard run, for the frantic gasping for oxygen, the body doubled over, wracked. It is at these moments that I feel the profundity of being; it is at these moments I know I am alive.

In the desert, I ran in the evening as the rocks turned red in the setting sun. In New Orleans, I run in the early morning through the Quarter's "half-deserted streets," past people still out from the night before, streetcleaners working to erase the night's frenzy, merchants opening up their stalls; I run along the streetcar lines of St. Charles, past white mansions and wrought-iron gates, Loyola's arches and Tulane's austere façade, under the arching oaks. I think of E. M. Forster's plea to "Only connect" and know that I have, that I am a part.

As a woman, I run for autonomy, an assertion of control over my body, a body that is lithe and strong, that belongs to me. I run as a statement of female strength, not that of nurturing or childbirth, but of will and defiance. I will run at night; I will run alone; I will run untouched by catcalls and cars honking; I will stare down the lecherous glance; I run and keep running and I run fast.

I run also because in running all is equal. Here is no handicapping, no excuses. Running is objective. It is a test of character; the option of quitting, of losing contact with your competition, with the earth, with your body, is always present. Running is a constant lesson in self-respect. Self-delusion is impossible; if you quit, you must stare in the face of your weakness, no matter how you may hide it from others. If you quit, you have to find the strength to start again, that run, that day, that week.

I run also because I can, because I am lucky, because I am able-bodied, and because I am immensely grateful for my life.

Born in Oxford, England, Radcliffe Morris currently resides in the United States, where she is a university faculty member in English Literature and one of the premier women runners in her state. Initiated into Wicca by Kala Trobe at the age of eighteen, Dr. Morris believes there is a symbiotic relationship between mind, spirit, and body. Her present activities include writing, teaching, coaching, and training to qualify for the 2004 Olympic marathon trials.

twenty-one

The Witch and Food

OUR RELATIONSHIP WITH FOOD IS not simple. It ought to be a case of picking out what is nourishing and delicious, eating it, and feeling great as a result (assuming, that is, that we live in a country in which food is readily available)—but no. For a start, there are the pitfalls of chemically enhanced and sprayed foods, things that ought to be vegetarian but have bits of animal lurking in them (pork gelatin in some desserts, for example), plus the temptations of a thousand attractively packaged junk foods.

Labels should be read, yes, in order to avoid the pitfalls of gelatin or monosodium glutamate if these upset you, but my own view is that it is best to be reasonably relaxed with one's food intake. I suspect that it would cause as much harm through the stress of seeking out pure foods as it might consuming them. By this, I don't mean trying to survive on potato chips and chocolate alone, but a bit of what you like goes a long way.

Vegetarianism is big in witchcraft and Wicca—indeed, in spiritual disciplines in general. The Theosophists adopted the habit of not eating karmically polluting flesh from the Hindus. Many witches now are either vegetarian or vegan.

The subject of vegetarianism is a big bugbear amongst the spiritually inclined. As far as Craft history goes, Traditional (Hereditary) witches would no doubt have eaten animals hunted by themselves and respectfully treated (possibly thanking the animal for giving up its body as food), whereas many of the Theosophists who influenced modern witchcraft/Wicca were vegetarian. This came from the Hindu and Buddhist beliefs that so infiltrated Theosophy. The concept of karma came with them, and the thought that perhaps it is unwise to perpetuate the suffering of other species by raising them for slaughter, especially when it is not necessary to eat meat in order to live.

Witches and magickians have always held differing opinions on this one. Crowley, who was renowned for his hunting activities and "Do What Thou Wilt" attitude, came up with the brilliantly imaginative excuse that, by eating meat, we are doing the animals concerned a favour, as we are assimilating their flesh into the organism of a higher order, thereby elevating their matter. Most of the magickally inclined, however, agree that it comes down to the individual to decide.

Personally I do not eat meat or fish, but I do eat dairy products, including eggs. I actually agree with the principles of a vegan diet (no milk or egg derivatives whatever), but find it unsuitable to my constitution. To me, meat seems polluting, and carries bad karma. However, a functional witch is one at ease with her own conscience, and it is a personal decision, like all aspects of the Craft. However, this is a personal choice, and not something I believe one should ever be evangelical about.

Food is the world passing through us. Therefore it is sensible to concentrate on pure, clean foods like fresh vegetables and pulses, and to eat when the body requires it rather than for its own sake (except occasionally, of course!). Even this common-sense statement causes a big problem for many people, some witches included (see the section entitled "The Witch and Eating Disorders" in chapter 6).

I am a useless cook. I simply don't have the time or patience to dedicate to it. Eating, on the other hand . . . well, that's another story.

My friend Syd is an adept at magickally nourishing food. I know—I've staggered to her apartment after a hectic day or night in London a thousand times, and been fed foods that are psychically as well as physically rejuvenating—amazing. Here, she tells you how to make some of her favourite magickal and sabbatical recipes.

The Witch's Cauldron: The Alchemy of Food
by Syd Moore

Forget the celebrity chefs! Burn those Women's Institute recipes! Lose those frumpy associations with the kitchen and domesticity! Cookery is cool. Cookery is magick! But I'm a convert, and like most newcomers, I'm almost evangelical about the positive aspects of cooking. I have such a busy life, cookery really does exert a positive influence over me. It helps me wind down, destress, and meditate. Cooking with seasonal fare is also a fantastic way for urban Pagans, like me, to stay in touch with the cycles of nature.

I didn't always see it like this. In fact, in my teenage years, I hated cooking. Back then, cookery just seemed like a boring, fussy way of transforming raw elements into something edible. Yet as I grew older, flew the nest, and was forced to fend for myself, I began to perceive cookery as something more than pure survivalism. I started to notice the effects that my cookery had on other people (sometimes good, sometimes embarrassingly bad), and discerned that it also brought out my more creative and expressive side. The more I cooked, the more I realised cookery's positive properties and potential.

Then, when I learnt about Wicca, I spotted the parallels between cuisine and spellcraft: in both, one uses an athame, a cauldron (it is no coincidence that the witch's cauldron and chef's cooking pot are the same shape), and natural ingredients; one exerts one's own will on nature to bring about the desired results. After a while, I realised that cookery is a word for food *alchemy*. That knowledge is a potent thing.

My grandmother, however, always understood the power of food and cookery. As well as being an excellent cook, Nan was also a rare and talented pastry maker. Any nonprofessional chef who has ever attempted to make puff pastry from scratch will know that it requires a very light touch and a swift hand that few possess. Nan, however, perfected her own personal technique so much so that she became renowned in her local community as an expert pastry chef. In fact, in later years as a widow living by herself, she was able to trade premade pastry for favours.

Yet for me, my sister, and brother, Nan's greatest talent was her ability to unlock and inspire our infant imaginations with food and stories. The highlight of our visits to her was the serving up of the fairy cakes. These small winged cupcakes were filled with variously coloured buttercreams, and were dished up with cordials and also, most importantly, an enthralling fairy tale. At the end of each story, Nan would instruct us to go down to the bottom of the garden and leave the crumbs of our cakes for the fairy folk who lived there. It may have been a good way to get three excitable children out of the house so that she could clear up unhindered, but for us it was a wonderful, magickal experience that exhilarated our childhood years and stimulated our psyches. Though she passed over a few years ago, I still can't look at a fairy cake without recalling elves, shoemakers, fairy godmothers, and goblin balls.

Many of her recipes and her enthusiasm for cooking were handed down to my mother, who inherited Nan's gift for exceptional cake-making as well. Not only did Mum provide us with a good balanced and nutritious diet that produced three strong, healthy, and happy children, she also ran her own catering business. Though this was demanding, she continued to ensure that the three of us were regularly packed off to school with pastries and sweets that delighted and charmed. Often, when word got around that I had brought in a packed lunch filled with Mum's or Nan's homemade cakes, I would miraculously become the most popular kid on the playground. I was also never ever short of friends who wanted to come home to tea! Such was the pull of these magickal delicacies.

I, myself, am still experimenting with this alchemical practice, but I have a hunch that I, too, may have been lucky enough to receive this hereditary flair. However, to ensure that readers of this book get the best they can from this chapter, I have asked Mum for her collaboration and the gift of certain special recipes, for which I am very grateful. Yet, like most children, I have rebelled slightly with regards to one thing: regimented recipes that demand you *unerringly* observe precise instructions. Obviously this presents a bit of a problem when it comes to cookery. So I have adjusted the recipes to my own requirements. Thus you will find very few recipes in this chapter that require weighing and measuring. (Please note: What amounts do appear are in British units. Where necessary, American readers will find conversions in parentheses.) I urge you to remember two words that have helped me weave my way around the culinary world: *intuition* and *nutrition*.

Nature has a way of letting you know how much of what you should use. For instance, ingredients that you need just a touch of to flavour your meal are always tiny, little creations like chillies (the smaller the hotter, generally) or spices and herbs. On the other hand, nutritious produce that you can use cartloads of in most meals are always big, in plentiful supply, and brightly coloured (the brighter the more nutritious). See what I mean? Intuition and nutrition.

So if you get a gut instinct about an ingredient that you think might enhance your dish, go with it. Unless your psychic antenna's a bit skewed, your recipe will change for the better and you'll create something new and uniquely yours. Sounds a little bit like magick, doesn't it? Well, I think cooking is magickal. It's transformative, meditative, and has tangible results.

Okay, so here we go with the recipes. Happy weaving!

A Point on Stock

Now, some of the recipes in this chapter require vegetable stock. I know the thought of making stock seems strangely intimidating to a number of people, so it's absolutely fine, if you prefer, to use stock cubes or powders. There are some very good professional products out there, the best being on sale in health/organic food shops. However, I do believe a good homemade stock will jazz up and transform most soups, vegetarian sauces, and broths, adding texture, nutrition, and a gorgeous subtlety that the preproduced stocks just don't supply. In addition to this, stock is incredibly easy to make, ultraeconomic, and most importantly, a very soothing experience. Often at the weekends, especially if I've been socialising wildly, there is nothing I like better than making a big cauldron of stock. There really is something amazingly satisfying about rounding up the week's redundant vegetables, and alchemically converting them into something useful. Plus, the aromatherapeutic effects are sublime. As you cook, the smell of fresh vegetables and spices simmering away stretches round corners and creeps under doors, weaving and wrapping its comforting memories and wholesome associations round the members of the household, uplifting even the most bleary-eyed. I wouldn't say it is a total hangover cure, but it certainly seems to help the blues.

So, to business. This is a very basic recipe. As with all my recipes, feel free to add different vegetables according to season and mood.

VEGETABLE STOCK

3 stalks celery	3 or 4 peppercorns
8 mushrooms, any variety	Fresh herbs, any that you like or
3 or 4 carrots	have in the house
2 leeks	6 to 7 pints (3½ to 4¼ U.S.
3 medium onions	quarts) water
1 average-sized potato	Other vegetables to add can be:
2 cloves garlic	cabbage, lettuce, fennel
2 bay leaves	Vinegar or lemon juice (optional)

Roughly chop the vegetables and herbs and place them in the stockpot. Add the water (and a dash of vinegar or lemon juice if you like your food a little zingy) and slowly bring the liquid to a boil. Turn the heat to the lowest setting and let it simmer away gently for about an hour. From time to time return to the pot and skim off any impurities that may have risen to the surface. After an hour, add the peppercorns, let simmer for ten more minutes, then pour the stock through a sieve and strain well.

If you are not using this for another recipe, you can either refrigerate the stock for three to four days or freeze it.

Mum's Tip: Use old plastic soft drink bottles to store the stock in. They fit into the fridge perfectly and freeze well.

Staples and Tips

1. Each recipe is meant to serve roughly three to four people, although there will often be a quantity left that you can freeze.

2. Get a big, big pot. My big blue pot is my cauldron. It's great for cooking in bulk, and it feels wonderful to stir.

3. Always keep the following in your cupboard: soy sauce, chilli sauce, vinegar, and lemon juice. They are great flavour enhancers and can liven up many a dull meal.

4. Most of the best meals can be knocked together with a few simple ingredients. I always keep pastas, canned tomatoes, onions, and cheese in the house so that, should unexpected guests turn up, I can produce an Italian pasta dish at the drop of a hat. It's very easy to make and pleases most tastes.

5. Excessive use of salt can lead to high blood pressure, so you are best advised to keep your daily intake limited to one teaspoon, or 2,300 mg.

6. Try to season with sea salt and freshly milled black peppercorns. They have a supremely superior taste to the preground type.

7. Also, whenever possible, use cold pressed extra virgin olive oil. It's more expensive than most other oils, but it is one of the few fats that is not bad for you.

8. Healthy adults are meant to eat approximately four to five portions of fruit and vegetables every day. Personally I find this a difficult target to meet, so I try to add fruit and vegetables to my diet whenever I can. For instance, I always eat fruit yoghurts; whenever I go shopping I buy spinach pasta as opposed to egg pasta; I also pop the odd sliced banana into any creamy curries I make (nobody really notices them, but I find they add sweetness to the taste and a thickness to the texture). If I'm out, I try and drink juices: a vodka and orange is better than a vodka and tonic.

Imbolc

At last, spring is on its way! Soon new shoots will be pushing up through the soil, flowers will start to bud, and the old majestic trees will unfurl their lush, curvaceous leaves. What better time is there to go out and embrace the freshness in the air, and for this celebratory Imbolc recipe you will have to do exactly that. Although there is a profusion of the main ingredient everywhere (in urban parks and the countryside too!), I can't think of any retail outlet that sells them.

NETTLE SOUP

It may sound strange, but folks have been using stinging nettles for food, dyes, and medicines since the Bronze Age. It is a wonderfully hardy plant and grows all over the world. In Italy, nettles have been used for centuries as a substitute for spinach. High in calcium, iron, and vitamin C, they are wholesome, tasty, and also wonderfully detoxifying. This soup is, therefore, a delicious way to cleanse your body of the wintery excesses and to prepare yourself for the purity of spring.

Don't be put off by the fact that they sting. When cooked, the nettles' stings are completely destroyed. Just ensure that, when you go out and collect them, you are armed with plastic gloves and plastic bags. Remember to keep your gloves on when you're washing and preparing the nettles too.

The best parts of the nettle are the youngest leaves at the top. Pick the uppermost four leaves and avoid the larger leaves, which may turn out a little rough. Do not pick from nettles that have flowered. If you are an urban practitioner, make sure you pick from patches that are well away from polluted roadsides.

2 tablespoons salty butter	Pinch of paprika
2 to 3 cloves garlic, finely chopped	Pinch of ground nutmeg
1 onion, finely chopped	1 teaspoon lemon juice
5 medium-sized potatoes, chopped roughly into cubes	Salt and pepper
6 or 7 handfuls nettle leaves, washed twice and *destemmed*	3 to 4 tablespoons Greek yoghurt, soya milk, or fresh double cream
2 pints (4¾ U.S. cups) vegetable stock	Freshly grated Parmesan cheese
	4 eggs

Melt the butter on a gentle heat. Chop the garlic and the onion and throw it into the pot. Cook until the onion becomes translucent.

Add the chopped potatoes to the pot along with the nettles. Sauté for a couple of minutes. Pour enough stock into the pan so that the vegetables are covered. Cover and simmer very gently for about ten to fifteen minutes. In the meantime, hard-boil the eggs.

When ready, you can either liquidise the whole potful, or simply process half of it. I prefer to liquidise half of it, and return the purée to the broth in the stockpot. This gives the soup a chunkier farmhouse texture to it.

Peel the eggs and halve them.

Just before you are ready to serve, season with the paprika, nutmeg, lemon juice, salt, and pepper, and remove from heat. Stir in the yoghurt/soya/cream.

Ladle the liquid into individual soup bowls. Float two egg halves on the surface of the soup and then sprinkle with a little Parmesan cheese. Serve to a delighted audience.

Ostara (Easter)

Out of everyone I know, I think Ostara, or Easter, has the most positive effect on my mum. Though energetic and upbeat by nature, this solstice sees her really skip about the place with renewed bounce and vigour. Ask her why and she'll tell you, "This festival is really important to me. It's the time of year when we can visibly see growth and the nurturing forces of nature; the flora that dies in the winter is reborn. All around me I see flowers like the crocus and daffodil pushing up through the hard earth. Trees, too, begin to bloom and flourish. I walk through the world with an ever-enlarging feeling of hope for new beginnings and a sense of security in the continuum of life. This is a time when we should celebrate life over death and rejoice in the world of the spirit." Which about sums it up.

Watercress flan is ideal for this time of year, as this plant comes into season quickly now, like a harbinger of change, bringing goodness and bounty. This recipe also incorporates eggs, the most potent symbol of new ideas and new life.

STELLA'S WATERCRESS FLAN

Pastry

2 full cups wholemeal flour
2 tablespoons butter or
   margarine

2 teaspoons baking powder
3 tablespoons cold water

The trick to making good pastry is cold hands, so before starting, try running cold water over your wrists for thirty seconds or so. Sift the baking powder into the flour. Lightly rub the fat into the flour until it resembles breadcrumbs. Don't overdo the kneading, as it's important that the dough stays cool to keep its lightness.

Next, very gradually mix in the cold water. Keep this cold in the fridge until you roll it out for the flan.

Filling

2 bunches watercress	3 eggs
9 ounces wholemeal shortcrust pastry	3 tablespoons milk
	Pinch of cayenne pepper
12 ounces cottage cheese, sieved	Salt and pepper

Line a 9-inch flan tin with the pastry. Prick the base with a fork and bake at Gas Mark 3–4 (170 degrees Celsius, or 325–350 degrees Fahrenheit) for ten to fifteen minutes.

Meanwhile, finely chop the watercress and beat the eggs.

Mix the cottage cheese, watercress, beaten eggs, and milk together well with a fork. Add the cayenne pepper, salt, and pepper.

Put filling into the partially cooked pastry case and bake at Gas Mark 3–4 (325–350 degrees Fahrenheit) for thirty-five minutes, or until the top is firm and a lovely golden brown.

Beltane

This recipe involves small green chillies, which are quite possibly hottest of the lot, so use with caution. They have a real kick and not just on the taste buds: chillies are circulatory stimulants and help improve your blood flow enormously. As Beltane is a time for coming out of your shell and into the light, embracing energy and new ideas, this recipe should really help you fire up your verve and add power to your resolve.

GREEN CURRY PASTE

2 cloves garlic	1 small bunch coriander (cilantro)
3 small green chillies	
1 small onion	1 small piece of ginger root, 1 to 2 inches long
1 tablespoon soy sauce	
1 stalk lemon grass	Juice of 1 lime
1 teaspoon cumin	Rind of ½ lime, grated
	2 teaspoons olive oil

Peel the ginger and garlic and chop into small chunks. Slice up the remaining ingredients finely. Throw into a blender.

Squeeze the juice of the lime into the blender, and then grate half of the rind over the mixture.

Spoon in the olive oil and blend until you have a fine paste.

THAI GREEN CURRY

3 to 4 tablespoons green curry paste, or to taste

Juice of 1 lime

2 sprigs of coriander (cilantro)

1 bunch green beans, topped and tailed

2 leeks, quartered

1 green pepper, diced

8 spring onions, chopped

2 large handfuls baby spinach leaves

2 handfuls spring greens, roughly chopped

1 small banana, finely sliced

1 carrot

8 small mushrooms, any kind

½ cup vegetable stock

1 can (400 millilitres, or 13½ U.S. ounces) coconut milk

2 teaspoons olive oil

Pour the oil into your wok or pan and heat gently.

Cut the coriander stalks finely, but leave off the leaves to decorate the meal. Add the stalks to the pan.

Toss the chopped spring onions into the wok. Add the green curry paste.

Add the green beans, leeks, green pepper, spring greens, banana, and carrot all to the cauldron. Pour the juice of the lime into the pot and turn up the heat.

Stir-fry for three to four minutes. Next, add the vegetable stock and stir for one minute.

Cut up the mushrooms. Add the coconut milk, the baby spinach, and mushrooms, and simmer for three to four minutes more.

Serve up with rice and garnish with coriander leaves (cilantro).

Summer Solstice

When we were young, during the summer holidays, my sister Josie and I would often be sent to the north of England to stay with our grandparents. They lived in a large old house with a big sprawling, mature garden full of vegetables and flowers, at the center of which stood a magnificent oak complete with tree house. It was the perfect environment for two very urbanized little girls to cavort and frolic in.

With such a wonderful playground, we would often become rather overexcited and rowdy. On these occasions, our grandparents would try and barter us into a quieter, more submissive state with the promise of elderflower champagne if we were good. The light texture, bubbles, and sugary taste of the fizz were such a delicious treat that on most occasions Josie and I would instantly transform ourselves into sweet little angels.

Afterwards, however, Josie and I would return to a more unruly state. Despite its name, elderflower champagne is merely a cordial mixed with sparkling water, but the powers of suggestion constitute a magickal spell when you're nine. After imbibing the delicacy, my sister and I would consequently stagger round the garden pretending to be drunk, wrecking the vegetable patch, and falling out of the tree house. Ah, those halcyon days!

Little did I know, however, I was setting a precedent of behaviour that would stay with me for the rest of my life! Since then, summer has been associated in my mind with cheerful hedonism, fun, and fizz.

This recipe has been supplied by my good friend Kathleen Smith, who assures me that it's just as good as the stuff Granddad used to make. However, as it's completely harmless, I've also added my dad's recipe for carrot wine. I warn you: the latter is an adaptation of a formula from one of England's late, great wine-makers, C. J. Berry, and should only be attempted by amateur wine-makers.

Both of these drinks form a wonderful accompaniment to any salads or light meals you may be making for the solstice.

ELDERFLOWER CORDIAL

22 to 23 elderflower heads
1.75 kilograms (8⅔ U.S. cups) castor sugar
1.8 litres (7⅔ U.S. cups) water
50 grams (¼ U.S. cup) tartaric acid
2 lemons, sliced
2 oranges, sliced

Boil the water to purify it and leave to cool. When it is cold, add the sugar, acid, oranges, lemons, and elderflowers, and then stir occasionally over twenty-four hours.

After a day, return to the cauldron. Strain out the mixture and then bottle it. Don't forget that this is a cordial, so you should dilute it with water. The mixture should keep for a good month. If you want to make "champagne" simply add carbonated water!

DAD'S CARROT WINE

1 gallon (1¼ U.S. gallons) water

35 medium-sized (6 pounds) carrots

1 pound brewer's wheat (you can usually buy this from a health food shop)

3 pounds (6¾ U.S. cups plus 5 teaspoons) white sugar

2 lemons, sliced

2 oranges, sliced

1 teaspoon granulated brewer's yeast

Gently wash the carrots. Slice them up, submerge them in the water, and boil them until they are soft and tender. Eat the carrots, strain the water, and keep it.

Take a separate bowl and ladle in the sugar, oranges, and lemons and give it a stir. Empty this into a large receptacle with a lid. Pour the hot water over this, and add enough water to make the liquid mix up to one gallon (1¼ U.S. gallons). Stir it. Let stand until the liquid temperature is lukewarm. Throw in the wheat. Sprinkle with the yeast.

Leave to ferment, closely covered with a lid, for fifteen days stirring twice daily (or as Dad says, "As many times as you can manage—it's such a lovely smell!"). After fifteen days, decant the liquid into a fermentation jar with an airlock. Ferment until the liquid is clear and fermentation has finished (up to a year).

Lughnassah

As I approach the harvest, I find my body starts to yearn for more earthy food such as corn, grains, milk, and bread. This recipe always seems to satisfy me at this time. Although the majority of ingredients are good solid foods, the dish is quite an indulgence so it goes down well with all my Leo friends, who are at their most ebullient at this time of year.

For this recipe you will need a small baking dish and a larger oven-proof basin, or Bain-Marie.

CHOCOLATE BREAD AND BUTTER PUDDING

3½ soft, nutty, wholemeal petit pains or baguettes

Butter or margarine

3 eggs

2 ounces (4 tablespoons plus 2 teaspoons) castor sugar

Pinch of ground nutmeg

4 squares of dark chocolate

¾ pint (1¾ U.S. cups) milk
3 fluid ounces double cream
Chocolate spread, like Nutella

1 handful pecan halves
Pinch of drinking chocolate
  powder

Butter your baking dish. Cut the bread into slices of about two centimeters (¾ inch) thickness. Spread liberally with butter and chocolate spread. Arrange, slightly overlapping, in the smaller dish.

Combine the eggs, castor sugar, and nutmeg and whisk. Next, pour in the cream and the milk and whisk again.

Scatter the pecan halves and grate the chocolate over the bread. Pour the liquid mixture over the bread. Press down on the bread lightly with a potato masher, and leave to soak for fifteen minutes.

Fill the large baking dish with water and float the smaller one inside it (or use a Bain-Marie). Bake at Gas Mark 3 (170 degrees Celsius, or 325 degrees Fahrenheit) for about forty minutes or until the middle of the pudding is set.

Dust with drinking chocolate powder and serve with cream.

Mabon

My mum, though Christian in belief, has always been interested in folk culture and music. Mabon, or Harvest Festival, really draws out her strong Pagan impulse, so that every year she will gather round the family and celebrate this solstice in the true Celtic tradition with lashings of drink and a cornucopia of scrumptious dishes. One dessert that always turns up at this time when apples are at their most plentiful is wild honey and apple tart. It seemed only natural then, that I should ask her to supply that old family favourite for this sabbat.

WILD HONEY AND APPLE TART

The perfect combination of sweet (wild honey) and sour (lemon juice), this appetizing dish is also very good for you, incorporating, as it does, one of nature's most plentiful fruits: the apple. Mum always used to tell us that "An apple a day keeps the doctor away," and now, after years of research, scientists are at last conceding this is probably true. Apples are not only full of goodness and nutrition, they also contain pectin, a fibre that reduces cholesterol and lowers the chances of cancer. See, those old wives do have a true tale or two!

> 3 medium-sized cooking apples
>   (approximately)
> ¼ pint (⅔ U.S. cups) wild honey
> 1 lemon
> 1 handful icing (powdered) sugar
>
> 2 handfuls wholemeal bread-
>   crumbs (or more if you prefer
>   a thicker texture)
> 9 ounces shortcrust pastry

Grease an 8-inch oven-proof flan dish, and line it with the pastry.

Squeeze the juice of the lemon into a bowl. Grate the apples and lemon rind, then mix this together with the juice of the lemon and the honey. Put the mixture into the flan dish and sprinkle breadcrumbs over it. Some should sink into the mixture. Cut any leftover pastry into leaf shapes and use them to decorate the top of the flan.

Put the dish into an oven preheated to 200 degrees Celsius (400 degrees Fahrenheit, or Gas Mark 6). Bake for thirty minutes or until firm to the touch.

Remove from the oven. Leave to cool and sift a light coat of icing sugar across the top to decorate.

Samhain

Samhain is all about colour, warmth, and cheer before we enter the long dark winter. At this time of year, it also pays to be practical. With the cold months approaching, it is important that we refuel and stay warm, so I have used barley in this recipe. Originally from Mesopotamia, barley was often administered to invalids. Our ancestors obviously had their antennae working properly, as we now know that this grain is actually a great source of protein, carbohydrates, calcium, and vitamin B. Barley, however, takes approximately one to one and a half hours to cook, so it's worth boiling it before you start the rest of the preparations (or even the night before).

Samhain is mostly about magick, and pumpkins, nature's biggest fruit, have always been linked to enchantment. To me as a child, the pumpkin represented spells and glamour, turning, as it did, into a coach and transporting Cinderella off to the biggest night of her life. As an adult, I look at a pumpkin and see a symbol of abundance—a big orange ball of warmth and energy. It's a lovely solid vegetable related to the squash family and an essential provider of vitamins A, C, and E. So this Samhain recipe combines the visual and nutritional elements of the pumpkin and barley grain, providing you with all the major vitamins and also a spectacular serving vessel with which to impress your guests!

I'm usually so excited about Samhain that once I've stirred in my spells, I spend the rest of the time dancing around the kitchen to Motown. But I really don't expect you to do that. The main thing about this meal, though, is the vigour and the concentration with which you cook. Remember that Samhain is a celebration. Tonight, more than any other night, the Veil between worlds is at its thinnest. I often find the air full of expectation and a sense of drama lurking in the most unlikely places, such as my cupboards and pots! The intense energy that you will be experiencing as you cook this meal will be soaked up by the food and transmitted to those eating it, so it's important to feel positive, upbeat, and strong. Also, be careful. Watch your hands over the flames, and be vigilant as you carve and scrape the pumpkin. Mischief abounds tonight!

Not including the boiling of the pearl barley, from chopping the vegetables to serving up, this recipe takes about an hour and a half to make, so you have plenty of time to chant incantations and meditate as you cook. Only use the tomato paste if you like a rich, tomatoey taste. If you prefer a sweetness to your food, you can substitute tomato ketchup for the paste.

PUMPKIN STEW

1 large pumpkin (jack-o'-lantern variety)

2 handfuls cashew nuts

2 leeks, chopped

12 mushrooms, any kind, roughly sliced

2 carrots, chopped

1 can (400 grams, or 14 ounces) chopped tomatoes

2 small red chillies, or pinch of chilli powder

2 cloves garlic, roughly chopped

1 large onion, roughly chopped

1 red pepper, sliced and chopped

1 tablespoon tomato paste (optional)

2 handfuls pearl barley

Pinch of saffron

2 teaspoons olive oil

Pinch of paprika

1 pint (2⅓ U.S. cups) vegetable stock

2 tablespoons plain yoghurt or crème fraîche

2 tablespoons grated cheese (I find mature cheddar best)

Dash of soy sauce

Salt and pepper

First, cook the barley. It's best to get the type that doesn't need soaking beforehand. Rinse it, then boil it until it is soft. This usually takes about one hour. Drain and leave to one side.

Arrange the cashew nuts on a baking tray and very lightly drizzle one of the tea-spoons of olive oil over them. Toast them under the grill until they start to brown (approximately six to seven minutes).

Carve a zigzag around the top of the pumpkin and remove the top. This will be the lid to your pumpkin serving pot. Carefully scrape out the seeds and stringy flesh and simmer this up with the vegetable stock for fifteen minutes. Pour through a sieve, discard the seeds and tissue, and put the liquid to one side.

Next, using an athame or sharp knife, cut or scrape out most of the pumpkin flesh, but remember to leave a good sturdy shell. Chop up the flesh into bite-sized cubes.

Add the other teaspoon of olive oil to a big pot (cauldron, stockpot, or wok will do) and heat gently. Add the chopped onion and sauté until translucent. Then add the garlic, the chillies, the tomato paste (or ketchup), and the spices, and stir for another two minutes. Add the remaining vegetables except the mushrooms (carrots, leeks, and pepper). Sauté for another five minutes.

Add the can of chopped tomatoes, the barley, and the pumpkin stock. Turn down the heat and simmer gently for another twenty to twenty-five minutes, returning frequently to stir. Add the mushrooms and cook for five minutes more uncovered. You can now either roughly chop the cashew nuts or throw them in whole.

Next, taste the stew and season with salt and pepper and a dash of soy sauce. Remove from heat and ladle the mixture into the empty pumpkin shell. Stir in the grated cheese so that it melts into the stew. Then add the crème fraîche or yoghurt, replace the pumpkin lid, and serve.

There should be enough stew left over to leave out for any visiting spirits. Alternatively, you can refrigerate it and blend in vegetable stock to make a delicious pumpkin-based soup within two to three days.

I would suggest, as an accompaniment to this meal, saffron-flavoured rice, baked potatoes, or hot crusty bread. You can make the bread yourself according to your own recipe, but if you buy some rolls or a loaf from someone who makes it for a living, you will have more time to pray, play, and prance about on this the most exciting of nights.

Yule

December sees us arrive in the darkest, coldest season of the year. With the days at their shortest and the temperature dropping steeply, a wholesome, tasty meal using the fruits of our harvested bounty is exactly what we need to raise our spirits. This hearty recipe, with its plethora of tasty and health-imparting ingredients, will not fail to bring a vigorous dose of cheeriness at this time.

You can use canned chestnuts for this recipe, but if you are going to go out and pick chestnuts, choose the ones that have already dropped onto the floor and fallen out of their spiky casings. Also make sure that you peel them before you start cooking. It's a very fiddly job: shelling thirty chestnuts can take up to an hour and a half. The same advice goes for the walnuts. Also, this makes a huge amount of filling, so use a large pie dish. I generally use any leftover filling to make an extra smaller pie, or use it as a base for a stew the following day.

CHESTNUT PIE

30 chestnuts (approximately)

15 mushrooms, any variety

20 walnuts, undried if possible

2 large onions, finely sliced

2 carrots, diced

1 parsnip, cubed

½ small turnip, cubed

2 leeks, quartered

3 cups (2¾ U.S. cups plus
   2 tablespoons) strong ale
   (brown beer)

1 tablespoon olive oil

3 bay leaves

1 cup vegetable stock

1 clove garlic, chopped

Pinch of mustard seeds

1 ounce (3 tablespoons plus
   1 teaspoon) plain flour

Black pepper

Fresh parsley

1 egg, beaten

Premade shortcrust pastry
   (enough to cover your pie
   dish)

Boil the chestnuts until soft (should take about twenty minutes).

Gently sauté the onion until translucent, then add the garlic and the mustard seeds and sauté for another minute. Add the carrots, turnip, and parsnip, and sauté for another two minutes. Add the flour to the pan and gradually stir in the ale and vegetable stock. Then add the bay leaves and simmer for twenty minutes. Turn your oven on and set the temperature to 200 degrees Celsius (Gas Mark 6, or 400 degrees Fahrenheit).

Next, add the chestnuts and the mushrooms. Simmer for another three minutes. Add ground black pepper to the mixture, and turn into your pie dish.

Roll out the pastry and cover the pie dish. Pattern the pie, and brush the top with a whisked egg to give it a shine. Bake in the oven for forty minutes.

Serve with green beans.

Syd Moore has been a Pagan for fifteen years. During that time, she has travelled extensively throughout Europe, southeast Asia, and Australia. She has been a stand-up performance poet, film actress, writer, publicist, cabaret artiste, and full-on glitz chick. Most recently she has worked in marketing for Random House publishers, and in television, presenting her own book programme, U.K. channel 4's Pulp. She lives in London where she is directing a short film, finishing her first novel, handcrafting soaps, and raising her son, Riley. What a woman!

twenty-two

The Witch and Wealth

WE ALL KNOW THE OCCULT clichés about trading one's soul for wealth and power—the moral lesson taught in Goethe's *Faust*. Magickal history contains more than its fair share of such shenanigans—indeed, most magick was developed in order to satisfy immediate physical needs. It was not until Victorian times through the Golden Dawn (many of whose members were already amply provided for on this level) that Western magick became truly spiritualised. That's not to say that the primitive/mediaeval mindset doesn't still prevail in many occultists—it does—but we shall leave these practitioners to their own devices and look instead at the more wholesome attitude of the modern witch/Wiccan.

A witch's greatest wealth is her ingenuity. This enables her to approach any situation with a win-win attitude. If she can tackle a problem in the normal manner, she will do so. If not, she can take recourse to her spellcraft. The spell is not necessarily intended to bend fate to her will. On the contrary, it is designed to bring optimum positives to all concerned by working with natural tides.

A friend of mine was keen to get a promotion at work, where she felt she was being overlooked. She was also in need of the extra money a raise would bring in. However, she did not wish to magickally interlope on the promotional possibilities open to the others in the office. She cast a spell for career success, adding the proviso that it should be to the benefit of all.

She cast her spell at the new moon, adding a little energy to it every day as the moon waxed. On the third day before the full moon, she was told that she was to be moved to the PR department, which meant a pay increase. Within the next month, due partly to a contact she had made in her new role, her old office was shifted around and everybody was given an improved post. A couple of her closest friends also received pay increases. The gentle working of her will with the tides of the moon had worked to enhance all of their situations. Stagnation and dissatisfaction are true poverty.

Regarding money, the witch enjoys it when it is there—she knows how to treat herself and her friends—but does not fret much when it is not. She knows that the Goddess will provide, and She always does. One of the happiest times of my life was when I was penniless in London. I was young, free, and had complete trust in the powers that be. I eked out a living reading Tarot, sometimes for little more than a cup of coffee, but felt so karmically strong that I knew—just *knew*—that I would be fine. Admittedly, if one is born into poverty, that is a different matter—but here I am concentrating on the ability of the grown adult to improvise. When you ask the gods to assist you, and then do everything within your power to help yourself, you have a winning combination. Every witch knows this.

Because she is a very down-to-earth creature at the end of the day, the witch does not care too much for wealth. She likes to have the basics at hand, as do we all, and the occasional luxury is welcome. However, materialistic she certainly is not. Money is not the driving force of the metaphysicist. If you want that, you become a broker in the city, not a witch. There are some wealthy witches around, but that is incidental. Financially successful people who become interested in the Craft want what poorer witches have: magick, and immunity to social expectations. No witch bends to the rules of materialism—this would be anathema to the witching spirit. Spiritual wealth—most notably wisdom and compassion—is true richness. Experience and insight are the currency of the sorceress, and we trade fairly. This way, we stay karmically clean and carry our wealth onto the next level, which few other mortals can claim.

Though wealth has the power to change the world, it rarely does. Those who possess it often become too introspective to use it meaningfully. Traditionally, for this reason, spiritually minded people are poor on the material planes. Saints and prophets, who often become anti-materialist to the point of poverty, have transformed more lives than many a millionaire.

The *sense* of abundance is true affluence. The rich and famous can feel just as unfulfilled as the rest of us, either because greater things are craved, or because of scarcity in other realms (especially emotional). Hollywood provides us with more than one example of this.

The following technique is an example of the creative faculties the witch employs to bring meaningful wealth and abundance into her life. It is a classically Wiccan spell, and an example of sympathetic-style magick (see chapter 18, "Magickal Techniques and Spell-casting").

MONEY TREE SPELL

Take a money tree and place it on your altar or in a place special to you, such as a magickal spot in your garden. Make sure it has plenty of light, wherever it is.

These succulent plants only need to be lightly watered twice a month or so, so this simple spell is best performed every time it is watered.

This tree will represent your fortunes. As well as a physical organism, make it an astral image in your mind. Imagine the tree flourishing, its leaves representing money and abundance. Beginning under the darkness of a new moon, burn a green candle, and as you sprinkle the water, invest the plant with energy and see it growing in your mind. Talk to the tree, tell it what you want, and thank it. Imagine that every time you take money from your astral money tree, it instantly grows back and redoubles.

Now bury a small silver coin in the pot. Next time you return to water the plant, repeat the ritual, but retrieve the last coin you buried. Be sure to replace it with a new one. Give the coin to someone you love.

The Witch and Employment

The witch is famed for her versatility. After all, if changing shape and fortune are possible, so, too, is adjustment to any given situation. I have worked in all manner of jobs, with everybody from other witches (Tarot reading), to Oxford dons (bookshop), to entirely uneducated sixteen-year-olds (cafes and shops). It is not always easy, and it is not always pleasant, but it is always possible.

The creative witch may at times feel stultified by the necessity of working a normal job—I certainly have. Sometimes the excess of banality counteracts magickal thought processes and leaves one feeling bereft of real purpose in the world. This is especially relevant to sales- and marketing-related jobs, and any profession in which one is serving "clients" and "customers" rather than "people." Caring professions are, of course, an entirely different matter. Nursing, counselling, working for worthy causes, and so on, are probably the most rewarding job sectors for anybody, particularly the witch.

It is important to integrate with the "outside world." The witch does not confine her magick to her own sphere, she uses it to subtly help others. Sitting on the bus close to a distressed mother, she might surround the screaming child in fluffy pink light until it calms down, and project calming energy at the mother. When she sees an old, lonely person in the street, she tries to connect his or her life lines with those of friendly spirits in both realms. She confers a blessing everywhere she goes, and this is her real full-time employment.

Witches today work in every profession imaginable. Many you would not recognise as witches at first, but a closer inspection of their auras and of the pendants round their necks might reveal more. Perhaps a small pentagram will be found, or an ankh. Of course, not everyone who wears these symbols is a witch. Many people (especially teens and goths) wear them as decoration merely.

Witches are computer programmers, shop assistants, university lecturers, writers, members of the police, and school teachers. They may not be able to wear their beliefs openly, especially the latter (many school computers have firewalls against New Age and esoteric subjects and sites), but they will subtly apply their knowledge to any task at hand. (See the work of Kerr Cuhulain for more about the Wiccan cop.)

The witch at work has to guard against using her powers through anger or frustration, but she has the advantage of being able to psychically and psychologically protect herself. Most of us encounter problems in our working life, whether they be caused by difficult colleagues, bosses, or clients. The witch is able to use her spellcraft to turn the tides of fortune in her favour, or at least to help her bear up in adverse circumstances.

The witch sees the symbolism inherent in her situation, and that of others, and tries to work intuitively and spiritually with the given circumstances. She abides by the normal rules and fits in, but when she can subtly help another person psychologically or magickally without interfering—"An' it Harm None"—she will do so. Apart from that, as far as the outside world is concerned, she is an ordinary citizen.

Glossary

Throughout this book I have used Qabalistic terms for which you will find detailed explanations in their relevant sections. See below for a quick and easy version. I also include definitions of terms that may not be familiar to some readers.

Aura—The energy that emanates from the spiritual and physical bodies, and is visible (with third-eye perception, usually) to some people.

Binah—The third sphere of the Qabalistic Tree of Life, which is concerned with death, dissolution, integrating, and thus higher understanding. The spirit of the sphere is feminine and restrictive.

Chakra—An energy-vortex on the astral/etheric body. There are seven main chakras, which are detailed in chapter 11, "The Chakra System and Auras."

Chesed/Chesedic—The fourth sphere of the Qabalistic Tree of Life, which corresponds to love and mercy. Its nature is masculine and expansive.

Chokmah—The second sphere of the Qabalistic Tree of Life, which represents driving force (in a metaphysical sense), wisdom, and the supreme masculine principle. Chokmah is the counterpart of Binah.

Deosil—Clockwise. This term is usually used to refer to the direction of a witch's dance or Circle-casting.

Geburah/Geburic—Geburah is the fifth sphere on the Qabalistic Tree of Life, and represents strength, severity, and power—the qualities of Mars. Its flip side is violence and wanton destruction.

Great Rite—In Wicca and magick in general, the Great Rite refers to the union of the male and female. This may be performed symbolically (for example, by using an athame and chalice as representations of male and female energies, respectively), or literally (as ritual sex).

Hod—This is the eighth sephirah on the Qabalistic Tree of Life. Hod corresponds to the qualities of intellect, honesty, and academic evolution emanating from a spiritual source.

Kether/Ketheric—Pertaining to the first sphere on the Qabalistic Tree of Life, which is situated at the top of the Middle Pillar, sometimes referred to as the "Inscrutable Height." Its qualities are those of the loftiest spiritual attainment, such as Samadhi, or Union with God.

Malkuth/Malkuthic—This refers to the tenth or lowest sphere on the Qabalistic Tree of Life, or physically, the earth plane that we inhabit. In its highest sense it is the gateway to the higher spheres—that is, to spiritual experience. Its negative qualities include the reverence of material form over inner qualities, while its virtues include discrimination and spiritual aspiration.

Moot—The name given to a meeting, usually of Neo-Pagans.

Netzach/Netzachian—This is the sphere of Venus on the Qabalistic Tree of Life, thus it represents the qualities of nature, beauty, sexual love, and procreation. Netzach sits as the seventh sphere on the Tree of Life, the counterpart of Hod.

'Obby 'oss—The Old English folk term for "hobby horse."

Qabalah/Qabalistic—Of or pertaining to the Jewish Tree of Life, as adapted by the Western Mystery Tradition.

Sephirah—Another word for a sphere or station on the Qabalistic Tree of Life diagram. The plural is *sephiroth*.

Skyclad—Naked, usually in ritual.

Telesmatic—Pertaining to the building up of an image from a word (such as the name of a Qabalistic angel) letter by letter, according to the attributes of each glyph.

Tiphareth—The sixth sephirah of the Qabalah, which is the mystical heart of the system. Tiphareth corresponds with sacrifice in the cause for higher good, and thus to such deities as Krishna, Jesus as Christ, and, mythologically, Prometheus. It is represented by the sun.

Widdershins—Anti-clockwise.

Yesod/Yesodic—Yesod is the astral, lunar sphere of the Tree of Life, situated between Tiphareth and Malkuth on the Middle Pillar. Its negative side includes delusion and laziness, while in the positive it corresponds with the faculties of independent thought and action.

Bibliography
and Resources

Bailey, Alice A. *The Seven Rays of Life.* London: Lucis Publishing Trust, 1995.

———. *Unfinished Autobiography.* London: Lucis Publishing Trust, 1994.

Balyoz, Harold. *Three Remarkable Women.* Sedona, Ariz.: Altai Publishers, 2000.

Baudelaire, Charles. *Les Fleurs Du Mal.* Paris: Classiques Francais, 1993.

Beskin, Geraldine, and John Bonner, eds. *Austin Osman Spare: Artist, Occultist, Sensualist.* Exhibition catalogue. Suffolk, England: Beskin Press, 1999.

Blake, William. *Selected Poems and Prose.* London: Penguin Group, 1982.

Bloom, William. *The Sacred Magician: A Ceremonial Diary.* Glastonbury, England: Gothic Image Publications, 1992.

Bonner, John. *Qabalah: A Primer.* London: Skoob Esoterica, 1995.

Brennan, Barbara Ann. *Hands of Light.* New York: Bantam Books, 1987.

Buckland, Raymond. *The Buckland Romani Tarot.* St. Paul, Minn.: Llewellyn Publications, 2001.

———. *Complete Book of Witchcraft.* St. Paul, Minn.: Llewellyn Publications, 2001.

Cabot, Laurie. *Power of the Witch.* London: Michael Joseph, 1990.

Cooper, Quentin, and Paul Sullivan. *Maypoles, Martyrs and Mayhem.* London: Bloomsbury Publishing Plc., 1995.

Crowley, Aleister. *The Complete Astrological Writings.* London: Duckworth, 1988.

———. *Magick.* London: Guild Publishing, 1988.

———. *777 and Other Qabalistic Writings.* York Beach, Maine: Samuel Weiser, Inc., 1998.

Crowther, Patricia. *Lid off the Cauldron.* York Beach, Maine: Samuel Weiser, Inc., 1992.

Cuhulain, Kerr. *Wiccan Warrior.* St. Paul, Minn.: Llewellyn Publications, 2000.

Drury, Neville. *Echoes From the Void.* Dorset, England: Prism Press, 1994.

Edwards, Gill. *Stepping into the Magic.* London: Judy Piatkus Publishers Ltd., 1993.

Farrar, Janet, and Stewart Farrar. *A Witch's Bible: The Complete Witch's Handbook.* Washington, D.C.: Phoenix Publishing, Inc., 1984.

Farrar, Stewart. *What Witches Do.* Washington, D.C.: Phoenix Publishing, Inc., 1983.

Fielding, Charles, and Carr Collins. *The Story of Dion Fortune.* Dallas, Tex.: Star and Cross Publications, 1985.

Firth, Violet. *The Problem of Purity.* London: Rider & Co., 1928.

———. *Psychology of the Servant Problem.* London: C. W. Daniel Company Ltd., 1925.

Fitch, Ed. *Magical Rites from the Crystal Well.* St. Paul, Minn.: Llewellyn Publications, 1988.

Fortune, Dion. *Applied Magic and Aspects of Occultism.* Northants, England: Aquarian Press, 1987.

———. *The Demon Lover.* York Beach, Maine: Samuel Weiser, Inc., 1994.

———. *The Goat-Foot God.* London: Star Books, 1976.

———. *Moon Magic.* London: Society of the Inner Light, n.d.

———. *The Mystical Qabalah.* Northants, England: Aquarian Press, 1987.

———. *The Sea Priestess.* Northants, England: Aquarian Press, 1979.

———. *The Secrets of Doctor Taverner.* Northants, England: Aquarian Press, 1989.

———. *The Winged Bull.* Northants, England: Aquarian Press, 1989.

González-Wippler, Migene. *A Kabbalah for the Modern World*. St. Paul, Minn.: Llewellyn Publications, 1997.

Goodman, Frederick. *Magic Symbols*. London: Brian Trodd Publishing House Limited, 1989.

Grant, Kenneth. *Hecate's Fountain*. London: Skoob Books Publishing, 1991.

———. *The Magical Revival*. London: Skoob Books Publishing, 1991.

Graves, Robert. *The Greek Myths*. Vols. 1 and 2. London: Penguin Books, 1984.

———. *The White Goddess*. London: Faber and Faber, 1994.

Gray, William G. *Ladder of Lights*. York Beach, Maine: Samuel Weiser, Inc., 1981.

Greer, Mary K. *Women of the Golden Dawn: Rebels and Priestesses*. Rochester, Vt.: Park Street Press, 1995.

Grimassi, Raven. *Encyclopedia of Wicca and Witchcraft*. St. Paul, Minn.: Llewellyn Publications, 2000.

Hawke, Elen. *In the Circle: Crafting the Witch's Path*. St. Paul, Minn.: Llewellyn Worldwide, 2001.

Hurwitz, Sigmund. *Lilith, the First Eve*. Zurich, Switzerland: Daimon Verlag, 1992.

Jung, Carl. *Man and His Symbols*. London: Picador, 1964.

K, Amber. *True Magick*. St. Paul, Minn.: Llewellyn Publications, 2000.

Kaplan, Aryeh. *Sefer Yetzirah*. York Beach, Maine: Samuel Weiser, Inc., 1997.

King, Francis. *Modern Ritual Magic*. Dorset, England: Prism Press, 1990.

Knight, Gareth. *Dion Fortune and the Inner Light*. Leicestershire, England: Thoth Publications, 2000.

———. *A Practical Guide to Qabalistic Symbolism*. Vols. 1 and 2. N.p.: Kahn & Averil, 1997–1998.

———. *The Practise of Ritual Magic*. Oceanside, Calif.: Sun Chalice Books, 1996.

Konstantinos. *Nocturnal Witchcraft*. St. Paul, Minn.: Llewellyn Publications, 2002.

———. *Summoning Spirits*. St. Paul, Minn.: Llewellyn Publications, 1995.

Larousse Encyclopaedia of Mythology. N.p.: Paul Hamlyn Limited, 1959.

Latrobe, Benjamin Henry Boneval. *The Journals 1799–1820: From Philadelphia to New Orleans.* New Haven, Conn.: Yale University Press, 1980.

Lemesurier, Peter. *The Healing of the Gods: The Magic of Symbols and the Practise of Theotherapy.* Dorset, England: Element Books Limited, 1988.

Levi, Eliphas. *Transcendental Magic: Its Doctrine and Ritual.* London: William Rider & Son, 1923.

Lloyd Jones, Hugh. *The Justice of Zeus.* N.p.: University of California Press, 1971.

Lutyens, Mary. *Krishnamurti: The Years of Awakening.* Cambridge, Mass.: Shambhala Publications, Inc., 1975.

Mathers, S. Liddell MacGregor. *Book of the Sacred Magic of Abramelin the Mage.* New York: Dover Publications, Inc., 1975.

———. *The Key of Solomon the King.* York Beach, Maine: Samuel Weiser, Inc., 2000.

Moon, Akasha. *The Little Book of Pocket Spells.* London: Rider, 2001.

Moore, Daphna. *Rabbi's Tarot.* St. Paul, Minn.: Llewellyn Publications, 1992.

Morrison, Sarah Lyddon. *The Modern Witch's Spellbook.* Secaucus, N.J.: Citadel Press, 1971.

Parfitt, Will. *The Elements of the Qabalah.* Dorset, England: Element Books Ltd., 1997.

RavenWolf, Silver. *Witches' Night Out.* St. Paul, Minn.: Llewellyn Publications, 2000.

Reed, Ellen Cannon. *The Witches Tarot.* St. Paul, Minn.: Llewellyn Publications, 1997.

———. *The Witches Qabalah.* York Beach, Maine: Samuel Weiser, Inc., 1997.

Regardie, Israel. *A Garden of Pomegranates.* London: Rider & Co., 1932.

Richardson, Alan. *Dancers to the Gods.* Leicestershire, England: Thoth Publications, N.d.

———. *Priestess: The Life and Magic of Dion Fortune.* Northamptonshire, England: Aquarian Press, 1987.

Roman, Sanaya. *Personal Power Through Awareness.* N.p.: H. J. Kramer, Inc., 1986.

Roman, Sanaya, and Duane Packer. *Opening to Channel.* N.p.: H. J. Kramer Inc., 1986.

Rosenberg, David. *Dreams of Being Eaten Alive: The Literary Core of the Kabbalah.* New York: Harmony Books, 2000.

————. *The Lost Book of Paradise.* New York: Hyperion, 1993.

Saraydarian, Torkom. *Symphony of the Zodiac.* Sedona, Ariz.: Aquarian Educational Group, 1988.

Sargent, Carl. *Personality, Divination and the Tarot.* Rochester, Vt.: Destiny Books, 1988.

Skelton, Robin. *Spellcraft: A Manual of Verbal Magic.* London: Routledge & Kegan Paul Ltd., 1978.

Symonds, John, and Kenneth Grant, eds. *The Confessions of Aleister Crowley.* London: Arkana, Penguin Group, 1989.

Tallant, Robert. *Voodoo in New Orleans.* New Orleans, La.: Pelican Publishing Company, 1998.

Trobe, Kala. *Invoke the Goddess.* St. Paul, Minn.: Llewellyn Publications, 2000.

————. *Invoke the Gods.* St. Paul, Minn.: Llewellyn Publications, 2001.

————. *Magic of Qabalah.* St. Paul, Minn.: Llewellyn Publications, 2001.

Waite, A. E. *The Key to the Tarot.* London: Rider, 1991.

Westcott, Wynn, trans. *Sepher Yetzirah.* Bath, England: Robert Fryar, 1887.

Willis, Tony. *Discover Runes.* London: Aquarian Press, 1986.

Wilson, Colin. *Aleister Crowley: The Nature of the Beast.* Northants, England: Aquarian Press, 1987.

Yogananda, Paramahansa. *Autobiography of a Yogi.* Los Angeles: Self-Realization Fellowship, 1990.

————. *Awake in the Cosmic Dream.* Los Angeles: Self-Realization Fellowship, 1998.

Zalewski, Pat. *Golden Dawn Enochian Magic.* St. Paul, Minn.: Llewellyn Publications, 1994.

Zwi Werblowsky, R. J. *Cabala.* Man, Myth and Magic series. London: Purnell, n.d.

Website Resources

There are many excellent websites out there that will further the research of the witch—far too many to name here. The following are just a few that are recommended. Following links is always a good way of discovering new and related sites.

Witchcraft and Paganism

www.witchvox.com
www.witchcraft.org

High Magick

www.hermetic.com
www.hermeticgoldendawn.com
www.thelemicgoldendawn.org

Spiritual Research/Development Groups

www.servantsofthelight.com
www.theosophy.org
www.yogananda-srf.org

There are links through to other sites of interest via my own at:
www.witchguide.com

Index

abundance, 37, 110, 131, 133, 172, 202,
 228, 346–347, 354–355, 369–370,
 432, 438–439
Ace, 221, 223, 228, 233, 239, 246
Agrippa, Cornelius, 268, 274
air, 3, 21, 34, 36, 81, 95, 103, 117, 124, 160,
 164, 176, 181, 188, 196, 198,
 200–201, 203–204, 221, 230, 261,
 281, 286, 320, 336–337, 340–341,
 343–345, 348, 356, 361–362, 365,
 374, 396, 403, 424, 433
Akasha, 137, 143, 150, 159, 167, 204, 279,
 288, 351, 356
alcohol, 16, 69, 91, 94, 96–98, 152, 296,
 405, 408, 413
altar, 48, 55, 77, 113–114, 200, 244, 254,
 258, 263, 276, 335–336, 339, 343,
 354, 373, 391, 439
Amaterasu, 140, 143
amrita, 93, 146
angel, 20, 66, 101, 153–154, 177, 179,
 194–195, 198, 212, 219–220, 255,
 269–272, 289, 294, 312, 316, 329,
 352, 354, 358–360, 364–365,
 381–382, 429
anorexia, 82–83
Anubis, 140–141
Apollo, 59, 138, 141, 148–149, 159, 199,
 206, 220, 373

Arcana
 Major, 123, 150, 191–192, 198–199,
  219, 221–222
 Minor, 150, 191, 198, 219, 221
art, 29, 50, 149, 158, 192–193, 223,
 253–254, 280, 289, 297, 305–306,
 315, 317, 325, 328, 339–340, 347,
 349, 367, 373, 378, 390
Artemis, 59, 128, 141–142, 156, 332, 395,
 403, 410–411, 415–416
Asgard, 146, 151
astral
 magick, 131, 189, 350–351, 368
 plane, 7, 53, 71, 85, 102, 131, 159, 244,
  350, 368, 372–373
 projection, 103, 314, 395
astrology, 63, 80, 127, 138, 244, 260,
 268–269, 272, 286, 341, 346–348,
 352, 354, 360
Atum, 145
aura, 48, 78, 81, 91, 153, 166–167,
 170–176, 197, 199, 201, 203, 259,
 291, 358, 366, 386, 390–391, 398,
 400, 405, 407

Bailey, Alice, 45, 57–58, 165, 260, 279–280,
 282–284, 297, 300–303, 318
banishing, 101, 346, 353, 357, 393

bath, ritual, 30, 46, 80–81, 113, 155, 170,
    174–175, 187, 189, 195, 285,
    340–341, 354, 356, 382, 387, 392,
    401, 403–404
beauty, 43, 54, 59, 84, 93, 101, 104, 129,
    141, 146, 154, 157, 162, 182,
    184–185, 188–189, 192, 197, 201,
    203, 205, 208–210, 232, 252, 255,
    257–258, 269, 286, 306, 309,
    327–328, 345, 401, 411
Beltane, 13, 35, 109–110, 113, 130, 160,
    344, 427
Besant, Annie, 165, 218, 260, 282–284
besom, *see* broomstick
Binah, 35, 50, 177–180, 187–189, 202,
    395–396
binding, 11, 104, 122, 177, 341–342,
    351–352, 365
bisexuality, 58–59, 214, 295, 306
Blake, William, 14, 75, 192, 272–274, 279,
    295
Blavatsky, Helena, 74, 137, 153, 165, 260,
    268, 277–284, 288–289, 302–303, 318
body, 7, 11, 17, 25, 41–42, 45, 48, 51,
    53–55, 58, 76–77, 81–84, 88, 92,
    95–97, 100, 102–104, 118, 122–123,
    129, 132, 142, 160–161, 165–169,
    171, 174–176, 179, 196, 199,
    204–205, 211–212, 219–220, 228,
    234, 236–237, 260–262, 272–273,
    277, 280, 286, 303, 314, 319, 324,
    330, 340–341, 349, 351, 359,
    361–362, 364, 367–368, 370, 372,
    377, 383–385, 387, 390, 394, 398,
    404–405, 409–410, 412–417,
    419–420, 425, 430
Boehme, Jacob, 272–273
Brahma, 142–143, 149–150, 164, 373
Brigit, 143–144
broomstick, 61, 84, 337
Buddhism, 24, 26–27, 36, 73–74, 86, 133,
    158, 160, 165, 211, 260, 280, 294,
    302, 371, 373, 419

Buffy, 67, 329–331
bulimia, 82–83
Butler, W. E., 27, 288, 303, 318, 322

Campbell, Joseph, 137, 152
candle magick, 338, 353–355
cauldron, 13, 48, 50, 119, 129, 262, 335,
    338–339, 342, 370, 373–374,
    420–421, 423–424, 428–429, 434
Cernunnos, 21–22, 119, 370
chakras, xvii, 165–171, 173, 175, 260, 283,
    350, 372
chalice, 56, 69, 101, 113, 195, 212, 222,
    228–231, 254, 262, 335, 338–339,
    351, 399
chanting, 11–12, 15, 21–22, 120, 151, 159,
    245, 260, 264, 321, 332, 342, 357,
    362, 371–374, 391, 433
Chaos Magick, 266
Chariot, the, 193–194, 196, 206–207, 364
Charmed, 329, 331, 421
Chesed, 34, 76, 110, 177–179, 186–189, 312
Chokmah, 50, 178–180, 187–189
Christ, 109, 112, 116, 143, 179, 258,
    300–302, 342
Circle, casting, 8, 10, 15–17, 175, 352,
    354–355, 357, 379, 382, 391, 400
cleansing, 48, 81, 141, 155, 160, 162, 170,
    174–175, 262, 343, 353–354, 378,
    386–387, 391, 400–401, 425
cocaine, 91, 94, 291, 295
Cone of Power, 357
Couzyn, Jeni, 51, 377–378
creative visualisation, 47, 100, 149, 360,
    365
crisis
    global, 40
    personal, 47
Crowley, Aleister, 4, 18, 31, 58–59, 65, 91,
    97, 153, 163, 177, 191, 220, 226, 260,
    262–263, 266, 270, 277, 282,
    291–297, 305–307, 311, 313–314,
    316, 318–321, 363–364, 397–398, 420

Crowther, Patricia, 262, 265, 316
crystals, 47, 364, 369, 384, 392
Cups, 52, 180, 198–199, 221–223, 228–234, 339
Cybele, 327–328

Da'ath, 189
Dana, 128, 143
dance, 11–12, 16, 40, 98, 115, 120–122, 124–128, 131, 143, 159, 183, 202, 220, 228, 231, 258, 261, 342, 347, 357, 371, 373, 377, 385, 433
Davenport, Paul, 40, 114, 116, 126
de Leon, Moses, 132, 185, 267–268, 277, 285, 399
Death, 4, 6–7, 10, 26, 30, 34–35, 40–42, 46, 50, 53, 73–75, 84, 86–87, 89, 95, 99–105, 109–111, 113–115, 117, 119, 121, 123, 125, 127–131, 133, 135, 140–141, 147, 151, 154, 157, 159–161, 175, 194–195, 209–213, 215, 219, 231, 237, 248, 254, 256–257, 259, 268, 295–296, 306–307, 313–314, 316, 320–322, 324, 326, 328, 330, 338, 342, 385, 394–395, 397–400, 426
Dee, Dr. John, 255, 268–272, 359, 363–365
Demeter, 33, 87, 112, 140, 159–160, 203
Devil, the, 195–198, 200, 213–214, 222, 235, 265, 299
divination, 14, 57, 110–111, 127, 138, 146, 152, 191, 193, 195, 197, 199, 201, 203, 205, 207, 209, 211, 213, 215, 217, 219, 221, 223, 225, 227, 229, 231, 233, 235, 237, 239, 241, 243–247, 249, 251, 269, 296, 320, 339, 344, 346, 384, 388, 393, 399
doll, 11, 48, 352, 381, 387, 389, 392
drugs, 16–17, 37, 91–95, 97, 103, 212–213, 265, 296, 303, 310–311, 327, 330, 348, 385

Earth, 3, 6–8, 10, 21, 24, 31–40, 43, 53, 56, 63–64, 75, 81, 84, 88, 99, 101, 109–110, 112, 120, 129–130, 140, 151, 154–155, 160, 163–164, 168, 175–176, 179, 181, 193–194, 200–205, 212, 215–216, 219, 221, 261–262, 266, 276, 280, 283, 299–302, 306, 312, 314, 325, 336, 339, 341, 343, 351, 355–356, 363, 394, 396, 398, 415–416, 426
eating disorders, 82–84, 420
Ecstasy, 37, 93–94, 129, 306, 325, 328
elixir, 195, 327
Emperor, the, 39, 192–193, 197, 203–204, 227
employment, 200, 439–440
Empress, the, 192–193, 197, 202–203, 227, 239
Enochia, 266, 269–271, 359, 363–365, 376, 401
esbat, 8, 35, 127–135, 216, 335
Eve, 113, 155, 398–399
evocation, 22, 51, 66, 134, 187, 276, 342, 356–357, 364–365, 382, 391

faery, 8, 113, 183–184, 270
Farr, Florence, 47, 71, 105, 161, 261, 265, 285, 290, 293, 304–306, 316–317, 321, 330–331, 344
Farrar, Janet, 47, 71, 105, 316, 321, 330
Farrar, Stewart, 47, 71, 105, 161, 261, 265, 316, 321, 330, 344
fetch, 368
fetish, 54, 258–259, 387, 389
fire, 3, 13, 21, 30, 34, 36, 48, 81, 84, 111, 113, 117–118, 130, 140, 143, 147, 154, 159–160, 162, 164, 174, 176, 181, 196, 198, 201, 203–204, 221, 248, 303, 317, 335–336, 338–339, 341, 343–344, 355–356, 373–374, 381, 383–384, 396, 399, 427
fith-fath, 387, 389
fitness, 415

Fludd, Robert, 271–272

folk magick, 40, 114, 116, 337

folklore, 14, 116, 126–127, 156, 253, 317, 331, 391–392

food, 39, 67, 83, 110, 119, 253, 255, 316, 337–338, 419–423, 425, 427, 429–431, 433, 435

Fool, the, 155, 158, 192–201, 203, 209, 211, 213, 216, 218–220, 237

Fortune, Dion, 27, 32–33, 35, 53, 57, 69, 71, 86, 88–90, 92, 97, 104, 115, 120, 177, 183, 190, 194, 196–197, 200, 207–208, 222, 225, 231, 237, 251, 260, 276, 282, 288, 291, 295, 303–304, 307–314, 319–320, 322, 328, 332, 341, 351, 359, 368, 379–381, 393, 439–440

Ganesh, 127, 144

Gardner, Gerald, 5, 8–9, 11–12, 14, 16–19, 22, 26, 58, 260–263, 265–266, 315–316, 320–322, 331, 343

garment, 379

Geburah, 76, 110, 178–179, 185–189, 204, 312, 371, 403–404

God, 5–6, 8, 17, 22, 26, 33–35, 37, 44, 52–54, 58–59, 64, 69, 73, 99–101, 109–115, 133–134, 139–145, 147, 149–153, 155, 159–160, 162, 164, 179–180, 188–189, 206, 219, 254–255, 261–262, 265–266, 268, 271–274, 279, 283, 290, 292, 301, 308–309, 311, 313–315, 335, 355, 361, 366, 370, 378, 394, 399

Goddess, 5–8, 10, 12–14, 16–17, 20–22, 30, 32–37, 47, 54–55, 58, 80, 87, 90, 99–100, 109–114, 118, 123, 128–129, 139–140, 142–144, 146, 148, 154–155, 158–161, 164, 199, 201–202, 206, 212, 217, 254–256, 261–262, 265–266, 279, 295, 310, 316, 327–328, 335, 338–339, 345, 355, 360, 365, 367, 370, 372, 375, 394–395, 397, 399–400, 415, 438

godform, 87, 90, 138–139, 147, 151, 179, 254, 263, 360–361, 370, 383

golem, 360

Gonne, Maud, 288–290, 304, 316–317

Goya, 26, 31, 323–328, 332

Graves, Robert, 137, 159, 198, 201, 218, 372, 375–376

Greek, ancient, 5, 30, 33, 59, 93, 99, 101, 110, 137, 141–144, 146–147, 149–150, 152, 154, 156–157, 159, 162, 171, 191, 201, 204, 206, 208, 220, 253–254, 324–325, 339, 360, 373, 375, 399, 425

handfasting, 59–61, 337, 342

Hecate, 7, 99, 110, 254, 295, 375, 394, 398–400

Hera, 37, 93, 112, 119, 144, 147, 153–154, 157, 162, 202, 205, 212, 219, 258, 295, 359, 361

herbs, 37, 41, 81, 150, 253, 255, 336–337, 339–340, 368, 374, 392, 422–423

Hermes, 138, 149–150, 152, 201

hex, 8, 390

Hierophant, 193, 195, 204, 219, 223, 290

High Priestess, 22, 60–61, 69, 99, 113, 128, 192–193, 195, 197, 201–203, 217, 219, 232, 258, 263–264, 290, 320, 368

Hinduism, 26–27, 36, 39, 67, 73–74, 86–87, 93, 133, 137, 140, 142, 144, 146, 149, 155, 157, 159–160, 162–166, 179, 209, 211, 260, 279–281, 283, 286, 293–294, 303, 318, 328, 360, 366–367, 373, 397, 403, 419

Hod, 178–179, 183, 185, 188–189, 213, 312, 396

Horniman, Annie, 287, 304, 317

Horus, 58, 144, 147–148, 150, 153, 164, 260, 263, 266, 295

incense, 13, 22, 98, 144, 188, 335–336, 339–340, 346, 350, 352, 354–355, 358, 360, 379, 382, 400

initiation, 9–10, 30, 55, 68, 87, 100, 150, 152, 161, 210–211, 226, 237, 239, 265, 291, 328, 343, 385, 394, 396

invocation, 10, 47, 87, 90, 139, 151, 260, 276, 300–302, 357, 360–361, 368, 370, 374

Isis, 128, 139–140, 144–145, 147–148, 150, 152, 156, 164, 188, 199, 279, 287, 290, 310, 361, 367

Judaism, 36, 65, 73, 100, 154, 177, 188, 260, 267, 287, 289, 294, 302, 318, 399

Judgement, 74–75, 102, 140–141, 206, 209–211, 218–220, 275, 284, 309

Jung, Carl, 137, 152, 209, 273, 275, 288, 293

Justice, 29, 44, 46, 130, 133, 147, 186–187, 193, 203, 205–207, 211, 219, 244, 247

Kabbalah, 177, 190, 260, 267–268, 293

Kala, 190, 417

Kali, 102, 104, 159, 328, 397–399, 403

karma, 4, 6, 34, 37, 39, 56, 64, 70, 73–78, 84, 86, 88–89, 93, 96, 102, 104, 146, 158, 172, 189, 206, 208, 211–212, 219, 247–248, 311–312, 320, 329, 367, 408, 419–420

Kether, 32, 53, 101, 103, 105, 178–180, 186–189, 325

Khephri, 140, 145

Knight, Gareth, 71, 190, 217, 307, 322, 382

Krishnamurti, 74, 165, 218, 282–284

Laksmi, 146, 355

Lammas, 109, 114–115, 131–132

Latrobe, Benjamin, 256

Leadbeater, Charles, 165, 218, 260, 283–284

Levi, Eliphas, 27, 71, 102, 161, 177, 230, 260, 274–277, 282, 323, 361

Lilith, 161, 295, 327, 332, 398–399

love, 3, 6, 9–10, 12–14, 19–20, 35, 43–44, 46, 49–53, 55, 57–61, 64–66, 70, 76–77, 85, 99, 105, 114, 122, 127–129, 148, 162, 166–169, 172, 174, 184–186, 189, 192, 195, 198, 203, 205, 228–233, 248, 253, 274, 280, 282, 287, 289, 291, 294, 300–302, 306, 312–314, 316–317, 321, 327–329, 342, 345, 347, 351–354, 357, 369, 371, 387–388, 405, 439

Lovers, the, 4, 50, 60, 193, 205, 244, 258, 264, 296, 313, 392

Maat, 149, 153

Mabon, 115, 431

Magician, xvii, 183, 192, 196, 200–201, 203, 244, 370

magickian, 19, 29, 31, 56–57, 64–65, 85, 97, 102, 138, 150–151, 155–156, 183, 273, 275, 286, 296, 306, 309, 311, 313, 316, 328, 351, 358–359, 361, 364, 366, 372, 386, 389, 393, 398

Malkuth, 32, 63, 67, 88, 97, 101, 138, 178–183, 185–186, 188–190, 204, 231, 325, 396, 399

marriage, 59, 113, 115, 144, 205, 249, 269, 275, 291, 299, 312, 314, 320, 370, 411

Mathers, Moina, 276, 285, 287–291, 304, 312, 317–318

Mathers, Samuel MacGregor, 22, 177, 260, 268, 285, 287–290, 293–294, 304–305, 312, 317–318, 349, 358, 364

maya, 73, 75, 131, 133, 142, 149, 184, 279, 281

Maypole, 113

media, the witch in, 323, 325, 327, 329–331

menstrual magick, 393

menstruation, 100, 393–400, 404

mescaline, 16, 91

minerals, 83, 394

monogamy, 59–60

monogram, 56, 151, 325, 352–353, 386, 401–402

moods, mood swings, 11, 24, 29, 32, 50, 76, 79–80, 82, 171, 216, 230–231, 239, 339, 356, 367, 371–372, 381, 385, 392, 395, 410, 423

Moon, 4, 9, 12, 15, 21–22, 33, 35–36, 47, 53–54, 65, 69, 79–80, 92, 99–100, 115, 121, 127–135, 144–145, 148–149, 156, 179, 182, 184, 197, 202, 216–219, 233, 246, 251, 254–255, 270, 272, 303, 307, 309–310, 314, 325, 328, 338, 345, 347, 352–353, 355, 360, 362, 369, 375, 379, 387, 391–393, 395, 397, 399–400, 437–439

Moore, Syd, 365, 370, 420, 436

Morae, the, 146, 208

Morris, Radcliffe, 410, 417

Morris, 120–121, 126, 264, 320

music(k), 40, 92, 103, 122, 125–126, 128, 139, 141, 195, 200, 202, 244, 272, 280, 305, 342, 360, 362, 366, 371–373, 381, 385, 391–392, 404–405, 431

nature, 3, 5-10, 15-16, 25-26, 29, 31-33, 35, 37-38, 40, 44, 46, 51, 55, 68, 84, 99–100, 109, 114-115, 129-130, 132, 134, 137, 139, 142, 153, 156, 161, 167, 169, 172, 174, 180, 182-186, 188-189, 195, 197, 201-202, 210, 213, 216-218, 220, 222, 226, 229, 232, 239, 247-249, 253-256, 261, 264, 268, 272-273, 293-295, 309-310, 312, 316-317, 324, 327, 331, 336-337, 349, 354, 358, 360-361, 371, 374, 377-378, 383, 386,

395, 398, 409, 420-422, 426, 431-432

Netzach, 35, 178–179, 183–184, 188–189, 202, 312, 320, 360, 405

Norns, the, 146, 151, 208

Norton, Rosaleen, 326

'Obby 'oss, 337

Odin, 146–147, 151–152, 156, 210

oil, 30, 34, 46, 48, 81, 95, 338, 340–341, 345–346, 353–354, 358, 365, 369–370, 386, 388, 391–392, 400–401, 405, 424, 427–428, 433–435

Osiris, 101, 104, 109, 140, 144–145, 147, 150–151, 156, 164, 263, 361

pentacle, 14, 21, 52, 150, 179, 198–199, 204, 221–227, 244, 336, 338, 341–342, 379

Pentacles, 52, 150, 179, 198, 221–227, 244

Persephone, 37, 87, 104, 112, 118

poetry, 51, 151–152, 293, 327, 372, 376–378, 388, 391

Prometheus, 147

psychic, 4, 7, 11, 15–17, 20, 24, 27, 30, 33, 41, 47, 53, 56–57, 59, 71, 86, 94, 100, 102, 127, 131, 134, 139, 156–160, 166, 169–170, 172, 175, 181, 185, 198, 202, 252, 283, 299, 301, 308–310, 313–314, 317, 328, 332, 337–341, 343–344, 348, 352–353, 359–360, 364, 367, 369–371, 373, 379–380, 382–385, 387, 391, 394–395, 400, 407, 410–411, 415, 422

psychic self-protection, 382

purification, 86, 110, 113, 141, 145, 154–155, 159, 264, 291, 341, 343, 345, 356, 369, 371, 382, 392, 401, 403, 429

Qabalah, xvii, 29, 34–35, 50, 63, 67, 76,
        103, 110, 114, 177, 179–181, 183,
        185, 187, 189–190, 199, 201–202,
        204, 213, 217, 226, 260, 265,
        267–268, 270, 272, 277, 284–289,
        293, 302, 304–305, 307, 312, 314,
        318–320, 322, 350, 360, 364, 371,
        376–377, 381, 395–396, 399, 403
Qlipoth, 177, 181, 204, 313, 327, 399

Ra, 101, 140, 144–145, 149–150, 260, 399,
        403
RavenWolf, Silver, 57, 330
Rays, 81, 140–141, 174, 204, 210,
        280–281, 300–302, 314, 353, 362,
        369
recipe, 349, 369, 420–424, 426–427,
        429–430, 432–435
Regardie, Israel, 18, 71, 104, 177, 261, 287,
        318–320, 365
Rhiannon, 148
ritual, 5, 7–11, 14, 16, 18, 22, 40, 47,
        52–57, 59, 63, 65, 67–69, 85, 87,
        89–90, 92–93, 102, 104, 111,
        113–115, 118–121, 126, 129,
        138–139, 149–150, 152, 154–155,
        170, 172, 175, 177, 204, 216, 246,
        254–255, 261–264, 266, 273–274,
        276–277, 281, 285, 287–290, 294,
        296, 304–305, 312, 314, 316–317,
        319–321, 324–325, 330–332,
        335–337, 339–340, 342–343, 346,
        349–350, 352, 354, 358–361, 368,
        371–374, 376–377, 388–389,
        392–393, 395, 398, 401, 404, 409,
        411, 439
runes, 12, 15, 21–22, 147, 151, 230,
        245–252, 338, 376, 386, 401
running, 23, 39, 44, 61, 77, 82, 84, 92, 112,
        124, 127, 142, 148, 165–166, 173,
        196, 202, 215, 227, 235–236, 271,
        303, 327, 375–376, 391, 405,
        410–416, 426

sabbat, 6–8, 14, 34–35, 40, 110–116, 122,
        127–129, 131, 133, 138, 160, 265,
        273, 323, 331, 335, 337, 360, 420,
        431
Samhain, 6, 34–35, 46, 99, 104, 110–111,
        113, 130, 133–134, 154, 432–433
Sanders, Alex, 5, 8–9, 23, 26, 67, 177,
        260–261, 263–265, 268, 292, 320,
        331, 343, 360
Sanders, Maxine, 260, 264–265, 320–321
scourge, 21, 336, 343
script, 246, 285, 363, 386, 388, 401
sephiroth, 76, 110, 154, 177, 179–181, 184,
        187–189, 202, 204, 226, 285–286,
        302, 305, 312, 371
Seth, 58, 147, 150, 263, 279
sex, 18, 23, 31, 37, 49, 51, 53–59, 61, 70, 83,
        93, 100, 113, 146, 161–162, 169,
        171–172, 174, 205, 213–214, 249,
        257, 262–263, 287, 306, 312–314,
        316, 318, 320, 323, 325–326, 329,
        350, 353, 379, 386, 395, 397, 399, 407
Shadows, Book of, 9, 191, 315–316, 321,
        329, 336
Shakespeare, William, 63, 88, 121, 125,
        254, 270, 373–376
Shakti, 143
Shinto, 140
sigils, 56, 151, 226, 246, 285, 306, 325, 338,
        355, 386
Siva, 104, 140, 142, 148, 159, 164, 397
skrying, 152, 174, 304, 317, 384
skyclad, 7, 9, 31, 161, 261, 330
smoking, 48, 94–96, 175, 318, 340, 379,
        384, 413
sorcery, 79, 84, 87, 128, 144, 217, 253,
        324–326, 328, 358, 362, 438
space, sacred, 11, 15–17, 61, 155, 357, 391
Spare, Austin Osman, 56, 305–307,
        324–326, 358, 367, 386, 393
spellcraft, 36, 51, 64, 78, 148, 264, 349,
        371–373, 375–376, 378, 388, 402,
        421, 437, 440

spells, xvii, 4–7, 11, 15–16, 18, 20–23,
        30–31, 43, 48–52, 54, 63–65, 67,
        77–78, 80, 82, 89–90, 125, 127–128,
        141, 149–150, 177, 189–190, 236,
        244–245, 325, 331, 335, 338,
        341–342, 345–346, 349–354,
        357–358, 360, 365, 368–369,
        371–379, 382, 386, 388–389,
        391–393, 400, 402–404, 409, 429,
        432–433, 437, 439
spirit, 3, 7, 19, 36, 42, 45–47, 59, 65, 75, 81,
        92, 100–104, 114, 128–129,
        131–133, 142, 147, 153, 158–160,
        175, 181, 186, 192–193, 214–215,
        217, 227, 237, 239, 245, 255, 272,
        276–277, 280, 300, 304, 307,
        309–311, 313, 319–320, 324–325,
        336, 341, 344, 349, 356–357, 359,
        361, 366–368, 370, 382, 385–386,
        396, 405, 410, 415–417, 426, 438
Star, the, 196–198, 215–217, 233, 241, 245
suicide, 44, 46, 75, 82, 84–88, 264
Sun, 15, 21–22, 33, 36, 101, 109, 111–112,
        114–115, 119, 122–123, 127,
        129–135, 140–141, 144–145, 147,
        149, 161, 176, 184, 197–198,
        210–211, 218–219, 237, 240, 248,
        252–254, 270, 272, 303, 329, 344,
        346–347, 353, 355, 358, 362, 373,
        375, 377, 407, 416
sword, 21, 73, 119, 160, 198, 206, 276, 312,
        330, 336, 343–344, 356, 360
Swords, 46, 179, 198–199, 221–223,
        233–238, 244, 291
symbols, 13–14, 16, 30–32, 36, 50, 56, 59,
        67, 87, 112–113, 119, 138–139, 143,
        145, 148, 152–154, 157–162, 166,
        177, 179–180, 191–193, 206,
        209–210, 212, 219, 228, 250–251,
        254–255, 268, 270, 272, 274–275,
        289, 291, 305, 310, 325, 336–339,
        341–342, 351–353, 355, 363, 367,
        370, 386, 388–389, 399, 426, 432, 440

Tarot, 12, 46, 101, 111, 123, 132, 138, 150,
        155, 158, 160, 174, 179–180,
        191–192, 198–199, 201–202,
        204–205, 208–214, 216–219, 221,
        223, 244, 246, 248, 277, 288, 291,
        293, 296, 322, 339, 364, 384, 390,
        438–439
tattoo, 370
telepathy, 111, 168–169, 173, 387, 389–390
Temperance, 115, 194–196, 212–213, 215,
        234, 244
Theosophy, 27, 57, 74, 153, 165, 260, 265,
        268, 272, 277, 279, 281–285,
        288–289, 293, 297, 300–301, 303,
        314, 318, 419
Thoth, 140, 145, 148–152, 156, 191, 220,
        226, 296, 307, 322, 361–363
thoughtform, 53, 187, 256, 389, 391
Tiphareth, 36, 114, 178–179, 184–185,
        188–189, 213, 302
Tower, the, 46, 160, 196–197, 213–215,
        217, 235, 237, 248, 390
Traditional Witchcraft, 8, 11, 354
Tree of Life, 35, 101, 146, 154, 163,
        177–179, 199, 204, 226, 228, 286,
        302, 319, 394, 396
tree, 8, 13, 35, 43, 51, 59, 109–110, 117,
        125, 133, 146–147, 151, 154, 163,
        174, 179–181, 184, 188, 194, 196,
        210, 215, 220, 229, 241, 246, 251,
        273, 326, 344, 372, 424, 426,
        428–429, 439

Vac, 143
Valhalla, 151
Valiente, Doreen, 11–12, 262, 265,
        315–316, 321–322, 331
Valkyries, 151
vampire, 313, 327, 329–330
verbal magick, 371
Vishnu, 142–143, 164, 188, 283–284
Voodoo, 256, 258–259, 366, 381–382, 387,
        389

wand, 21, 25, 38, 82, 160, 180, 198–200,
    207, 221–222, 239–243, 246,
    335–337, 344, 356, 360
Wands, 180, 198–199, 221–222, 239–243,
    246
wart spell, 391
water, 3, 11, 16, 21, 36, 39, 51, 66, 69,
    76–77, 80–81, 83, 98, 122, 135, 151,
    155, 157, 160, 164, 174–176, 181,
    195–196, 201, 203–204, 212, 215,
    219, 221, 235–237, 239, 251, 296,
    336, 338–339, 341, 343, 355–356,
    362, 378, 387, 404–405, 423, 426,
    429–431, 439
Westcott, Wynn, 268, 284–287, 289–290,
    293, 304
Western Mystery Tradition, xvii, 27, 177,
    179–180, 190, 199, 260, 268, 277,
    284, 304, 307
Wheel of Fortune, 86, 88–90, 194, 200,
    207–208, 222
Wicca, xvii, 6–11, 15–16, 19, 22, 32, 36,
    40, 52, 54–55, 60, 67–71, 74, 91,
    100–101, 109, 111, 128, 255,
    260–266, 268, 293, 315–316,
    320–321, 329–331, 335, 340,
    342–343, 410, 417, 419, 421

Witch's Rune, 12, 15, 21–22
witchcraft, xvii–xviii, 5–9, 11, 13, 20,
    23–24, 26, 31, 36, 40, 52–54, 59–60,
    64, 67, 85, 87, 101, 104, 107, 110,
    158, 160, 177, 221, 253, 255–257,
    259–263, 265–266, 284, 288,
    315–316, 320–321, 323–324, 326,
    329–333, 335, 340, 343, 345, 350,
    354, 365, 368, 373, 378, 380, 387,
    394, 419
Wodan, 146–147, 151–152, 156, 210
World, the, 150, 192–198, 204, 207–208,
    211, 217–221, 227, 232, 237, 240
Wyrd, 146

Yeats, W. B., 274, 288–290, 293, 304–305,
    316–318
Yesod, 29, 178–179, 182–184, 187–189,
    217, 321, 325, 327, 395–396, 405
Yggdrasill, 146–147, 151, 163, 210
Yogananda, Paramahansa, 44, 71, 73,
    272–274
Yugas, 143
Yule, 13, 34, 111, 134, 265, 434

Zeus, 144, 147, 162, 399
zodiac, 112, 129, 134, 353, 365, 388

To Write to the Author

If you wish to contact the author or would like more information about this book, please write to the author in care of Llewellyn Worldwide and we will forward your request. Both the author and publisher appreciate hearing from you and learning of your enjoyment of this book and how it has helped you. Llewellyn Worldwide cannot guarantee that every letter written to the author can be answered, but all will be forwarded. Please write to:

Kala Trobe
℅ Llewellyn Worldwide
P.O. Box 64383, Dept. 0-7387-0200-5
St. Paul, MN 55164-0383, U.S.A.

Please enclose a self-addressed stamped envelope for reply,
or $1.00 to cover costs. If outside U.S.A., enclose
international postal reply coupon.

Many of Llewellyn's authors have websites with additional information and resources. For more information, please visit our website at:

http://www.llewellyn.com